Griffith and Johnson as Tribulation and Ananias
in " The Alchemist "

Act 3   Scene 2   —p. 571

From the painting by Peter Van Bleeck

THE HARVARD CLASSICS
EDITED BY CHARLES W ELIOT LL D

ELIZABETHAN DRAMA

VOLUME II

DEKKER · JONSON

BEAUMONT AND FLETCHER

WEBSTER · MASSINGER

WITH INTRODUCTIONS, NOTES
AND ILLUSTRATIONS

"DR ELIOT'S FIVE-FOOT SHELF OF BOOKS"

P F COLLIER & SON
NEW YORK

CONTENTS

INTRODUCTORY NOTE

THOMAS DEKKER'S *career is an extreme instance of the hazardous life led by the professional author in the time of Shakespeare. Born in London about 1570, Dekker first appears certainly as a dramatist about 1598, when we find him working on plays in collaboration with other dramatists in the pay of the manager, Henslowe. He wrote, in partnership or alone, many dramas; and when the market for these was dull he turned to the writing of entertainments, occasional verses, and prose pamphlets on a great variety of subjects. But all his activity seems to have failed to supply a decent livelihood, for he was often in prison for debt, at one time for a period of three years; and most of the biographical details about him which have come down to us are connected with borrowing money or getting into jail or out of it. He disappears from view in the thirties of the seventeenth century.*

"The Shoemaker's Holiday," first acted in 1599, is a good example of Dekker's work in the drama. The story is taken from Thomas Deloney's "Gentle Craft," and gives an opportunity for a picture of life among the trades-people of London at a period when the frequency in the drama of Italian Dukes and Cardinals is liable to make us forget that, in spite of vice and frivolity in high places, the world was still kept going by decent work-people who attended to their business. The play is full of an atmosphere of pleasant mirth, varied with characteristic touches of pathos; and it contains in the figure of Simon Eyre a creation of marked individuality and hilarious humor. It is striking that the most high-spirited picture of London life in the time of Elizabeth should come from the pen of the author who seems to have been more hardly treated by fortune than any of his contemporaries.

THE SHOEMAKER'S HOLIDAY

[DRAMATIS PERSONÆ

THE KING.
THE EARL OF CORNWALL.
SIR HUGH LACY, Earl of Lincoln.
ROWLAND LACY,
  otherwise HANS, } His Nephews.
ASKEW,
SIR ROGER OATELEY, Lord Mayor of London.
Master HAMMON,
Master WARNER, } Citizens of London.
Master SCOTT,
SIMON EYRE, the Shoemaker.

ROGER, commonly
  called HODGE, } EYRE's Jour-
FIRK, } neymen.
RALPH,
LOVELL, a Courtier.
DODGER, Servant to the EARL OF LINCOLN.
A DUTCH SKIPPER.
A BOY.

ROSE, Daughter of SIR ROGER.
SYBIL, her Maid.
MARGERY, Wife of SIMON EYRE.
JANE, Wife of RALPH.

Courtiers, Attendants, Officers, Soldiers, Hunters, Shoemakers, Apprentices, Servants.

SCENE—*London and Old Ford*]

ACT I

SCENE I[1]

Enter the LORD MAYOR *and the* EARL OF LINCOLN

Lincoln

MY lord mayor, you have sundry times
  Feasted myself and many courtiers more;
  Seldom or never can we be so kind
To make requital of your courtesy.
But leaving this, I hear my cousin Lacy
Is much affected to[2] your daughter Rose.

 L. MAYOR. True, my good lord, and she loves him so well
That I mislike her boldness in the chase.

 LINCOLN. Why, my lord mayor, think you it then a shame,

---

[1] A street in London. [2] In love with.

447

To join a Lacy with an Oateley's name?

    L. MAYOR. Too mean is my poor girl for his high birth;
Poor citizens must not with courtiers wed,
Who will in silks and gay apparel spend
More in one year than I am worth, by far:
Therefore your honour need not doubt[3] my girl.

    LINCOLN. Take heed, my lord, advise you what you do!
A verier unthrift lives not in the world,
Than is my cousin; for I'll tell you what:
'Tis now almost a year since he requested
To travel countries for experience.
I furnished him with coin, bills of exchange,
Letters of credit, men to wait on him,
Solicited my friends in Italy
Well to respect him. But to see the end:
Scant had he journey'd through half Germany,
But all his coin was spent, his men cast off,
His bills embezzl'd,[4] and my jolly coz,[5]
Asham'd to show his bankrupt presence here,
Became a shoemaker in Wittenberg,
A goodly science for a gentleman
Of such descent! Now judge the rest by this:
Suppose your daughter have a thousand pound,
He did consume me more in one half year;
And make him heir to all the wealth you have
One twelvemonth's rioting will waste it all.
Then seek, my lord, some honest citizen
To wed your daughter to.

    L. MAYOR.   I thank your lordship.
[*Aside.*] Well, fox, I understand your subtilty.—
As for your nephew, let your lordship's eye
But watch his actions, and you need not fear,
For I have sent my daughter far enough.
And yet your cousin Rowland might do well,
Now he hath learn'd an occupation;
And yet I scorn to call him son-in-law.

    LINCOLN. Ay, but I have a better trade for him.
I thank his grace, he hath appointed him

---

        [3] Fear.   [4] Wasted.
        [5] Cousin; used of any relative not of one's immediate family.

Chief colonel of all those companies
Must'red in London and the shires about,
To serve his highness in those wars of France.
See where he comes!—

Enter LOVELL, LACY, *and* ASKEW

                        Lovell, what news with you?
  LOVELL. My Lord of Lincoln, 'tis his highness' will,
That presently[6] your cousin ship for France
With all his powers; he would not for a million,
But they should land at Dieppe within four days.
  LINCOLN. Go certify his grace, it shall be done.
                             Exit LOVELL.
Now, cousin Lacy, in what forwardness
Are all your companies?
  LACY.   All well prepared.
The men of Hertfordshire lie at Mile-end,
Suffolk and Essex train in Tothill-fields,
The Londoners and those of Middlesex,
All gallantly prepar'd in Finsbury,
With frolic spirits long for their parting hour.
  L. MAYOR. They have their imprest,[7] coats, and furniture;[8]
And, if it please your cousin Lacy come
To the Guildhall, he shall receive his pay;
And twenty pounds besides my brethren
Will freely give him, to approve our loves
We bear unto my lord, your uncle here.
  LACY. I thank your honour.
  LINCOLN.   Thanks, my good lord mayor.
  L. MAYOR. At the Guildhall we will expect your coming.
                                 Exit.
  LINCOLN. To approve your loves to me? No subtilty!
Nephew, that twenty pound he doth bestow
For joy to rid you from his daughter Rose.
But, cousins both, now here are none but friends,
I would not have you cast an amorous eye
Upon so mean a project as the love
Of a gay, wanton, painted citizen.
I know, this churl even in the height of scorn

      [6] At once.   [7] Regimental badge.   [8] Equipment.

Doth hate the mixture of his blood with thine.
I pray thee, do thou so! Remember, coz,
What honourable fortunes wait on thee.
Increase the king's love, which so brightly shines,
And gilds thy hopes. I have no heir but thee,—
And yet not thee, if with a wayward spirit
Thou start from the true bias[9] of my love.

    LACY. My lord, I will for honour, not desire
Of land or livings, or to be your heir,
So guide my actions in pursuit of France,
As shall add glory to the Lacys' name.

    LINCOLN. Coz, for those words here's thirty Portuguese,[10]
And, nephew Askew, there's a few for you.
Fair Honour, in her loftiest eminence,
Stays in France for you, till you fetch her thence.
Then, nephews, clap swift wings on your designs.
Begone, begone, make haste to the Guildhall;
There presently I'll meet you. Do not stay:
Where honour beckons, shame attends delay.   *Exit.*

    ASKEW. How gladly would your uncle have you gone!

    LACY. True, coz, but I'll o'erreach his policies.
I have some serious business for three days,
Which nothing but my presence can dispatch.
You, therefore, cousin, with the companies,
Shall haste to Dover; there I'll meet with you:
Or, if I stay past my prefixed time,
Away for France; we'll meet in Normandy.
The twenty pounds my lord mayor gives to me
You shall receive, and these ten Portuguese,
Part of mine uncle's thirty. Gentle coz,
Have care to our great charge; I know, your wisdom
Hath tried itself in higher consequence.

    ASKEW. Coz, all myself am yours: yet have this care,
To lodge in London with all secrecy;
Our uncle Lincoln hath, besides his own,
Many a jealous eye, that in your face
Stares only to watch means for your disgrace.

    LACY. Stay, cousin, who be these?

---

[9] Inclination.
[10] A gold coin, worth about three pounds twelve shillings.

Enter SIMON EYRE, MARGERY *his wife,* HODGE, FIRK, JANE,
and RALPH *with a piece*[11]

EYRE. Leave whining, leave whining! Away with this
whimpering, this puling, these blubbering tears, and these
wet eyes! I'll get thy husband discharg'd, I warrant thee,
sweet Jane; go to!

HODGE. Master, here be the captains.

EYRE. Peace, Hodge; hush, ye knave, hush!

FIRK. Here be the cavaliers and the colonels, master.

EYRE. Peace, Firk; peace, my fine Firk! Stand by with your
pishery-pashery,[12] away! I am a man of the best presence;
I'll speak to them, an[13] they were Popes.—Gentlemen, captains, colonels, commanders! Brave men, brave leaders, may
it please you to give me audience. I am Simon Eyre, the
mad shoemaker of Tower Street; this wench with the mealy
mouth that will never tire, is my wife, I can tell you; here's
Hodge, my man and my foreman; here's Firk, my fine firk-
ing[14] journeyman, and this is blubbered Jane. All we come
to be suitors for this honest Ralph. Keep him at home, and
as I am a true shoemaker and a gentleman of the gentle
craft, buy spurs yourselves, and I'll find ye boots these seven
years.

MARG. Seven years, husband?

EYRE. Peace, midriff,[15] peace! I know what I do. Peace!

FIRK. Truly, master cormorant,[16] you shall do God good
service to let Ralph and his wife stay together. She's a
young new-married woman; if you take her husband away
from her a-night, you undo her; she may beg in the day-
time; for he's as good a workman at a prick and an awl, as
any is in our trade.

JANE. O let him stay, else I shall be undone.

FIRK. Ay, truly, she shall be laid at one side like a pair
of old shoes else, and be occupied for no use.

LACY. Truly, my friends, it lies not in my power:
The Londoners are press'd,[17] paid, and set forth
By the lord mayor; I cannot change a man.

HODGE. Why, then you were as good be a corporal as a

---

[11] Piece of leather.   [12] Twiddle-twaddle.   [13] If.   [14] Frisky, tricky.
[15] Used as a term of contempt.   [16] Quibbling on *colonel.*
[17] Impressed into service.

colonel, if you cannot discharge one good fellow; and I tell
you true, I think you do more than you can answer, to press
a man within a year and a day of his marriage.

EYRE. Well said, melancholy Hodge; gramercy, my fine
foreman.

MARG. Truly, gentlemen, it were ill done for such as you,
to stand so stiffly against a poor young wife, considering
her case, she is new-married, but let that pass. I pray, deal
not roughly with her; her husband is a young man, and but
newly ent'red, but let that pass.

EYRE. Away with your pishery-pashery, your pols and your
edipols![18] Peace, midriff; silence, Cicely Bumtrinket! Let
your head speak.

FIRK. Yea, and the horns too, master.

EYRE. Too soon, my fine Firk, too soon! Peace, scoundrels! See you this man? Captains, you will not release
him? Well, let him go; he's a proper shot; let him vanish!
Peace, Jane, dry up thy tears, they'll make his powder
dankish.[19] Take him, brave men; Hector of Troy was an
hackney to him, Hercules and Termagant[20] scoundrels, Prince
Arthur's Round-table—by the Lord of Ludgate—ne'er fed
such a tall, such a dapper swordsman; by the life of Pharaoh,
a brave, resolute swordsman! Peace, Jane! I say no more,
mad knaves.

FIRK. See, see, Hodge, how my master raves in commendation of Ralph!

HODGE. Ralph, th'art a gull,[21] by this hand, an thou goest
not.

ASKEW. I am glad, good Master Eyre, it is my hap
To meet so resolute a soldier.
Trust me, for your report and love to him,
A common slight regard shall not respect him.

LACY. Is thy name Ralph?

RALPH.   Yes, sir.

LACY.   Give me thy hand;
Thou shalt not want, as I am a gentleman.
Woman, be patient; God, no doubt, will send
Thy husband safe again; but he must go,
His country's quarrel says it shall be so.

[18] Solemn declarations.   [19] Damp.   [20] An imaginary Saracen god.   [21] Fool.

HODGE. Th'art a gull, by my stirrup, if thou dost not go.
I will not have thee strike thy gimlet into these weak vessels;
prick thine enemies, Ralph.

Enter DODGER

DODGER. My lord, your uncle on the Tower-hill
Stays with the lord mayor and the aldermen,
And doth request you with all speed you may,
To hasten thither.

ASKEW.   Cousin, let's go.

LACY. Dodger, run you before, tell them we come.—
This Dodger is mine uncle's parasite,   *Exit* DODGER.
The arrant'st varlet that e'er breath'd on earth;
He sets more discord in a noble house
By one day's broaching of his pickthank tales,[22]
Than can be salv'd[23] again in twenty years,
And he, I fear, shall go with us to France,
To pry into our actions.

ASKEW.   Therefore, coz,
It shall behove you to be circumspect.

LACY. Fear not, good cousin.—Ralph, hie to your colours.
                              [*Exit* LACY *and* ASKEW.]

RALPH. I must, because there's no remedy;
But, gentle master and my loving dame,
As you have always been a friend to me,
So in mine absence think upon my wife.

JANE. Alas, my Ralph.

MARG. She cannot speak for weeping.

EYRE. Peace, you crack'd groats,[24] you mustard tokens,[25]
disquiet not the brave soldier. Go thy ways, Ralph!

JANE. Ay, ay, you bid him go; what shall I do
When he is gone?

FIRK. Why, be doing with me or my fellow Hodge; be
not idle.

EYRE. Let me see thy hand, Jane. This fine hand, this
white hand, these pretty fingers must spin, must card, must
work; work, you bombast-cotton-candle-quean; work for
your living, with a pox to you.—Hold thee, Ralph, here's **five**

----

[22] Tales told to curry favor.   [23] Healed.   [24] Fourpenny-pieces.
[25] Yellow spots on the body denoting the infection of the plague.

sixpences for thee; fight for the honour of the gentle craft,
for the gentlemen shoemakers, the courageous cordwainers,
the flower of St. Martin's, the mad knaves of Bedlam, Fleet
Street, Tower Street and Whitechapel; crack me the crowns
of the French knaves; a pox on them, crack them; fight, by
the Lord of Ludgate; fight, my fine boy!

FIRK. Here, Ralph, here's three twopences: two carry
into France, the third shall wash our souls at parting, for
sorrow is dry. For my sake, firk the *Basa mon cues*.

HODGE. Ralph, I am heavy at parting; but here's a shilling
for thee. God send[26] thee to cram thy slops[27] with French
crowns, and thy enemies' bellies with bullets.

RALPH. I thank you, master, and I thank you all.
Now, gentle wife, my loving lovely Jane,
Rich men, at parting, give their wives rich gifts,
Jewels and rings, to grace their lily hands.
Thou know'st our trade makes rings for women's heels:
Here take this pair of shoes, cut out by Hodge,
Stitch'd by my fellow Firk, seam'd by myself,
Made up and pink'd[28] with letters for thy name.
Wear them, my dear Jane, for thy husband's sake,
And every morning, when thou pull'st them on,
Remember me, and pray for my return.
Make much of them; for I have made them so
That I can know them from a thousand mo.
Drum sounds. Enter the LORD MAYOR, *the* Earl *of* LINCOLN,
    LACY, ASKEW, DODGER, *and* Soldiers. *They pass over
    the stage;* RALPH *falls in amongst them;* FIRK *and the
    rest cry* " Farewell," *etc., and so exeunt.*

ACT II

SCENE I[1]

Enter ROSE, *alone, making a garland*

ROSE. Here sit thou down upon this flow'ry bank,
And make a garland for thy Lacy's head.
These pinks, these roses, and these violets,
These blushing gilliflowers, these marigolds,

---

[26] Grant.   [27] Breeches (-pockets).   [28] Perforated.
[1] A garden at Old Ford.

The fair embroidery of his coronet,
Carry not half such beauty in their cheeks,
As the sweet countenance of my Lacy doth.
O my most unkind father! O my stars,
Why lower'd you so at my nativity,
To make me love, yet live robb'd of my love?
Here as a thief am I imprisoned
For my dear Lacy's sake within those walls,
Which by my father's cost were builded up
For better purposes. Here must I languish
For him that doth as much lament, I know,
Mine absence, as for him I pine in woe.

Enter Sybil

Sybil. Good morrow, young mistress. I am sure you make that garland for me; against[2] I shall be Lady of the Harvest.

Rose. Sybil, what news at London?

Sybil. None but good; my lord mayor, your father, and master Philpot, your uncle, and Master Scot, your cousin, and Mistress Frigbottom by Doctors' Commons, do all, by my troth, send you most hearty commendations.

Rose. Did Lacy send kind greetings to his love?

Sybil. O yes, out of cry, by my troth. I scant knew him; here 'a wore a scarf; and here a scarf, here a bunch of feathers, and here precious stones and jewels, and a pair of garters,—O, monstrous! like one of our yellow silk curtains at home here in Old Ford House here, in Master Belly-mount's chamber. I stood at our door in Cornhill, look'd at him, he at me indeed, spake to him, but he not to me, not a word; marry go-up, thought I, with a wanion![3] He passed by me as proud—Marry foh! are you grown humorous,[4] thought I; and so shut the door, and in I came.

Rose. O Sybil, how dost thou my Lacy wrong!
My Rowland is as gentle as a lamb,
No dove was ever half so mild as he.

Sybil. Mild? yea, as a bushel of stamped crabs.[5] He looked upon me as sour as verjuice.[6] Go thy ways, thought

---

[2] In preparation.   [3] With a vengeance.   [4] Capricious.
[5] Crushed crab apples.   [6] Juice of green fruits.

I; thou may'st be much in my gaskins,[7] but nothing in my nether-stocks.[8] This is your fault, mistress, to love him that loves not you; he thinks scorn to do as he's done to; but if I were as you, I'd cry, 'Go by, Jeronimo, go by!'[9]

> I'd set mine old debts against my new driblets,
> And the hare's foot against the goose giblets,
> For if ever I sigh, when sleep I should take,
> Pray God I may lose my maidenhead when I wake.

ROSE. Will my love leave me then, and go to France?

SYBIL. I know not that, but I am sure I see him stalk before the soldiers. By my troth, he is a proper man; but he is proper that proper doth. Let him go snick-up,[10] young mistress.

ROSE. Get thee to London, and learn perfectly
Whether my Lacy go to France, or no.
Do this, and I will give thee for thy pains
My cambric apron and my Romish gloves,
My purple stockings and a stomacher.
Say, wilt thou do this, Sybil, for my sake?

SYBIL. Will I, quoth'a? At whose suit? By my troth, yes, I'll go. A cambric apron, gloves, a pair of purple stockings, and a stomacher! I'll sweat in purple, mistress, for you; I'll take anything that comes a' God's name. O rich! a cambric apron! Faith, then have at 'up tails all.' I'll go jiggy-joggy to London, and be here in a trice, young mistress.　　　　　*Exit.*

ROSE. Do so, good Sybil. Meantime wretched I
Will sit and sigh for his lost company.　　　　　*Exit.*

SCENE II[1]

Enter LACY, *disguised as a Dutch Shoemaker*

LACY. How many shapes have gods and kings devis'd,
Thereby to compass their desired loves!
It is no shame for Rowland Lacy, then,

[7] Wide trousers.
[8] Stockings. The meaning seems to be that though we may be acquainted, we are not intimate friends.　　[9] A phrase from Kyd's *Spanish Tragedy.*
[10] Go and be hanged!
[1] A street in London.

To clothe his cunning with the gentle craft,
That, thus disguis'd, I may unknown possess
The only happy presence of my Rose.
For her have I forsook my charge in France,
Incurr'd the king's displeasure, and stirr'd up
Rough hatred in mine uncle Lincoln's breast.
O love, how powerful art thou, that canst change
High birth to baseness, and a noble mind
To the mean semblance of a shoemaker!
But thus it must be. For her cruel father,
Hating the single union of our souls,
Has secretly convey'd my Rose from London,
To bar me of her presence; but I trust,
Fortune and this disguise will further me
Once more to view her beauty, gain her sight.
Here in Tower Street with Eyre the shoemaker
Mean I a while to work; I know the trade,
I learnt it when I was in Wittenberg.
Then cheer thy hoping spirits, be not dismay'd,
Thou canst not want: do Fortune what she can,
The gentle craft is living for a man.   *Exit.*

SCENE III[1]

Enter EYRE, *making himself ready*[2]

EYRE. Where be these boys, these girls, these drabs, these
scoundrels? They wallow in the fat brewiss[3] of my bounty,
and lick up the crumbs of my table, yet will not rise to see
my walks cleansed. Come out, you powder-beef[4] queans!
What, Nan! what, Madge Mumble-crust. Come out, you
fat midriff-swag-belly-whores, and sweep me these kennels[5]
that the noisome stench offend not the noses of my neighbours. What, Firk, I say; what, Hodge! Open my shop-
windows! What, Firk, I say!

[1] Before Eyre's house.   [2] Dressing himself.
[3] Beef broth.   [4] Salted beef.   [5] Gutters.

Enter FIRK

FIRK. O master, is't you that speak bandog[6] and Bed-lam[7] this morning? I was in a dream, and mused what madman was got into the street so early. Have you drunk this morning that your throat is so clear?

EYRE. Ah, well said, Firk; well said, Firk. To work, my fine knave, to work! Wash thy face, and thou't be more blest.

FIRK. Let them wash my face that will eat it. Good master, send for a souse-wife,[8] if you'll have my face cleaner.

Enter HODGE

EYRE. Away, sloven! avaunt, scoundrel!—Good-morrow, Hodge; good-morrow, my fine foreman.

HODGE. O master, good-morrow; y'are an early stirrer. Here's a fair morning.—Good-morrow, Firk, I could have slept this hour. Here's a brave day towards.[9]

EYRE. Oh, haste to work, my fine foreman, haste to work.

FIRK. Master, I am dry as dust to hear my fellow Roger talk of fair weather; let us pray for good leather, and let clowns and ploughboys and those that work in the fields pray for brave days. We work in a dry shop; what care I if it rain?

Enter MARGERY

EYRE. How now, Dame Margery, can you see to rise? Trip and go, call up the drabs, your maids.

MARG. See to rise? I hope 'tis time enough, 'tis early enough for any woman to be seen abroad. I marvel how many wives in Tower Street are up so soon. Gods me, 'tis not noon,—here's a yawling![10]

EYRE. Peace, Margery, peace! Where's Cicely Bum-trinket, your maid? She has a privy fault, she farts in her sleep. Call the quean up; if my men want shoe-thread, I'll swinge her in a stirrup.

FIRK. Yet, that's but a dry beating; here's still a sign of drought.

---

[6] Watch-dog.   [7] Madman.
[8] A woman who washed and pickled pigs' faces.
[9] Coming.   [10] Bawling.

Enter LACY *disguised, singing*

LACY. *Der was een bore van Gelderland*
   Frolick sie byen;
   He was als dronck he cold nyet stand,
   Upsolce sie byen.
   Tap eens de canneken,
   Drincke, schone mannekin.[11]

FIRK. Master, for my life, yonder's a brother of the gentle craft; if he bear not Saint Hugh's bones,[12] 'I'll forfeit my bones; he's some uplandish workman: hire him, good master, that I may learn some gibble-gabble; 'twill make us work the faster.

EYRE. Peace, Firk! A hard world! Let him pass, let him vanish; we have journeymen enow. Peace, my fine Firk!

MARG. Nay, nay, y'are best follow your man's counsel; you shall see what will come on't. We have not men enow, but we must entertain every butter-box;[13] but let that pass.

HODGE. Dame, 'fore God, if my master follow your counsel, he'll consume little beef. He shall be glad of men an he can catch them.

FIRK. Ay, that he shall.

HODGE. 'Fore God, a proper man, and I warrant, a fine workman. Master, farewell; dame, adieu; if such a man as he cannot find work, Hodge is not for you.   *Offers to go.*

EYRE. Stay, my fine Hodge.

FIRK. Faith, an your foreman go, dame, you must take a journey to seek a new journeyman; if Roger remove, Firk follows. If Saint Hugh's bones shall not be set a-work, I may prick mine awl in the walls, and go play. Fare ye well, master; good-bye, dame.

EYRE. Tarry, my fine Hodge, my brisk foreman! Stay, Firk! Peace, pudding-broth! By the Lord of Ludgate, I

[11] The language is, of course, meant for Dutch.
   ' There was a boor from Gelderland,
       Jolly they be;
   He was so drunk he could not stand,
       Drunken (?) they be:
   Clink then the cannikin,
   Drink, pretty mannikin! '
[12] The bones of St. Hugh, the patron saint of shoemakers, were supposed to have been made into shoemaker's tools.
[13] Dutchman.

love my men as my life. Peace, you gallimafry![14] Hodge, if he want work, I'll hire him. One of you to him; stay,—he comes to us.

LACY. *Goeden dach, meester, ende u vro oak.*[15]

FIRK. Nails,[16] if I should speak after him without drinking, I should choke. And you, friend Oake, are you of the gentle craft?

LACY. *Yaw, yaw, ik bin den skomawker.*[17]

FIRK. *Den skomaker,* quoth a! And hark you, *skomaker,* have you all your tools, a good rubbing-pin, a good stopper, a good dresser, your four sorts of awls, and your two balls of wax, your paring knife, your hand- and thumb-leathers, and good St. Hugh's bones to smooth up your work?

LACY. *Yaw, yaw; be niet vorveard. Ik hab all de dingen voour mack skooes groot and cleane.*[18]

FIRK. Ha, ha! Good master, hire him; he'll make me laugh so that I shall work more in mirth than I can in earnest.

EYRE. Hear ye, friend, have ye any skill in the mystery of cordwainers?

LACY. *Ik weet niet wat yow seg; ich verstaw you niet.*[19]

FIRK. Why, thus, man: [*Imitating by gesture a shoemaker at work.*] *Ich verste u niet,* quoth'a.

LACY. *Yaw, yaw, yaw; ick can dat wel doen.*[20]

FIRK. *Yaw, yaw!* He speaks yawing like a jackdaw that gapes to be fed with cheese-curds. Oh, he'll give a villanous pull at a can of double-beer; but Hodge and I have the vantage, we must drink first, because we are the eldest journeymen.

EYRE. What is thy name?

LACY. Hans—Hans Meulter.

EYRE. Give me thy hand; th'art welcome.—Hodge, entertain him; Firk, bid him welcome; come, Hans. Run, wife, bid your maids, your trullibubs,[21] make ready my fine men's breakfasts. To him, Hodge!

[14] A dish of different hashed meats. Many of Eyre's words have no particular appropriateness.   [15] Good day, master, and your wife too.
[16] An oath.   [17] Yes, yes, I am a shoemaker.
[18] Yes, yes; be not afraid. I have everything to make boots big and little.
[19] I don't know what you say; I don't understand you.
[20] Yes, yes, yes; I can do that well.   [21] Slatterns.

HODGE. Hans, th'art welcome; use thyself friendly, for we are good fellows; if not, thou shalt be fought with, wert thou bigger than a giant.

FIRK. Yea, and drunk with, wert thou Gargantua. My master keeps no cowards, I tell thee.—Ho, boy, bring him an heel-block, here's a new journeyman.

Enter Boy

LACY. *O, ich wersto you; ich moet een halve dossen cans betaelen; here, boy, nempt dis skilling, tap eens freelicke.*[22]

Exit Boy.

EYRE. Quick, snipper-snapper, away! Firk, scour thy throat; thou shalt wash it with Castilian liquor.

Enter Boy

Come, my last of the fives, give me a can. Have to thee, Hans; here, Hodge; here, Firk; drink, you mad Greeks, and work like true Trojans, and pray for Simon Eyre, the shoemaker.—Here, Hans, and th'art welcome.

FIRK. Lo, dame, you would have lost a good fellow that will teach us to laugh. This beer came hopping in well.

MARG. Simon, it is almost seven.

EYRE. Is't so, Dame Clapper-dudgeon?[23] Is't seven a clock, and my men's breakfast not ready? Trip and go, you soused conger,[24] away! Come, you mad hyperboreans; follow me, Hodge; follow me, Hans; come after, my fine Firk; to work, to work a while, and then to breakfast! [*Exit.*

FIRK. Soft! *Yaw, yaw,* good Hans, though my master have no more wit but to call you afore me, I am not so foolish to go behind you, I being the elder journeyman.

[*Exeunt.*

SCENE IV[1]

Holloaing within. Enter Master WARNER *and* Master HAMMON, *attired as Hunters*

HAM. Cousin, beat every brake, the game's not far,
This way with winged feet he fled from death,

[22] O, I understand you; I must pay for half-a-dozen cans; here, boy, take this shilling, tap this once freely.   [23] Slang for beggar.   [24] Conger-eel.
[1] A field near Old Ford.

Whilst the pursuing hounds, scenting his steps,
Find out his highway to destruction.
Besides, the miller's boy told me even now,
He saw him take soil,[2] and he holloaed him,
Affirming him to have been so embost[3]
That long he could not hold.

WARN. If it be so,
'Tis best we trace these meadows by Old Ford.

A noise of Hunters *within.* *Enter a* Boy

HAM. How now, boy? Where's the deer? speak, saw'st
thou him?

BOY. O yea; I saw him leap through a hedge, and then
over a ditch, then at my lord mayor's pale, over he skipp'd
me, and in he went me, and "holla" the hunters cried,
and "there, boy; there, boy!" But there he is, a' mine
honesty.

HAM. Boy, Godamercy. Cousin, let's away;
I hope we shall find better sport to-day. *Exeunt.*

SCENE V[1]

[*Hunting within.*] *Enter* ROSE *and* SYBIL

ROSE. Why, Sybil, wilt thou prove a forester?

SYBIL. Upon some, no. Forester? Go by; no, faith,
mistress. The deer came running into the barn through
the orchard and over the pale; I wot well, I looked as
pale as a new cheese to see him. But whip, says Goodman Pin-close, up with his flail, and our Nick with a prong,
and down he fell, and they upon him, and I upon them.
By my troth, we had such sport; and in the end we ended
him; his throat we cut, flayed him, unhorn'd him, and my
lord mayor shall eat of him anon, when he comes.

Horns sound within.

ROSE. Hark, hark, the hunters come; y'are best take heed,
They'll have a saying to you for this deed.

---

[2] Cover.   [3] Exhausted.
[1] The garden at Old Ford.

Enter Master HAMMON, Master WARNER, Huntsmen,
and Boy

HAM. God save you, fair ladies.

SYBIL.   Ladies! O gross![2]

WARN. Came not a buck this way?

ROSE.   No, but two does.

HAM. And which way went they? Faith, we'll hunt at
those.

SYBIL. At those? Upon some, no. When, can you tell?

WARN. Upon some, ay.

SYBIL.   Good Lord!

WARN.   Wounds![3] Then farewell!

HAM. Boy, which way went he?

BOY.   This way, sir, he ran.

HAM. This way he ran indeed, fair Mistress Rose;

Our game was lately in your orchard seen.

WARN. Can you advise, which way he took his flight?

SYBIL. Follow your nose; his horns will guide you right.

WARN. Th'art a mad wench.

SYBIL.   O, rich!

ROSE.   Trust me, not I.

It is not like that the wild forest-deer

Would come so near to places of resort;

You are deceiv'd, he fled some other way.

WARN. Which way, my sugar-candy, can you shew?

SYBIL. Come up, good honeysops, upon some, no.

ROSE. Why do you stay, and not pursue your game?

SYBIL. I'll hold my life, their hunting-nags be lame.

HAM. A deer more dear is found within this place.

ROSE. But not the deer, sir, which you had in chase.

HAM. I chas'd the deer, but this dear chaseth me.

ROSE. The strangest hunting that ever I see.

But where's your park?   *She offers to go away.*

HAM.   'Tis here: O stay!

ROSE. Impale me, and then I will not stray.

WARN. They wrangle, wench; we are more kind than they.

SYBIL. What kind of hart is that dear heart, you seek?

WARN. A hart, dear heart.

[2] Stupid.   [3] An oath.

SYBIL.   Who ever saw the like?

ROSE. To lose your heart, is't possible you can?

HAM. My heart is lost.

ROSE.   Alack, good gentleman!

HAM. This poor lost hart would I wish you might find.

ROSE. You, by such luck, might prove your hart a hind.

HAM. Why, Luck had horns, so have I heard some say.

ROSE. Now, God, an't be his will, send Luck into your way

Enter the LORD MAYOR *and* Servants

L. MAYOR. What, Master Hammon? Welcome to Old
   Ford!

SYBIL. Gods pittikins,[4] Hands off, sir! Here's my lord.

L. MAYOR. I hear you had ill luck, and lost your game.

HAM. Tis true, my lord.

L. MAYOR.   I am sorry for the same.
What gentleman is this?

HAM.   My brother-in-law.

L. MAYOR. Y'are welcome both; sith Fortune offers you
Into my hands, you shall not part from hence,
Until you have refresh'd your wearied limbs.
Go, Sybil, cover the board! You shall be guest
To no good cheer, but even a hunter's feast.

HAM. I thank your lordship.—Cousin, on my life,
For our lost venison I shall find a wife.

                          Exeunt [*all but* MAYOR].

L. MAYOR. In, gentlemen; I'll not be absent long.—
This Hammon is a proper gentleman,
A citizen by birth, fairly allied;
How fit an husband were he for my girl!
Well, I will in, and do the best I can,
To match my daughter to this gentleman.   *Exit.*

---

[4] By God's pity.

ACT III

Scene I[1]

Enter Lacy [*as* Hans], Skipper, Hodge, *and* Firk

Skip. *Ick sal yow wat seggen, Hans; dis skip, dat comen from Candy, is al vol, by Got's sacrament, van sugar, civet, almonds, cambrick, end alle dingen, towsand towsand ding. Nempt it, Hans, nempt it vor v meester. Daer be de bils van laden. Your meester Simon Eyre sal hae good copen. Wat seggen yow, Hans?*[2]

Firk. *Wat seggen de reggen de copen, slopen*—laugh, Hodge, laugh!

Hans. *Mine liever broder Firk, bringt Meester Eyre tot det signe vn Swannekin; daer sal yow finde dis skipper end me. Wat seggen yow, broder Firk? Doot it, Hodge.*[3]
Come, skipper.   *Exeunt.*

Firk. Bring him, quoth you? Here's no knavery, to bring my master to buy a ship worth the lading of two or three hundred thousand pounds. Alas, that's nothing; a trifle, a bauble, Hodge.

Hodge. The truth is, Firk, that the merchant owner of the ship dares not shew his head, and therefore this skipper that deals for him, for the love he bears to Hans, offers my master Eyre a bargain in the commodities. He shall have a reasonable day of payment; he may sell the wares by that time, and be an huge gainer himself.

Firk. Yea, but can my fellow Hans lend my master twenty porpentines as an earnest penny?

Hodge. Portuguese,[4] thou wouldst say; here they be, Firk; hark, they jingle in my pocket like St. Mary Overy's bells.

---

[1] A room in Eyre's house.
[2] I'll tell you what, Hans; this ship that is come from Candia, is quite full, by God's sacrament, of sugar, civet, almonds, cambric, and all things; a thousand, thousand things. Take it, Hans, take it for your master. There are the bills of lading. Your master, Simon Eyre, shall have a good bargain. What say you, Hans?
[3] My dear brother Firk, bring Master Eyre to the sign of the Swan; there shall you find this skipper and me. What say you, brother Firk? Do it, Hodge.
[4] A coin worth about three pounds twelve shillings.

Enter EYRE *and* MARGERY

FIRK. Mum, here comes my dame and my master. She'll scold, on my life, for loitering this Monday; but all's one, let them all say what they can, Monday's our holiday.

MARG. You sing, Sir Sauce, but I beshrew your heart,
    I fear, for this your singing we shall smart.

FIRK. Smart for me, dame; why, dame, why?

HODGE. Master, I hope you'll not suffer my dame to take down your journeymen.

FIRK. If she take me down, I'll take her up; yea, and take her down too, a button-hole lower.

EYRE. Peace, Firk; not I, Hodge; by the life of Pharaoh, by the Lord of Ludgate, by this beard, every hair whereof I value at a king's ransom, she shall not meddle with you.— Peace, you bombast-cotton-candle-quean; away, queen of clubs; quarrel not with me and my men, with me and my fine Firk; I'll firk you, if you do.

MARG. Yea, yea, man, you may use me as you please; but let that pass.

EYRE. Let it pass, let it vanish away; peace! Am I not Simon Eyre? Are not these my brave men, brave shoe-makers, all gentlemen of the gentle craft? Prince am I none, yet am I nobly born, as being the sole son of a shoe-maker. Away, rubbish! vanish, melt; melt like kitchen-stuff.

MARG. Yea, yea, 'tis well; I must be call'd rubbish, kitchen-stuff, for a sort⁵ of knaves.

FIRK. Nay, dame, you shall not weep and wail in woe for me. Master, I'll stay no longer; here's an inventory of my shop-tools. Adieu, master; Hodge, farewell.

HODGE. Nay, stay, Firk; thou shalt not go alone.

MARG. I pray, let them go; there be more maids than Mawkin, more men than Hodge, and more fools than Firk.

FIRK. Fools? Nails! if I tarry now, I would my guts might be turn'd to shoe-thread.

HODGE. And if I stay, I pray God I may be turn'd to a Turk, and set in Finsbury⁶ for boys to shoot at.— Come, Firk.

⁵ Set.   ⁶ Finsbury was a famous practising ground for archery.

EYRE. Stay, my fine knaves, you arms of my trade, you pillars of my profession. What, shall a tittle-tattle's words make you forsake Simon Eyre?—Avaunt, kitchen-stuff! Rip, you brown-bread Tannikin; out of my sight! Move me not! Have not I ta'en you from selling tripes in East-cheap, and set you in my shop, and made you hail-fellow with Simon Eyre, the shoemaker? And now do you deal thus with my journeymen? Look, you powder-beef-quean, on the face of Hodge, here's a face for a lord.

FIRK. And here's a face for any lady in Christendom.

EYRE. Rip, you chitterling, avaunt! Boy, bid the tapster of the Boar's Head fill me a dozen cans of beer for my journeymen.

FIRK. A dozen cans? O, brave! Hodge, now I'll stay.

EYRE. [*In a low voice to the* Boy]. An the knave fills any more than two, he pays for them. [*Exit* Boy. *Aloud.*] —A dozen cans of beer for my journeymen. [*Re-enter* Boy.] Here, you mad Mesopotamians, wash your livers with this liquor. Where be the odd ten? No more, Madge, no more.—Well said. Drink and to work!—What work dost thou, Hodge? What work?

HODGE. I am a making a pair of shoes for my lord mayor's daughter, Mistress Rose.

FIRK. And I a pair of shoes for Sybil, my lord's maid. I deal with her.

EYRE. Sybil? Fie, defile not thy fine workmanly fingers with the feet of kitchenstuff and basting-ladles. Ladies of the court, fine ladies, my lads, commit their feet to our apparelling; put gross work to Hans. Yark and seam, yark[7] and seam!

FIRK. For yarking and seaming let me alone, an I come to't.

HODGE. Well, master, all this is from the bias.[8] Do you remember the ship my fellow Hans told you of? The skipper and he are both drinking at the Swan. Here be the Portuguese to give earnest. If you go through with it, you cannot choose but be a lord at least.

FIRK. Nay, dame, if my master prove not a lord, and you a lady, hang me.

[7] Prepare.   [8] Beside the point.

MARG. Yea, like enough, if you may loiter and tipple thus.

FIRK. Tipple, dame? No, we have been bargaining with Skellum Skanderbag:[9] can you Dutch spreaken for a ship of silk Cyprus, laden with sugar-candy.

Enter Boy *with a velvet coat and an Alderman's gown.* EYRE *puts them on*

EYRE. Peace, Firk; silence, Tittle-tattle! Hodge, I'll go through with it. Here's a seal-ring, and I have sent for a guarded gown[10] and a damask cassock. See where it comes; look here, Maggy; help me, Firk; apparel me, Hodge; silk and satin, you mad Philistines, silk and satin.

FIRK. Ha, ha, my master will be as proud as a dog in a doublet, all in beaten[11] damask and velvet.

EYRE. Softly, Firk, for rearing[12] of the nap, and wearing threadbare my garments. How dost thou like me, Firk? How do I look, my fine Hodge?

HODGE. Why, now you look like yourself, master. I warrant you, there's few in the city but will give you the wall,[13] and come upon you with[14] the right worshipful.

FIRK. Nails, my master looks like a threadbare cloak new turned and dressed. Lord, Lord, to see what good raiment doth! Dame, dame, are you not enamoured?

EYRE. How say'st thou, Maggy, am I not brisk? Am I not fine?

MARG. Fine? By my troth, sweetheart, very fine! By my troth, I never liked thee so well in my life, sweetheart; but let that pass. I warrant, there be many women in the city have not such handsome husbands, but only for their apparel; but let that pass too.

Re-enter HANS *and* Skipper

HANS. *Godden day, mester. Dis be de skipper dat heb de skip van marchandice; de commodity ben good; nempt it, master, nempt it.*[15]

---

[9] German: Schelm, a scoundrel. Skanderbag, or Scander Beg (*i. e.* Lord Alexander), a Turkish name for John Kastriota, the Albanian hero, who freed his country from the yoke of the Turks (1443—1467).—*Warnke and Proescholdt.*
[10] A robe ornamented with guards or facings. [11] Stamped. [12] Ruffling.
[13] Yield precedence. [14] Address you as.
[15] Good day, master. This is the skipper that has the ship of merchandise; the commodity is good; take it, master, take it.

EYRE. Godamercy, Hans; welcome, skipper. Where lies this ship of merchandise?

SKIP. *De skip ben in revere; dor be van Sugar, cyvet, al-monds, cambrick, and a towsand, towsand tings, gotz sacra-ment; nempt it, mester: ye sal heb good copen.*[16]

FIRK. To him, master! O sweet master! O sweet wares! Prunes, almonds, sugar-candy, carrot-roots, turnips, O brave fatting meat! Let not a man buy a nutmeg but yourself.

EYRE. Peace, Firk! Come, skipper, I'll go aboard with you.—Hans, have you made him drink?

SKIP. *Yaw, yaw, ic heb veale gedrunck.*[17]

EYRE. Come, Hans, follow me. Skipper, thou shalt have my countenance in the city.   *Exeunt.*

FIRK. *Yaw heb veale gedrunck,* quoth a. They may well be called butter-boxes, when they drink fat veal and thick beer too. But come, dame, I hope you'll chide us no more.

MARG. No, faith, Firk; no, perdy,[18] Hodge. I do feel honour creep upon me, and which is more, a certain rising in my flesh; but let that pass.

FIRK. Rising in your flesh do you feel, say you? Ay, you may be with child, but why should not my master feel a rising in his flesh, having a gown and a gold ring on? But you are such a shrew, you'll soon pull him down.

MARG. Ha, ha! prithee, peace! Thou mak'st my worship laugh; but let that pass. Come, I'll go in; Hodge, prithee, go before me; Firk, follow me.

FIRK. Firk doth follow: Hodge, pass out in state.

Exeunt.

SCENE II[1]

Enter the EARL OF LINCOLN *and* DODGER

LINCOLN. How now, good Dodger, what's the news in France?

DODGER. My lord, upon the eighteenth day of May
The French and English were prepar'd to fight;
Each side with eager fury gave the sign

---

[16] The ship lies in the river; there are sugar, civet, almonds, cambric, and a thousand thousand things. By God's sacrament, take it, master; you shall have a good bargain.   [17] Yes, yes, I have drunk well.
[18] Fr. *Par Dieu.*
[1] London: a room in Lincoln's house.

Of a most hot encounter. Five long hours
Both armies fought together; at the length
The lot of victory fell on our side.
Twelve thousand of the Frenchmen that day died,
Four thousand English, and no man of name
But Captain Hyam and young Ardington,
Two gallant gentlemen, I knew them well.

    LINCOLN. But Dodger, prithee, tell me, in this fight
How did my cousin Lacy bear himself?

    DODGER. My lord, your cousin Lacy was not there.

    LINCOLN. Not there?

    DODGER.   No, my good lord.

    LINCOLN.   Sure, thou mistakest.
I saw him shipp'd, and a thousand eyes beside
Were witnesses of the farewells which he gave,
When I, with weeping eyes, bid him adieu.
Dodger, take heed.

    DODGER.   My lord, I am advis'd[2]
That what I spake is true: to prove it so,
His cousin Askew, that supplied his place,
Sent me for him from France, that secretly
He might convey himself thither.

    LINCOLN.   Is't even so?
Dares he so carelessly venture his life
Upon the indignation of a king?
Has he despis'd my love, and spurn'd those favours
Which I with prodigal hand pour'd on his head?
He shall repent his rashness with his soul;
Since of my love he makes no estimate,
I'll make him wish he had not known my hate.
Thou hast no other news?

    DODGER.   None else, my lord.

    LINCOLN. None worse I know thou hast.—Procure the
        king
To crown his giddy brows with ample honours,
Send him chief colonel, and all my hope
Thus to be dash'd! But 'tis in vain to grieve,
One evil cannot a worse relieve.
Upon my life, I have found out his plot;

[2] Certainly informed.

That old dog, Love, that fawn'd upon him so,
Love to that puling girl, his fair-cheek'd Rose,
The lord mayor's daughter, hath distracted him,
And in the fire of that love's lunacy
Hath he burnt up himself, consum'd his credit,
Lost the king's love, yea, and I fear, his life,
Only to get a wanton to his wife,
Dodger, it is so.
 DODGER.   I fear so, my good lord.
 LINCOLN. It is so—nay, sure it cannot be!
I am at my wits' end. Dodger!
 DODGER.   Yea, my lord.
 LINCOLN. Thou art acquainted with my nephew's haunts.
Spend this gold for thy pains; go seek him out;
Watch at my lord mayor's—there if he live,
Dodger, thou shalt be sure to meet with him.
Prithee, be diligent.—Lacy, thy name
Liv'd once in honour, now 'tis dead in shame.—
Be circumspect.   *Exit.*
 DODGER. I warrant you, my lord. *Exit.*

SCENE III[1]

Enter the LORD MAYOR *and* Master SCOTT

 L. MAYOR. Good Master Scott, I have been bold with you,
To be a witness to a wedding-knot
Betwixt young Master Hammon and my daughter.
O, stand aside; see where the lovers come.

Enter MASTER HAMMON *and* ROSE

 ROSE. Can it be possible you love me so?
No, no, within those eyeballs I espy
Apparent likelihoods of flattery.
Pray now, let go my hand.
 HAM.   Sweet Mistress Rose,
Misconstrue not my words, nor misconceive
Of my affection, whose devoted soul
Swears that I love thee dearer than my heart.

    [1] London: a room in the Lord Mayor's house.

Rose. As dear as your own heart? I judge it right,
Men love their hearts best when th'are out of sight.

Ham. I love you, by this hand.

Rose.   Yet hands off now!
If flesh be frail, how weak and frail's your vow!

Ham. Then by my life I swear.

Rose.   Then do not brawl;
One quarrel loseth wife and life and all.
Is not your meaning thus?

Ham.   In faith, you jest.

Rose. Love loves to sport; therefore leave love, y'are
    best,

L. Mayor. What? square[2] they, Master Scott?

Scott.   Sir, never doubt,
Lovers are quickly in, and quickly out.

Ham. Sweet Rose, be not so strange in fancying me.
Nay, never turn aside, shun not my sight:
I am not grown so fond, to fond[3] my love
On any that shall quit it with disdain;
If you will love me, so—if not, farewell.

L. Mayor. Why, how now, lovers, are you both agreed?

Ham. Yes, faith, my lord.

L. Mayor.   'Tis well, give me your hand.
Give me yours, daughter.—How now, both pull back!
What means this, girl?

Rose.   I mean to live a maid.

Ham. But not to die one; pause, ere that be said. *Aside.*

L. Mayor. Will you still cross me, still be obstinate?

Ham. Nay, chide her not, my lord, for doing well;
If she can live an happy virgin's life,
'Tis far more blessed than to be a wife.

Rose. Say, sir, I cannot: I have made a vow,
Whoever be my husband, 'tis not you.

L. Mayor. Your tongue is quick; but Master Hammon,
    know,
I bade you welcome to another end.

Ham. What, would you have me pule and pine and
        pray,
    With 'lovely lady,' 'mistress of my heart,'

----

[2] Quarrel.   [3] Found, set; a pun upon fond.

'Pardon your servant,' and the rhymer play,
    Railing on Cupid and his tyrant's-dart;
Or shall I undertake some martial spoil,
Wearing your glove at tourney and at tilt,
And tell how many gallants I unhors'd—
Sweet, will this pleasure you?
    Rose.   Yea, when wilt begin?
What, love rhymes, man? Fie on that deadly sin!
    L. Mayor. If you will have her, I'll make her agree.
    Ham. Enforced love is worse than hate to me.
[Aside.] There is a wench keeps shop in the Old Change,
To her will I; it is not wealth I seek,
I have enough; and will prefer her love
Before the world.—[Aloud.] My good lord mayor, adieu.
Old love for me, I have no luck with new.   Exit.
    L. Mayor. Now, mammet,° you have well behav'd yourself,
But you shall curse your coyness if I live.—
Who's within there? See you convey your mistress
Straight to th' Old Ford! I'll keep you straight enough.
Fore God, I would have sworn the puling girl
Would willingly accepted Hammon's love;
But banish him, my thoughts!—Go, minion, in!   Exit Rose.
Now tell me, Master Scott, would you have thought
That Master Simon Eyre, the shoemaker,
Had been of wealth to buy such merchandise?
    Scott. 'Twas well, my lord, your honour and myself
Grew partners with him; for your bills of lading
Shew that Eyre's gains in one commodity
Rise at the least to full three thousand pound
Besides like gain in other merchandise.
    L. Mayor. Well, he shall spend some of his thousands
        now,
For I have sent for him to the Guildhall.

Enter Eyre

See, where he comes.—Good morrow, Master Eyre.
    Eyre. Poor Simon Eyre, my lord, your shoemaker.
    L. Mayor. Well, well, it likes° yourself to term you so.

° Puppet, doll.   ° Pleases.

Enter DODGER

Now, Master Dodger, what's the news with you?

DODGER. I'd gladly speak in private to your honour.

L. MAYOR You shall, you shall.—Master Eyre and Master
 Scott,

I have some business with this gentleman;
I pray, let me entreat you to walk before
To the Guildhall; I'll follow presently.
Master Eyre, I hope ere noon to call you sheriff.

EYRE. I would not care, my lord, if you might call me
King of Spain.—Come, Master Scott.

        [Exeunt EYRE *and* SCOTT.]

 L. MAYOR. Now, Master Dodger, what's the news you
bring?

DODGER. The Earl of Lincoln by me greets your lordship,
And earnestly requests you, if you can,
Inform him where his nephew Lacy keeps.

 L. MAYOR. Is not his nephew Lacy now in France?

DODGER. No, I assure your lordship, but disguis'd
Lurks here in London.

 L. MAYOR   London? Is't even so?
It may be; but upon my faith and soul,
I know not where he lives, or whether he lives:
So tell my Lord of Lincoln.—Lurks in London?
Well, Master Dodger, you perhaps may start him;
Be but the means to rid him into France,
I'll give you a dozen angels[6] for your pains:
So much I love his honour, hate his nephew.
And, prithee, so inform thy lord from me.

 DODGER. I take my leave.   *Exit* DODGER.

 L. MAYOR.   Farewell, good Master Dodger.
Lacy in London? I dare pawn my life,
My daughter knows thereof, and for that cause
Deni'd young Master Hammon in his love.
Well, I am glad I sent her to Old Ford.
Gods Lord, 'tis late; to Guildhall I must hie;
I know my brethren stay[r] my company.   *Exit.*

    [6] Coins worth about 10s. each.   [r] Wait for.

Enter FIRK, MARGERY, [LACY *as*] HANS, *and* ROGER

MARG. Thou goest too fast for me, Roger. O, Firk!

FIRK. Ay, forsooth.

MARG. I pray thee, run—do you hear?—run to Guildhall, and learn if my husband, Master Eyre, will take that worshipful vocation of Master Sheriff upon him. Hie thee, good Firk.

FIRK. Take it? Well, I go; an he should not take it, Firk swears to forswear him. Yes, forsooth, I go to Guildhall.

MARG. Nay, when? Thou art too compendious and tedious.

FIRK. O rare, your excellence is full of eloquence; how like a new cart-wheel my dame speaks, and she looks like an old musty ale-bottle[2] going to scalding.

MARG. Nay, when? Thou wilt make me melancholy.

FIRK. God forbid your worship should fall into that humour;—I run. *Exit.*

MARG. Let me see now, Roger and Hans.

HODGE. Ay, forsooth, dame—mistress I should say, but the old term so sticks to the roof of my mouth, I can hardly lick it off.

MARG. Even what thou wilt, good Roger; dame is a fair name for any honest Christian; but let that pass. How dost thou, Hans?

HANS. *Mee tanck you, vro.*[3]

MARG. Well, Hans and Roger, you see, God hath blest your master, and, perdy, if ever he comes to be Master Sheriff of London—as we are all mortal—you shall see, I will have some odd thing or other in a corner for you: I will not be your back-friend;[4] but let that pass. Hans, pray thee, tie my shoe.

HANS. *Yaw, ic sal, vro.*[5]

MARG. Roger, thou know'st the length of my foot; as it is none of the biggest, so I thank God, it is handsome enough; prithee, let me have a pair of shoes made, cork, good Roger, wooden heel too.

HODGE. You shall.

---

[1] London: a room in Eyre's house. [2] Ale-kegs, made of wood.
[3] I thank you, mistress! [4] Faithless friend. [5] Yes, I shall, mistress!

MARG. Art thou acquainted with never a farthingale-maker, nor a French hood-maker? I must enlarge my bum, ha, ha! How shall I look in a hood, I wonder! Perdy, oddly, I think.

HODGE. [*Aside.*] As a cat out of a pillory.—Very well, I warrant you, mistress.

MARG. Indeed, all flesh is grass; and, Roger, canst thou tell where I may buy a good hair?

HODGE. Yes, forsooth, at the poulterer's in Gracious Street.

MARG. Thou art an ungracious wag; perdy, I mean a false hair for my periwig.

HODGE. Why, mistress, the next time I cut my beard, you shall have the shavings of it; but they are all true hairs.

MARG. It is very hot, I must get me a fan or else a mask.

HODGE. [*Aside.*] So you had need, to hide your wicked face.

MARG. Fie, upon it, how costly this world's calling is; perdy, but that it is one of the wonderful works of God, I would not deal with it.—Is not Firk come yet? Hans, be not so sad, let it pass and vanish, as my husband's worship says.

HANS. *Ick bin vrolicke, lot see yow soo.*[6]

HODGE. Mistress, will you drink[7] a pipe of tobacco?

MARG. Oh, fie upon it, Roger, perdy! These filthy tobacco-pipes are the most idle slavering baubles that ever I felt. Out upon it! God bless us, men look not like men that use them.

Enter RALPH, *lame*

HODGE. What, fellow Ralph? Mistress, look here, Jane's husband! Why, how now, lame? Hans, make much of him, he's a brother of our trade, a good workman, and a tall soldier.

HANS. You be welcome, broder.

MARG. Perdy, I knew him not. How dost thou, good Ralph? I am glad to see thee well.

RALPH. I would to God you saw me, dame, as well As when I went from London into France.

MARG. Trust me, I am sorry, Ralph, to see thee impotent. Lord, how the wars have made him sunburnt! The left leg is not well; 'twas a fair gift of God the infirmity took not

[6] I am merry; let's see you so too!   [7] Smoke.

hold a little higher, considering thou camest from France; but let that pass.

RALPH. I am glad to see you well, and I rejoice
To hear that God hath blest my master so
Since my departure.

MARG. Yea, truly, Ralph, I thank my Maker; but let that pass.

HODGE. And, sirrah Ralph, what news, what news in France?

RALPH. Tell me, good Roger, first, what news in England?
How does my Jane? When didst thou see my wife?
Where lives my poor heart? She'll be poor indeed,
Now I want limbs to get whereon to feed.

HODGE. Limbs? Hast thou not hands, man? Thou shalt never see a shoemaker want bread, though he have but three fingers on a hand.

RALPH. Yet all this while I hear not of my Jane.

MARG. O Ralph, your wife,—perdy, we know not what's become of her. She was here a while, and because she was married, grew more stately than became her; I checked her, and so forth; away she flung, never returned, nor said bye nor bah; and, Ralph, you know, "ka me, ka thee."[8] And so, as I tell ye——Roger, is not Firk come yet?

HODGE. No, forsooth.

MARG. And so, indeed, we heard not of her, but I hear she lives in London; but let that pass. If she had wanted, she might have opened her case to me or my husband, or to any of my men; I am sure, there's not any of them, perdy, but would have done her good to his power. Hans, look if Firk be come.

HANS. *Yaw, ik sal, vro.*[9]   *Exit* HANS.

MARG. And so, as I said—but, Ralph, why dost thou weep? Thou knowest that naked we came out of our mother's womb, and naked we must return; and, therefore, thank God for all things.

HODGE. No, faith, Jane is a stranger here; but, Ralph, pull up a good heart, I know thou hast one. Thy wife, man, is in London; one told me, he saw her a while ago very brave[10] and neat; we'll ferret her out, an London hold her.

MARG. Alas, poor soul, he's overcome with sorrow; he

---

[8] Scratch me, and I'll scratch thee.   [9] Yes, I shall, dame!   [10] Fine.

does but as I do, weep for the loss of any good thing. But, Ralph, get thee in, call for some meat and drink, thou shalt find me worshipful towards thee.

RALPH. I thank you, dame; since I want limbs and lands, I'll trust to God, my good friends, and my hands.   *Exit.*

Enter HANS *and* FIRK *running*

FIRK. Run, good Hans! O Hodge, O mistress! Hodge, heave up thine ears; mistress, smug up[11] your looks; on with your best apparel; my master is chosen, my master is called, nay, condemned by the cry of the country to be sheriff of the city for this famous year now to come. And time now being, a great many men in black gowns were asked for their voices and their hands, and my master had all their fists about his ears presently, and they cried 'Ay, ay, ay, ay,'—and so I came away—
      Wherefore without all other grieve
      I do salute you, Mistress Shrieve,[12]

HANS. *Yaw, my mester is de groot man, de shrieve.*

HODGE. Did not I tell you, mistress? Now I may boldly say: Good-morrow to your worship.

MARG. Good-morrow, good Roger. I thank you, my good people all.—Firk, hold up thy hand: here's a three-penny piece for thy tidings.

FIRK. 'Tis but three-half-pence, I think. Yes, 'tis three-pence, I smell the rose.[13]

HODGE. But, mistress, be rul'd by me, and do not speak so pulingly.

FIRK. 'Tis her worship speaks so, and not she. No, faith, mistress, speak me in the old key: 'To it, Firk,' 'there, good Firk,' 'ply your business, Hodge,' 'Hodge, with a full mouth,' 'I'll fill your bellies with good cheer, till they cry twang.'

Enter EYRE *wearing a gold chain*

HANS. *See, myn liever broder, heer compt my meester.*[14]

MARG. Welcome home, Master Shrieve; I pray God continue you in health and wealth.

---

[11] Brighten up.   [12] Sheriff.
[13] "The three-farthing silver pieces of Queen Elizabeth had the profile of the sovereign with a rose at the back of her head."—*Dyce.*
[14] See, my dear brothers, here comes my master.

EYRE. See here, my Maggy, a chain, a gold chain for Simon Eyre. I shall make thee a lady; here's a French hood for thee; on with it, on with it! dress thy brows with this flap of a shoulder of mutton,[15] to make thee look lovely. Where be my fine men? Roger, I'll make over my shop and tools to thee; Firk, thou shalt be the foreman; Hans, thou shalt have an hundred for twenty.[16] Be as mad knaves as your master Sim Eyre hath been, and you shall live to be Sheriffs of London.—How dost thou like me, Margery? Prince am I none, yet am I princely born. Firk, Hodge, and Hans!

ALL THREE. Ay forsooth, what says your worship, Master Sheriff?

EYRE. Worship and honour, you Babylonian knaves, for the gentle craft. But I forgot myself, I am bidden by my lord mayor to dinner to Old Ford; he's gone before, I must after. Come, Madge, on with your trinkets! Now, my true Trojans, my fine Firk, my dapper Hodge, my honest Hans, some device, some odd crotchets, some morris, or such like, for the honour of the gentlemen shoemakers. Meet me at Old Ford, you know my mind. Come, Madge, away. Shut up the shop, knaves, and make holiday.   *Exeunt.*

FIRK. O rare! O brave! Come, Hodge; follow me, Hans; We'll be with them for a morris-dance.   *Exeunt.*

SCENE V[1]

Enter the LORD MAYOR, [ROSE,] EYRE, MARGERY *in a French hood,* SYBIL, *and other* Servants

L. MAYOR. Trust me, you are as welcome to Old Ford As I myself.

MARG. Truly, I thank your lordship.

L. MAYOR. Would our bad cheer were worth the thanks you give.

EYRE. Good cheer, my lord mayor, fine cheer! A fine house, fine walls, all fine and neat.

L. MAYOR. Now, by my troth, I'll tell thee, Master Eyre, It does me good, and all my brethren,

---

[15] The flap of a hood trimmed with fur or sheep's wool.—*Rhys.*
[16] *I. e.,* for the twenty Portuguese previously lent.
[1] A room at Old Ford.

That such a madcap fellow as thyself
Is ent'red into our society.

MARG. Ay, but, my lord, he must learn now to put on
gravity.

EYRE. Peace, Maggy, a fig for gravity! When I go to
Guildhall in my scarlet gown, I'll look as demurely as a
saint, and speak as gravely as a justice of peace; but now I
am here at Old Ford, at my good lord mayor's house, let it
go by, vanish, Maggy, I'll be merry; away with flip-flap, these
fooleries, these gulleries. What, honey? Prince am I none,
yet am I princely born. What says my lord mayor?

L. MAYOR. Ha, ha, ha! I had rather than a thousand
pound, I had an hear⁺ but half so light as yours.

EYRE. Why, what should I do, my lord? A pound of care
pays not a dram of debt. Hum, let's be merry, whiles we are
young; old age, sack and sugar will steal upon us, ere we
be aware.

THE FIRST THREE-MEN'S SONG

O the month of May, the merry month of May,
   So frolick, so gay, and so green, so green, so green!
O, and then did I unto my true love say:
   "Sweet Peg, thou shalt be my summer's queen!"

"Now the nightingale, the pretty nightingale,
   The sweetest singer in all the forest's choir,
Entreats thee, sweet Peggy, to hear thy true love's tale;
   Lo, yonder she sitteth, her breast against a brier.

"But O, I spy the cuckoo, the cuckoo, the cuckoo;
   See where she sitteth: come away, my joy;
Come away, I prithee: I do not like the cuckoo
   Should sing where my Peggy and I kiss and toy."

O the month of May, the merry month of May,
   So frolick, so gay, and so green, so green, so green!
And then did I unto my true love say:
   "Sweet Peg, thou shalt be my summer's queen!"

L. Mayor. It's well done; Mistress Eyre, pray, give good
    counsel
To my daughter.

Marg. I hope, Mistress Rose will have the grace to take
nothing that's bad.

L. Mayor. Pray God she do; for i' faith, Mistress Eyre,
I would bestow upon that peevish girl
A thousand marks more than I mean to give her
Upon condition she'd be rul'd by me.
The ape still crosseth me. There came of late
A proper gentleman of fair revenues,
Whom gladly I would call son-in-law:
But my fine cockney would have none of him.
You'll prove a coxcomb for it, ere you die:
A courtier, or no man must please your eye.

Eyre. Be rul'd, sweet Rose: th'art ripe for a man. Marry
not with a boy that has no more hair on his face than thou
hast on thy cheeks. A courtier, wash, go by, stand not upon
pishery-pashery: those silken fellows are but painted images,
outsides, outsides, Rose; their inner linings are torn. No,
my fine mouse, marry me with a gentleman grocer like my
lord mayor, your father; a grocer is a sweet trade: plums,
plums. Had I a son or daughter should marry out of the gen-
eration and blood of the shoemakers, he should pack; what,
the gentle trade is a living for a man through Europe,
through the world. *A noise within of a tabor and a pipe.*

L. Mayor. What noise is this?

Eyre. O my lord mayor, a crew of good fellows that for
love to your honour are come hither with a morris-dance.
Come in, my Mesopotamians, cheerily.

Enter Hodge, Hans, Ralph, Firk, *and other* Shoemakers,
    in a morris; after a little dancing the Lord Mayor
    speaks:

L. Mayor. Master Eyre, are all these shoemakers?

Eyre. All cordwainers, my good lord mayor.

Rose. [*Aside.*] How like my Lacy looks yond shoemaker!

Hans. [*Aside.*] O that I durst but speak unto my love!

L. Mayor. Sybil, go fetch some wine to make these drink.
You are all welcome.

ALL. We thank your lordship.

          ROSE *takes a cup of wine and goes to* HANS.

ROSE. For his sake whose fair shape thou represent'st,
Good friend, I drink to thee.

HANS. *Ic bedancke, good frister.*[2]

MARG. I see, Mistress Rose, you do not want judgment;
you have drunk to the properest man I keep.

FIRK. Here be some have done their parts to be as proper
as he.

L. MAYOR. Well, urgent business calls me back to London.
Good fellows, first go in and taste our cheer;
And to make merry as you homeward go,
Spend these two angels in beer at Stratford-Bow.

EYRE. To these two, my mad lads, Sim Eyre adds another;
then cheerily, Firk; tickle it, Hans, and all for the honour
of shoemakers.   *All go dancing out.*

L. MAYOR. Come, Master Eyre, let's have your company.

                    Exeunt.

ROSE. Sybil, what shall I do?

SYBIL. Why, what's the matter?

ROSE. That Hans the shoemaker is my love Lacy,
Disguis'd in that attire to find me out.
How should I find the means to speak with him?

SYBIL. What, mistress, never fear; I dare venture my
maidenhead to nothing, and that's great odds, that Hans the
Dutchman, when we come to London, shall not only see and
speak with you, but in spite of all your father's policies steal
you away and marry you. Will not this please you?

ROSE. Do this, and ever be assured of my love.

SYBIL. Away, then, and follow your father to London, lest
your absence cause him to suspect something:

        To morrow, if my counsel be obey'd,
        I'll bind you prentice to the gentle trade. [*Exeunt.*]

               [2] I thank you, good maid!

ACT IV

Scene I[1]

Jane in a Seamster's shop, working; enter Master Hammon,
muffled; he stands aloof

Ham. Yonder's the shop, and there my fair love sits.
She's fair and lovely, but she is not mine.
O, would she were! Thrice have I courted her,
Thrice hath my hand been moist'ned with her hand,
Whilst my poor famish'd eyes do feed on that
Which made them famish. I am unfortunate:
I still love one, yet nobody loves me.
I muse in other men what women see
That I so want! Fine Mistress Rose was coy,
And this too curious! Oh, no, she is chaste,
And for she thinks me wanton, she denies
To cheer my cold heart with her sunny eyes.
How prettily she works, oh pretty hand!
Oh happy work! It doth me good to stand
Unseen to see her. Thus I oft have stood
In frosty evenings, a light burning by her,
Enduring biting cold, only to eye her.
One only look hath seem'd as rich to me
As a king's crown; such is love's lunacy.
Muffled I'll pass along, and by that try
Whether she know me.

Jane.   Sir, what is't you buy?
What is't you lack, sir, calico, or lawn,
Fine cambric shirts, or bands, what will you buy?

Ham. [*Aside.*] That which thou wilt not sell. Faith, yet
     I'll try:
How do you sell this handkerchief?

Jane.   Good cheap.

Ham. And how these ruffs?

Jane.   Cheap too.

Ham.   And how this band?

Jane. Cheap too.

Ham.   All cheap; how sell you then this hand?

---

[1] A street in London.

JANE. My hands are not to be sold.

HAM. To be given then!
Nay, faith, I come to buy.

JANE. But none knows when.

HAM. Good sweet, leave work a little while; let's play.

JANE. I cannot live by keeping holiday.

HAM. I'll pay you for the time which shall be lost.

JANE. With me you shall not be at so much cost.

HAM. Look, how you wound this cloth, so you wound me.

JANE. It may be so.

HAM. 'Tis so.

JANE. What remedy?

HAM. Nay, faith, you are too coy.

JANE. Let go my hand.

HAM. I will do any task at your command,
I would let go this beauty, were I not
In mind to disobey you by a power
That controls kings: I love you!

JANE. So, now part.

HAM. With hands I may, but never with my heart.
In faith, I love you.

JANE. I believe you do.

HAM. Shall a true love in me breed hate in you?

JANE. I hate you not.

HAM. Then you must love?

JANE. I do.
What are you better now? I love not you.

HAM. All this, I hope, is but a woman's fray,
That means, "Come to me," when she cries, "Away!"
In earnest, mistress, I do not jest,
A true chaste love hath ent'red in my breast.
I love you dearly, as I love my life,
I love you as a husband loves a wife;
That, and no other love, my love requires,
Thy wealth, I know, is little; my desires
Thirst not for gold. Sweet, beauteous Jane, what's mine
Shall, if thou make myself thine, all be thine.
Say, judge, what is thy sentence, life or death?
Mercy or cruelty lies in thy breath.

JANE. Good sir, I do believe you love me well;

For 'tis a silly conquest, silly pride
For one like you—I mean a gentleman—
To boast that by his love-tricks he hath brought
Such and such women to his amorous lure;
I think you do not so, yet many do,
And make it even a very trade to woo.
I could be coy, as many women be,
Feed you with sunshine smiles and wanton looks,
But I detest witchcraft; say that I
Do constantly believe, you constant have——

HAM. Why dost thou not believe me?

JANE.   I believe you;
But yet, good sir, because I will not grieve you
With hopes to taste fruit which will never fall,
In simple truth this is the sum of all:
My husband lives, at least, I hope he lives.
Press'd was he to these bitter wars in France;
Bitter they are to me by wanting him.
I have but one heart, and that heart's his due.
How can I then bestow the same on you?
Whilst he lives, his I live, be it ne'er so poor,
And rather be his wife than a king's whore.

HAM. Chaste and dear woman, I will not abuse thee,
Although it cost my life, if thou refuse me.
Thy husband, press'd for France, what was his name?

JANE. Ralph Damport.

HAM.   Damport?—Here's a letter sent
From France to me, from a dear friend of mine,
A gentleman of place; here he doth write
Their names that have been slain in every fight.

JANE. I hope death's scroll contains not my love's name.

HAM. Cannot you read?

JANE.   I can.

HAM.   Peruse the same.
To my remembrance such a name I read
Amongst the rest. See here.

JANE.   Ay me, he's dead!
He's dead! If this be true, my dear heart's slain!

HAM. Have patience dear love.

JANE.   Hence, hence!

HAM.   Nay, sweet Jane,
Make not poor sorrow proud with these rich tears.
I mourn thy husband's death, because thou mourn'st.
  JANE. That bill is forg'd; 'tis sign'd by forgery.
  HAM. I'll bring thee letters sent besides to many,
Carrying the like report: Jane, 'tis too true.
Come, weep not: mourning, though it rise from love,
Helps not the mourned, yet hurts them that mourn.
  JANE. For God's sake, leave me.
  HAM.   Whither dost thou turn?
Forget the dead, love them that are alive;
His love is faded, try how mine will thrive.
  JANE. 'Tis now no time for me to think on love.
  HAM. 'Tis now best time for you to think on love,
Because your love lives not.
  JANE.   Though he be dead,
My love to him shall not be buried;
For God's sake, leave me to myself alone.
  HAM. 'Twould kill my soul, to leave thee drown'd in moan
Answer me to my suit, and I am gone;
Say to me yea or no.
  JANE.   No.
  HAM.   Then farewell!
One farewell will not serve, I come again;
Come, dry these wet cheeks; tell me, faith, sweet Jane,
Yea or no, once more.
  JANE.   Once more I say: no;
Once more be gone, I pray; else will I go.
  HAM. Nay, then I will grow rude, by this white hand,
Until you change that cold " no "; here I'll stand
Till by your hard heart——
  JANE.   Nay, for God's love, peace!
My sorrows by your presence more increase.
Not that you thus are present, but all grief
Desires to be alone; therefore in brief
Thus much I say, and saying bid adieu:
If ever I wed man, it shall be you.
  HAM. O blessed voice! Dear Jane, I'll urge no more,
Thy breath hath made me rich.
  JANE.   Death makes me poor. *Exeunt.*

Scene II[1]

Hodge, at his shop-board, Ralph, Firk, Hans, and a Boy at work

ALL. Hey, down a down, down derry.

HODGE. Well said, my hearts; ply your work to-day, we loit'red yesterday; to it pell-mell, that we may live to be lord mayors, or aldermen at least.

FIRK. Hey, down a down, derry.

HODGE. Well said, i' faith! How say'st thou, Hans, doth not Firk tickle it?

HANS. *Yaw, mester.*

FIRK. Not so neither, my organ-pipe squeaks this morning for want of liquoring. Hey, down a down, derry!

HANS. *Forward, Firk, tow best un jolly yongster. Hort, I, mester, ic bid yo, cut me un pair vampres vor Mester Jeffre's boots.*[2]

HODGE. Thou shalt, Hans.

FIRK. Master!

HODGE. How now, boy?

FIRK. Pray, now you are in the cutting vein, cut me out a pair of counterfeits,[3] or else my work will not pass current; hey, down a down!

HODGE. Tell me, sirs, are my cousin Mrs. Priscilla's shoes done?

FIRK. Your cousin? No, master; one of your aunts, hang her; let them alone.

RALPH. I am in hand with them; she gave charge that none but I should do them for her.

FIRK. Thou do for her? Then 'twill be a lame doing, and that she loves not. Ralph, thou might'st have sent her to me, in faith, I would have yearked and firked your Priscilla. Hey, down a down, derry. This gear will not hold.

HODGE. How say'st thou, Firk, were we not merry at Old Ford?

FIRK. How, merry! Why, our buttocks went jiggy-joggy

---

[1] London: a street before Hodge's shop.
[2] "Forward, Firk, thou art a jolly youngster. Hark, ay, master, I pray you cut me a pair of vamps for Master Jeffrey's boots." Vamps are the upper leathers of a shoe.   [3] Counterfeits sometimes means vamps.

like a quagmire. Well, Sir Roger Oatmeal, if I thought all meal of that nature, I would eat nothing but bagpuddings.

RALPH. Of all good fortunes my fellow Hans had the best.

FIRK. 'Tis true, because Mistress Rose drank to him.

HODGE. Well, well, work apace. They say, seven of the aldermen be dead, or very sick.

FIRK. I care not, I'll be none.

RALPH. No, nor I; but then my Master Eyre will come quickly to be lord mayor.

Enter SYBIL

FIRK. Whoop, yonder comes Sybil.

HODGE. Sybil, welcome, i'faith; and how dost thou, mad wench?

FIRK. Sybil, welcome to London.

SYBIL. Godamercy, sweet Firk; good lord, Hodge, what a delicious shop you have got! You tickle it, i'faith.

RALPH. Godamercy, Sybil, for our good cheer at Old Ford.

SYBIL. That you shall have, Ralph.

FIRK. Nay, by the mass, we had tickling cheer, Sybil; and how the plague dost thou and Mistress Rose and my lord mayor? I put the women in first.

SYBIL. Well, Godamercy; but God's me, I forget myself, where's Hans the Fleming?

FIRK. Hark, butter-box, now you must yelp out some *spreken*.

HANS. *Wat begaie you? Vat vod you, Frister?*[4]

SYBIL. Marry, you must come to my young mistress, to pull on her shoes you made last.

HANS. *Vare ben your egle fro, vare ben your mistris?*[5]

SYBIL. Marry, here at our London house in Cornhill.

FIRK. Will nobody serve her turn but Hans?

SYBIL. No, sir. Come, Hans, I stand upon needles.

HODGE. Why then, Sybil, take heed of pricking.

[4] What do you want, what would you, girl?
[5] Where is your noble lady, where is your mistress?

SYBIL. For that let me alone. I have a trick in my budget. Come, Hans.

HANS. *Yaw, yaw, ic sall meete yo gane.*[6]

Exit HANS *and* SYBIL.

HODGE. Go, Hans, make haste again. Come, who lacks work?

FIRK. I, master, for I lack my breakfast; 'tis munching-time, and past.

HODGE. Is't so? Why, then leave work, Ralph. To breakfast! Boy, look to the tools. Come, Ralph; come, Firk. *Exeunt.*

SCENE III[1]

Enter a Serving-man

SERV. Let me see now, the sign of the Last in Tower Street. Mass, yonder's the house. What, haw! Who's within?

Enter RALPH

RALPH. Who calls there? What want you, sir?

SERV. Marry, I would have a pair of shoes made for a gentlewoman against to-morrow morning. What, can you do them?

RALPH. Yes, sir, you shall have them. But what length's her foot?

SERV. Why, you must make them in all parts like this shoe; but, at any hand, fail not to do them, for the gentlewoman is to be married very early in the morning.

RALPH. How? by this shoe must it be made? By this? Are you sure, sir, by this?

SERV. How, by this? Am I sure, by this? Art thou in thy wits? I tell thee, I must have a pair of shoes, dost thou mark me? A pair of shoes, two shoes, made by this very shoe, this same shoe, against to-morrow morning by four a clock. Dost understand me? Canst thou do't?

RALPH. Yes, sir, yes—I—I—I can do't. By this shoe, you say? I should know this shoe. Yes, sir, yes, by this

[6] Yes, yes, I shall go with you.
[1] The same.

shoe, I can do't. Four a clock, well. Whither shall I bring them?

SERV. To the sign of the Golden Ball in Watling Street; enquire for one Master Hammon, a gentleman, my master.

RALPH. Yea, sir; by this shoe, you say?

SERV. I say, Master Hammon at the Golden Ball; he's the bridegroom, and those shoes are for his bride.

RALPH. They shall be done by this shoe. Well, well, Master Hammon at the Golden Shoe—I would say, the Golden Ball; very well, very well. But I pray you, sir, where must Master Hammon be married?

SERV. At Saint Faith's Church, under Paul's. But what's that to thee? Prithee, dispatch those shoes, and so farewell.   *Exit.*

RALPH. By this shoe, said he. How am I amaz'd
At this strange accident! Upon my life,
This was the very shoe I gave my wife,
When I was press'd for France; since when, alas!
I never could hear of her. It is the same,
And Hammon's bride no other but my Jane.

Enter FIRK

FIRK. 'Snails,* Ralph, thou hast lost thy part of three pots, a countryman of mine gave me to breakfast.

RALPH. I care not; I have found a better thing.

FIRK. A thing? Away! Is it a man's thing, or a woman's thing?

RALPH. Firk, dost thou know this shoe?

FIRK. No, by my troth; neither doth that know me! I have no acquaintance with it, 'tis a mere stranger to me.

RALPH. Why, then I do; this shoe, I durst be sworn,
Once covered the instep of my Jane.
This is her size, her breadth, thus trod my love;
These true-love knots I pricked. I hold my life,
By this old shoe I shall find out my wife.

FIRK. Ha, ha! Old shoe, that wert new! How a murrain came this ague-fit of foolishness upon thee?

RALPH. Thus, Firk: even now here came a serving-man:
By this shoe would he have a new pair made

* A corruption of " God's nails."

Against to-morrow morning for his mistress,
That's to be married to a gentleman.
And why may not this be my sweet Jane?

FIRK. And why may'st not thou be my sweet ass?
Ha, ha!

RALPH. Well, laugh and spare not! But the truth is this:
Against to-morrow morning I'll provide
A lusty crew of honest shoemakers,
To watch the going of the bride to church.
If she prove Jane, I'll take her in despite
From Hammon and the devil, were he by.
If it be not my Jane, what remedy?
Hereof I am sure, I shall live till I die,
Although I never with a woman lie.   *Exit.*

FIRK. Thou lie with a woman to build nothing but Cripple-
gates! Well, God sends fools fortune, and it may be, he
may light upon his matrimony by such a device; for wedding
and hanging goes by destiny.   *Exit.*

SCENE IV[1]

Enter HANS *and* ROSE, *arm in arm*

HANS. How happy am I by embracing thee!
Oh, I did fear such cross mishaps did reign,
That I should never see my Rose again.

ROSE. Sweet Lacy, since fair opportunity
Offers herself to further our escape,
Let not too over-fond esteem of me
Hinder that happy hour. Invent the means,
And Rose will follow thee through all the world.

HANS. Oh, how I surfeit with excess of joy,
Made happy by thy rich perfection!
But since thou pay'st sweet interest to my hopes,
Redoubling love on love, let me once more
Like to a bold-fac'd debtor crave of thee,
This night to steal abroad, and at Eyre's house,
Who now by death of certain aldermen
Is mayor of London, and my master once,

---

[1] London: a room in the Lord Mayor's house.

Meet thou thy Lacy, where in spite of change,
Your father's anger, and mine uncle's hate,
Our happy nuptials will we consummate.

Enter SYBIL

SYBIL. Oh God, what will you do, mistress? Shift for
yourself, your father is at hand! He's coming, he's coming!
Master Lacy, hide yourself in my mistress! For God's sake,
shift for yourselves!

HANS. Your father come, sweet Rose—what shall I do?
Where shall I hide me? How shall I escape?

ROSE. A man, and want wit in extremity?
Come, come, be Hans still, play the shoemaker,
Pull on my shoe.

Enter the LORD MAYOR

HANS.   Mass, and that's well rememb'red.

SYBIL. Here comes your father.

HANS. *Forware, metresse, 'tis un good skow, it sal vel
dute, or ye sal neit betallen.*[2]

ROSE. Oh God, it pincheth me; what will you do?

HANS. [*Aside.*] Your father's presence pincheth, not the
    shoe.

L. MAYOR. Well done; fit my daughter well, and she shall
please thee well.

HANS. *Yaw, yaw, ick weit dat well; forware, 'tis un
good skoo, 'tis gimait van neits leither; se euer, mine here.*[3]

Enter a Prentice

L. MAYOR. I do believe it.—What's the news with you?

PRENTICE. Please you, the Earl of Lincoln at the gate
Is newly lighted, and would speak with you.

L. MAYOR. The Earl of Lincoln come to speak with me?
Well, well, I know his errand. Daughter Rose,
Send hence your shoemaker, dispatch, have done!
Syb, make things handsome! Sir boy, follow me.   *Exit.*

HANS. Mine uncle come! Oh, what may this portend?
Sweet Rose, this of our love threatens an end.

---

[2] Indeed, mistress, 'tis a good shoe, it shall fit well, or you shall not pay.

[3] Yes, yes, I know that well; indeed, 'tis a good shoe, 'tis made of neat's
leather, see here, good sir!

Rose. Be not dismay'd at this; whate'er befall,
Rose is thine own. To witness I speak truth,
Where thou appoint'st the place, I'll meet with thee.
I will not fix a day to follow thee,
But presently⁴ steal hence. Do not reply:
Love which gave strength to bear my father's hate,
Shall now add wings to further our escape.   *Exeunt.*

Scene V¹

Enter the Lord Mayor *and the* Earl of Lincoln

L. Mayor. Believe me, on my credit, I speak truth:
Since first your nephew Lacy went to France,
I have not seen him. It seem'd strange to me,
When Dodger told me that he stay'd behind,
Neglecting the high charge the king imposed.

Lincoln. Trust me, Sir Roger Oateley, I did think
Your counsel had given head to this attempt,
Drawn to it by the love he bears your child.
Here I did hope to find him in your house;
But now I see mine error, and confess,
My judgment wrong'd you by conceiving so.

L. Mayor. Lodge in my house, say you? Trust me,
        my lord,
I love your nephew Lacy too too dearly,
So much to wrong his honour; and he hath done so,
That first gave him advice to stay from France.
To witness I speak truth, I let you know,
How careful I have been to keep my daughter
Free from all conference or speech of him;
Not that I scorn your nephew, but in love
I bear your honour, lest your noble blood
Should by my mean worth be dishonoured.

Lincoln. [*Aside.*] How far the churl's tongue wanders
        from his heart!
Well, well, Sir Roger Oateley, I believe you,
With more than many thanks for the kind love
So much you seem to bear me. But, my lord,

---

⁴ Immediately.
¹ Another room in the same house.

Let me request your help to seek my nephew,
Whom if I find, I'll straight embark for France.
So shall your Rose be free, my thoughts at rest,
And much care die which now lies in my breast.

Enter SYBIL

SYBIL. Oh Lord! Help, for God's sake! My mistress; oh, my young mistress!

L. MAYOR. Where is thy mistress? What's become of her?

SYBIL. She's gone, she's fled!

L. MAYOR. Gone! Whither is she fled?

SYBIL. I know not, forsooth; she's fled out of doors with Hans the shoemaker; I saw them scud, scud, scud, apace, apace!

L. MAYOR. Which way? What, John! Where be my men? Which way?

SYBIL. I know not, an it please your worship.

L. MAYOR. Fled with a shoemaker? Can this be true?

SYBIL. Oh Lord, sir, as true as God's in Heaven.

LINCOLN. Her love turn'd shoemaker? I am glad of this.

L. MAYOR. A Fleming butter-box, a shoemaker!
Will she forget her birth, requite my care
With such ingratitude? Scorn'd she young Hammon
To love a honniken,[2] a needy knave?
Well, let her fly, I'll not fly after her,
Let her starve, if she will; she's none of mine.

LINCOLN. Be not so cruel, sir.

Enter FIRK *with shoes*

SYBIL.   I am glad, she's scap'd.

L. MAYOR. I'll not account of her as of my child.
Was there no better object for her eyes
But a foul drunken lubber, swill-belly,
A shoemaker? That's brave!

FIRK. Yea, forsooth; 'tis a very brave shoe, and as fit as a pudding.

L. MAYOR. How now, what knave is this? From whence comest thou?

[2] Simpleton (?).

FIRK. No knave, sir. I am Firk the shoemaker, lusty Roger's chief lusty journeyman, and I have come hither to take up the pretty leg of sweet Mistress Rose, and thus hoping your worship is in as good health, as I was at the making hereof, I bid you farewell, yours, Firk.

L. MAYOR. Stay, stay, Sir Knave!

LINCOLN. Come hither, shoemaker!

FIRK. 'Tis happy the knave is put before the shoemaker, or else I would not have vouchsafed to come back to you. I am moved, for I stir.

L. MAYOR. My lord, this villain calls us knaves by craft.

FIRK. Then 'tis by the gentle craft, and to call one knave gently, is no harm. Sit your worship merry! Syb, your young mistress—I'll so bob[3] them, now my Master Eyre is lord mayor of London.

L. MAYOR. Tell me, sirrah, whose man are you?

FIRK. I am glad to see your worship so merry. I have no maw to this gear, no stomach as yet to a red petticoat.

Pointing to SYBIL.

LINCOLN. He means not, sir, to woo you to his maid,
But only doth demand whose man you are.

FIRK. I sing now to the tune of Rogero. Roger, my fellow, is now my master.

LINCOLN. Sirrah, know'st thou one Hans, a shoemaker?

FIRK. Hans, shoemaker? Oh yes, stay, yes, I have him. I tell you what, I speak it in secret: Mistress Rose and he are by this time—no, not so, but shortly are to come over one another with "Can you dance the shaking of the sheets?" It is that Hans—[*Aside.*] I'll so gull[3] these diggers![4]

L. MAYOR. Know'st thou, then, where he is?

FIRK. Yes, forsooth; yea, marry!

LINCOLN. Canst thou, in sadness[5]——

FIRK. No, forsooth; no, marry!

L. MAYOR. Tell me, good honest fellow, where he is,
And thou shalt see what I'll bestow on thee.

FIRK. Honest fellow? No, sir; not so, sir; my profession is the gentle craft; I care not for seeing, I love feeling; let me feel it here; *aurium tenus,* ten pieces of gold;

---

[3] Fool.   [4] *I. e.,* diggers for information.   [5] Seriously.

genuum tenus, ten pieces of silver; and then Firk is your man—[*aside*] in a new pair of stretchers.[6]

L. MAYOR. Here is an angel, part of thy reward,
Which I will give thee; tell me where he is.

FIRK. No point. Shall I betray my brother? No! Shall I prove Judas to Hans? No! Shall I cry treason to my corporation? No, I shall be firked and yerked then. But give me your angel; your angel shall tell you.

LINCOLN. Do so, good fellow; 'tis no hurt to thee.

FIRK. Send simpering Syb away.

L. MAYOR. Huswife, get you in.   *Exit* SYBIL.

FIRK. Pitchers have ears, and maids have wide mouths; but for Hans Prauns, upon my word, to-morrow morning he and young Mistress Rose go to this gear, they shall be married together, by this rush, or else turn Firk to a firkin of butter, to tan leather withal.

L. MAYOR. But art thou sure of this?

FIRK. Am I sure that Paul's steeple is a handful higher than London Stone,[7] or that the Pissing-Conduit[8] leaks nothing but pure Mother Bunch?[9] Am I sure I am lusty Firk? God's nails, do you think I am so base to gull you?

LINCOLN. Where are they married? Dost thou know the church?

FIRK. I never go to church, but I know the name of it; it is a swearing church—stay a while, 'tis—ay, by the mass, no, no,—'tis—ay, by my troth, no, nor that; 'tis—ay, by my faith, that, that, 'tis, ay, by my Faith's Church under Paul's Cross. There they shall be knit like a pair of stockings in matrimony; there they'll be inconie.[10]

LINCOLN. Upon my life, my nephew Lacy walks
In the disguise of this Dutch shoemaker.

FIRK. Yes, forsooth.

LINCOLN. Doth he not, honest fellow?

FIRK. No, forsooth; I think Hans is nobody but Hans, no spirit.

L. MAYOR. My mind misgives me now, 'tis so, indeed.

LINCOLN. My cousin speaks the language, knows the trade.

---

[6] Stretchers of the truth, lies.
[7] A stone which marked the center from which the old Roman roads radiated.   [8] A small conduit near the Royal Exchange.
[9] Mother Bunch was a well-known ale-wife.   [10] A pretty sight.

L. MAYOR. Let me request your company, my lord;
Your honourable presence may, no doubt,
Refrain their headstrong rashness, when myself
Going alone perchance may be o'erborne.
Shall I request this favour?

LINCOLN.   This, or what else.

FIRK. Then you must rise betimes, for they mean to fall
to their hey-pass and repass,[11] pindy-pandy, which hand will
you have, very early.

L. MAYOR. My care shall every way equal their haste.
This night accept your lodging in my house,
The earlier shall we stir, and at Saint Faith's
Prevent this giddy hare-brain'd nuptial.
This traffic of hot love shall yield cold gains:
They ban[12] our loves, and we'll forbid their banns.   *Exit.*

LINCOLN. At Saint Faith's Church thou say'st?

FIRK. Yes, by their troth.

LINCOLN. Be secret, on thy life.   *Exit.*

FIRK. Yes, when I kiss your wife! Ha, ha, here's no
craft in the gentle craft. I came hither of purpose with
shoes to Sir Roger's worship, whilst Rose, his daughter, be
cony-catched by Hans. Soft now; these two gulls will be at
Saint Faith's Church to-morrow morning, to take Master
Bridegroom and Mistress Bride napping, and they, in the
mean time, shall chop up the matter at the Savoy. But the
best sport is, Sir Roger Oateley will find my fellow lame
Ralph's wife going to marry a gentleman, and then he'll
stop her instead of his daughter. Oh brave! there will be
fine tickling sport. Soft now, what have I to do? Oh, I
know; now a mess of shoemakers meet at the Woolsack
in Ivy Lane, to cozen[13] my gentleman of lame Ralph's wife,
that's true.

> Alack, alack!
> Girls, hold out tack!
> For now smocks for this jumbling
> Shall go to wrack.   *Exit.*

[11] Conjuring terms.   [12] Curse.   [13] Cheat.

ACT V

Scene I[1]

Enter EYRE, MARGERY, HANS, *and* ROSE

EYRE. This is the morning, then; stay, my bully, my honest Hans, is it not?

HANS. This is the morning that must make us two happy or miserable; therefore, if you——

EYRE. Away with these ifs and ands, Hans, and these et caeteras! By mine honour, Rowland Lacy, none but the king shall wrong thee. Come, fear nothing, am not I Sim Eyre? Is not Sim Eyre lord mayor of London? Fear nothing, Rose: let them all say what they can; dainty, come thou to me— laughest thou?

MARG. Good my lord, stand her friend in what thing you may.

EYRE. Why, my sweet Lady Madgy, think you Simon Eyre can forget his fine Dutch journeyman? No, vah! Fie, I scorn it, it shall never be cast in my teeth, that I was un-thankful. Lady Madgy, thou had'st never covered thy Sara-cen's head with this French flap, nor loaden thy bum with this farthingale, ('tis trash, trumpery, vanity); Simon Eyre had never walked in a red petticoat, nor wore a chain of gold, but for my fine journeyman's Portuguese.—And shall I leave him? No! Prince am I none, yet bear a princely mind.

HANS. My lord, 'tis time for us to part from hence.

EYRE. Lady Madgy, Lady Madgy, take two or three of my pie-crust-eaters, my buff-jerkin varlets, that do walk in black gowns at Simon Eyre's heels; take them, good Lady Madgy; trip and go, my brown queen of periwigs, with my delicate Rose and my jolly Rowland to the Savoy; see them link'd, countenance the marriage; and when it is done, cling, cling together, you Hamborow turtle-doves. I'll bear you out, come to Simon Eyre; come, dwell with me, Hans, thou shalt eat minced-pies and marchpane.[2] Rose, away, cricket; trip and go, my Lady Madgy, to the Savoy; Hans, wed, and to bed; kiss, and away! Go, vanish!

MARG. Farewell, my lord.

---

[1] A room in Eyre's house.   [2] A sweetmeat made of sugar and almonds.

Rose. Make haste, sweet love.

Marg.   She'd fain the deed were done.

Hans. Come, my sweet Rose; faster than deer we'll run.

Exeunt Hans, Rose, *and* Margery.

Eyre. Go, vanish, vanish! Avaunt, I say! By the Lord of Ludgate, it's a mad life to be a lord mayor; it's a stirring life, a fine life, a velvet life, a careful life. Well, Simon Eyre, yet set a good face on it, in the honour of Saint Hugh. Soft, the king this day comes to dine with me, to see my new buildings; his majesty is welcome, he shall have good cheer, delicate cheer, princely cheer. This day, my fellow prentices of London come to dine with me too, they shall have fine cheer, gentlemanlike cheer. I promised the mad Cappadocians, when we all served at the Conduit together, that if ever I came to be mayor of London, I would feast them all, and I'll do't, I'll do't, by the life of Pharaoh; by this beard, Sim Eyre will be no flincher. Besides, I have procur'd that upon every Shrove-Tuesday, at the sound of the pancake bell, my fine dapper Assyrian lads shall clap up their shop windows, and away. This is the day, and this day they shall do't, they shall do't.

Boys, that day are you free, let masters care,
And prentices shall pray for Simon Eyre.   *Exit.*

Scene II[1]

Enter Hodge, Firk, Ralph, *and five or six* Shoemakers, *all with cudgels or such weapons*

Hodge. Come, Ralph; stand to it, Firk. My masters, as we are the brave bloods of the shoemakers, heirs apparent to Saint Hugh, and perpetual benefactors to all good fellows, thou shalt have no wrong; were Hammon a king of spades, he should not delve in thy close without thy sufferance. But tell me, Ralph, art thou sure 'tis thy wife?

Ralph. Am I sure this is Firk? This morning, when I stroked[2] on her shoes, I looked upon her, and she upon me, and sighed, asked me if ever I knew one Ralph. Yes, said I. For his sake, said she—tears standing in her eyes—and for

---

[1] A street near St. Faith's Church.   [2] Fitted.

thou art somewhat like him, spend this piece of gold. I took it; my lame leg and my travel beyond sea made me unknown. All is one for that: I know she's mine.

FIRK. Did she give thee this gold? O glorious glittering gold! She's thine own, 'tis thy wife, and she loves thee; for I'll stand to't, there's no woman will give gold to any man, but she thinks better of him than she thinks of them she gives silver to. And for Hammon, neither Hammon nor hangman shall wrong thee in London. Is not our old master Eyre, lord mayor? Speak, my hearts.

ALL. Yes, and Hammon shall know it to his cost.

Enter HAMMON, *his* Serving-man, JANE *and* Others

HODGE. Peace, my bullies; yonder they come.

RALPH. Stand to't, my hearts. Firk, let me speak first.

HODGE. No, Ralph, let me.—Hammon, whither away so early?

HAM. Unmannerly, rude slave, what's that to thee?

FIRK. To him, sir? Yes, sir, and to me, and others. Goodmorrow, Jane, how dost thou? Good Lord, how the world is changed with you! God be thanked!

HAM. Villains, hands off! How dare you touch my love?

ALL. Villains? Down with them! Cry clubs for prentices![a]

HODGE. Hold, my hearts! Touch her, Hammon? Yea, and more than that: we'll carry her away with us. My masters and gentlemen, never draw your bird-spits; shoemakers are steel to the back, men every inch of them, all spirit.

THOSE OF HAMMON'S SIDE. Well, and what of all this?

HODGE. I'll show you.—Jane, dost thou know this man? 'Tis Ralph, I can tell thee; nay, 'tis he in faith, though he be lam'd by the wars. Yet look not strange, but run to him, fold him about the neck and kiss him.

JANE. Lives then my husband? Oh God, let me go, Let me embrace my Ralph.

HAM.					What means my Jane?

JANE. Nay, what meant you, to tell me, he was slain?

HAM. Pardon me, dear love, for being misled.

[a] "Clubs" was the rallying cry of the London apprentices.

[To RALPH.] 'Twas rumour'd here in London, thou wert
   dead.

FIRK. Thou seest he lives. Lass, go, pack home with him.
Now, Master Hammon, where's your mistress, your wife?

SERV. 'Swounds, master, fight for her! Will you thus
lose her?

ALL. Down with that creature! Clubs! Down with him!

HODGE. Hold, hold!

HAM. Hold, fool! Sirs, he shall do no wrong.
Will my Jane leave me thus, and break her faith?

FIRK. Yea, sir! She must, sir! She shall, sir! What
then? Mend it!

HODGE. Hark, fellow Ralph, follow my counsel: set the
wench in the midst, and let her choose her man, and let
her be his woman.

JANE. Whom should I choose? Whom should my thoughts
   affect
But him whom Heaven hath made to be my love?
Thou art my husband, and these humble weeds
Makes thee more beautiful than all his wealth.
Therefore, I will but put off his attire,
Returning it into the owner's hand,
And after ever be thy constant wife.

HODGE. Not a rag, Jane! The law's on our side; he that
sows in another man's ground, forfeits his harvest. Get thee
home, Ralph; follow him, Jane; he shall not have so much
as a busk-point[4] from thee.

FIRK. Stand to that, Ralph; the appurtenances are thine
own. Hammon, look not at her!

SERV. O, swounds, no!

FIRK. Blue coat, be quiet, we'll give you a new livery
else; we'll make Shrove Tuesday Saint George's Day for you.
Look not, Hammon, leer not! I'll firk you! For thy head
now, one glance, one sheep's eye, anything, at her! Touch
not a rag, lest I and my brethren beat you to clouts.

SERV. Come, Master Hammon, there's no striving here.

HAM. Good fellows, hear me speak; and, honest Ralph,
Whom I have injured most by loving Jane,

---

[4] A lace with a tag, which fastened the busk, or piece of wood or whale-
bone, used to keep the stays in position.

Mark what I offer thee: here in fair gold
Is twenty pound, I'll give it for thy Jane;
If this content thee not, thou shalt have more.

HODGE. Sell not thy wife, Ralph; make her not a whore.

HAM. Say, wilt thou freely cease thy claim in her,
And let her be my wife?

ALL.   No, do not, Ralph.

RALPH. Sirrah Hammon, Hammon, dost thou think a
shoemaker is so base to be a bawd to his own wife for commodity? Take thy gold, choke with it! Were I not lame,
I would make thee eat thy words.

FIRK. A shoemaker sell his flesh and blood?   Oh
indignity!

HODGE. Sirrah, take up your pelf, and be packing.

HAM. I will not touch one penny, but in lieu
Of that great wrong I offered thy Jane,
To Jane and thee I give that twenty pound.
Since I have fail'd of her, during my life,
I vow, no woman else shall be my wife.
Farewell, good fellows of the gentle trade:
Your morning mirth my mourning day hath made.   *Exit.*

FIRK. [*To the* Serving-man.] Touch the gold, creature,
if you dare! Y'are best be trudging. Here, Jane, take
thou it. Now let's home, my hearts.

HODGE. Stay! Who comes here? Jane, on again with
thy mask!

Enter the EARL OF LINCOLN, *the* LORD MAYOR *and*
Servants

LINCOLN. Yonder's the lying varlet mocked us so.

L. MAYOR. Come hither, sirrah!

FIRK. I, sir? I am sirrah? You mean me, do you not?

LINCOLN. Where is my nephew married?

FIRK. Is he married? God give him joy, I am glad of
it. They have a fair day, and the sign is in a good planet,
Mars in Venus.

L. MAYOR. Villain, thou toldst me that my daughter Rose
This morning should be married at Saint Faith's;
We have watch'd there these three hours at the least,
Yet see we no such thing.

FIRK. Truly, I am sorry for't; a bride's a pretty thing.

HODGE. Come to the purpose. Yonder's the bride and bridegroom you look for, I hope. Though you be lords, you are not to bar by your authority men from women, are you?

L. MAYOR. See, see, my daughter's masked.

LINCOLN.   True, and my nephew, To hide his guilt, counterfeits him lame.

FIRK. Yea, truly; God help the poor couple, they are lame and blind.

L. MAYOR. I'll ease her blindness.

LINCOLN.   I'll his lameness cure.

FIRK. Lie down, sirs, and laugh! My fellow Ralph is taken for Rowland Lacy, and Jane for Mistress Damask Rose. This is all my knavery.

L. MAYOR. What, have I found you, minion?

LINCOLN.   O base wretch Nay, hide thy face, the horror of thy guilt Can hardly be washed off. Where are thy powers? What battles have you made? O yes, I see, Thou fought'st with Shame, and Shame hath conquer'd thee. This lameness will not serve.

L. MAYOR.   Unmask yourself.

LINCOLN. Lead home your daughter.

L. MAYOR.   Take your nephew hence.

RALPH. Hence! Swounds, what mean you? Are you mad? I hope you cannot enforce my wife from me. Where's Hammon?

L. MAYOR. Your wife?

LINCOLN. What, Hammon?

RALPH. Yea, my wife; and, therefore, the proudest of you that lays hands on her first, I'll lay my crutch 'cross his pate.

FIRK. To him, lame Ralph! Here's brave sport!

RALPH. Rose call you her? Why, her name is Jane. Look here else; do you know her now? [*Unmasking* JANE.]

LINCOLN. Is this your daughter?

L. MAYOR.   No, nor this your nephew. My Lord of Lincoln, we are both abus'd By this base, crafty varlet.

FIRK. Yea, forsooth, no varlet; forsooth, no base; forsooth, I am but mean; no crafty neither, but of the gentle craft.

L. MAYOR. Where is my daughter Rose? Where is my child?

LINCOLN. Where is my nephew Lacy married?

FIRK. Why, here is good lac'd mutton,[5] as I promis'd you.

LINCOLN. Villain, I'll have thee punish'd for this wrong.

FIRK. Punish the journeyman villain, but not the journeyman shoemaker.

Enter DODGER

DODGER. My lord, I come to bring unwelcome news.
Your nephew Lacy and your daughter Rose
Early this morning wedded at the Savoy,
None being present but the lady mayoress.
Besides, I learnt among the officers,
The lord mayor vows to stand in their defence
'Gainst any that shall seek to cross the match.

LINCOLN. Dares Eyre the shoemaker uphold the deed?

FIRK. Yes, sir, shoemakers dare stand in a woman's quarrel, I warrant you, as deep as another, and deeper too.

DODGER. Besides, his grace to-day dines with the mayor;
Who on his knees humbly intends to fall
And beg a pardon for your nephew's fault.

LINCOLN. But I'll prevent him! Come, Sir Roger Oateley;
The king will do us justice in this cause.
Howe'er their hands have made them man and wife,
I will disjoin the match, or lose my life.   *Exeunt.*

FIRK. Adieu, Monsieur Dodger! Farewell, fools! Ha, ha! Oh, if they had stay'd, I would have so lamb'd[6] them with flouts! . . . But let that pass, as my lady mayoress says.

HODGE. This matter is answer'd. Come, Ralph; home with thy wife. Come, my fine shoemakers, let's to our master's, the new lord mayor, and there swagger this Shrove-Tuesday. I'll promise you wine enough, for Madge keeps the cellar.

ALL. O rare! Madge is a good wench.

FIRK. And I'll promise you meat enough, for simp'ring

---

[5] A slang term for a woman.   [6] Whipped.

Susan keeps the larder. I'll lead you to victuals, my brave soldiers; follow your captain. O brave! Hark, hark!

Bell rings.

ALL. The pancake-bell[7] rings, the pancake-bell! Trilill, my hearts!

FIRK. Oh brave! Oh sweet bell! O delicate pancakes! Open the doors, my hearts, and shut up the windows! keep in the house, let out the pancakes! Oh rare, my hearts! Let's march together for the honour of Saint Hugh to the great new hall[8] in Gracious Street-corner, which our master, the new lord mayor, hath built.

RALPH. O the crew of good fellows that will dine at my lord mayor's cost to-day!

HODGE. By the Lord, my lord mayor is a most brave man. How shall prentices be bound to pray for him and the honour of the gentlemen shoemakers! Let's feed and be fat with my lord's bounty.

FIRK. O musical bell, still! O Hodge, O my brethren! There's cheer for the heavens: venison-pasties walk up and down piping hot, like sergeants; beef and brewess[9] comes marching in dry-vats,[10] fritters and pancakes comes trowling in in wheel-barrows; hens and oranges hopping in porters'-baskets, collops and eggs in scuttles,[11] and tarts and custards comes quavering in in malt-shovels.

Enter more Prentices

ALL. Whoop, look here, look here!

HODGE. How now, mad lads, whither away so fast?

1ST PRENTICE. Whither? Why, to the great new hall, know you not why? The lord mayor hath bidden all the prentices in London to breakfast this morning.

ALL. Oh brave shoemakers, oh brave lord of incomprehensible good-fellowship! Whoo! Hark you! The pancake-bell rings.

Cast up caps.

FIRK. Nay, more, my hearts! Every Shrove-Tuesday is our year of jubilee; and when the pancake-bell rings, we are as free as my lord mayor; we may shut up our

---

[7] A bell rung on the morning of Shrove Tuesday.   [8] Leadenhall.
[9] Beef broth.   [10] Barrels.   [11] Hods.

shops, and make holiday. I'll have it called Saint Hugh's Holiday.

ALL. Agreed, agreed! Saint Hugh's Holiday.

HODGE. And this shall continue for ever.

ALL. Oh brave! Come, come, my hearts! Away, away!

FIRK. O eternal credit to us of the gentle craft! March fair, my hearts! Oh rare! *Exeunt.*

SCENE III[1]

Enter the KING *and his* Train *across the stage*

KING. Is our lord mayor of London such a gallant?

NOBLEMAN. One of the merriest madcaps in your land.
Your grace will think, when you behold the man,
He's rather a wild ruffian than a mayor.
Yet thus much I'll ensure your majesty.
In all his actions that concern his state,
He is as serious, provident, and wise,
As full of gravity amongst the grave,
As any mayor hath been these many years.

KING. I am with child,[2] till I behold this huff-cap.[3]
But all my doubt is, when we come in presence,
His madness will be dashed clean out of countenance.

NOBLEMAN. It may be so, my liege.

KING   Which to prevent,
Let some one give him notice, 'tis our pleasure
That he put on his wonted merriment.
Set forward!

ALL. On afore! *Exeunt.*

SCENE IV[1]

Enter EYRE, HODGE, FIRK, RALPH, *and other* Shoemakers,
all with napkins on their shoulders

EYRE. Come, my fine Hodge, my jolly gentlemen shoe-makers; soft, where be these cannibals, these varlets, my officers? Let them all walk and wait upon my brethren; for my meaning is, that none but shoemakers, none but the

---

[1] A street in London.   [2] In suspense.   [3] Swaggerer.
[1] A great hall.

livery of my company shall in their satin hoods wait upon the trencher of my sovereign.

FIRK. O my lord, it will be rare!

EYRE. No more, Firk; come, lively! Let your fellow-prentices want no cheer; let wine be plentiful as beer, and beer as water. Hang these penny-pinching fathers, that cram wealth in innocent lamb-skins. Rip, knaves, avaunt! Look to my guests!

HODGE. My lord, we are at our wits' end for room; those hundred tables will not feast the fourth part of them.

EYRE. Then cover me those hundred tables again, and again, till all my jolly prentices be feasted. Avoid, Hodge! Run, Ralph! Frisk about, my nimble Firk! Carouse me fathom-healths to the honour of the shoemakers. Do they drink lively, Hodge? Do they tickle it, Firk?

FIRK. Tickle it? Some of them have taken their liquor standing so long that they can stand no longer; but for meat, they would eat it, an they had it.

EYRE. Want they meat? Where's this swag-belly, this greasy kitchenstuff cook? Call the varlet to me! Want meat? Firk, Hodge, lame Ralph, run, my tall men, be-leaguer the shambles, beggar all Eastcheap, serve me whole oxen in chargers, and let sheep whine upon the tables like pigs for want of good fellows to eat them. Want meat? Vanish, Firk! Avaunt, Hodge!

HODGE. Your lordship mistakes my man Firk; he means, their bellies want meat, not the boards; for they have drunk so much, they can eat nothing.

THE SECOND THREE MEN'S SONG

Cold's the wind, and wet's the rain,
　Saint Hugh be our good speed:
Ill is the weather that bringeth no gain,
　Nor helps good hearts in need.

Trowl² the bowl, the jolly nut-brown bowl,
　And here, kind mate, to thee:
Let's sing a dirge for Saint Hugh's soul,
　And down it merrily.

² Pass.

Down a down heydown a down,
   (*Close with the tenor boy*)
Hey derry derry, down a down!
Ho, well done; to me let come!
Ring, compass, gentle joy.

Trowl the bowl, the nut-brown bowl,
   And here, kind mate, to thee: etc.
   [*Repeat as often as there be men to drink; and
      at last when all have drunk, this verse:*

Cold's the wind, and wet's the rain,
   Saint Hugh be our good speed:
Ill is the weather that bringeth no gain,
   Nor helps good hearts in need.

Enter HANS, ROSE, *and* MARGERY

MARG. Where is my lord?

EYRE. How now, Lady Madgy?

MARG. The king's most excellent majesty is new come; he sends me for thy honour; one of his most worshipful peers bade me tell thou must be merry, and so forth; but let that pass.

EYRE. Is my sovereign come? Vanish, my tall shoemakers, my nimble brethren; look to my guests, the prentices. Yet stay a little! How now, Hans? How looks my little Rose?

HANS. Let me request you to remember me.
I know, your honour easily may obtain
Free pardon of the king for me and Rose,
And reconcile me to my uncle's grace.

EYRE. Have done, my good Hans, my honest journeyman; look cheerily! I'll fall upon both my knees, till they be as hard as horn, but I'll get thy pardon.

MARG. Good my lord, have a care what you speak to his grace.

EYRE. Away, you Islington whitepot![3] hence, you barley-pudding, full of maggots! you broiled carbonado![4] avaunt, avaunt, avoid, Mephistophiles! Shall Sim Eyre learn to speak

[3] "A dish, made of milk, eggs and sugar, baked in a pot."—*Webster.*
[4] A steak cut crossways.

of you, Lady Madgy? Vanish, Mother Miniver-cap; vanish, go, trip and go; meddle with your partlets[5] and your pishery-pashery, your flewes[6] and your whirligigs; go, rub,[7] out of mine alley! Sim Eyre knows how to speak to a Pope, to Sultan Soliman, to Tamburlaine, an he were here, and shall I melt, shall I droop before my sovereign? No, come, my Lady Madgy! Follow me, Hans! About your business, my frolic free-booters! Firk, frisk about, and about, and about, for the honour of mad Simon Eyre, lord mayor of London.

FIRK. Hey, for the honour of the shoemakers. *Exeunt.*

SCENE V[1]

A long flourish, or two. Enter the KING, Nobles, EYRE, MARGERY, LACY, ROSE. LACY *and* ROSE *kneel*

KING. Well, Lacy, though the fact was very foul
Of your revolting from our kingly love
And your own duty, yet we pardon you.
Rise both, and, Mistress Lacy, thank my lord mayor
For your young bridegroom here.

EYRE. So, my dear liege, Sim Eyre and my brethren, the gentlemen shoemakers, shall set your sweet majesty's image cheek by jowl by Saint Hugh for this honour you have done poor Simon Eyre. I beseech your grace, pardon my rude behaviour; I am a handicraftsman, yet my heart is without craft; I would be sorry at my soul, that my boldness should offend my king.

KING. Nay, I pray thee, good lord mayor, be even as merry
As if thou wert among thy shoemakers;
It does me good to see thee in this humour.

EYRE. Say'st thou me so, my sweet Dioclesian? Then, humph! Prince am I none, yet am I princely born. By the Lord of Ludgate, my liege, I'll be as merry as a pie.[2]

KING. Tell me, in faith, mad Eyre, how old thou art.

EYRE. My liege, a very boy, a stripling, a younker; you

---

[5] Ruffs for the neck.   [6] Flaps; as resembling the hanging chaps of a hound.   [7] Obstruction, a term in bowling.
[1] An open yard before the hall.   [2] Magpie.

see not a white hair on my head, not a gray in this beard.
Every hair, I assure thy majesty, that sticks in this beard,
Sim Eyre values at the King of Babylon's ransom, Tamar
Cham's beard was a rubbing brush to't: yet I'll shave it off,
and stuff tennis-balls with it, to please my bully king.

KING. But all this while I do not know your age.

EYRE. My liege, I am six and fifty year old, yet I can
cry humph! with a sound heart for the honour of Saint
Hugh. Mark this old wench, my king: I danc'd the shaking
of the sheets with her six and thirty years ago, and yet I
hope to get two or three young lord mayors, ere I die. I
am lusty still, Sim Eyre still. Care and cold lodging brings
white hairs. My sweet Majesty, let care vanish, cast it upon
thy nobles, it will make thee look always young like Apollo,
and cry humph! Prince am I none, yet am I princely born.

KING. Ha, ha!
Say, Cornwall, didst thou ever see his like?

CORNWALL. Not I, my lord.

Enter the EARL OF LINCOLN *and the* LORD MAYOR

KING.   Lincoln, what news with you?

LINCOLN. My gracious lord, have care unto yourself,
For there are traitors here.

ALL. Traitors? Where? Who?

EYRE. Traitors in my house? God forbid! Where be my
officers? I'll spend my soul, ere my king feel harm.

KING. Where is the traitor, Lincoln?

LINCOLN.   Here he stands.

KING. Cornwall, lay hold on Lacy!—Lincoln, speak,
What canst thou lay unto thy nephew's charge?

LINCOLN. This, my dear liege: your Grace, to do me
           honour,
Heap'd on the head of this degenerate boy
Desertless favours; you made choice of him,
To be commander over powers in France.
But he——

KING. Good Lincoln, prithee, pause a while!
Even in thine eyes I read what thou wouldst speak.
I know how Lacy did neglect our love,
Ran himself deeply, in the highest degree,

Into vile treason——

    LINCOLN.   Is he not a traitor?

    KING. Lincoln, he was; now have we pard'ned him.
'Twas not a base want of true valour's fire,
That held him out of France, but love's desire.

    LINCOLN. I will not bear his shame upon my back.

    KING. Nor shalt thou, Lincoln; I forgive you both.

    LINCOLN. Then, good my liege, forbid the boy to wed
One whose mean birth will much disgrace his bed.

    KING. Are they not married?

    LINCOLN.   No, my liege.

    BOTH.   We are.

    KING. Shall I divorce them then? O be it far,
That any hand on earth should dare untie
The sacred knot, knit by God's majesty;
I would not for my crown disjoin their hands
That are conjoin'd in holy nuptial bands.
How say'st thou, Lacy, wouldst thou lose thy Rose?

    LACY. Not for all India's wealth, my sovereign.

    KING. But Rose, I am sure, her Lacy would forego?

    ROSE. If Rose were asked that question, she'd say no.

    KING. You hear them, Lincoln?

    LINCOLN.   Yea, my liege, I do.

    KING. Yet canst thou find i'th' heart to part these two?
Who seeks, besides you, to divorce these lovers?

    L. MAYOR. I do, my gracious lord, I am her father.

    KING. Sir Roger Oateley, our last mayor, I think?

    NOBLEMAN. The same, my liege.

    KING.   Would you offend Love's laws?
Well, you shall have your wills, you sue to me,
To prohibit the match. Soft, let me see—
You both are married, Lacy, art thou not?

    LACY. I am, dread sovereign.

    KING.   Then, upon thy life,
I charge thee, not to call this woman wife.

    L. MAYOR. I thank your grace.

    ROSE.   O my most gracious lord!
                              Kneels.

    KING. Nay, Rose, never woo me; I tell you true,
Although as yet I am a bachelor,

Yet I believe, I shall not marry you.

ROSE. Can you divide the body from the soul,
Yet make the body live?

KING.   Yea, so profound?
I cannot, Rose, but you I must divide.
This fair maid, bridegroom, cannot be your bride.
Are you pleas'd, Lincoln? Oateley, are you pleas'd?

BOTH. Yes, my lord.

KING.   Then must my heart be eas'd;
For, credit me, my conscience lives in pain,
Till these whom I divorc'd, be join'd again.
Lacy, give me thy hand; Rose, lend me thine!
Be what you would be! Kiss now! So, that's fine.
At night, lovers, to bed!—Now, let me see,
Which of you all mislikes this harmony.

L. MAYOR. Will you then take from me my child perforce?

KING. Why, tell me, Oateley: shines not Lacy's name
As bright in the world's eye as the gay beams
Of any citizen?

LINCOLN.   Yea, but, my gracious lord,
I do mislike the match far more than he;
Her blood is too too base.

KING.   Lincoln, no more.
Dost thou not know that love respects no blood,
Cares not for difference of birth or state?
The maid is young, well born, fair, virtuous,
A worthy bride for any gentleman.
Besides, your nephew for her sake did stoop
To bare necessity, and, as I hear,
Forgetting honours and all courtly pleasures,
To gain her love, became a shoemaker.
As for the honour which he lost in France,
Thus I redeem it: Lacy, kneel thee down!—
Arise, Sir Rowland Lacy! Tell me now,
Tell me in earnest, Oateley, canst thou chide,
Seeing thy Rose a lady and a bride?

L. MAYOR. I am content with what your grace hath done.

LINCOLN. And I, my liege, since there's no remedy.

KING. Come on, then, all shake hands: I'll have you
friends;

Where there is much love, all discord ends.
What says my mad lord mayor to all this love?

EYRE. O my liege, this honour you have done to my fine
journeyman here, Rowland Lacy, and all these favours
which you have shown to me this day in my poor house,
will make Simon Eyre live longer by one dozen of warm
summers more than he should.

KING. Nay, my mad lord mayor, that shall be thy name;
If any grace of mine can length thy life,
One honour more I'll do thee: that new building,[*]
Which at thy cost in Cornhill is erected,
Shall take a name from us; we'll have it call'd
The Leadenhall, because in digging it
You found the lead that covereth the same.

EYRE. I thank your majesty.

MARG. God bless your grace!

KING. Lincoln, a word with you!

Enter HODGE, FIRK, RALPH, *and more* Shoemakers

EYRE. How now, my mad knaves? Peace, speak softly,
yonder is the king.

KING. With the old troop which there we keep in pay,
We will incorporate a new supply.
Before one summer more pass o'er my head,
France shall repent, England was injured.
What are all those?

LACY.   All shoemakers, my liege,
Sometime my fellows; in their companies
I liv'd as merry as an emperor.

KING. My mad lord mayor, are all these shoemakers?

EYRE. All shoemakers, my liege; all gentlemen of the
gentle craft, true Trojans, courageous cordwainers; they all
kneel to the shrine of holy Saint Hugh.

ALL THE SHOEMAKERS. God save your majesty!

KING. Mad Simon, would they anything with us?

EYRE. Mum, mad knaves! Not a word! I'll do't; I warrant you. They are all beggars, my liege; all for them-

[*] "A. D. 1419. This year Sir Symon Eyre built Leadenhall, at his
proper expense, as it now appears, and gave the same to the City to be
employed as a public granary for laying up corn against a time of scarcity."
—*Maitland*, ii., p. 187, quoted by Rhys.

selves, and I for them all on both my knees do entreat, that for the honour of poor Simon Eyre and the good of his brethren, these mad knaves, your grace would vouchsafe some privilege to my new Leadenhall, that it may be lawful for us to buy and sell leather there two days a week.

KING. Mad Sim, I grant your suit, you shall have patent
To hold two market-days in Leadenhall,
Mondays and Fridays, those shall be the times.
Will this content you?

ALL. Jesus bless your grace!

EYRE. In the name of these my poor brethren shoe-makers, I most humbly thank your grace. But before I rise, seeing you are in the giving vein and we in the begging, grant Sim Eyre one boon more.

KING. What is it, my lord mayor?

EYRE. Vouchsafe to taste of a poor banquet that stands sweetly waiting for your sweet presence.

KING. I shall undo thee, Eyre, only with feasts;
Already have I been too troublesome;
Say, have I not?

EYRE. O my dear king, Sim Eyre was taken unawares upon a day of shroving,[4] which I promised long ago to the prentices of London.

> For, an't please your highness, in time past,
> I bare the water-tankard,[5] and my coat
> Sits not a whit the worse upon my back;
> And then, upon a morning, some mad boys,
> It was Shrove Tuesday, even as 'tis now,

gave me my breakfast, and I swore then by the stopple of my tankard, if ever I came to be lord mayor of London, I would feast all the prentices. This day, my liege, I did it, and the slaves had an hundred tables five times covered; they are gone home and vanished;

> Yet add more honour to the gentle trade,
> Taste of Eyre's banquet, Simon's happy made.

KING. Eyre, I will taste of thy banquet, and will say,
I have not met more pleasure on a day.

---

[4] Merry-making.   [5] As an apprentice.

Friends of the gentle craft, thanks to you all,
Thanks, my kind lady mayoress, for our cheer.—
Come, lords, a while let's revel it at home!
When all our sports and banquetings are done,
Wars must right wrongs which Frenchmen have begun.

Exeunt.

THE ALCHEMIST

BY
BEN JONSON

INTRODUCTORY NOTE

BEN JONSON *was born of poor parents at Westminster in 1573. Through the influence of Camden, the antiquary, he got a good education at Westminster School; but he does not seem to have gone to a University, though later both Oxford and Cambridge gave him degrees. In his youth he practised for a time his stepfather's trade of bricklaying, and he served as a soldier in Flanders.*

It was probably about 1595 that he began to write for the stage, and within a few years he was recognized as a distinguished playwright. His comedy of "Every Man in His Humour" was not only a great immediate success, but founded a school of satirical drama in England. "Sejanus" and "Catiline" were less popular, but are impressive pictures of Roman life, less interesting but more accurate than the Roman plays of Shakespeare.

For the court of James I, Jonson wrote a large number of masques, which procured him substantial rewards in the form of pensions.

But it was between 1605 and 1614 that Jonson's greatest work was done. "Volpone," "Epicœne," "The Alchemist," and "Bartholomew Fair" belong to this period, and are all masterpieces.

After the accession of Charles I, Jonson fell into adversity. His plays were less successful and he had enemies at court; but he continued to hold his position of leadership among his fellow authors.

A specimen of Jonson's prose will be found in the volume of "English Essays" in the Harvard Classics, and a number of his graceful lyrics in the first volume of "English Poetry."

Jonson died in 1637, and was celebrated in a volume of elegies to which all the chief poets of the day contributed.

"The Alchemist" is perhaps the most perfect technically of Jonson's plays, and is an admirable satire on the quacks and humbugs of the day. It contains, at the same time, so much universal human nature, and is so excellent in art, that it holds a place among the first of those Elizabethan works that have held the interest of posterity.

ARGUMENT

THE sickness hot,[1] a master quit, for fear,
H is house in town, and left one servant there;
E ase him corrupted, and gave means to know

A Cheater and his punk;[2] who now brought low,
L eaving their narrow practice, were become
C oz'ners[3] at large; and only wanting some
H ouse to set up, with him they here contract,
E ach for a share, and all begin to act.
M uch company they draw, and much abuse,[4]
I n casting figures,[5] telling fortunes, news,
S elling of flies,[6] flat bawdry, with the stone,[7]
T ill it, and they, and all in fume[8] are gone.

[1] The plague raging.　　[2] Mistress.　　[3] Swindlers.　　[4] Deceive.
[5] Calculating the future.　　[6] Familiar spirits.　　[7] Philosopher's stone
[8] Smoke.

PROLOGUE

FORTUNE, that favours fools, these two short hours
   We wish away, both for your sakes and ours,
Judging spectators; and desire, in place,
   To th' author justice, to ourselves but grace.
Our scene is London, 'cause we would make known,
   No country's mirth is better than our own:
No clime breeds better matter for your whore,
   Bawd, squire, impostor, many persons more,
Whose manners, now call'd humours, feed the stage;
   And which have still been subject for the rage
Or spleen of comic writers. Though this pen
   Did never aim to grieve, but better men;
Howe'er the age he lives in doth endure
   The vices that she breeds, above their cure.
But when the wholesome remedies are sweet,
   And in their working gain and profit meet,
He hopes to find no spirit so much diseas'd,
   But will with such fair correctives be pleas'd:
For here he doth not fear who can apply.
   If there be any that will sit so nigh
Unto the stream, to look what it doth run,
   They shall find things, they'd think or wish were done;
They are so natural follies, but so shown,
   As even the doers may see, and yet not own.

THE ALCHEMIST

DRAMATIS PERSONÆ

SUBTLE, the ALCHEMIST.
FACE, the House-keeper.
DOL COMMON, their colleague.
DAPPER, a Lawyer's clerk.
DRUGGER, a Tobacco-man.
LOVEWIT, Master of the House.
Sir EPICURE MAMMON, a Knight.

PERTINAX SURLY, a Gamester.
TRIBULATION WHOLESOME, a Pastor of Amsterdam.
ANANIAS, a Deacon there.
KASTRILL, the angry boy.
Dame PLIANT, his sister, a Widow.
Neighbours.

Officers, Mutes.

THE SCENE—*London*

ACT I

SCENE I[1]

[*Enter*] FACE, [*in a captain's uniform, with his sword drawn, and*] SUBTLE [*with a vial, quarrelling, and followed by*] DOL COMMON

Face

BELIEVE 't, I will.
   SUB.   Thy worst.
   DOL. Have you your wits? why, gentlemen! for love——
   FACE. Sirrah, I'll strip you——
   SUB.   What to do?
   FACE. Rogue, rogue!—out of all your sleights.[2]
   DOL. Nay, look ye, sovereign, general, are you madmen?
   SUB. O, let the wild sheep loose. I'll gum your silks
With good strong water, an you come.
   DOL.   Will you have
The neighbours hear you? Will you betray all?

---

[1] A room in Lovewit's house.   [2] Drop your tricks.

521

Hark! I hear somebody.

FACE.   Sirrah——

SUB.   I shall mar
All that the tailor has made if you approach.

FACE. You most notorious whelp, you insolent slave,
Dare you do this?

SUB.   Yes, faith; yes, faith.

FACE.   Why, who
Am I, my mongrel, who am I?

SUB.   I'll tell you,
Since you know not yourself.

FACE.   Speak lower, rogue.

SUB. Yes, you were once (time's not long past) the good,
Honest, plain, livery-three-pound-thrum,[3] that kept
Your master's worship's house here in the Friars,[4]
For the vacations——

FACE.   Will you be so loud?

SUB. Since, by my means, translated suburb-captain.

FACE. By your means, doctor dog!

SUB.   Within man's memory,
All this I speak of.

FACE.   Why, I pray you, have I
Been countenanc'd by you, or you by me?
Do but collect, sir, where I met you first.

SUB. I do not hear well.

FACE.   Not of this, I think it.
But I shall put you in mind, sir;—at Pie-corner,
Taking your meal of steam in, from cooks' stalls,
Where, like the father of hunger, you did walk
Piteously costive, with your pinch'd-horn-nose,
And your complexion of the Roman wash,[5]
Stuck full of black and melancholic worms,
Like powder-corns[6] shot at the artillery-yard.

SUB. I wish you could advance your voice a little.

FACE. When you went pinn'd up in the several rags
You had rak'd and pick'd from dunghills, before day;
Your feet in mouldy slippers, for your kibes;[7]
A felt of rug,[8] and a thin threaden cloak,

---

[3] Poorly paid servant. [4] The precinct of Blackfriars. [5] *I. e.*, sallow.
[6] Grains of powder. [7] Chilblains. [8] A hat of coarse material.

That scarce would cover your no-buttocks——

SUB.   So, sir!

FACE. When all your alchemy, and your algebra,
Your minerals, vegetals, and animals,
Your conjuring, coz'ning;[9] and your dozen of trades,
Could not relieve your corpse with so much linen
Would make you tinder, but to see a fire;
I ga' you count'nance, credit for your coals,
Your stills, your glasses, your materials;
Built you a furnace, drew you customers,
Advanc'd all your black arts; lent you, beside,
A house to practise in——

SUB.   Your master's house!

FACE. Where you have studied the more thriving skill
Of bawdry since.

SUB.   Yes, in your master's house.
You and the rats here kept possession.
Make it not strange.[10] I know you were one could keep
The buttery-hatch still lock'd, and save the chippings,
Sell the dole beer to aqua-vitæ men,[11]
The which, together with your Christmas vails[12]
At post-and-pair,[13] your letting out of counters,[14]
Made you a pretty stock, some twenty marks,
And gave you credit to converse with cobwebs,
Here, since your mistress' death hath broke up house.

FACE. You might talk softlier, rascal.

SUB.   No, you scarab.
I'll thunder you in pieces: I will teach you
How to beware to tempt a Fury again
That carries tempest in his hand and voice.

FACE. The place has made you valiant.

SUB.   No, your clothes.
Thou vermin, have I ta'en thee out of dung,
So poor, so wretched, when no living thing
Would keep thee company, but a spider or worse?
Rais'd thee from brooms, and dust, and wat'ring-pots,
Sublim'd thee, and exalted thee, and fix'd thee
In the third region,[15] call'd our state of grace?

---

[9] Swindling.   [10] Don't pretend to forget.   [11] Sell the beer intended for the poor to liquor-dealers.   [12] Tips.   [13] A game of cards.   [14] I. e., to the card-players.   [15] Technical jargon of alchemy.

Wrought thee to spirit, to quintessence, with pains
Would twice have won me the philosopher's work?
Put thee in words and fashion, made thee fit
For more than ordinary fellowships?
Giv'n thee thy oaths, thy quarrelling dimensions,
Thy rules to cheat at horse-race, cock-pit, cards,
Dice, or whatever gallant tincture[16] else?
Made thee a second in mine own great art?
And have I this for thanks! Do you rebel?
Do you fly out i' the projection?[17]
Would you be gone now?

DOL.   Gentlemen, what mean you?
Will you mar all?

SUB. Slave, thou hadst had no name——

DOL. Will you undo yourselves with civil war?

SUB. Never been known, past *equi clibanum,*
The heat of horse-dung, under ground, in cellars,
Or an ale-house darker than deaf John's; been lost
To all mankind, but laundresses and tapsters,
Had not I been.

DOL.   Do you know who hears you, sovereign?

FACE. Sirrah——

DOL. Nay, general, I thought you were civil.

FACE. I shall turn desperate, if you grow thus loud.

SUB. And hang thyself, I care not.

FACE.   Hang thee, collier,
And all thy pots and pans, in picture, I will,
Since thou hast mov'd me——

DOL. [*Aside*]   O, this 'll o'erthrow all.

FACE. Write thee up bawd in Paul's, have all thy tricks
Of coz'ning with a hollow cole, dust, scrapings,
Searching for things lost, with a sieve and shears,
Erecting figures in your rows of houses,[18]
And taking in of shadows with a glass,
Told in red letters; and a face cut for thee,
Worse than Gamaliel Ratsey's.[19]

DOL.   Are you sound?
Ha' you your senses, masters?

---

[16] Accomplishment.   [17] At the moment when success is near.
[18] Astrological tricks.   [19] A notorious highwayman.

FACE.   I will have
A book, but barely reckoning thy impostures,
Shall prove a true philosopher's stone to printers.

SUB. Away, you trencher-rascal!

FACE.   Out, you dog-leech!
The vomit of all prisons——

DOL.   Will you be
Your own destructions, gentlemen?

FACE.   Still spew'd out
For lying too heavy on the basket.[20]

SUB.   Cheater!

FACE. Bawd!

SUB.   Cow-herd!

FACE.   Conjurer!

SUB.   Cutpurse!

FACE.   Witch!

DOL.   O me!
We are ruin'd, lost! Ha' you no more regard
To your reputations? Where's your judgment? 'Slight,
Have yet some care of me, o' your republic——

FACE. Away, this brach![21] I'll bring thee, rogue, within
The statute of sorcery, tricesimo tertio
Of Harry the Eighth:[22] ay, and perhaps thy neck
Within a noose, for laund'ring gold and barbing it.[23]

DOL. You'll bring your head within a cockscomb,[24] will
    you?

> *She catcheth out* FACE *his sword, and breaks*
> SUBTLE's *glass.*

And you, sir, with your menstrue![25]—Gather it up.
'Sdeath, you abominable pair of stinkards,
Leave off your barking, and grow one again,
Or, by the light that shines, I'll cut your throats.
I'll not be made a prey unto the marshal
For ne'er a snarling dog-bolt of you both.
Ha' you together cozen'd all this while,
And all the world, and shall it now be said,
You've made most courteous shift to cozen yourselves?

[20] Eating more than his share of rations.   [21] Bitch.
[22] 33 Henry VIII, the first act against witchcraft in England.
[23] "Sweating" and clipping the coinage.   [24] Halter.
[25] A liquid which dissolves solids.

You will accuse him! You will "bring him in   [*to* FACE.]
Within the statute!"   Who shall take your word?
A whoreson, upstart, apocryphal captain,
Whom not a Puritan in Blackfriars will trust
So much as for a feather: and you, too,   [*to* SUBTLE.]
Will give the cause, forsooth! You will insult,
And claim a primacy in the divisions!
You must be chief! As if you only had
The powder to project[26] with, and the work
Were not begun out of equality?
The venture tripartite? All things in common?
Without priority? 'Sdeath! you perpetual curs,
Fall to your couples again, and cozen kindly,
And heartily, and lovingly, as you should,
And lose not the beginning of a term,
Or, by this hand, I shall grow factious too,
And take my part, and quit you.

  FACE.   'Tis his fault;
He ever murmurs, and objects his pains,
And says, the weight of all lies upon him.

  SUB. Why, so it does.

  DOL.   How does it? Do not we
Sustain our parts?

  SUB.   Yes, but they are not equal.

  DOL. Why, if your part exceed to-day, I hope
Ours may to-morrow match it.

  SUB.   Ay, they *may*.

  DOL. May, murmuring mastiff! Ay, and do. Death
    on me!
Help me to throttle him.   [*Seizes* SUB. *by the throat.*]

  SUB.   Dorothy! Mistress Dorothy!
'Ods precious, I'll do anything. What do you mean?

  DOL. Because o' your fermentation and cibation?[27]

  SUB. Not I, by heaven——

  DOL.   Your Sol and Luna——help me.
                        [*To* FACE.]

  SUB. Would I were hang'd then! I'll conform myself.

  DOL. Will you, sir? Do so then, and quickly: swear.

  SUB. What should I swear?

---

[26] Transmute metals.   [27] Alchemical terms.

DOL.   To leave your faction, sir,
And labour kindly in the common work.

SUB. Let me not breathe if I meant aught beside.
I only us'd those speeches as a spur
To him.

DOL. I hope we need no spurs, sir. Do we?

FACE. 'Slid, prove to-day who shall shark best.

SUB.   Agreed.

DOL. Yes, and work close and friendly.

SUB.   'Slight, the knot
Shall grow the stronger for this breach, with me.

[They shake hands.]

DOL. Why, so, my good baboons! Shall we go make
A sort of sober, scurvy, precise neighbours,
That scarce have smil'd twice sin' the king came in,[28]
A feast of laughter at our follies? Rascals,
Would run themselves from breath, to see me ride,
Or you t' have but a hole to thrust your heads in,[29]
For which you should pay ear-rent?[30] No, agree.
And may Don Provost ride a feasting long,
In his old velvet jerkin and stain'd scarfs,
My noble sovereign, and worthy general,
Ere we contribute a new crewel[31] garter
To his most worsted[31] worship.

SUB.   Royal Dol!
Spoken like Claridiana,[32] and thyself.

FACE. For which at supper, thou shalt sit in triumph,
And not be styl'd Dol Common, but Dol Proper,
Dol Singular: the longest cut at night,
Shall draw thee for his Dol Particular. *[Bell rings without.]*

SUB. Who's that? One rings. To the window, Dol:
    [Exit DOL.]—pray heav'n,
The master do not trouble us this quarter.

FACE. O, fear not him. While there dies one a week
O 'the plague, he's safe from thinking toward London.
Beside, he's busy at his hop-yards now;
I had a letter from him. If he do,
He'll send such word, for airing o' the house,

---

[28] Seven years before.   [29] In the pillory.   [30] Have your ears cut off.
[31] Familiar puns.   [32] The heroine of the " Mirror of Knighthood."

As you shall have sufficient time to quit it:
Though we break up a fortnight, 'tis no matter.

Re-enter DOL.

SUB. Who is it, Dol?
DOL.   A fine young quodling.[88]
FACE.   O,
My lawyer's clerk, I lighted on last night,
In Holborn, at the Dagger. He would have
(I told you of him) a familiar,
To rifle with at horses, and win cups.
    DOL. O, let him in.
    SUB.   Stay. Who shall do't?
    FACE.   Get you
Your robes on; I will meet him, as going out.
    DOL. And what shall I do?
    FACE.   Not be seen; away!
                                [*Exit* DOL.]
Seem you very reserv'd.
    SUB.   Enough.   [*Exit.*]
    FACE. [*aloud and retiring.*] God be wi' you, sir,
I pray you let him know that I was here:
His name is Dapper. I would gladly have staid, but——

SCENE II[1]

FACE, *alone*

DAP. [*within.*] Captain, I am here.
FACE.   Who's that?—He's come, I think, doctor.

[*Enter* DAPPER.]

Good faith, sir, I was going away.
    DAP.   In truth,
I am very sorry, captain.
    FACE.   But I thought
Sure I should meet you.
    DAP.   Ay, I am very glad.
I had a scurvy writ or two to make,

---

        [88] Green apple, a youth.
        [1] The same. The scene-divisions are Jonson's.

And I had lent my watch last night to one
That dines to-day at the sheriff's, and so was robb'd
Of my pass-time.[2]

     [*Re-enter* SUBTLE *in his velvet cap and gown*]
              Is this the cunning-man?

FACE. This is his worship.
DAP.   Is he a doctor?
FACE.   Yes.
DAP. And ha' you broke[8] with him, captain?
FACE.   Ay.
DAP.   And how?
FACE. Faith, he does make the matter, sir, so dainty,[4]
I know not what to say.
DAP.   Not so, good captain.
FACE. Would I were fairly rid on 't, believe me.
DAP. Nay, now you grieve me, sir. Why should you
    wish so?
I dare assure you, I'll not be ungrateful.
FACE. I cannot think you will, sir. But the law
Is such a thing——and then he says, Read's[5] matter
Falling so lately.
DAP.   Read! he was an ass,
And dealt, sir, with a fool.
FACE.   It was a clerk, sir.
DAP. A clerk!
FACE.   Nay, hear me, sir. You know the law
Better, I think——
DAP.   I should, sir, and the danger:
You know, I show'd the statute to you.
FACE.   You did so.
DAP. And will I tell then! By this hand of flesh,
Would it might never write good courthand more,
If I discover.[6] What do you think of me,
That I am a chiaus?[7]
FACE.   What's that?
DAP.   The Turk was, here—
As one would say, do you think I am a Turk?

    [2] Watch.   [3] Opened the matter.   [4] Has such scruples.   [5] A magician
recently convicted.   [6] Reveal.   [7] A Turkish interpreter, like the one
who had recently cheated some merchants.

FACE. I'll tell the doctor so.

DAP.   Do, good sweet captain.

FACE. Come, noble doctor, pray thee let's prevail;
This is the gentleman, and he is no chiaus.

SUB. Captain, I have return'd you all my answer.
I would do much, sir, for your love—— But this
I neither may, nor can.

FACE.   Tut, do not say so.
You deal now with a noble fellow, doctor,
One that will thank you richly; and he is no chiaus:
Let that, sir, move you.

SUB.   Pray you, forbear——

FACE.   He has
Four angels here.

SUB.   You do me wrong, good sir.

FACE. Doctor, wherein? To tempt you with these spirits?

SUB. To tempt my art and love, sir, to my peril.
'Fore heav'n, I scarce can think you are my friend,
That so would draw me to apparent danger.

FACE. I draw you! A horse draw you, and a halter,
You, and your flies[8] together——

DAP.   Nay, good captain.

FACE. That know no difference of men.

SUB.   Good words, sir.

FACE. Good deeds, sir, doctor dogs'-meat. 'Slight, I bring
        you
No cheating Clim o' the Cloughs[9] or Claribels,[10]
That look as big as five-and-fifty, and flush;[11]
And spit out secrets like hot custard——

DAP.   Captain!

FACE. Nor any melancholic underscribe,
Shall tell the vicar; but a special gentle,
That is the heir to forty marks a year,
Consorts with the small poets of the time,
Is the sole hope of his old grandmother;
That knows the law, and writes you six fair hands,
Is a fine clerk, and has his ciph'ring perfect.

---

[8] Familiar spirits.   [9] An outlaw hero.
[10] Probably a hero of romance. The name occurs in Spenser.
[11] Five-and-fifty was the highest number to stand on at the old game of
Primero. If a flush accompanied this, the hand swept the table.—*Gifford.*

Will take his oath o' the Greek Xenophon,[12]
If need be, in his pocket; and can court
His mistress out of Ovid.

DAP.   Nay, dear captain——

FACE. Did you not tell me so?

DAP.   Yes; but I'd ha' you
Use master doctor with some more respect.

FACE. Hang him, proud stag, with his broad velvet head!——
But for your sake, I'd choke ere I would change
An article of breath with such a puck-fist![13]
Come, let's be gone.   [*Going.*]

SUB.   Pray you le' me speak with you.

DAP. His worship calls you, captain.

FACE.   I am sorry
I e'er embark'd myself in such a business.

DAP. Nay, good sir; he did call you.

FACE.   Will he take then?

SUB. First, hear me——

FACE.   Not a syllable, 'less you take.

SUB. Pray ye, sir——

FACE.   Upon no terms but an *assumpsit*.[14]

SUB. Your humour must be law.   *He takes the money.*

FACE.   Why now, sir, talk.
Now I dare hear you with mine honour. Speak.
So may this gentleman too.

SUB.   Why, sir—— [*Offering to whisper* FACE.]

FACE.   No whispering.

SUB. 'Fore heav'n, you do not apprehend the loss
You do yourself in this.

FACE.   Wherein? for what?

SUB. Marry, to be so importunate for one
That, when he has it, will undo you all:
He'll win up all the money i' the town.

FACE. How?

SUB.   Yes, and blow up gamester after gamester,
As they do crackers in a puppet-play.
If I do give him a familiar,
Give you him all you play for; never set[15] him:

---

[12] The Quarto reads *Testament*.   [13] Niggard.
[14] That he has undertaken the affair.   [15] Stake against.

For he will have it.

FACE.   You're mistaken, doctor.
Why, he does ask one but for cups and horses,
A rifling[16] fly; none o' your great familiars.

DAP. Yes, captain, I would have it for all games.

SUB. I told you so.

FACE. [*taking* DAP. *aside.*] 'Slight, that is a new business!
I understood you, a tame bird, to fly
Twice in a term, or so, on Friday nights,
When you had left the office; for a nag
Of forty or fifty shillings.

DAP.   Ay, 'tis true, sir;
But I do think, now, I shall leave the law,
And therefore——

FACE.   Why, this changes quite the case.
Do you think that I dare move him?

DAP.   If you please, sir;
All's one to him, I see.

FACE.   What! for that money?
I cannot with my conscience; nor should you
Make the request, methinks.

DAP.   No, sir, I mean
To add consideration.

FACE.   Why then, sir,
I'll try. [*Goes to* SUBTLE.] Say that it were for all games,
      doctor?

SUB. I say then, not a mouth shall eat for him
At any ordinary,[17] but on the score,[18]
That is a gaming mouth, conceive me.

FACE.   Indeed!

SUB. He'll draw you all the treasure of the realm,
If it be set him.

FACE.   Speak you this from art?

SUB. Ay, sir, and reason too, the ground of art.
He is of the only best complexion,
The queen of Fairy loves.

FACE.   What! is he?

SUB.   Peace.

[16] To be used in raffles.   [17] Table d'hôte restaurant.
[18] The gamblers (who frequented ordinaries) will be so impoverished
through his winnings that they will have to eat on credit.

He'll overhear you.   Sir, should she but see him——
    FACE. What?
    SUB.   Do not you tell him.
    FACE.   Will he win at cards too?
    SUB. The spirits of dead Holland, living Isaac,[19]
You'd swear, were in him; such a vigorous luck
As cannot be resisted. 'Slight, he'll put
Six of your gallants to a cloak,[20] indeed.
    FACE. A strange success, that some man shall be born to!
    SUB. He hears you, man——
    DAP.   Sir, I'll not be ingrateful.
    FACE. Faith, I have confidence in his good nature:
You hear, he says he will not be ingrateful.
    SUB. Why, as you please; my venture follows yours.
    FACE. Troth, do it, doctor; think him trusty, and make him.
He may make us both happy in an hour;
Win some five thousand pound, and send us two on't.
    DAP. Believe it, and I will, sir.
    FACE.   And you shall, sir.
You have heard all?
    DAP.   No, what was't? Nothing, I, sir.
                    FACE *takes him aside.*
    FACE. Nothing!
    DAP.   A little, sir.
    FACE.   Well, a rare star
Reign'd at your birth.
    DAP.   At mine, sir! No.
    FACE.   The doctor
Swears that you are——
    SUB.   Nay, captain, you'll tell all now.
    FACE. Allied to the queen of Fairy.
    DAP.   Who! That I am?
Believe it, no such matter——
    FACE.   Yes, and that
You were born with a caul on your head.
    DAP.   Who says so?
    FACE.   Come,
You know it well enough, though you dissemble it.

[19] Supposed to refer to two alchemists, but the dates do not agree.
[20] Strip to the cloak.

DAP. I' fac,[21] I do not; you are mistaken.

FACE.   How!
Swear by your fac,[21] and in a thing so known
Unto the doctor? How shall we, sir, trust you
I' the other matter; can we ever think,
When you have won five or six thousand pound,
You'll send us shares in't by this rate?

DAP.   By Jove, sir,
I'll win ten thousand pound, and send you half.
I' fac's no oath.

SUB.   No, no, he did but jest.

FACE. Go to.   Go thank the doctor: he's your friend,
To take it so.

DAP.   I thank his worship.

FACE.   So!
Another angel.

DAP.   Must I?

FACE.   Must you! 'slight,
What else is thanks? Will you be trivial?—Doctor,
                    [DAPPER *gives him the money*.]
When must he come for his familiar?

DAP. Shall I not ha' it with me?

SUB.   O, good sir!
There must a world of ceremonies pass;
You must be bath'd and fumigated first:
Besides, the queen of Fairy does not rise
Till it be noon.

FACE.   Not, if she danc'd, to-night.

SUB. And she must bless it.

FACE.   Did you never see
Her royal grace yet?

DAP.   Whom?

FACE.   Your aunt of Fairy?

SUB. Not since she kist him in the cradle, captain;
I can resolve you that.

FACE.   Well, see her grace,
Whate'er it cost you, for a thing that I know.
It will be somewhat hard to compass; but
However, see her. You are made, believe it,

[21] Faith.

THE ALCHEMIST

If you can see her. Her grace is a lone woman,
And very rich; and if she take a fancy,
She will do strange things. See her, at any hand.
'Slid, she may hap to leave you all she has:
It is the doctor's fear.

DAP.   How will't be done, then?

FACE. Let me alone, take you no thought. Do you
But say to me, " Captain, I'll see her grace."

DAP. " Captain, I'll see her grace."

FACE.   Enough. *One knocks without.*

SUB.   Who's there?

Anon.—Conduct him forth by the back way.

                          [*Aside to* FACE.]

—Sir, against one o'clock prepare yourself;
Till when you must be fasting; only take
Three drops of vinegar in at your nose,
Two at your mouth, and one at either ear;
Then bathe your fingers' ends and wash your eyes,
To sharpen your five senses, and cry *hum*
Thrice, and then *buz* as often; and then come.   [*Exit.*]

FACE. Can you remember this?

DAP.   I warrant you.

FACE. Well then, away. It is but your bestowing
Some twenty nobles 'mong her grace's servants,
And put on a clean shirt. You do not know
What grace her grace may do you in clean linen.

                [*Exeunt* FACE *and* DAPPER.]

SCENE III[1]

SUB. [*within.*] Come in! Good wives, I pray you forbear
     me now;
Troth, I can do you no good till afternoon—

      [*Enter* SUBTLE, *followed by* DRUGGER]

SUB. What is your name, say you? Abel Drugger?

DRUG.   Yes, sir.

SUB. A seller of tobacco?

         [1] The same.

DRUG.   Yes, sir.

SUB.   Umph!

Free of the grocers?[3]

DRUG.   Ay, an't please you.

SUB.   Well——

Your business, Abel?

DRUG.   This, an't please your worship;
I am a young beginner, and am building
Of a new shop, an't like your worship, just
At corner of a street:—Here is the plot[3] on't——
And I would know by art, sir, of your worship,
Which way I should make my door, by necromancy,
And where my shelves; and which should be for boxes,
And which for pots. I would be glad to thrive, sir:
And I was wish'd[4] to your worship by a gentleman,
One Captain Face, that says you know men's planets,
And their good angels, and their bad.

SUB.   I do,
If I do see 'em——

[*Enter* FACE]

FACE.   What! my honest Abel?
Thou art well met here.

DRUG.   Troth, sir, I was speaking,
Just as your worship came here, of your worship:
I pray you speak for me to master doctor.

FACE. He shall do anything. Doctor, do you hear?
This is my friend, Abel, an honest fellow;
He lets me have good tobacco, and he does not
Sophisticate it with sack-lees or oil,
Nor washes it in muscadel and grains,
Nor buries it in gravel, under ground,
Wrapped up in greasy leather, or piss'd clouts:
But keeps it in fine lily pots, that, open'd,
Smell like conserve of roses, or French beans.
He has his maple block,[5] his silver tongs,
Winchester pipes, and fire of juniper:[6]
A neat, spruce, honest fellow, and no goldsmith.[7]

---

[3] *I. e.*, a member of the Grocers' Company.   [3] Plan.
[4] Recommended.   [5] On which tobacco was shredded.
[6] The coals of which were used to light pipes.   [7] Usurer.

Sub. He's a fortunate fellow, that I am sure on.

Face. Already, sir, ha' you found it? Lo thee, Abel!

Sub. And in right way toward riches——

Face.   Sir!

Sub.   This summer.
He will be of the clothing of his company,[8]
And next spring call'd to the scarlet;[9] spend what he can.

Face. What, and so little beard?

Sub.   Sir, you must think,
He may have a receipt to make hair come:
But he'll be wise, preserve his youth, and fine for 't;
His fortune looks for him another way.

Face. 'Slid, doctor, how canst thou know this so soon?
I am amus'd[10] at that.

Sub.   By a rule, captain,
In metoposcopy,[11] which I do work by;
A certain star i' the forehead, which you see not.
Your chestnut or your olive-colour'd face
Does never fail: and your long ear doth promise.
I knew 't, by certain spots, too, in his teeth,
And on the nail of his mercurial finger.

Face.   Which finger's that?

Sub. His little finger. Look.
You were born upon a Wednesday?

Drug.   Yes, indeed, sir.

Sub. The thumb, in chiromancy, we give Venus;
The forefinger to Jove; the midst to Saturn;
The ring to Sol; the least to Mercury,
Who was the lord, sir, of his horoscope,
His house of life being Libra; which foreshow'd
He should be a merchant, and should trade with balance.

Face. Why, this is strange! Is it not, honest Nab?

Sub. There is a ship now coming from Ormus,
That shall yield him such a commodity
Of drugs——This is the west, and this the south?

                                [Pointing to the plan.]

Drug. Yes, sir.

Sub.   And those are your two sides?

Drug.   Ay, sir.

[8] Wear the **livery**.   [9] **Be sheriff**.   [10] Amazed.   [11] A branch of physiognomy

SUB. Make me your door then, south; your broad side,
    west:
And on the east side of your shop, aloft,
Write Mathlai, Tarmiel, and Baraborat;
Upon the north part, Rael, Velel, Thiel.
They are the names of those Mercurial spirits
That do fright flies from boxes.

DRUG.   Yes, sir.

SUB.   And
Beneath your threshold, bury me a loadstone
To draw in gallants that wear spurs: the rest,
They'll seem[12] to follow.

FACE.   That's a secret, Nab!

SUB. And, on your stall, a puppet, with a vice
And a court-fucus,[13] to call city-dames:
You shall deal much with minerals.

DRUG.   Sir, I have.
At home, already——

SUB.   Ay, I know you have arsenic,
Vitriol, sal-tartar, argaile,[14] alkali,
Cinoper:[15] I know all.—This fellow, captain,
Will come, in time, to be a great distiller,
And give a say[16]—I will not say directly,
But very fair—at the philosopher's stone.

FACE. Why, how now, Abel! is this true?

DRUG.   [Aside to FACE.] Good captain,
What must I give?

FACE.   Nay, I'll not counsel thee.
Thou hear'st what wealth (he says, spend what thou canst),
Thou'rt like to come to.

DRUG.   I would gi' him a crown.

FACE. A crown! and toward such a fortune? Heart,
Thou shalt rather gi' him thy shop. No gold about thee?

DRUG. Yes, I have a portague,[17] I ha' kept this half-year.

FACE. Out on thee, Nab! 'Slight, there was such an offer—
Shalt keep't no longer, I'll give't him for thee. Doctor,
Nab prays your worship to drink this, and swears
He will appear more grateful, as your skill

----

[12] Be seen.   [13] Paint for the face.   [14] Tartar deposited by wine.
[15] Cinnabar, mercuric sulphid.   [16] Assay.
[17] A gold coin worth about three pounds twelve shillings.

Does raise him in the world.

DRUG.   I would entreat
Another favour of his worship.

FACE.   What is't, Nab?

DRUG. But to look over, sir, my almanac,
And cross out my ill-days,[18] that I may neither
Bargain, nor trust upon them.

FACE.   That he shall, Nab:
Leave it, it shall be done, 'gainst afternoon.

SUB. And a direction for his shelves.

FACE.   Now, Nab,
Art thou well pleas'd, Nab?

DRUG.   'Thank, sir, both your worships.

FACE.   Away. [*Exit* DRUGGER.]
Why, now, you smoaky persecutor of nature!
Now do you see, that something 's to be done,
Beside your beech-coal, and your cor'sive[19] waters,
Your crosslets,[20] crucibles, and cucurbites?[21]
You must have stuff, brought home to you, to work on:
And yet you think, I am at no expense
In searching out these veins, then following them,
Then trying 'em out. 'Fore God, my intelligence
Costs me more money than my share oft comes to,
In these rare works.

SUB.   You're pleasant, sir.—How now!

SCENE IV[1]

FACE. SUBTLE. [*Enter*] DOL.

SUB. What says my dainty Dolkin?

DOL.   Yonder fish-wife
Will not away. And there's your giantess,
The bawd of Lambeth.

SUB.   Heart, I cannot speak with 'em.

DOL. Not afore night, I have told 'em in a voice,
Thorough the trunk, like one of your familiars.
But I have spied Sir Epicure Mammon——

[18] Unlucky days.   [19] Corrosive.   [20] Crucibles.
[21] Glass retort, shaped like a gourd.
[1] The same.

SUB.   Where?
DOL. Coming along, at far end of the lane,
Slow of his feet, but earnest of his tongue
To one that's with him.
    SUB.   Face, go you and shift.
Dol, you must presently make ready too.   [*Exit* FACE.]
    DOL. Why, what's the matter?
    SUB.   O, I did look for **him**
With the sun's rising: marvel he could sleep.
This is the day I am to perfect for him
The magisterium, our great work, the stone;
And yield it, made, into his hands: of which
He has, this month, talk'd as he were possess'd.
And now he's dealing pieces on't away.
Methinks I see him ent'ring ordinaries,
Dispensing for the pox, and plaguy houses,
Reaching his dose, walking Moorfields for lepers,
And off'ring citizens' wives pomander[2]-bracelets,
As his preservative, made of the elixir;
Searching the spittle, to make old bawds young;
And the highways, for beggars, to make rich.
I see no end of his labours. He will make
Nature asham'd of her long sleep: when art,
Who's but a step-dame, shall do more than she,
In her best love to mankind, ever could.
If his dream last, he'll turn the age to gold.   [*Exeunt.*]

ACT II

SCENE I[1]

[*Enter*] Sir EPICURE MAMMON *and* SURLY

MAM. Come on, sir. Now you set your foot on shore
In *Novo Orbe;*[2] here's the rich Peru:
And there within, sir, are the golden mines,
Great Solomon's Ophir! He was sailing to't
Three years, but we have reach'd it in ten months.
This is the day wherein, to all my friends,

---

    [2] A ball of perfume carried against infection.
    [1] An outer room in Lovewit's house.   [2] The New World.

I will pronounce the happy word, BE RICH;
THIS DAY YOU SHALL BE SPECTATISSIMI.[3]
You shall no more deal with the hollow die,
Or the frail card. No more be at charge of keeping
The livery-punk[4] for the young heir, that must
Seal, at all hours, in his shirt: no more,
If he deny, ha' him beaten to't, as he is
That brings him the commodity. No more
Shall thirst of satin, or the covetous hunger
Of velvet entrails[5] for a rude-spun cloak,
To be display'd at Madam Augusta's, make
The sons of Sword and Hazard fall before
The golden calf, and on their knees, whole nights,
Commit idolatry with wine and trumpets:
Or go a feasting after drum and ensign.
No more of this. You shall start up young viceroys.
And unto thee I speak it first, BE RICH.
Where is my Subtle, there? Within, ho!

　　[FACE, *within*.]   Sir,
He'll come to you by and by.

　　MAM.   That is his fire-drake,[6]
His Lungs, his Zephyrus, he that puffs his coals,
Till he firk[7] nature up, in her own centre.
You are not faithful,[8] sir. This night I'll change
All that is metal in my house to gold:
And, early in the morning, will I send
To all the plumbers and the pewterers,
And buy their tin and lead up; and to Lothbury
For all the copper.

　　SUR.   What, and turn that, too?

　　MAM. Yes, and I'll purchase Devonshire and Cornwall,
And make them perfect Indies! You admire now?

　　SUR. No, faith.

　　MAM. But when you see th' effects of the Great Med'cine,
Of which one part projected on a hundred
Of Mercury, or Venus, or the moon,
Shall turn it to as many of the sun;[9]
Nay, to a thousand, so *ad infinitum:*

---

[3] Most gazed at. [4] Female accomplice in swindling heirs out of property.
[5] Lining. [6] Dragon. [7] Stir, rouse. [8] Believing.
[9] Turn mercury, copper, or silver into gold.

You will believe me.

SUR.   Yes, when I see't, I will.
But if my eyes do cozen me so, and I
Giving them no occasion, sure I'll have
Them out next day.

MAM.   Ha ! why ?
Do you think I fable with you ? I assure you,
He that has once the flower of the sun,
The perfect ruby, which we call elixir,
Not only can do that, but by its virtue,
Can confer honour, love, respect, long life;
Give safety, valour, yea, and victory,
To whom he will. In eight and twenty days,
I'll make an old man of fourscore, a child.

SUR. No doubt; he's that already.

MAM.   Nay, I mean,
Restore his years, renew him, like an eagle,
To the fifth age; make him get sons and daughters,
Young giants; as our philosophers have done,
The ancient patriarchs, afore the flood,
But taking, once a week, on a knife's point,
The quantity of a grain of mustard of it;
Become stout Marses, and beget young Cupids.

SUR. The decay'd vestals of Pickt-hatch[10] would thank you,
That keep the fire alive there.

MAM.   'Tis the secret
Of nature naturiz'd 'gainst all infections,
Cures all diseases coming of all causes;
A month's grief in a day, a year's in twelve;
And, of what age soever, in a month:
Past all the doses of your drugging doctors.
I'll undertake, withal, to fright the plague
Out o' the kingdom in three months.

SUR.   And I'll
Be bound, the players shall sing your praises then,
Without their poets.[11]

MAM.   Sir, I'll do't. Meantime,
I'll give away so much unto my man,

---

[10] A disreputable locality.
[11] The theatres were closed when the plague was prevalent.

Shall serve th' whole city with preservative
Weekly; each house his dose, and at the rate——
   Sur. As he that built the Water-work does with water?
   Mam. You are incredulous.
   Sur.   Faith, I have a humour,
I would not willingly be gull'd.[12] Your stone
Cannot transmute me.
   Mam.   Pertinax Surly,
Will you believe antiquity? Records?
I'll show you a book where Moses, and his sister,
And Solomon have written of the art;
Ay, and a treatise penn'd by Adam——
   Sur.   How!
   Mam. Of the philosopher's stone, and in High Dutch.
   Sur. Did Adam write, sir, in High Dutch?
   Mam.   He did;
Which proves it was the primitive tongue.
   Sur.   What paper?
   Mam. On cedar board.
   Sur.   O that, indeed, they say,
Will last 'gainst worms.
   Mam.   'Tis like your Irish wood,
'Gainst cobwebs. I have a piece of Jason's fleece too,
Which was no other than a book of alchemy,
Writ in large sheepskin, a good fat ram-vellum.
Such was Pythagoras' thigh, Pandora's tub,
And all that fable of Medea's charms,
The manner of our work; the bulls, our furnace,
Still breathing fire; our argent-vive,[13] the dragon:
The dragon's teeth, mercury sublimate,
That keeps the whiteness, hardness, and the biting;
And they are gather'd into Jason's helm,
The alembic, and then sow'd in Mars his field,
And thence sublim'd so often, till they're fix'd.
Both this, th' Hesperian garden, Cadmus' story,
Jove's shower, the boon of Midas, Argus' eyes,
Boccace his Demogorgon,[14] thousands more,
All abstract riddles of our stone.—How now!

[12] Fooled.   [13] Quick-silver.
[14] According to Boccaccio, the ancestor of all the gods.

Scene II[1]

MAMMON, SURLY. [*Enter*] FACE, [*as a Servant*]

MAM. Do we succeed? Is our day come? And holds it?

FACE. The evening will set red upon you, sir;
You have colour for it, crimson: the red ferment
Has done his office; three hours hence prepare you
To see projection.

MAM.   Pertinax, my Surly.
Again I say to thee, aloud, BE RICH.
This day thou shalt have ingots; and to-morrow
Give lords th' affront.—Is it, my Zephyrus, right?
Blushes the bolt's-head?[2]

FACE.   Like a wench with child, sir,
That were but now discover'd to her master.

MAM. Excellent witty Lungs!—My only care is
Where to get stuff enough now, to project on;[3]
This town will not half serve me.

FACE.   No, sir! buy
The covering off o' churches.

MAM.   That's true.

FACE.   Yes.
Let 'em stand bare, as do their auditory;[4]
Or cap 'em new with shingles.

MAM.   No, good thatch:
Thatch will lie light upo' the rafters, Lungs.—
Lungs, I will manumit thee from the furnace;
I will restore thee thy complexion, Puff,
Lost in the embers; and repair this brain,
Hurt with the fume o' the metals.

FACE.   I have blown, sir,
Hard, for your worship; thrown by many a coal,
When 'twas not beech; weigh'd those I put in, just,
To keep your heat still even. These blear'd eyes
Have wak'd to read your several colours, sir,
Of the pale citron, the green lion, the crow,
The peacock's tail, the plumed swan.

MAM.   And lastly,

---

[1] The same. [2] A kind of flask. [3] Transmute. [4] Congregation.

Thou hast descried the flower, the *sanguis agni?*

FACE. Yes, sir.

MAM.   Where's master?

FACE.   At's prayers, sir, he;
Good man, he's doing his devotions
For the success.

MAM.   Lungs, I will set a period
To all thy labours; thou shalt be the master
Of my seraglio.

FACE.   Good, sir.

MAM.   But do you hear?
I'll geld you, Lungs.

FACE.   Yes, sir.

MAM.   For I do mean
To have a list of wives and concubines
Equal with Solomon, who had the stone
Alike with me; and I will make me a back
With the elixir that shall be as tough
As Hercules, to encounter fifty a night.—
Thou'rt sure thou saw'st it blood?

FACE.   Both blood and spirit, sir.

MAM. I will have all my beds blown up, not stuft;
Down is too hard: and then, mine oval room
Fill'd with such pictures as Tiberius took
From Elephantis, and dull Aretine
But coldly imitated. Then, my glasses
Cut in more subtle angles, to disperse
And multiply the figures, as I walk
Naked between my succubæ. My mists
I'll have of perfume, vapour'd 'bout the room,
To lose our selves in; and my baths, like pits
To fall into; from whence we will come forth,
And roll us dry in gossamer and roses.—
Is it arrived at ruby?——Where I spy
A wealthy citizen, or [a] rich lawyer,
Have a sublim'd pure wife, unto that fellow
I'll send a thousand pound to be my cuckold.

FACE. And I shall carry it?

MAM.   No. I'll ha' no bawds
But fathers and mothers: they will do it best,

Best of all others. And my flatterers
Shall be the pure and gravest of divines,
That I can get for money. My mere fools,
Eloquent burgesses, and then my poets
The same that writ so subtly of the fart,
Whom I will entertain still for that subject.
The few that would give out themselves to be
Court and town-stallions, and, each-where, bely
Ladies who are known most innocent, for them,
Those will I beg, to make me eunuchs of:
And they shall fan me with ten estrich tails
A-piece, made in a plume to gather wind.
We will be brave, Puff, now we ha' the med'cine.
My meat shall all come in, in Indian shells,
Dishes of agate set in gold, and studded
With emeralds, sapphires, hyacinths, and rubies.
The tongues of carps, dormice, and camels' heels,
Boil'd i' the spirit of sol, and dissolv'd pearl
(Apicius' diet, 'gainst the epilepsy):
And I will eat these broths with spoons of amber,
Headed with diamond and carbuncle.
My foot-boy shall eat pheasants, calver'd salmons,[5]
Knots,[6] godwits, lampreys: I myself will have
The beards of barbel serv'd, instead of salads;
Oiled mushrooms; and the swelling unctuous paps
Of a fat pregnant sow, newly cut off,
Drest with an exquisite and poignant sauce;
For which, I'll say unto my cook, *There's gold,*
Go forth, and be a knight.
    FACE.   Sir, I'll go look
A little, how it heightens.   [*Exit.*]
    MAM.   Do.—My shirts
I'll have of taffeta-sarsnet,[7] soft and light
As cobwebs; and for all my other raiment,
It shall be such as might provoke the Persian,
Were he to teach the world riot anew.
My gloves of fishes and birds' skins, perfum'd
With gums of paradise, and Eastern air——
    SUR. And do you think to have the stone with this?

---

    [5] Salmon elaborately prepared.   [6] Robin-snipes.   [7] Soft silk.

MAM. No, I do think t' have all this with the stone.

SUR. Why, I have heard he must be *homo frugi,*[8]
A pious, holy, and religious man,
One free from mortal sin, a very virgin.

MAM. That makes it, sir; he is so: but I buy it;
My venture brings it me. He, honest wretch,
A notable, superstitious, good soul,
Has worn his knees bare, and his slippers bald,
With prayer and fasting for it: and, sir, let him
Do it alone, for me, still. Here he comes.
Not a profane word afore him; 'tis poison.—

SCENE III[1]

MAMMON, SURLY. [*Enter*] SUBTLE

MAM. Good morrow, father.

SUB.   Gentle son, good morrow,
And to your friend there. What is he, is with you?

MAM. An heretic, that I did bring along,
In hope, sir, to convert him.

SUB.   Son, I doubt
You 're covetous, that thus you meet your time
I' the just[2] point, prevent[3] your day at morning.
This argues something worthy of a fear
Of importune and carnal appetite.
Take heed you do not cause the blessing leave you,
With your ungovern'd haste. I should be sorry
To see my labours, now e'en at perfection,
Got by long watching and large patience,
Not prosper where my love and zeal hath plac'd them.
Which (heaven I call to witness, with your self,
To whom I have pour'd my thoughts) in all my ends,
Have look'd no way, but unto public good,
To pious uses, and dear charity
Now grown a prodigy with men. Wherein
If you, my son, should now prevaricate,
And to your own particular lusts employ

[8] A virtuous man.
[1] The same.   [2] Exact.   [3] Anticipate.

So great and catholic a bliss, be sure
A curse will follow, yea, and overtake
Your subtle and most secret ways.

MAM.   I know, sir;
You shall not need to fear me; I but come
To ha' you confute this gentleman.

SUR.   Who is,
Indeed, sir, somewhat costive of belief
Toward your stone; would not be gull'd.

SUB.   Well, son,
All that I can convince him in, is this,
The work is done, bright Sol is in his robe.
We have a med'cine of the triple soul,
The glorified spirit. Thanks be to heaven,
And make us worthy of it!—𝕵𝖑𝖊𝖓 𝕾𝖕𝖎𝖊𝖌𝖊𝖑! [4]

FACE. [*within.*] Anon, sir.

SUB.   Look well to the register.
And let your heat still lessen by degrees,
To the aludels. [5]

FACE. [*within.*] Yes, sir.

SUB.   Did you look
O' the bolt's head yet?

FACE. [*within.*] Which? On D, sir?

SUB.   Ay;
What's the complexion?

FACE. [*within.*] Whitish.

SUB.   Infuse vinegar,
To draw his volatile substance and his tincture:
And let the water in glass E be filt'red,
And put into the gripe's egg. [6] Lute [7] him well;
And leave him clos'd *in balneo.* [8]

FACE. [*within.*]   I will, sir.

SUR. What a brave language here is! next to canting. [9]

SUB. I have another work you never saw, son,
That three days since past the philosopher's wheel,
In the lent heat of Athanor; [10] and's become
Sulphur o' Nature.

[4] The hero of a well-known German jest-book.
[5] A pear-shaped vessel, open at both ends.
[6] An egg-shaped vessel. Gripe is griffin.
[7] Seal with clay.   [8] A dish of warm water.
[9] Rogues' slang.   [10] An alchemical furnace.

MAM.   But 'tis for me?
SUB.   What need you?
You have enough, in that is, perfect.
MAM.   O, but——
SUB. Why, this is covetise!
MAM.   No, I assure you,
I shall employ it all in pious uses,
Founding of colleges and grammar schools,
Marrying young virgins, building hospitals,
And now and then a church.

[Re-enter FACE]

SUB.   How now!
FACE.   Sir, please you,
Shall I not change the filter?
SUB.   Marry, yes;
And bring me the complexion of glass B.   *[Exit* FACE.]
MAM. Ha' you another?
SUB.   Yes, son; were I assur'd
Your piety were firm, we would not want
The means to glorify it: but I hope the best.
I mean to tinct C in sand-heat to-morrow,
And give him imbibition.[11]
MAM.   Of white oil?
SUB. No, sir, of red. F is come over the helm too,
I thank my maker, in S. Mary's bath,
And shows *lac virginis*. Blessed be heaven!
I sent you of his fæces there calcin'd:
Out of that calx, I ha' won the salt of mercury.
MAM. By pouring on your rectified water?
SUB. Yes, and reverberating in Athanor.

[Re-enter FACE]

How now! what colour says it?
FACE.   The ground black, sir.
MAM. That's your crow's head?
SUR.   Your cock's-comb's, is it not?
SUB. No, 'tis not perfect. Would it were the crow!

[11] **Absorption.**

That work wants something.

SUR.   [*Aside.*]   O, I look'd for this,
The hay's[12] a pitching.

SUB.   Are you sure you loos'd 'em
In their own menstrue?[13]

FACE.   Yes, sir, and then married 'em,
And put 'em in a bolt's-head nipp'd to digestion,
According as you bade me, when I set
The liquor of Mars to circulation
In the same heat.

SUB.   The process then was right.

FACE. Yes, by the token, sir, the retort brake,
And what was sav'd was put into the pellican,
And sign'd with Hermes' seal.

SUB.   I think 'twas so.
We should have a new amalgama.

SUR.   [*Aside.*]   O, this ferret
Is rank as any polecat.

SUB.   But I care not:
Let him e'en die; we have enough beside,
In embrion. H has his white shirt on?

FACE.   Yes, sir,
He's ripe for inceration, he stands warm,
In his ash-fire. I would not you should let
Any die now, if I might counsel, sir,
For luck's sake to the rest: it is not good.

MAM. He says right.

SUR.   [*Aside.*]   Ah, are you boîted?

FACE.   Nay, I know't, sir,
I have seen the ill fortune. What is some three ounces
Of fresh materials?

MAM.   Is't no more?

FACE.   No more, sir,
Of gold, t' amalgam with some six of mercury.

MAM. Away, here's money. What will serve?

FACE.   Ask him, sir.

MAM. How much?

SUB.   Give him nine pound: you may gi' him ten.

SUR. Yes, twenty, and be cozen'd, do.

---

[12] A net for catching rabbits.   [13] Dissolving fluids.

MAM. There 'tis [*Gives* FACE *the money.*]

SUB. This needs not; but that you will have it so,
To see conclusions of all: for two
Of our inferior works are at fixation,
A third is in ascension. Go your ways.
Ha' you set the oil of luna in kemia?

FACE. Yes, sir.

SUB. And the philosopher's vinegar?

FACE. Ay. [*Exit.*]

SUR. We shall have a salad!

MAM. When do you make projection?

SUB. Son, be not hasty, I exalt our med'cine,
By hanging him *in balneo vaporoso,*
And giving him solution; then congeal him;
And then dissolve him; then again congeal him;
For look, how oft I iterate the work,
So many times I add unto his virtue.
As if at first one ounce convert a hundred,
After his second loose, he'll turn a thousand;
His third solution, ten; his fourth, a hundred;
After his fifth, a thousand thousand ounces
Of any imperfect metal, into pure
Silver or gold, in all examinations,
As good as any of the natural mine.
Get you your stuff here against afternoon,
Your brass, your pewter, and your andirons.

MAM. Not those of iron?

SUB. Yes, you may bring them too;
We'll change all metals.

SUR. I believe you in that.

MAM. Then I may send my spits?

SUB. Yes, and your racks.

SUR. And dripping-pans, and pot-hangers, and hooks?
Shall he not?

SUB. If he please.

SUR. —To be an ass.

SUB. How, sir!

MAM. This gent'man you must bear withal:
I told you he had no faith.

SUR. And little hope, sir;

But much less charity, should I gull myself.

SUB. Why, what have you observ'd, sir, in our art,
Seems so impossible?

SUR.   But your whole work, no more.
That you should hatch gold in a furnace, sir,
As they do eggs in Egypt!

SUB.   Sir, do you
Believe that eggs are hatch'd so?

SUR.   If I should?

SUB. Why, I think that the greater miracle.
No egg but differs from a chicken more
Than metals in themselves.

SUR.   That cannot be.
The egg's ordain'd by nature to that end,
And is a chicken *in potentia*.

SUB. The same we say of lead and other metals,
Which would be gold if they had time.

MAM.   And that
Our art doth further.

SUB.   Ay, for 'twere absurd
To think that nature in the earth bred gold
Perfect i' the instant: something went before.
There must be remote matter.

SUR.   Ay, what is that?

SUB. Marry, we say——

MAM.   Ay, now it heats: stand, father,
Pound him to dust.

SUB.   It is, of the one part,
A humid exhalation, which we call
Materia liquida, or the unctuous water;
On th' other part, a certain crass and viscous
Portion of earth; both which, concorporate,
Do make the elementary matter of gold;
Which is not yet *propria materia,*
But common to all metals and all stones;
For, where it is forsaken of that moisture,
And hath more dryness, it becomes a stone:
Where it retains more of the humid fatness,
It turns to sulphur, or to quicksilver,
Who are the parents of all other metals.

Nor can this remote matter suddenly
Progress so from extreme unto extreme,
As to grow gold, and leap o'er all the means.
Nature doth first beget th' imperfect, then
Proceeds she to the perfect. Of that airy
And oily water, mercury is engend'red;
Sulphur o' the fat and earthy part; the one,
Which is the last, supplying the place of male,
The other, of the female, in all metals.
Some do believe hermaphrodeity,
That both do act and suffer. But these two
Make the rest ductile, malleable, extensive.
And even in gold they are; for we do find
Seeds of them by our fire, and gold in them;
And can produce the species of each metal
More perfect thence, than nature doth in earth.
Beside, who doth not see in daily practice
Art can beget bees, hornets, beetles, wasps,
Out of the carcases and dung of creatures;
Yea, scorpions of an herb, being rightly plac'd?
And these are living creatures, far more perfect
And excellent than metals.

   Mam.   Well said, father!
Nay, if he take you in hand, sir, with an argument,
He'll bray you in a mortar.

   Sur.   Pray you, sir, stay.
Rather than I'll be bray'd, sir, I'll believe
That Alchemy is a pretty kind of game,
Somewhat like tricks o' the cards, to cheat a man
With charming.

   Sub.   Sir?

   Sur.   What else are all your terms,
Whereon no one o' your writers 'grees with other?
Of your elixir, your *lac virginis,*
Your stone, your med'cine, and your chrysosperm,
Your sal, your sulphur, and your mercury,
Your oil of height, your tree of life, your blood,
Your marchesite, your tutie, your magnesia,
Your toad, your crow, your dragon, and your panther;
Your sun, your moon, your firmament, your adrop,

Your lato, azoch, zernich, chibrit, heautarit,
And then your red man, and your white woman,
With all your broths, your menstrues, and materials
Of piss and egg-shells, women's terms, man's blood,
Hair o' the head, burnt clouts, chalk, merds, and clay,
Powder of bones, scalings of iron, glass,
And worlds of other strange ingredients,
Would burst a man to name?

SUB.   And all these nam'd,
Intending but one thing; which art our writers
Us'd to obscure their art.

MAM.   Sir, so I told him—
Because[14] the simple idiot should not learn it,
And make it vulgar.

SUB.   Was not all the knowledge
Of the Ægyptians writ in mystic symbols?
Speak not the scriptures oft in parables?
Are not the choicest fables of the poets,
That were the fountains and first springs of wisdom,
Wrapt in perplexed allegories?

MAM.   I urg'd that,
And clear'd to him, that Sisyphus was damn'd
To roll the ceaseless stone, only because
He would have made ours common. (DOL *appears at the
    door.*)—Who is this?

SUB. 'Sprecious!—What do you mean? Go in, good lady,
Let me entreat you. [DOL *retires.*]—Where's this varlet?

[*Re-enter* FACE]

FACE.   Sir.
SUB. You very knave! do you use me thus?
FACE.   Wherein, sir?
SUB. Go in and see, you traitor. Go!   [*Exit* FACE.]
MAM.   Who is it, sir?
SUB. Nothing, sir; nothing.
MAM.   What's the matter, good sir?
I have not seen you thus distemp'red: who is't?

[14] In order that.

Sub. All arts have still had, sir, their adversaries;
But ours the most ignorant.—

Re-enter Face
                    What now?

Face. 'Twas not my fault, sir; she would speak with you.
Sub. Would she, sir! Follow me.   [*Exit.*]
Mam. [*stopping him.*] Stay, Lungs.
Face.   I dare not, sir.
Mam. How! pray thee, stay.
Face.   She's mad, sir, and sent hither—
Mam. Stay, man; what is she?
Face.   A lord's sister, sir.
He'll be mad too.—
    Mam.   I warrant thee.—
                                  Why sent hither?

Face. Sir, to be cur'd.
Sub.   [*within.*] Why, rascal!
Face.   Lo you!—Here, sir! *Exit.*
Mam. 'Fore God, a Bradamante, a brave piece.
Sur. Heart, this is a bawdy-house! I 'll be burnt else.
Mam. O, by this light, no: do not wrong him. He's
Too scrupulous that way: it is his vice.
No, he's a rare physician, do him right,
An excellent Paracelsian, and has done
Strange cures with mineral physic. He deals all
With spirits, he; he will not hear a word
Of Galen; or his tedious recipes.—

Re-enter Face
                        How now, Lungs!

Face. Softly, sir; speak softly. I meant
To have told your worship all. This must not hear.
    Mam. No, he will not be gull'd; let him alone.
    Face. You're very right, sir; she is a most rare scholar
And is gone mad with studying Broughton's[15] works.
If you but name a word touching the Hebrew,
She falls into her fit, and will discourse

                15 A learned eccentric of the time.

So learnedly of genealogies,
As you would run mad too, to hear her, sir.

 MAM. How might one do t' have conference with her,
  Lungs?

 FACE. O, divers have run mad upon the conference:
I do not know, sir. I am sent in haste
To fetch a vial.

 SUR.   Be not gull'd, Sir Mammon.

 MAM. Wherein? Pray ye, be patient.

 SUR.   Yes, as you are,
And trust confederate knaves and bawds and whores.

 MAM. You are too foul, believe it.—Come here, ULEN,
One word.

 FACE. I dare not, in good faith,   [*Going.*]

 MAM.   Stay, knave.

 FACE. He is extreme angry that you saw her, sir.

 MAM. Drink that. [*Gives him money.*] What is she when
  she's out of her fit?

 FACE. O, the most affablest creature, sir! so merry!
So pleasant! She'll mount you up, like quicksilver,
Over the helm; and circulate like oil,
A very vegetal: discourse of state,
Of mathematics, bawdry, anything——

 MAM. Is she no way accessible? no means,
No trick to give a man a taste of her——wit——
Or so?

 [SUB. *within.*] ULEN!

 FACE.   I'll come to you again, sir. [*Exit.*]

 MAM. Surly, I did not think one of your breeding
Would traduce personages of worth.

 SUR.   Sir Epicure,
Your friend to use; yet still loth to be gull'd:
I do not like your philosophical bawds.
Their stone is lechery enough to pay for,
Without this bait.

 MAM.   'Heart, you abuse yourself.
I know the lady, and her friends, and means,
The original of this disaster. Her brother
Has told me all.

 SUR.   And yet you ne'er saw her

Till now!

MAM. O yes, but I forgot. I have, believe it,
One o' the treacherousest memories, I do think,
Of all mankind.

SUR. What call you her brother?

MAM. My lord——
He wi' not have his name known, now I think on't.

SUR. A very treacherous memory!

MAM. On my faith——

SUR. Tut, if you ha' it not about you, pass it,
Till we meet next.

MAM. Nay, by this hand, 'tis true.
He's one I honour, and my noble friend;
And I respect his house.

SUR. Heart! can it be
That a grave sir, a rich, that has no need,
A wise sir, too, at other times, should thus,
With his own oaths, and arguments, make hard means
To gull himself? An this be your elixir,
Your *lapis mineralis,* and your lunary,
Give me your honest trick yet at primero,
Or gleek;[16] and take your *lutum sapientis,*
Your *menstruum simplex!* I'll have gold before you,
And with less danger of the quicksilver,
Or the hot sulphur.

[*Re-enter* FACE]

FACE. Here's one from Captain Face, sir. (*to* SURLY.)
Desires you meet him i' the Temple-church,
Some half-hour hence, and upon earnest business.
Sir, (*whispers* MAMMON) if you please to quit us now; and
    come
Again within two hours, you shall have
My master busy examining o' the works;
And I will steal you in unto the party,
That you may see her converse.—Sir, shall I say
You'll meet the captain's worship?

SUR. Sir, I will.— [*Walks aside.*]
But, by attorney, and to a second purpose.

[16] Games at cards.

Now, I am sure it is a bawdy-house;
I'll swear it, were the marshal here to thank me:
The naming this commander doth confirm it.
Don Face! why, he's the most authentic dealer
In these commodities, the superintendent
To all the quainter traffickers in town!
He is the visitor, and does appoint
Who lies with whom, and at what hour; what price;
Which gown, and in what smock; what fall;[17] what tire.[18]
Him will I prove, by a third person, to find
The subtleties of this dark labyrinth:
Which if I do discover, dear Sir Mammon,
You'll give your poor friend leave, though no philosopher,
To laugh: for you that are, 'tis thought, shall weep.

    FACE. Sir, he does pray you'll not forget.
    SUR.   I will not, sir.
Sir Epicure, I shall leave you.   [Exit.]
    MAM.   I follow you straight.
    FACE. But do so, good sir, to avoid suspicion.
This gent'man has a parlous head.
    MAM.   But wilt thou, ULEN,
Be constant to thy promise?
    FACE.   As my life, sir.
    MAM. And wilt thou insinuate what I am, and praise me,
And say I am a noble fellow?
    FACE.   O, what else, sir?
And that you'll make her royal with the stone,
An empress; and yourself King of Bantam.
    MAM. Wilt thou do this?
    FACE.   Will I, sir!
    MAM.   Lungs, my Lungs!
I love thee.
    FACE.   Send your stuff, sir, that my master
May busy himself about projection.
    MAM. Thou'st witch'd me, rogue: take, go.
                        [Gives him money.]
    FACE.   Your jack, and all, sir.
    MAM. Thou art a villain—I will send my jack,
And the weights too. Slave, I could bite thine ear.

        [17] A collar, or a veil.   [18] A head-dress.

Away, thou dost not care for me.

FACE. Not I, sir!

MAM. Come, I was born to make thee, my good weasel,
Set thee on a bench, and have thee twirl a chain
With the best lord's vermin of 'em all.

FACE. Away, sir.

MAM. A count, nay, a count palatine——

FACE. Good sir, go.

MAM. Shall not advance thee better: no, nor faster.

[*Exit.*]

SCENE IV[1]

FACE. [*Re-enter*] SUBTLE *and* DOL

SUB. Has he bit? has he bit?

FACE. And swallowed, too, my Subtle.
I have given him line, and now he plays, i' faith.

SUB. And shall we twitch him?

FACE. Thorough both the gills.
A wench is a rare bait, with which a man
No sooner's taken, but he straight firks mad.[2]

SUB. Dol, my Lord What'ts'hum's sister, you must now
Bear yourself *statelich*.

DOL. O, let me alone.
I'll not forget my race, I warrant you.
I'll keep my distance, laugh and talk aloud;
Have all the tricks of a proud scurvy lady,
And be as rude 's her woman.

FACE. Well said, sanguine![3]

SUB. But will he send his andirons?

FACE. His jack too,
And 's iron shoeing-horn; I have spoke to him. Well,
I must not lose my wary gamester yonder.

SUB. O, Monsieur Caution, that will not be gull'd?

FACE. Ay,
If I can strike a fine hook into him, now!—
The Temple-church, there I have cast mine angle.
Well, pray for me. I'll about it. (*Knocking without.*)

---

[1] The same.   [2] Runs mad.   [3] Red cheeks.

Sub. What, more gudgeons![4]

Dol, scout, scout! [Dol *goes to the window.*] Stay, Face,
    you must go to the door,
'Pray God it be my anabaptist—Who is't, Dol.

    Dol. I know him not: he looks like a gold-end-man.[5]

    Sub. Ods so! 'tis he, he said he would send—what call
    you him?
The sanctified elder, that should deal
For Mammon's jack and andirons. Let him in.
Stay, help me off, first, with my gown. [*Exit* Face *with the
    gown.*] Away,
Madam, to your withdrawing chamber. [*Exit.* Dol.] Now,
In a new tune, new gesture, but old language.—
This fellow is sent from one negotiates with me
About the stone too, for the holy brethren
Of Amsterdam, the exil'd saints, that hope
To raise their discipline[6] by it. I must use him
In some strange fashion now, to make him admire me.

Scene V[1]

Subtle.   [*Enter*] Ananias

Where is my drudge?   [*Aloud.*]

[*Enter*] Face

Face.   Sir!
Sub.   Take away the recipient,
And rectify your menstrue from the phlegma.
Then pour it on the Sol, in the cucurbite,
And let them macerate together.
Face.   Yes, sir.
And save the ground?
Sub.   No: *terra damnata*
Must not have entrance in the work.—Who are you?
    Ana. A faithful brother,[2] if it please you.
    Sub.   What's that?

---

[4] Easy dupes.   [5] A man who buys broken remnants of gold.
[6] Puritan form of church government.
[1] The same.   [2] A Puritan. Subtle wilfully misunderstands.

A Lullianist? a Ripley?[3] Filius artis?
Can you sublime and dulcify? Calcine?
Know you the sapor pontic? Sapor stiptic?
Or what is homogene, or heterogene?

ANA. I understand no heathen language, truly.

SUB. Heathen! You Knipper-doling?[4] Is Ars sacra,
Or chrysopœia, or spagyrica,
Or the pamphysic, or panarchic knowledge,
A heathen language?

ANA.   Heathen Greek, I take it.

SUB. How! Heathen Greek?

ANA.   All's heathen but the Hebrew.

SUB. Sirrah my varlet, stand you forth and speak to him
Like a philosopher: answer i' the language.
Name the vexations, and the martyrizations
Of metals in the work.

FACE.   Sir, putrefaction,
Solution, ablution, sublimation,
Cohobation, calcination, ceration, and
Fixation.

SUB.   This is heathen Greek, to you, now!—
And when comes vivification?

FACE.   After mortification.

SUB. What's cohobation?

FACE.   'Tis the pouring on
Your aqua regis, and then drawing him off,
To the trine circle of the seven spheres.

SUB. What's the proper passion of metals?

FACE.   Malleation.

SUB. What's your *ultimum supplicium auri?*

FACE.   Antimonium.

SUB. This is heathen Greek to you!—And what's your mer-
    cury?

FACE. A very fugitive, he will be gone, sir.

SUB. How know you him?

FACE.   By his viscosity,
His oleosity, and his suscitability.

SUB. How do you sublime him?

---

[3] A follower of Raymond Lully (1235-1315) or George Ripley (d. c.
1490), well-known alchemical writers.   [4] An Anabaptist leader.

FACE.   With the calce of egg-shells,
White marble, talc.

SUB.   Your magisterium now,
What's that?

FACE.   Shifting, sir, your elements,
Dry into cold, cold into moist, moist into hot,
Hot into dry.

SUB.   This is heathen Greek to you still!
Your *lapis philosophicus?*

FACE.   'Tis a stone,
And not a stone; a spirit, a soul, and a body:
Which if you do dissolve, it is dissolv'd;
If you coagulate, it is coagulated;
If you make it to fly, it flieth.

SUB.   Enough.   [*Exit* FACE.]
This is heathen Greek to you! What are you, sir?

ANA. Please you, a servant of the exil'd brethren,
That deal with widows' and with orphans' goods,
And make a just account unto the saints:
A deacon.

SUB. O, you are sent from Master Wholesome,
Your teacher?

ANA.   From Tribulation Wholesome,
Our very zealous pastor.

SUB.   Good! I have
Some orphans' goods to come here.

ANA.   Of what kind, sir?

SUB. Pewter and brass, andirons and kitchen-ware.
Metals, that we must use our med'cine on:
Wherein the brethren may have a penn'orth
For ready money.

ANA.   Were the orphans' parents
Sincere professors?

SUB.   Why do you ask?

ANA.   Because
We then are to deal justly, and give, in truth,
Their utmost value.

SUB.   'Slid, you'd cozen else,
An if their parents were not of the faithful!—
I will not trust you, now I think on it,

Till I ha' talk'd with your pastor. Ha' you brought money
To buy more coals?

ANA.   No, surely.

SUB.   No? How so?

ANA. The brethren bid me say unto you, sir,
Surely, they will not venture any more
Till they may see projection.

SUB.   How!

ANA.   You've had
For the instruments, as bricks, and lome, and glasses,
Already thirty pound; and for materials,
They say, some ninety more: and they have heard since,
That one, at Heidelberg, made it of an egg,
And a small paper of pin-dust.

SUB.   What's your name?

ANA. My name is Ananias.

SUB.   Out, the varlet
That cozen'd the apostles! Hence, away!
Flee, mischief! had your holy consistory
No name to send me, of another sound,
Than wicked Ananias? Send your elders
Hither, to make atonement for you, quickly,
And give me satisfaction; or out goes
The fire; and down th' alembecs, and the furnace,
Piger Henricus, or what not. Thou wretch!
Both sericon and bufo shall be lost,
Tell them. All hope of rooting out the bishops,
Or th' anti-Christian hierarchy shall perish,
If they stay threescore minutes: the aqueity,
Terreity, and sulphureity
Shall run together again, and all be annull'd,
Thou wicked Ananias! [*Exit* ANANIAS.] This will fetch
  'em,
And make 'em haste towards their gulling more.
A man must deal like a rough nurse, and fright
Those that are froward, to an appetite.

Scene VI[1]

Subtle [*Enter*] Face [*in his uniform, followed by*] Drugger

FACE. He's busy with his spirits, but we'll upon him.

SUB. How now! What mates, what Bayards[2] ha' we
  here?

FACE. I told you he would be furious.—Sir, here's Nab
Has brought you another piece of gold to look on;
—We must appease him. Give it me,—and prays you,
You would devise—what is it, Nab?

DRUG. A sign, sir.

FACE. Ay, a good lucky one, a thriving sign, doctor.

SUB. I was devising now.

FACE. [*Aside to* SUB.] 'Slight, do not say so,
He will repent he ga' you any more—
What say you to his constellation, doctor,
The Balance?

SUB. No, that way is stale and common.
A townsman born in Taurus, gives the bull,
Or the bull's head: in Aries, the ram,
A poor-device! No, I will have his name
Form'd in some mystic character; whose radii,
Striking the senses of the passers-by,
Shall, by a virtual[3] influence, breed affections,
That may result upon the party owns it:
As thus——

FACE. Nab!

SUB. He first shall have *a bell,* that's *Abel;*
And by it standing one whose name is *Dee,*[4]
In a *rug*[5] gown, there's *D,* and *Rug,* that's *drug:*
And right anenst him a dog snarling *er;*
There's Drugger, Abel Drugger. That's his sign.
And here's now mystery and hieroglyphic!

FACE. Abel, thou art made.

DRUG. Sir, I do thank his worship.

FACE. Six o' thy legs[6] more will not do it, Nab.
He has brought you a pipe of tobacco, doctor.

[1] The same. [2] Blind horses.
[3] Due to the virtue or power of the device.
[4] A reference to Dr. Dee, the famous magician and astrologer, who died
in 1608. [5] Of coarse frieze. [6] Bows.

DRUG. Yes, sir;
I have another thing I would impart——
FACE. Out with it, Nab.
DRUG. Sir, there is lodg'd, hard by me,
A rich young widow——
FACE. Good! a bona roba?[7]
DRUG. But nineteen at the most.
FACE. Very good, Abel.
DRUG. Marry, she's not in fashion yet; she wears
A hood, but 't stands a cop.[8]
FACE. No matter, Abel.
DRUG. And I do now and then give her a fucus[9]——
FACE. What! dost thou deal, Nab?
SUB. I did tell you, captain.
DRUG. And physic too, sometime, sir; for which she
    trusts me
With all her mind. She's come up here of purpose
To learn the fashion.
FACE. Good (his match too!)—On, Nab.
DRUG. And she does strangely long to know her fortune.
FACE. 'Ods lid, Nab, send her to the doctor, hither.
DRUG. Yes, I have spoke to her of his worship already;
But she's afraid it will be blown abroad,
And hurt her marriage.
FACE. Hurt it! 'tis the way
To heal it, if 'twere hurt; to make it more
Follow'd and sought. Nab, thou shalt tell her this.
She'll be more known, more talk'd of; and your widows
Are ne'er of any price till they be famous;
Their honour is their multitude of suitors.
Send her, it may be thy good fortune. What!
Thou dost not know.
DRUG. No, sir, she'll never marry
Under a knight: her brother has made a vow.
FACE. What! and dost thou despair, my little Nab,
Knowing what the doctor has set down for thee,
And seeing so many o' the city dubb'd?
One glass o' thy water, with a madam I know,

[7] Handsome girl.
[8] Peaked (?) or straight on the top of her head, instead of tilted (?).
[9] Paint for the face.

Will have it done, Nab. What's her brother, a knight?

DRUG. No, sir, a gentleman newly warm in's land, sir,
Scarce cold in his one and twenty, that does govern
His sister here; and is a man himself
Of some three thousand a year, and is come up
To learn to quarrel, and to live by his wits,
And will go down again, and die i' the country.

FACE. How! to quarrel?

DRUG.   Yes, sir, to carry quarrels,
As gallants do; to manage 'em by line.

FACE. 'Slid, Nab, the doctor is the only man
In Christendom for him. He has made a table,
With mathematical demonstrations,
Touching the art of quarrels: he will give him
An instrument to quarrel by. Go, bring 'em both,
Him and his sister. And, for thee, with her
The doctor happ'ly may persuade. Go to:
'Shalt give his worship a new damask suit
Upon the premises.

SUB.   O, good captain!

FACE.   He shall;
He is the honestest fellow, doctor. Stay not,
No offers; bring the damask, and the parties.

DRUG. I'll try my power, sir.

FACE.   And thy will too, Nab.

SUB. 'Tis good tobacco, this! What is't an ounce?

FACE. He'll send you a pound, doctor.

SUB.   O no.

FACE.   He will do't.
It is the goodest soul!—Abel, about it.
Thou shalt know more anon. Away, be gone. [*Exit* ABEL.]
A miserable rogue, and lives with cheese,
And has the worms. That was the cause, indeed,
Why he came now: he dealt with me in private,
To get a med'cine for 'em.

SUB.   And shall, sir. This works.

FACE. A wife, a wife for one on us, my dear Subtle!
We'll e'en draw lots, and he that fails, shall have
The more in goods.

SUB. Faith, best let's see her first, and then determine.

FACE. Content: but Dol must ha' no breath on't.

SUB.   Mum.
Away you, to your Surly yonder, catch him.

FACE. Pray God I ha' not staid too long.

SUB.   I fear it. [*Exeunt.*]

ACT III

SCENE I[1]

Enter TRIBULATION WHOLESOME *and* ANANIAS

TRI. These chastisements are common to the saints,
And such rebukes we of the separation
Must bear with willing shoulders, as the trials
Sent forth to tempt our frailties.

ANA.   In pure zeal,
I do not like the man; he is a heathen,
And speaks the language of Canaan, truly.

TRI. I think him a profane person indeed.

ANA.   He bears
The visible mark of the beast in his forehead.
And for his stone, it is a work of darkness,
And with philosophy blinds the eyes of man.

TRI. Good brother, we must bend unto all means,
That may give furtherance to the holy cause.

ANA. Which his cannot: the sanctified cause
Should have a sanctified course.

TRI.   Not always necessary:
The children of perdition are ofttimes
Made instruments even of the greatest works.
Beside, we should give somewhat to man's nature,
The place he lives in, still about the fire,
And fume of metals, that intoxicate
The brain of man, and make him prone to passion.
Where have you greater atheists than your cooks?
Or more profane, or choleric, than your glass-men?
More anti-Christian than your bell-founders?
What makes the devil so devilish, I would ask you,

[1] The lane before Lovewit's house.

Sathan, our common enemy, but his being
Perpetually about the fire, and boiling
Brimstone and arsenic? We must give, I say,
Unto the motives, and the stirrers up
Of humours in the blood. It may be so,
When as the work is done, the stone is made,
This heat of his may turn into a zeal,
And stand up for the beauteous discipline
Against the menstruous cloth and rag of Rome.
We must await his calling, and the coming
Of the good spirit. You did fault, t' upbraid him
With the brethren's blessing of Heidelberg, weighing
What need we have to hasten on the work,
For the restoring of the silenc'd saints,[2]
Which ne'er will be but by the philosopher's stone.
And so a learned elder, one of Scotland,
Assur'd me; *aurum potabile* being
The only med'cine for the civil magistrate,
T' incline him to a feeling of the cause;
And must be daily us'd in the disease.

    ANA. I have not edified more, truly, by man;
Not since the beautiful light first shone on me:
And I am sad my zeal hath so offended.

    TRI. Let us call on him then.

    ANA.   The motion's good,
And of the spirit; I will knock first. [*Knocks.*] Peace be
    within! [*The door is opened, and they enter.*]

SCENE II[1]

Enter SUBTLE, *followed by* TRIBULATION *and* ANANIAS

    SUB. O, are you come? 'Twas time. Your threescore
    minutes
Were at last thread, you see; and down had gone
Furnus acediæ, turris circulatorius:
Lembec, bolt's-head, retort, and pelican
Had all been cinders. Wicked Ananias!
Art thou return'd? Nay, then it goes down yet.

---

    [2] Non-conformist ministers not allowed to preach.
    [1] A room in Lovewit's house.

Tri. Sir, be appeased; he is come to humble
Himself in spirit, and to ask your patience,
If too much zeal hath carried him aside
From the due path.

Sub.   Why, this doth qualify!

Tri. The brethren had no purpose, verily,
To give you the least grievance; but are ready
To lend their willing hands to any project
The spirit and you direct.

Sub.   This qualifies more!

Tri. And for the orphans' goods, let them be valu'd,
Or what is needful else to the holy work,
It shall be numb'red; here, by me, the saints
Throw down their purse before you.

Sub.   This qualifies most!
Why, thus it should be, now you understand.
Have I discours'd so unto you of our stone,
And of the good that it shall bring your cause?
Show'd you (beside the main of hiring forces
Abroad, drawing the Hollanders, your friends,
From the Indies, to serve you, with all their fleet)
That even the med'cinal use shall make you a faction,
And party in the realm? As, put the case,
That some great man in state, he have the gout,
Why, you but send three drops of your elixir,
You help him straight: there you have made a friend.
Another has the palsy or the dropsy,
He takes of your incombustible stuff,
He's young again: there you have made a friend.
A lady that is past the feat of body,
Though not of mind, and hath her face decay'd
Beyond all cure of paintings, you restore,
With the oil of talc: there you have made a friend;
And all her friends. A lord that is a leper,
A knight that has the bone-ache, or a squire
That hath both these, you make 'em smooth and sound,
With a bare fricace[2] of your med'cine: still
You increase your friends.

Tri.   Ay, 't is very pregnant.

[2] Rubbing.

Sub. And then the turning of this lawyer's pewter
To plate at Christmas——

    Ana.   Christ-tide, I pray you.

    Sub. Yet, Ananias!

    Ana.   I have done.

    Sub.   Or changing
His parcel[3] gilt to massy gold. You cannot
But raise you friends. Withal, to be of power
To pay an army in the field, to buy
The King of France out of his realms, or Spain
Out of his Indies. What can you not do
Against lords spiritual or temporal,
That shall oppone[4] you?

    Tri.   Verily, 'tis true.
We may be temporal lords ourselves, I take it.

    Sub. You may be anything, and leave off to make
Long-winded exercises; or suck up
Your *ha!* and *hum!* in a tune. I not deny,
But such as are not graced in a state,
May, for their ends, be adverse in religion,
And get a tune to call the flock together:
For, to say sooth, a tune does much with women
And other phlegmatic people; it is your bell.

    Ana. Bells are profane; a tune may be religious.

    Sub. No warning with you? Then farewell my pa-
        tience.
'Slight, it shall down; I will not be thus tortur'd.

    Tri. I pray you, sir.

    Sub.   All shall perish. I have spoke it.

    Tri. Let me find grace, sir, in your eyes; the man
He stands corrected: neither did his zeal,
But as your self, allow a tune somewhere.
Which now, being tow'rd[5] the stone, we shall not need.

    Sub. No, nor your holy vizard,[6] to win widows
To give you legacies; or make zealous wives
To rob their husbands for the common cause:
Nor take the start of bonds broke but one day,
And say they were forfeited by providence.
Nor shall you need o'er night to eat huge meals,

---

    [3] Partly.   [4] Oppose.   [5] Near possession of.   [6] Set expression of face.

To celebrate your next day's fast the better;
The whilst the brethren and the sisters humbled,
Abate the stiffness of the flesh. Nor cast
Before your hungry hearers scrupulous bones;[7]
As whether a Christian may hawk or hunt,
Or whether matrons of the holy assembly
May lay their hair out, or wear doublets,
Or have that idol starch about their linen.
    ANA. It is indeed an idol.
    TRI.   Mind him not, sir.
I do command thee, spirit (of zeal, but trouble),
To peace within him! Pray you, sir, go on.
    SUB. Nor shall you need to libel 'gainst the prelates,
And shorten so your ears[8] against the hearing
Of the next wire-drawn grace. Nor of necessity
Rail against plays, to please the alderman
Whose daily custard you devour; nor lie
With zealous rage till you are hoarse. Not one
Of these so singular arts. Nor call yourselves
By names of Tribulation, Persecution,
Restraint, Long-patience, and such like, affected
By the whole family or wood[9] of you,
Only for glory, and to catch the ear
Of the disciple.
    TRI.   Truly, sir, they are
Ways that the godly brethren have invented,
For propagation of the glorious cause,
As very notable means, and whereby also
Themselves grow soon, and profitably famous.
    SUB. O, but the stone, all's idle to't! Nothing!
The art of angels, nature's miracle,
The divine secret that doth fly in clouds
From east to west: and whose tradition
Is not from men, but spirits.
    ANA.   I hate traditions;
I do not trust them——
    TRI.   Peace!
    ANA.   They are popish all.

---

[7] The dry bones of discussion on such scruples.
[8] Have your ears cut off in the pillory.   [9] Assembly.

I will not peace: I will not——

 Tri.   Ananias!

 Ana. Please the profane, to grieve the godly; I may not

 Sub. Well, Ananias, thou shalt overcome.

 Tri. It is an ignorant zeal that haunts him, sir:
But truly else a very faithful brother,
A botcher,[10] and a man by revelation
That hath a competent knowledge of the truth.

 Sub. Has he a competent sum there i' the bag
To buy the goods within? I am made guardian,
And must, for charity and conscience' sake,
Now see the most be made for my poor orphan;
Though I desire the brethren, too, good gainers:
There they are within. When you have view'd and
   bought 'em,
And ta'en the inventory of what they are,
They are ready for projection; there's no more
To do: cast on the med'cine, so much silver
As there is tin there, so much gold as brass,
I'll gi' it you in by weight.

 Tri.   But how long time,
Sir, must the saints expect yet?

 Sub.   Let me see,
How's the moon now? Eight, nine, ten days hence,
He will be silver potate; then three days
Before he citronise.[11] Some fifteen days,
The magisterium[12] will be perfected.

 Ana. About the second day of the third week,
In the ninth month?

 Sub.   Yes, my good Ananias.

 Tri. What will the orphans' goods arise to, think you?

 Sub. Some hundred marks, as much as fill'd three cars,
Unladed now: you'll make six millions of 'em——
But I must ha' more coals laid in.

 Tri.   How?

 Sub.   Another load,
And then we ha' finish'd. We must now increase
Our fire to *ignis ardens;*[13] we are past

---

[10] Tailor. But the term was used generally of Puritans.
[11] Become the color of citron—a stage in the process of producing the stone. [12] Full accomplishment. [13] Fiery heat.

Fimus equinus, balnei, cineris,[14]

And all those lenter[15] heats. If the holy purse
Should with this draught fall low, and that the saints
Do need a present sum, I have a trick
To melt the pewter, you shall buy now instantly,
And with a tincture make you as good Dutch dollars
As any are in Holland.

TRI.   Can you so?

SUB. Ay, and shall bide the third examination.

ANA. It will be joyful tidings to the brethren.

SUB. But you must carry it secret.

TRI.   Ay; but stay,
This act of coining, is it lawful?

ANA.   Lawful!
We know no magistrate: or, if we did,
This is foreign coin.

SUB.   It is no coining, sir.
It is but casting.

TRI.   Ha! you distinguish well:
Casting of money may be lawful.

ANA.   'Tis, sir.

TRI. Truly, I take it so.

SUB.   There is no scruple,
Sir, to be made of it; believe Ananias:
This case of conscience he is studied in.

TRI. I'll make a question of it to the brethren.

ANA. The brethren shall approve it lawful, doubt not.
Where shall it be done?

SUB. For that we'll talk anon.   *Knock without.*
There's some to speak with me. Go in, I pray you,
And view the parcels. That's the inventory.
I'll come to you straight. [*Exeunt* TRIB. *and* ANA.] Who
    is it?—Face! appear.

[14] Heat from horse-dung, warm bath, ashes.   [15] Milder.

Scene III[1]

Subtle. [*Enter*] Face [*in his uniform*]

How now! good prize?

Face.   Good pox! Yond' costive cheater
Never came on.

Sub.   How then?

Face.   I ha' walk'd the round
Till now, and no such thing.

Sub.   And ha' you quit him?

Face. Quit him! An hell would quit him too, he were
     happy.
'Slight! would you have me stalk like a mill-jade,
All day, for one that will not yield us grains?
I know him of old.

Sub.   O, but to ha' gull'd him,
Had been a mastery.

Face.   Let him go, black boy!
And turn thee, that some fresh news may possess thee.
A noble count, a don of Spain (my dear
Delicious compeer, and my party[2]-bawd),
Who is come hither private for his conscience
And brought munition with him, six great slops,[3]
Bigger than three Dutch hoys,[4] beside round trunks,[5]
Furnish'd with pistolets,[6] and pieces of eight,[7]
Will straight be here, my rogue, to have thy bath,
(That is the colour,[8]) and to make his battery
Upon our Dol, our castle, our cinqueport,
Our Dover pier, our what thou wilt. Where is she?
She must prepare perfumes, delicate linen,
The bath in chief, a banquet, and her wit,
Where is the doxy?

Sub.   I'll send her to thee:
And but despatch my brace of little John Leydens,[9]
And come again myself.

Face.   Are they within then?

Sub. Numbering the sum.

[1] The same.   [2] Partner.   [3] Large breeches.   [4] Ships.   [5] Trunk hose.
[3] A Spanish gold coin worth about 16sh. 8d.
[7] A coin worth about 4sh. 6d.   [8] Pretext.
[9] Puritans, from the name of the Anabaptist leader.

FACE.   How much?

SUB.   A hundred marks, boy. [*Exit.*]

FACE. Why, this is a lucky day. Ten pounds of Mammon!
Three o' my clerk! A portague o' my grocer!
This o' the brethren! Beside reversions
And states to come, i' the widow, and my count!
My share to-day will not be bought for forty——

[*Enter* DOL]

DOL.   What?

FACE. Pounds, dainty Dorothy! Art thou so near?

DOL. Yes; say, lord general, how fares our camp?

FACE. As with the few that had entrench'd themselves
Safe, by their discipline, against a world, Dol,
And laugh'd within those trenches, and grew fat
With thinking on the booties, Dol, brought in
Daily by their small parties. This dear hour,
A doughty don is taken with my Dol;
And thou mayst make his ransom what thou wilt
My Dousabel;[10] he shall be brought here fetter'd
With thy fair looks, before he sees thee; and thrown
In a down-bed, as dark as any dungeon;
Where thou shalt keep him waking with thy drum;
Thy drum, my Dol, thy drum; till he be tame
As the poor blackbirds were i' the great frost,
Or bees are with a bason; and so hive him
I' the swan-skin coverlid and cambric sheets,
Till he work honey and wax, my little God's-gift.[11]

DOL. What is he, general?

FACE.   An adalantado,[12]
A grandee, girl. Was not my Dapper here yet?

DOL. No.

FACE.   Nor my Drugger?

DOL.   Neither.

FACE.   A pox on 'em,
They are so long a furnishing! such stinkards
Would not be seen upon these festival days.—

---

[10] *I. e., douce et belle;* sweetheart.
[11] Referring to the literal meaning of *Dorothea.*
[12] A Spanish governor.

[*Re-enter* SUBTLE]

How now! ha' you done?

SUB.   Done.   They are gone: the sum
Is here in bank, my Face.   I would we knew
Another chapman who would buy 'em outright.

FACE.   'Slid, Nab shall do't against he ha' the widow,
To furnish household.

SUB.   Excellent, well thought on:
Pray God he come.

FACE.   I pray he keep away
Till our new business be o'erpast.

SUB.   But, Face,
How camst thou by this secret don?

FACE.   A spirit
Brought me th' intelligence in a paper here,
As I was conjuring yonder in my circle
For Surly; I ha' my flies[13] abroad.   Your bath
Is famous, Subtle, by my means.   Sweet Dol,
Tickle him with thy mother tongue.   His great
Verdugoship[14] has not a jot of language;
So much the easier to be cozen'd, my Dolly.
He will come here in a hir'd coach, obscure,
And our own coachman, whom I have sent as guide,
No creature else.   (*One knocks.*)   Who's that? [*Exit* DOL.]

SUB.   It is not he?

FACE. O no, not yet this hour.

Re-enter DOL

SUB.   Who is't?

DOL.   Dapper,
Your clerk.

FACE.   God's will then, Queen of Fairy,
On with your tire; [*Exit* DOL.] and, doctor, with your
    robes.
Let's despatch him for God's sake.

SUB.   .   'Twill be long.

FACE. I warrant you, take but the cues I give you,

---

[13] Familiars.
[14] Verdugo is a Spanish name, but the precise allusion is uncertain.

It shall be brief enough. [*Goes to the window.*] 'Slight,
    here are more!
Abel, and I think the angry boy, the heir,
That fain would quarrel.

    SUB.   And the widow?

    FACE.   No,
Not that I see. Away!   [*Exit* SUB.]

SCENE IV[1]

FACE. [*Enter*] DAPPER

    FACE.   O, sir, you are welcome.
The doctor is within a moving for you;
I have had the most ado to win him to it!—
He swears you'll be the darling o' the dice:
He never heard her highness dote till now.[2]
Your aunt has giv'n you the most gracious words
That can be thought on.

    DAP.   Shall I see her grace?

    FACE. See her, and kiss her too.—

[*Enter* ABEL, *followed by* KASTRIL]
                   What, honest Nab!
Hast brought the damask?

    NAB.   No, sir; here's tobacco.

    FACE. 'Tis well done, Nab; thou'lt bring the damask too?

    DRUG. Yes. Here's the gentleman, captain, Master Kastril,
I have brought to see the doctor.

    FACE.   Where's the widow?

    DRUG. Sir, as he likes, his sister, he says, shall come.

    FACE. O, is it so? Good time. Is your name Kastril, sir?

    KAS. Ay, and the best of the Kastrils, I'd be sorry else,
By fifteen hundred a year.[3] Where is this doctor?
My mad tobacco-boy here tells me of one
That can do things. Has he any skill?

    FACE.   Wherein, sir?

    KAS. To carry a business, manage a quarrel fairly,
Upon fit terms.

    FACE.   It seems, sir, you're but young
About the town, that can make that a question.

---

[1] The same.   [2] Folio adds (*he says*).
[3] *I. e.,* he is £1,500 a year richer than any other of the Kastrils.

Kas. Sir, not so young but I have heard some speech
Of the angry boys,[4] and seen 'em take tobacco;
And in his shop; and I can take it too.
And I would fain be one of 'em, and go down
And practise i' the country.

Face.   Sir, for the duello,
The doctor, I assure you, shall inform you,
To the least shadow of a hair; and show you
An instrument he has of his own making,
Wherewith, no sooner shall you make report
Of any quarrel, but he will take the height on't
Most instantly, and tell in what degree
Of safety it lies in, or mortality.
And how it may be borne, whether in a right line,
Or a half circle; or may else be cast
Into an angle blunt, if not acute:
And this he will demonstrate. And then, rules
To give and take the lie by.

Kas.   How! to take it?

Face. Yes, in oblique he'll show you, or in circle;[5]
But never in diameter.[6] The whole town
Study his theorems, and dispute them ordinarily
At the eating academies.

Kas.   But does he teach
Living by the wits too?

Face.   Anything whatever.
You cannot think that subtlety but he reads it.
He made me a captain. I was a stark pimp,
Just o' your standing, 'fore I met with him;
It's not two months since. I'll tell you his method:
First, he will enter you at some ordinary.

Kas. No, I'll not come there: you shall pardon me.

Face. For why, sir?

Kas.   There's gaming there, and tricks.

Face. Why, would you be
A gallant, and not game?

Kas.   Ay, 'twill spend a man.

Face. Spend you! It will repair you when you are spent.
How do they live by their wits there, that have vented

---

[4] Roysterers, young bloods. [5] The lie circumstantial. [6] The lie direct.

Six times your fortunes?

KAS.   What, three thousand a year!

FACE. Ay, forty thousand.

KAS.   Are there such?

FACE.   Ay, sir,

And gallants yet. Here's a young gentleman
Is born to nothing,—[*points to* DAPPER.] forty marks a year
Which I count nothing:—he is to be initiated,
And have a fly o' the doctor. He will win you
By unresistible luck, within this fortnight,
Enough to buy a barony. They will set him
Upmost, at the groom porter's,[7] all the Christmas:
And for the whole year through at every place
Where there is play, present him with the chair,
The best attendance, the best drink, sometimes
Two glasses of Canary, and pay nothing;
The purest linen and the sharpest knife,
The partridge next his trencher: and somewhere
The dainty bed, in private, with the dainty.
You shall ha' your ordinaries bid for him,
As playhouses for a poet; and the master
Pray him aloud to name what dish he affects,
Which must be butter'd shrimps: and those that drink
To no mouth else, will drink to his, as being
The goodly president mouth of all the board.

KAS. Do you not gull one?

FACE.   'Ods my life! Do you think it?
You shall have a cast commander, (can but get
In credit with a glover, or a spurrier,
For some two pair of either's ware aforehand,)
Will, by most swift posts, dealing [but] with him,
Arrive at competent means to keep himself,
His punk, and naked boy, in excellent fashion,
And be admir'd for't.

KAS.   Will the doctor teach this?

FACE. He will do more, sir: when your land is gone,
(As men of spirit hate to keep earth long),
In a vacation,[8] when small money is stirring,

---

[7] An officer of the royal household, having charge of the cards, dice, etc.
He had the privilege of keeping open table at Christmas.
[8] Of the law-courts.

And ordinaries suspended till the term,
He'll show a perspective,[9] where on one side
You shall behold the faces and the persons
Of all sufficient young heirs in town,
Whose bonds are current for commodity;[10]
On th' other side, the merchants' forms, and others,
That without help of any second broker,
Who would expect a share, will trust such parcels:
In the third square, the very street and sign
Where the commodity dwells, and does but wait
To be deliver'd, be it pepper, soap,
Hops, or tobacco, oatmeal, woad, or cheeses.
All which you may so handle, to enjoy
To your own use, and never stand oblig'd.
    KAS. I' faith! is he such a fellow?
    FACE.   Why, Nab here knows him.
And then for making matches for rich widows,
Young gentlewomen, heirs, the fortunat'st man!
He's sent to, far and near, all over England,
To have his counsel, and to know their fortunes.
    KAS. God's will, my suster shall see him.
    FACE.   I'll tell you, sir,
What he did tell me of Nab. It's a strange thing—
(By the way, you must eat no cheese, Nab, it breeds melan-
    choly,
And that same melancholy breeds worms) but pass it:—
He told me, honest Nab here was ne'er at tavern
But once in's life.
    DRUG.   Truth, and no more I was not.
    FACE. And then he was so sick——
    DRUG.   Could he tell you that too?
    FACE. How should I know it?
    DRUG.   In troth, we had been a shooting,
And had a piece of fat ram-mutton to supper,
That lay so heavy o' my stomach——
    FACE.   And he has no head
To bear any wine; for what with the noise o' the fiddlers,

---

[9] A magic glass.
[10] The reference is to the " commodity " fraud, in which a borrower was obliged to take part of a loan in merchandise, which the lender frequently bought back by agents for much less than it represented in the loan.

And care of his shop, for he dares keep no servants——

DRUG. My head did so ache——

FACE.   And he was fain to be brought home,
The doctor told me: and then a good old woman——

DRUG. Yes, faith, she dwells in Seacoal-lane,—did cure me,
With sodden ale, and pellitory[11] o' the wall;
Cost me but twopence. I had another sickness
Was worse than that.

FACE.   Ay, that was with the grief
Thou took'st for being cess'd[12] at eighteenpence,
For the waterwork.

DRUG.   In truth, and it was like
T' have cost me almost my life.

FACE.   Thy hair went off?

DRUG. Yes, sir; 'twas done for spite.

FACE.   Nay, so says the doctor.

KAS. Pray thee, tobacco-boy, go fetch my suster;
I'll see this learned boy before I go;
And so shall she.

FACE.   Sir, he is busy now:
But if you have a sister to fetch hither,
Perhaps your own pains may command her sooner;
And he by that time will be free.

KAS.   I go.   [*Exit.*]

FACE. Drugger, she's thine: the damask!—[*Exit* ABEL.]
        Subtle and I
Must wrastle for her. [*Aside.*] Come on, Master Dapper,
You see how I turn clients here away,
To give your cause dispatch; ha' you perform'd
The ceremonies were enjoin'd you?

DAP.   Yes, o' the vinegar,
And the clean shirt.

FACE.   'Tis well: that shirt may do you
More worship than you think. Your aunt's a-fire,
But that she will not show it, t' have a sight of you.
Ha' you provided for her grace's servants?

DAP. Yes, here are six score Edward shillings.

FACE.   Good!

DAP. And an old Harry's sovereign.

[11] A herb.   [12] Assessed, taxed.

FACE.   Very good!

DAP. And three James shillings, and an Elizabeth groat,
Just twenty nobles.[13]

FACE.   O, you are too just.
I would you had had the other noble in Maries.

DAP. I have some Philip and Maries.

FACE.   Ay, those same
Are best of all: where are they? Hark, the doctor.

SCENE V[1]

FACE, DAPPER. *Enter* SUBTLE, *disguised like a priest of
Fairy* [*with a strip of cloth*]

SUB. [*in a feigned voice.*] Is yet her grace's cousin
    come?

FACE.   He is come.

SUB. And is he fasting?

FACE.   Yes.

SUB.   And hath cried hum?

FACE. Thrice, you must answer.

DAP.   Thrice.

SUB.   And as oft buz?

FACE. If you have, say.

DAP.   I have.

SUB.   Then, to her cuz,
Hoping that he hath vinegar'd his senses,
As he was bid, the Fairy queen dispenses,
By me, this robe, the petticoat of fortune;
Which that he straight put on, she doth importune.
And though to fortune near be her petticoat,
Yet nearer is her smock, the queen doth note:
And therefore, even of that a piece she hath sent,
Which, being a child, to wrap him in was rent;
And prays him for a scarf he now will wear it,
With as much love as then her grace did tear it,
About his eyes, (*They blind him with the rag,*) to show he
    is fortunate.
And, trusting unto her to make his state,

[13] A noble was worth 6sh. 8d.
[1] The same.

He'll throw away all worldly pelf about him;
Which that he will perform, she doth not doubt him.
    FACE. She need not doubt him, sir. Alas, he has nothing
But what he will part withal as willingly,
Upon her grace's word—throw away your purse—
As she would ask it:—handkerchiefs and all—
She cannot bid that thing but he'll obey.—
If you have a ring about you, cast it off,
Or a silver seal at your wrist; her grace will send
                        (*He throws away, as they bid him.*)
Her fairies here to search you, therefore deal
Directly² with her highness: if they find
That you conceal a mite, you are undone.
    DAP. Truly, there's all.
    FACE.   All what?
    DAP.   My money; truly.
    FACE. Keep nothing that is transitory about you.
[*Aside to* SUBTLE.] Bid Dol play music.—Look, the elves are
        come.   [DOL. *plays on the cittern within.*
To pinch you, if you tell not truth. Advise you.
                                [*They pinch him.*]
    DAP. O! I have a paper with a spur-ryal³ in't.
    FACE.   *Ti, ti.*
They knew't, they say.
    SUB.   *Ti, ti, ti, ti.* He has more yet.
    FACE. *Ti, ti-ti-ti.* I' the other pocket?
    SUB.   *Titi, titi, titi, titi, titi.*
They must pinch him or he will never confess, they say.
                                [*They pinch him again.*
    DAP. O, O!
    FACE. Nay, pray you, hold: he is her grace's nephew,
Ti, ti, ti? What care you? good faith, you shall care.—
Deal plainly, sir, and shame the fairies. Show
You are innocent.
    DAP.   By this good light, I ha' nothing.
    SUB. *Ti, ti, ti, ti, to, ta.* He does equivocate she says:
Ti, ti do ti, ti ti do, ti da; and swears by the *light* when he
    is blinded.
    DAP. By this good *dark*, I ha' nothing but a half-crown

        ² **Uprightly.**   ³ **A gold coin worth 15sh.**

Of gold about my wrist, that my love gave me;
And a leaden heart I wore sin' she forsook me.

FACE. I thought 'twas something. And would you incur
Your aunt's displeasure for these trifles? Come,
I had rather you had thrown away twenty half-crowns.

                                              [*Takes it off.*]

You may wear your leaden heart still.—

                       [*Enter* DOL. *hastily*]

                                          How now!

SUB. What news, Dol?

DOL.   Yonder's your knight, Sir Mammon.

FACE. 'Ods lid, we never thought of him till now!
Where is he?

DOL.   Here hard by. He's at the door.

SUB. And you are not ready now! Dol, get his suit.

                                              [*Exit* DOL.]

He must not be sent back.

FACE.   O, by no means.
What shall we do with this same puffin[4] here,
Now he's on the spit?

SUB.   Why, lay him back awhile,
With some device.

                       [*Re-enter* DOL *with* FACE'S *clothes*]

        —*Ti, ti, ti, ti, ti, ti,* Would her grace speak with me?
I come.—Help, Dol!   *Knocking without.*

FACE. [*speaks through the keyhole.*]—Who's there? Sir
      Epicure,
My master's i' the way. Please you to walk
Three or four turns, but till his back be turn'd,
And I am for you.—Quickly, Dol!

SUB.   Her grace
Commends her kindly to you, Master Dapper.

DAP. I long to see her grace.

SUB.   She now is set
At dinner in her bed, and she has sent you
From her own private trencher, a dead mouse,

                       [4] A sort of gull.

And a piece of gingerbread, to be merry withal,
And stay your stomach, lest you faint with fasting:
Yet if you could hold out till she saw you, she says,
It would be better for you.

    FACE.   Sir, he shall
Hold out, an 'twere this two hours, for her highness;
I can assure you that. We will not lose
All we ha' done.——

    SUB.   He must not see, nor speak
To anybody, till then.

    FACE.   For that we'll put, sir,
A stay in's mouth.

    SUB.   Of what?

    FACE.   Of gingerbread.
Make you it fit. He that hath pleas'd her grace
Thus far, shall not now crinkle[6] for a little.——
Gape, sir, and let him fit you.

        [*They thrust a gag of gingerbread in his mouth.*]

    SUB.   Where shall we now
Bestow him?

    DOL.   I' the privy.

    SUB.   Come along, sir,
I must now show you Fortune's privy lodgings.

    FACE. Are they perfum'd, and his bath ready?

    SUB.   All:
Only the fumigation's somewhat strong.

    FACE. [*speaking through the keyhole.*] Sir Epicure, I am
      yours, sir, by and by.   [*Exeunt with* DAPPER.]

ACT IV

SCENE I[1]

Enter FACE *and* MAMMON

    FACE. O, sir, you're come i' the only finest time.——

    MAM. Where's master?

    FACE.   Now preparing for projection, sir.
Your stuff will be all chang'd shortly.

---

      [6] Turn aside from his purpose.
      [1] A room in Lovewit's house.

MAM. Into gold?

FACE. To gold and silver, sir.

MAM. Silver I care not for.

FACE. Yes, sir, a little to give beggars.

MAM. Where's the lady?

FACE. At hand here. I ha' told her such brave things o'
    you,
Touching your bounty and your noble spirit——

MAM. Hast thou?

FACE. As she is almost in her fit to see you.
But, good sir, no divinity i' your conference,
For fear of putting her in rage.——

MAM. I warrant thee.

FACE. Six men [sir] will not hold her down. And then,
If the old man should hear or see you——

MAM. Fear not.

FACE. The very house, sir, would run mad. You know it,
How scrupulous he is, and violent,
'Gainst the least act of sin. Physic or mathematics,
Poetry, state,[2] or bawdry, as I told you,
She will endure, and never startle; but
No word of controversy.

MAM. I am school'd, good ULEN.

FACE. And you must praise her house, remember that,
And her nobility.

MAM. Let me alone:
No herald, no, nor antiquary, Lungs,
Shall do it better. Go.

FACE. [*Aside*.] Why, this is yet
A kind of modern happiness,[3] to have
Dol Common for a great lady. [*Exit*.]

MAM. Now, Epicure,
Heighten thyself, talk to her all in gold;
Rain her as many showers as Jove did drops
Unto his Danäe; show the god a miser,
Compar'd with Mammon. What! the stone will do't.
She shall feel gold, taste gold, hear gold, sleep gold;
Nay, we will *concumbere* gold: I will be puissant,
And mighty in my talk to her.——

---

[2] Politics.   [3] Up-to-date appropriateness.

[*Re-enter* FACE *with* DOL *richly dressed*]

                    Here she comes.

FACE. To him, Dol, suckle him. This is the noble knight
I told your ladyship——

   MAM.   Madam, with your pardon,
I kiss your vesture.

   DOL.   Sir, I were uncivil
If I would suffer that; my lip to you, sir.

   MAM. I hope my lord your brother be in health, lady.

   DOL. My lord my brother is, though I no lady, sir.

   FACE. [*Aside.*] Well said, my Guinea bird.

   MAM.   .   Right noble madam——

   FACE. [*Aside.*] O, we shall have most fierce idolatry.

   MAM. 'Tis your prerogative.

   DOL.   Rather your courtesy.

   MAM. Were there nought else t' enlarge your virtues
      to me,
These answers speak your breeding and your blood.

   DOL. Blood we boast none, sir; a poor baron's daughter.

   MAM. Poor! and gat you? Profane not. Had your father
Slept all the happy remnant of his life
After that act, lien but there still, and panted,
He 'd done enough to make himself, his issue,
And his posterity noble.

   DOL.   Sir, although
We may be said to want the gilt and trappings,
The dress of honour, yet we strive to keep
The seeds and the materials.

   MAM.   I do see
The old ingredient, virtue, was not lost,
Nor the drug money us'd to make your compound.
There is a strange nobility i' your eye,
This lip, that chin! Methinks you do resemble
One o' the Austriac princes.

   FACE.   [*Aside.*] Very like!
Her father was an Irish costermonger.

   MAM. The house of Valois just had such a nose,
And such a forehead yet the Medici
Of Florence boast.

Dol.   Troth, and I have been lik'ned
To all these princes.

Face.   [*Aside.*] I'll be sworn, I heard it.

Mam. I know not how! it is not any one,
But e'en the very choice of all their features.

Face. [*Aside.*] I'll in, and laugh.   [*Exit.*]

Mam.   A certain touch, or air,
That sparkles a divinity beyond
An earthly beauty!

Dol.   O, you play the courtier.

Mam. Good lady, gi' me leave——

Dol.   In faith, I may not,
To mock me, sir.

Mam.   To burn i' this sweet flame;
The phœnix never knew a nobler death.

Dol. Nay, now you court the courtier, and destroy
What you would build. This art, sir, i' your words,
Calls your whole faith in question.

Mam.   By my soul——

Dol. Nay, oaths are made o' the same air, sir.

Mam.   Nature
Never bestow'd upon mortality
A more unblam'd, a more harmonious feature;
She play'd the step-dame in all faces else:
Sweet madam, le' me be particular——

Dol. Particular, sir! I pray you know your distance.

Mam. In no ill sense, sweet lady; but to ask
How your fair graces pass the hours? I see
You're lodg'd here, in the house of a rare man,
An excellent artist; but what's that to you?

Dol. Yes, sir; I study here the mathematics,
And distillation.

Mam.   O, I cry your pardon.
He's a divine instructor! can extract
The souls of all things by his art; call all
The virtues, and the miracles of the sun,
Into a temperate furnace; teach dull nature
What her own forces are. A man, the emp'ror
Has courted above Kelly;[a] sent his medals

[a] The partner of Dee, the astrologer.

And chains, t' invite him.

DOL.   Ay, and for his physic, sir——

MAM. Above the art of Æsculapius,
That drew the envy of the thunderer!
I know all this, and more.

DOL.   Troth, I am taken, sir,
Whole with these studies, that contemplate nature.

MAM. It is a noble humour; but this form
Was not intended to so dark a use.
Had you been crooked, foul, of some coarse mould,
A cloister had done well; but such a feature
That might stand up the glory of a kingdom,
To live recluse! is a mere solœcism,
Though in a nunnery. It must not be.
I muse, my lord your brother will permit it:
You should spend half my land first, were I he.
Does not this diamond better on my finger
Than i' the quarry?

DOL.   Yes.

MAM.   Why, you are like it.
You were created, lady, for the light.
Here, you shall wear it; take it, the first pledge
Of what I speak, to bind you to believe me.

DOL. In chains of adamant?

MAM.   Yes, the strongest bands.
And take a secret too.—Here, by your side,
Doth stand this hour the happiest man in Europe.

DOL. You are contented, sir?

MAM.   Nay, in true being,
The envy of princes and the fear of states.

DOL. Say you so, Sir Epicure?

MAM.   Yes, and thou shalt prove it,
Daughter of honour. I have cast mine eye
Upon thy form, and I will rear this beauty
Above all styles.

DOL.   You mean no treason, sir?

MAM. No, I will take away that jealousy.
I am the lord of the philosopher's stone,
And thou the lady.

DOL.   How, sir! ha' you that?

MAM. I am the master of the mastery.[5]
This day the good old wretch here o' the house
Has made it for us: now he's at projection.
Think therefore thy first wish now, let me hear it;
And it shall rain into thy lap, no shower,
But floods of gold, whole cataracts, a deluge,
To get a nation on thee.

DOL.   You are pleas'd, sir,
To work on the ambition of our sex.

MAM. I 'm pleas'd the glory of her sex should know,
This nook here of the Friars is no climate
For her to live obscurely in, to learn
Physic and surgery, for the constable's wife
Of some odd hundred in Essex; but come forth,
And taste the air of palaces; eat, drink
The toils of empirics, and their boasted practice;
Tincture of pearl, and coral, gold, and amber;
Be seen at feasts and triumphs; have it ask'd,
What miracle she is; set all the eyes
Of court a-fire, like a burning glass,
And work them into cinders, when the jewels
Of twenty states adorn thee, and the light
Strikes out the stars! that, when thy name is mention'd,
Queens may look pale; and we but showing our love,
Nero's Poppæa may be lost in story!
Thus will we have it.

DOL.   I could well consent, sir.
But in a monarchy, how will this be?
The prince will soon take notice, and both seize
You and your stone, it being a wealth unfit
For any private subject.

MAM.   If he knew it.

DOL. Yourself do boast it, sir.

MAM.   To thee, my life.

DOL. O, but beware, sir! You may come to end
The remnant of your days in a loath'd prison,
By speaking of it.

MAM.   'Tis no idle fear.
We'll therefore go with all, my girl, and live

[5] The art of transmutation.

In a free state, where we will eat our mullets,
Sous'd in high-country wines, sup pheasants' eggs,
And have our cockles boil'd in silver shells;
Our shrimps to swim again, as when they liv'd,
In a rare butter made of dolphins' milk,
Whose cream does look like opals; and with these
Delicate meats set ourselves high for pleasure,
And take us down again, and then renew
Our youth and strength with drinking the elixir,
And so enjoy a perpetuity
Of life and lust! And thou shalt ha' thy wardrobe
Richer than nature's, still to change thyself,
And vary oftener, for thy pride, than she,
Or art, her wise and almost-equal servant.

[*Re-enter* FACE]

FACE. Sir, you are too loud. I hear you every word
Into the laboratory. Some fitter place;
The garden, or great chamber above. How like you her?
    MAM. Excellent! Lungs. There's for thee.
                                [*Gives him money.*]
FACE.   But do you hear?
Good sir, beware, no mention of the rabbins.
    MAM. We think not on 'em.   [*Exeunt* MAM. *and* DOL.]
    FACE.   O, it is well, sir.—Subtle!

SCENE II[1]

FACE. [*Enter*] SUBTLE

Dost thou not laugh?
    SUB.   Yes; are they gone?
    FACE.   All's clear.
    SUB. The widow is come.
    FACE.   And your quarrelling disciple?
    SUB. Ay.
    FACE.   I must to my captainship again then.
    SUB. Stay, bring 'em in first.
    FACE.   So I meant. What is she?

---

[1] The same.

A bonnibel?

SUB.   I know not.

FACE.   We'll draw lots:
You'll stand to that?

SUB.   What else?

FACE.   O, for a suit,
To fall now like a curtain, flap!

SUB.   To th' door, man.

FACE. You'll ha' the first kiss, 'cause I am not ready.

                                         [*Exit.*]

SUB. Yes, and perhaps hit you through both the nostrils.[2]

FACE. [*within.*] Who would you speak with?

KAS.   [*within.*] Where's the captain?

FACE.   [*within.*] Gone, sir,
About some business.

KAS.   [*within.*] Gone!

FACE.   [*within.*] He'll return straight.
But, master doctor, his lieutenant, is here.

                [*Enter* KASTRIL, *followed by* Dame PLIANT]

SUB. Come near, my worshipful boy, *my terræ fili,*
That is, my boy of land; make thy approaches:
Welcome; I know thy lusts, and thy desires,
And I will serve and satisfy 'em. Begin,
Charge me from thence, or thence, or in this line;
Here is my centre: ground thy quarrel.

KAS.   You lie.

SUB. How, child of wrath and anger! the loud lie?
For what, my sudden boy?

KAS.   Nay, that look you to,
I am aforehand.

SUB.   O, this is no true grammar,
And as ill logic! You must render causes, child,
Your first and second intentions, know your canons
And your divisions, moods, degrees, and differences,
Your predicaments, substance, and accident,
Series extern and intern, with their causes,
Efficient, material, formal, final,
And ha' your elements perfect?

              [2] " Put your nose out of joint."

KAS.   What is this?
The angry[3] tongue he talks in?
    SUB.   That false precept,
Of being aforehand, has deceiv'd a number,
And made 'em enter quarrels oftentimes
Before they were aware; and afterward,
Against their wills.
    KAS.   How must I do then, sir?
    SUB. I cry this lady mercy; she should first
Have been saluted. (*Kisses her.*) I do call you lady,
Because you are to be one ere 't be long,
My soft and buxom widow.
    KAS.   Is she, i' faith?
    SUB. Yes, or my art is an egregious liar.
    KAS. How know you?
    SUB.   By inspection on her forehead,
And subtlety of her lip, which must be tasted
Often to make a judgment. (*Kisses her again.*) 'Slight,
        she melts
Like a myrobolane.[4] Here is yet a line,
In *rivo frontis*,[5] tells me he is no knight.
    DAME P. What is he then, sir?
    SUB.   Let me see your hand.
O, your *linea fortunæ* makes it plain;
And *stella* here *in monte Veneris*.
But, most of all, *junctura annularis*.[6]
He is a soldier, or a man of art, lady,
But shall have some great honour shortly.
    DAME P.   Brother,
He's a rare man, believe me!

[*Re-enter* FACE, *in his uniform*]
    KAS.   Hold your peace.
Here comes the t' other rare man.—'Save you, captain.
    FACE. Good Master Kastril! Is this your sister?
    KAS.   Ay, sir.
Please you to kiss her, and be proud to know her.
    FACE. I shall be proud to know you, lady.   [*Kisses her.*]

---

    [3] Swaggering.   [4] A kind of dried plum, esteemed as a sweetmeat.
    [5] Frontal vein.   [6] These are the cant phrases of palmistry.

DAME P.   Brother,
He calls me lady too.

KAS.   Ay, peace: I heard it.   [*Takes her aside.*]

FACE. The count is come.

SUB.   Where is he?

FACE.   At the door.

SUB. Why, you must entertain him.

FACE.   What will you do
With these the while?

SUB.   Why, have 'em up, and show 'em
Some fustian book, or the dark glass.

FACE.   'Fore God,
She is a delicate dabchick! I must have her.   [*Exit.*]

SUB. [*Aside.*] Must you! Ay, if your fortune will, you
        must.—
Come, sir, the captain will come to us presently:
I'll ha' you to my chamber of demonstrations,
Where I'll show you both the grammar and logic,
And rhetoric of quarrelling; my whole method
Drawn out in tables; and my instrument,
That hath the several scales upon't, shall make you
Able to quarrel at a straw's-breadth by moonlight.
And, lady, I'll have you look in a glass,
Some half an hour, but to clear your eyesight,
Against you see[7] your fortune; which is greater
Than I may judge upon the sudden, trust me.   [*Exeunt.*]

SCENE III[1]

[*Enter*] FACE

FACE. Where are you, doctor?

SUB.   [*within.*]   I'll come to you presently.

FACE. I will ha' this same widow, now I ha' seen her,
On any composition.

[*Enter* SUBTLE]

SUB.   What do you say?

FACE. Ha' you dispos'd of them?

[7] In preparation for seeing.
[1] The same.

Sub.   I ha' sent 'em up.

Face. Subtle, in troth, I needs must have this widow.

Sub. Is that the matter?

Face.   Nay, but hear me.

Sub.   Go to.
If you rebel once, Dol shall know it all:
Therefore be quiet, and obey your chance.

Face. Nay, thou art so violent now. Do but conceive,
Thou art old, and canst not serve——

Sub.   Who cannot? I?
'Slight, I will serve her with thee, for a——

Face.   ·   Nay,
But understand: I'll gi' you composition.[2]

Sub. I will not treat with thee. What! sell my fortune?
'Tis better than my birthright. Do not murmur:
Win her, and carry her. If you grumble, Dol
Knows it directly.

Face.   Well, sir, I am silent.
Will you go help to fetch in Don in state?   [*Exit.*]

Sub. I follow you, sir. We must keep Face in awe,
Or he will overlook us like a tyrant.

[*Re-enter* Face, *introducing*] Surly *disguised as a* Spaniard
Brain of a tailor! who comes here? Don John!

Sur. *Senores, beso las manos a vuestras mercedes.*[3]

Sub. Stab me; I shall never hold, man.
He looks in that deep ruff like a head in a platter,
Serv'd in by a short cloak upon two trestles.

Face. Or what do you say to a collar of brawn,[4] cut down
Beneath the souse,[5] and wriggled with a knife?

Sub. 'Slud, he does look too fat to be a Spaniard.

Face. Perhaps some Fleming or some Hollander got him
In d'Alva's time; Count Egmont's bastard.

Sub.   Don,
Your scurvy, yellow, Madrid face is welcome.

Sur. *Gratia.*

Sub.   He speaks out of a fortification.
Pray God he ha' no squibs in those deep sets.[6]

---

[2] Recompense.   [3] Spanish. " Gentlemen, I kiss your hands."
[4] Neck of a boar, or boar's flesh rolled.   [5] Ear.
[6] The deep plaits of his *ruff.*

Sur. *Por dios, senores, muy linda casa!*
Sub. What says he?
Face.   Praises the house, I think;
I know no more but 's action.
Sub.   Yes, the *casa,*
My precious Diego,⁹ will prove fair enough
To cozen you in. Do you mark? You shall
Be cozened, Diego.
Face.   Cozened, do you see,
My worthy Donzel,⁹ cozened.
Sur.   *Entiendo.*¹⁰
Sub. Do you intend it? So do we, dear Don.
Have you brought pistolets,¹¹ or portagues,
My solemn Don? [*to* Face.] Dost thou feel any?
Face. (*feels his pockets.*)   Full.
Sub. You shall be emptied, Don, pumped and drawn
Dry, as they say.
Face.   Milked, in troth, sweet Don.
Sub. See all the monsters; the great lion of all, Don.
Sur. *Con licencia, se puede ver a esta senora?*¹²
Sub. What talks he now?
Face.   Of the senora.
Sub.   O, Don,
This is the lioness, which you shall see
Also, my Don.
Face.   'Slid, Subtle, how shall we do?
Sub. For what?
Face.   Why, Dol's employ'd, you know.
Sub.   That's true.
'Fore heaven I know not: he must stay, that's all.
Face. Stay! that he must not by no means.
Sub.   No! why?
Face. Unless you'll mar all. 'Slight, he'll suspect it;
And then he will not pay, not half so well.
This is a travell'd punk-master, and does know
All the delays; a notable hot rascal,
And looks already rampant.

⁷ " Gad, sirs, a very pretty house."
⁸ Spaniard. Strictly, Spanish for James.   ⁹ Diminutive of Don.
¹⁰ " I understand."   ¹¹   Spanish gold coin, worth about 16sh. 8d.
¹² " If you please, may I see the lady? "

Sub.   'Sdeath, and Mammon
Must not be troubled.

Face.   Mammon! in no case.

Sub. What shall we do then?

Face.   Think: you must be sudden.[13]

Sur. *Entiendo que la senora es tan hermosa, que codicio
tan a verla, como la bien aventuranza de mi vida.*[14]

Face. *Mi vida!* 'Slid, Subtle, he puts me in mind o' the
    widow.
What dost thou say to draw her to't, ha!
And tell her 'tis her fortune? All our venture
Now lies upon't. It is but one man more,
Which on's chance to have her: and beside,
There is no maidenhead to be fear'd or lost.
What dost thou think on't, Subtle?

Sub.   Who, I? why——

Face. The credit of our house too is engag'd.[15]

Sub. You made me an offer for my share erewhile.
What wilt thou gi' me, i' faith?

Face.   O, by that light
I'll not buy now. You know your doom[16] to me.
E'en take your lot, obey your chance, sir; win her,
And wear her—out for me.

Sub.   'Slight, I'll not work her then.

Face. It is the common cause; therefore bethink you
Dol else must know it, as you said.

Sub.   I care not.

Sur. *Senores, porque se tarda tanto?*[17]

Sub. Faith, I am not fit, I am old.

Face.   That's now no reason, sir

Sur. *Puede ser de hazer burla de mi amor?*[18]

Face. You hear the Don too? by this air I call,
And loose the hinges. Dol!

Sub.   A plague of hell——

Face. Will you then do?

Sub.   You're a terrible rogue!
I'll think of this. Will you, sir, call the widow?

[13] Quick about it.
[14] "I understand that the lady is so handsome that I am as eager to see her as the good fortune of my life."   [15] Involved.   [16] Agreement.
[17] "Sirs, why so long delay?"
[18] "Can it be to make sport of my love?"

FACE. Yes, and I'll take her too with all her faults,
Now I do think on't better.

SUB.   With all my heart, sir;
Am I discharg'd o' the lot?

FACE.   As you please.

SUB.   Hands. [*They take hands.*]

FACE. Remember now, that upon any change,
You never claim her.

SUB.   Much good joy and health to you, sir,
Marry a whore! Fate, let me wed a witch first.

SUR. *Por estas honradas barbas*[19]——

SUB.   He swears by his beard.
Dispatch, and call the brother too   [*Exit* FACE.]

SUR. *Tengo duda, senores, que no me hagan alguna traycion.*[20]

SUB. How, issue on? yes, *præsto, senor.* Please you
Enthratha the *chambratha,* worthy don:
Where if you please the fates, in your *bathada,*
You shall be soak'd, and strok'd, and tubb'd, and rubb'd,
And scrubb'd, and fubb'd,[21] dear don, before you go.
You shall in faith, my scurvy baboon don,
Be curried, claw'd, and flaw'd,[22] and taw'd,[23] indeed.
I will the heartlier go about it now,
And make the widow a punk so much the sooner,
To be reveng'd on this impetuous Face:
The quickly doing of it is the grace.

                            [*Exeunt* SUB. *and* SURLY.]

SCENE IV[1]

[Enter] FACE, KASTRIL, *and* Dame PLIANT

FACE. Come, lady: I knew the doctor would not leave
Till he had found the very nick of her fortune.

KAS. To be a countess, say you?

[FACE.][2] A Spanish countess, sir.

DAME P. Why, is that better than an English countess?

FACE. Better! 'Slight, make you that a question, lady?

---

[19] "By this honored beard—"
[20] "I fear, sirs, that you are playing me some trick."
[21] Cheated.   [22] Cracked.   [23] Soaked, like a hide being tanned.
[1] Another room in the same.   [2] Folio gives this line also to Kastril

KAS. Nay, she is a fool, captain, you must pardon her.

FACE. Ask from your courtier to your inns-of-court-man,
To your mere milliner; they will tell you all,
Your Spanish jennet is the best horse; your Spanish
Stoop is the best garb;³ your Spanish beard
Is the best cut; your Spanish ruffs are the best
Wear; your Spanish pavin the best dance;
Your Spanish titillation in a glove
The best perfume: and for your Spanish pike,
And Spanish blade, let your poor captain speak.—
Here comes the doctor.

[*Enter* SUBTLE *with a paper*]

SUB.   My most honour'd lady,
For so I am now to style you, having found
By this my scheme,⁴ you are to undergo
An honourable fortune very shortly,
What will you say now, if some——

FACE.   I ha' told her all, sir,
And her right worshipful brother here, that she shall be
A countess; do not delay 'em, sir; a Spanish countess.

SUB. Still, my scarce-worshipful captain, you can keep
No secret! Well, since he has told you, madam,
Do you forgive him, and I do.

KAS.   She shall do that, sir;
I'll look to it, 'tis my charge.

SUB.   Well then: nought rests
But that she fit her love now to her fortune.

DAME P. Truly I shall never brook a Spaniard.

SUB.   No?

DAME P. Never sin' eighty-eight⁵ could I abide 'em,
And that was some three years afore I was born, in truth.

SUB. Come, you must love him, or be miserable;
Choose which you will.

FACE.   By this good rush, persuade her,
She will cry⁶ strawberries else within this twelve month.

SUB. Nay, shads and mackerel, which is worse.

FACE.   Indeed, sir!

---

³ Bodily carriage.   ⁴ Horoscope.
⁵ *I. e.*, since 1588, the year of the " Invincible Armada."
⁶ Sell on the street.

KAS. Gods lid, you shall love him, or I'll kick you.

DAME P. Why, I'll do as you will ha' me, brother.

KAS. Do, Or by this hand I'll maul you.

FACE. Nay, good sir, Be not so fierce.

SUB. No, my enragèd child; She will be rul'd. What, when she comes to taste The pleasures of a countess! to be courted——

FACE. And kiss'd, and ruffled!

SUB. Ay, behind the hangings.

FACE. And then come forth in pomp!

SUB. And know her state!

FACE. Of keeping all th' idolaters of the chamber Barer to her, than at their prayers!

SUB. Is served Upon the knee!

FACE. And has her pages, ushers, Footmen, and coaches——

SUB. Her six mares——

FACE. Nay, eight!

SUB. To hurry her through London, to th' Exchange,[7] Bethlem,[8] the china-houses[9]——

FACE. Yes, and have The citizens gape at her, and praise her tires,[10] And my lord's goose-turd[11] bands, that rides with her!

KAS. Most brave! By this hand, you are not my suster If you refuse.

DAME P. I will not refuse, brother.

[*Enter* SURLY]

SUR. *Que es esto, senores, que non se venga? Esta tardanza me mata!*[12]

FACE. It is the count come: The doctor knew he would be here, by his art.

SUB. *En gallanta madama, Don! gallantissima!*

---

[7] There were shops in the Royal Exchange.
[8] The madhouse was often visited for entertainment.
[9] Shops with merchandise from China.   [10] Head-dresses.
[11] In greenish-yellow liveries.
[12] "Why doesn't she come, sirs? This delay is killing me."

Sur. *Por todos los dioses, la mas acabada hermosura, que he visto en ma vida!*[13]

Face. Is't not a gallant language that they speak?

Kas. An admirable language! Is't not French?

Face. No, Spanish, sir.

Kas.   It goes like law French,
And that, they say, is the court-liest language.

Face.   List, sir.

Sur. *El sol ha perdido su lumbre, con el resplandor que trae esta dama! Valgame dios!*[14]

Face. H' admires your sister.

Kas.   Must not she make curt'sy.

Sub. 'Ods will, she must go to him, man, and kiss him!
It is the Spanish fashion, for the women
To make first court.

Face.   'Tis true he tells you, sir:
His art knows all.

Sur.   *Porque no se acude?*[15]

Kas. He speaks to her, I think.

Face.   That he does, sir.

Sur. *Por el amor de dios, que es esto que se tarda?*[16]

Kas. Nay, see: she will not understand him! Gull,
Noddy.

Dame P. What say you, brother?

Kas.   Ass, my suster,
Go kuss him, as the cunning man would have you;
I'll thrust a pin in your buttocks else.

Face.   O no, sir.

Sur. *Senora mia, mi persona muy indigna esta allegar a tanta hermosura.*[17]

Face. Does he not use her bravely?

Kas.   Bravely, i' faith!

Face. Nay, he will use her better.

Kas.   Do you think so?

Sur. *Senora, si sera servida, entremos.*[18]

                        [*Exit with* Dame Pliant.]

[13] " By all the gods, the most perfect beauty I have seen in my life!"
[14] " The sun has lost his light with the splendor this lady brings, so help me God."   [15] " Why don't you draw near? "
[16] " For the love of God, why this delay? "
[17] " Madam, my person is unworthy to approach such beauty."
[18] " Madam, at your service, let us go in."

KAS. Where does he carry her?

FACE.   Into the garden, sir;
Take you no thought: I must interpret for her.

SUB. Give Dol the word. [*Aside to* FACE *who goes out.*]
                              —Come, my fierce child, advance,
We'll to our quarrelling lesson again.

KAS.   Agreed.
I love a Spanish boy with all my heart.

SUB. Nay, and by this means, sir, you shall be brother
To a great count.

KAS.   Ay, I knew that at first,
This match will advance the house of the Kastrils.

SUB. 'Pray God your sister prove but pliant!

KAS.   Why,
Her name is so, by her other husband.

SUB.   How!

KAS. The Widow Pliant. Knew you not that?

SUB.   No, faith, sir;
Yet, by erection of her figure,[19] I guess'd it.
Come, let's go practise.

KAS.   Yes, but do you think, doctor,
I e'er shall quarrel well?

SUB.   I warrant you.   [*Exeunt.*]

SCENE V[1]

Enter DOL [*in her fit of raving, followed by*] MAMMON

DOL. *For after Alexander's death*[2]——

MAM.   Good lady——

DOL. *That Perdiccas and Antigonus were slain,*
The two that stood, Seleuc' and Ptolomy——

MAM.   Madam—

DOL. *Make up the two legs, and the fourth beast,*
That was Gog-north and Egypt-south: which after
Was call'd Gog-iron-leg and South-iron-leg——

MAM.   Lady——

DOL. *And then Gog-horned. So was Egypt, too:*

[19] By her horoscope, with a pun on her bearing.
[1] Another room in the same.
[2] Doll's ravings are taken almost at random from the headings of columns, preface, etc., of the "Concent of Scripture," by Hugh Broughton.

Then Egypt-clay-leg, and Gog-clay-leg——

MAM. Sweet madam——

DOL. *And last Gog-dust, and Egypt-dust, which fall*
In the last link of the fourth chain. And these
Be stars in story, which none see, or look at——

MAM. What shall I do?

DOL. *For,* as he says, *except*
We call the rabbins, and the heathen Greeks——

MAM. Dear lady——

DOL. *To come from Salem, and from Athens,*
And teach the people of Great Britain——

[*Enter* FACE *hastily, in his servant's dress*]

FACE. What's the matter, sir?

DOL. *To speak the tongue of Eber and Javan——*

MAM. O,
She's in her fit.

DOL. *We shall know nothing——*

FACE. Death, sir,
We are undone!

DOL. *Where then a learned linguist*
Shall see the ancient us'd communion
Of vowels and consonants——

FACE. My master will hear!

DOL. *A wisdom, which Pythagoras held most high——*

MAM. Sweet honourable lady!

DOL. *To comprise*
All sounds of voices, in few marks of letters.

FACE. Nay, you must never hope to lay her now.

(*They all speak together.*)

DOL. *And so we may arrive by Talmud skill,[3]*
And profane Greek, to raise the building up
Of Helen's house against the Ismaelite,
King of Thogarma, and his habergions
Brimstony, blue, and fiery; and the force
Of king Abaddon, and the beast of Cittim;
Which rabbi David Kimchi, Onkelos,
And Aben Ezra do interpret Rome.

---

[3] In the early editions this speech is printed in parallel columns with the dialogue immediately following, to indicate simultaneous utterance.

FACE. How did you put her into't?

MAM.   Alas, I talked
Of a fifth monarchy I would erect
With the philosopher's stone, by chance, and she
Falls on the other four straight.

FACE.   Out of Broughton!
I told you so. 'Slid, stop her mouth.

MAM.   Is't best

FACE. She'll never leave else. If the old man hear her,
We are but fæces, ashes.

SUB. [*within.*] What's to do there?

FACE. O, we are lost! Now she hears him, she is quiet.

Enter SUBTLE; *they run different ways*

MAM. Where shall I hide me!

SUB.   How! what sight is here?
Close[*] deeds of darkness, and that shun the light!
Bring him again. Who is he? What, my son!
O, I have liv'd too long.

MAM.   Nay, good, dear father,
There was no unchaste purpose.

SUB.   Not? and flee me
When I come in?

MAM.   That was my error.

SUB.   Error?
Guilt, guilt, my son; give it the right name. No marvel
If I found check in our great work within,
When such affairs as these were managing!

MAM. Why, have you so?

SUB.   It has stood still this half hour:
And all the rest of our less works gone back.
Where is the instrument of wickedness,
My lewd false drudge?

MAM.   Nay, good sir, blame not him;
Believe me, 'twas against his will or knowledge:
I saw her by chance.

SUB.   Will you commit more sin,
To excuse a varlet?

MAM.   By my hope, 'tis true, sir.

[*] Secret.

SUB. Nay, then I wonder less, if you, for whom
The blessing was prepar'd, would so tempt heaven,
And lose your fortunes.

MAM.   Why, sir?

SUB.   This will retard
The work a month at least.

MAM.   Why, if it do,
What remedy? But think it not, good father:
Our purposes were honest.[5]

SUB.   As they were,
So the reward will prove. (*A great crack and noise within.*)
    —How now! ay me!
God and all saints be good to us.——

[*Re-enter* FACE]
                              What's that?

FACE. O, sir, we are defeated! all the works
Are flown *in fumo,*[6] every glass is burst;
Furnace and all rent down, as if a bolt
Of thunder had been driven through the house.
Retorts, receivers, pelicans,[7] bolt-heads,[8]
All struck in shivers!   (SUBTLE *falls down as in a swoon.*)
                    Help, good sir! alas,
Coldness and death invades him. Nay, Sir Mammon,
Do the fair offices of a man! You stand,
As you were readier to depart than he.   (*One knocks.*)
Who's there? My lord her brother is come.

MAM.   Ha, Lungs!

FACE. His coach is at the door. Avoid his sight,
For he's as furious as his sister's mad.

MAM. Alas!   My brain is quite undone with the fume, sir,
I ne'er must hope to be mine own man again.

MAM. Is all lost, Lungs? Will nothing be preserv'd
Of all our cost?

FACE.   Faith, very little, sir;
A peck of coals or so, which is cold comfort, sir.

MAM. O, my voluptuous mind! I am justly punish'd.

---

[5] Chaste.   [6] Into smoke.   [7] An alembic of a particular shape.
[8] A globular flask.

FACE. And so am I, sir.

MAM.   Cast from all my hopes——

FACE. Nay, certainties, sir.

MAM.   By mine own base affections.

SUB. (*seeming to come to himself.*) O, the curst fruits of
    vice and lust!

MAM.   Good father,
It was my sin. Forgive it.

SUB.   Hangs my roof
Over us still, and will not fall, O justice,
Upon us, for this wicked man!

FACE.   Nay, look, sir,
You grieve him now with staying in his sight.
Good sir, the nobleman will come too, and take you,
And that may breed a tragedy.

MAM.   I'll go.

FACE. Ay, and repent at home, sir. It may be,
For some good penance you may ha' it yet;
A hundred pound to the box at Bethlem⁹——

MAM.   Yes.

FACE. For the restoring such as—ha' their wits.

MAM.   I'll do't.

FACE. I'll send one to you to receive it.

MAM.   Do.
Is no projection left?

FACE.   All flown, or stinks, sir.

MAM. Will nought be sav'd that's good for med'cine,
    think'st thou?

FACE. I cannot tell, sir. There will be perhaps
Something about the scraping of the shards,
Will cure the itch,—though not your itch of mind, sir.

                           [*Aside.*]
It shall be saved for you, and sent home. Good sir,
This way for fear the lord should meet you.

                       [*Exit* MAMMON.]

SUB.   [*raising his head.*] Face!

FACE. Ay.

SUB.   Is he gone?

FACE.   Yes, and as heavily

⁹ The lunatic asylum.

As all the gold he hop'd for were in's blood.
Let us be light though.

SUB. [*leaping up*.]   Ay, as balls, and bound
And hit our heads against the roof for joy:
There's so much of our care now cast away.

FACE. Now to our don.

SUB.   Yes, your young widow by this time
Is made a countess, Face; she's been in travail
Of a young heir for you.

FACE.   Good, sir.

SUB.   Off with your case,[10]
And greet her kindly, as a bridegroom should,
After these common hazards.

FACE.   Very well, sir.
Will you go fetch Don Diego off the while?

SUB. And fetch him over too, if you'll be pleas'd, sir.
Would Dol were in her place, to pick his pockets now!

FACE. Why, you can do't as well, if you would set to't.
I pray you prove your virtue.[11]

SUB.   For your sake, sir.   [*Exeunt.*]

SCENE VI[1]

[*Enter*] SURLY *and* Dame PLIANT

SUR. Lady, you see into what hands you are fall'n;
'Mongst what a nest of villains! and how near
Your honour was t'have catch'd a certain clap,
Through your credulity, had I but been
So punctually forward, as place, time,
And other circumstances would ha' made a man;
For you're a handsome woman: would you were wise too!
I am a gentleman come here disguis'd,
Only to find the knaveries of this citadel;
And where I might have wrong'd your honour, and have not,
I claim some interest in your love. You are,
They say, a widow, rich; and I'm a bachelor,
Worth nought: your fortunes may make me a man,

[10] His costume as Lungs.   [11] Capacity.
[1] Another room in the same.

As mine ha' preserv'd you a woman. Think upon it,
And whether I have deserv'd you or no.

DAME P.   I will, sir.

SUR. And for these household-rogues, let me alone
To treat with them.

[*Enter* SUBTLE.]

SUB.   How doth my noble Diego,
And my dear madam countess? Hath the count
Been courteous, lady? liberal and open?
Donzel,[2] methinks you look melancholic,
I do not like the dulness of your eye;
It hath a heavy cast, 'tis upsee Dutch,[3]
And says you are lumpish.
Be lighter, I will make your pockets so.

                        (*He falls to picking of them.*)

SUR. [*Throws open his cloak.*] Will you, don bawd and
     pick-purse? [*Strikes him down.*] How now! Reel
     you?
Stand up, sir, you shall find, since I am so heavy,
I'll give you equal weight.

SUB.   Help! murder!

SUR.   No, sir,
There's no such thing intended. A good cart[4]
And a clean whip shall ease you of that fear.
I am the Spanish don *that should be cozened,*
Do you see? Cozened? Where's your Captain Face,
That parcel[5]-broker, and whole-bawd, all rascal?

[*Enter* FACE *in his uniform.*] .

FACE. How, Surly!

SUR.   O, make your approach, good captain.
I have found from whence your copper rings and spoons
Come now, wherewith you cheat abroad in taverns.
'Twas here you learn'd t'anoint your boot with brimstone,
Then rub men's gold on't for a kind of touch,
And say 'twas naught, when you had changed the colour,
That you might ha't for nothing. And this doctor,

---

[2] Diminutive of Don.   [3] As if you had been drinking heavy Dutch beer.
[4] Referring to the punishment inflicted on bawds.   [5] Part.

Your sooty, smoky-bearded compeer, he
Will close you so much gold, in a bolt's-head,
And, on a turn, convey i' the stead another
With sublim'd mercury, that shall burst in the heat,
And fly out all *in fumo!* Then weeps Mammon;
Then swoons his worship. [FACE *slips out.*] Or, he is the Faustus,
That casteth figures[6] and can conjure, cures
Plagues, piles, and pox, by the ephemerides,[7]
And holds intelligence with all the bawds
And midwives of three shires: while you send in——
Captain!—what! is he gone?—damsels with child,
Wives that are barren, or the waiting-maid
With the green sickness. [*Seizes* SUBTLE *as he is retiring.*]
        —Nay, sir, you must tarry,
Though he be scap'd; and answer by the ears, sir.

SCENE VII[1]

[*Re-enter*] FACE *with* KASTRIL [*to*] SURLY *and* SUBTLE

FACE. Why, now's the time, if ever you will quarrel
Well, as they say, and be a true-born child:
The doctor and your sister both are abus'd.[2]
    KAS. Where is he? Which is he? He is a slave,
Whate'er he is, and the son of a whore.—Are you
The man, sir, I would know?
    SUR.   I should be loth, sir,
To confess so much.
    KAS.   Then you lie i' your throat.
    SUR.   How!
    FACE. [*to* KASTRIL.] A very arrant rogue, sir, and a cheater,
Employ'd here by another conjurer
That does not love the doctor, and would cross him
If he knew how.
    SUR.   Sir, you are abus'd.
    KAS.   You lie:
And 'tis no matter.

        [6] Horoscopes.   [7] Astrological almanacs.
        [1] The same.   [2] Cheated.

FACE.   Well said, sir!   He is
The impudent'st rascal——

SUR.   You are indeed.   Will you hear me, sir?

FACE. By no means: bid him be gone.

KAS.   Begone, sir, quickly.

SUR. This is strange!—Lady, do you inform your brother.

FACE. There is not such a foist[3] in all the town.
The doctor had him presently; and finds yet
The Spanish count will come here.—Bear up, Subtle.

                                    [*Aside.*]

SUB. Yes, sir, he must appear within this hour.

FACE. And yet this rogue would come in a disguise,
By the temptation of another spirit,
To trouble our art, though he could not hurt it!

KAS.   Ay,
I know—Away, [*to his sister.*]. you talk like a foolish
     mauther.[4]

SUR. Sir, all is truth she says.

FACE.   Do not believe him, sir.
He is the lying'st swabber!   Come your ways, sir.

SUR. You are valiant out of company!

KAS.   Yes, how then, sir?

       [*Enter* DRUGGER *with a piece of damask.*]

FACE. Nay, here's an honest fellow too that knows him,
And all his tricks.   Make good what I say, Abel,
This cheater would ha' cozen'd thee o' the widow.—

                            [*Aside to* DRUG.]
He owes this honest Drugger here seven pound,
He has had on him in twopenny'orths of tobacco.

DRUG. Yes, sir.   And he has damn'd himself three terms
     to pay me.

FACE. And what does he owe for lotium?[5]

DRUG.   Thirty shillings, sir;
And for six syringes.

SUR.   Hydra of villainy!

FACE. Nay, sir, you must quarrel him out o' the house.

KAS.   I will:

---

     [3] Rascal.   [4] Girl.   [5] A lotion.

—Sir, if you get not out o' doors, you lie;
And you are a pimp.

SUR.   Why, this is madness, sir,
Not valour in you; I must laugh at this.

KAS. It is my humour; you are a pimp and a trig.[6]
And an *Amadis de Gaul,* or a Don Quixote.

DRUG. Or a knight o' the curious coxcomb, do you see?

[*Enter* ANANIAS.]

ANA. Peace to the household!

KAS.   I'll keep peace for no man.

ANA. Casting of dollars is concluded lawful.

KAS. Is he the constable?

SUB.   Peace, Ananias.

FACE.   No, sir.

KAS. Then you are an otter, and a shad, a whit,
A very tim.[7]

SUR.   You'll hear me, sir?

KAS.   I will not.

ANA. What is the motive?

SUB.   Zeal in the young gentleman,
Against his Spanish slops.

ANA.   They are profane,
Lewd, superstitious, and idolatrous breeches.

SUR. New rascals!

KAS.   Will you be gone, sir?

ANA.   Avoid, Sathan!
Thou art not of the light! That ruff of pride
About thy neck, betrays thee; and is the same
With that which the unclean birds, in seventy-seven,[8]
Were seen to prank it with on divers coasts:
Thou look'st like antichrist, in that lewd hat.

SUR. I must give way.

KAS.   Be gone, sir.

SUR.   But I'll take
A course with you——

ANA.   Depart, proud Spanish fiend!

SUR. Captain and doctor.

[6] Dandy.   [7] Kastril's terms of abuse are not meant to be appropriate.
[8] The allusion here has not been explained.

ANA.   Child of perdition!

KAS. Hence, sir!—   [*Exit* SURLY.]
Did I not quarrel bravely?

FACE.   Yes, indeed, sir.

KAS. Nay, an I give my mind to't, I shall do't.

FACE. O, you must follow, sir, and threaten him tame:
He'll turn again else.

KAS.   ·   I'll re-turn him then.   [*Exit.*]

FACE. Drugger, this rogue prevented us, for thee:
We had determin'd that thou should'st ha' come
In a Spanish suit, and ha' carried her so; and he,
A brokerly slave, goes, puts it on himself.
Hast brought the damask?

DRUG.   Yes, sir.

FACE.   Thou must borrow
A Spanish suit. Hast thou no credit with the players?

DRUG. Yes, sir; did you never see me play the Fool?

FACE. I know not, Nab:—thou shalt, if I can help it.—
                                                [*Aside.*]
Hieronimo's[9] old cloak, ruff, and hat will serve;
I'll tell thee more when thou bring'st 'em.

                    [*Exit* DRUGGER.] SUBTLE *hath whisper'd with*
                         ANAN. *this while*

ANA.   Sir, I know.
The Spaniard hates the brethren, and hath spies
Upon their actions: and that this was one
I make no scruple.—But the holy synod
Have been in prayer and meditation for it;
And 'tis reveal'd no less to them than me,
That casting of money is most lawful.

SUB.   True.
But here I cannot do it: if the house
Should chance to be suspected, all would out,
And we be lock'd up in the Tower for ever,
To make gold there for th' state, never come out;
And then are you defeated.

ANA.   I will tell
This to the elders and the weaker brethren,
That the whole company of the separation

                    [9] In Kyd's *Spanish Tragedy.*

May join in humble prayer again.

SUB.   And fasting.

ANA. Yea, for some fitter place. The peace of mind
Rest with these walls!   [*Exit.*]

SUB.   Thanks, courteous Ananias.

FACE. What did he come for?

SUB.   About casting dollars,
Presently out of hand. And so I told him,
A Spanish minister came here to spy,
Against the faithful——

FACE.   I conceive. Come, Subtle,
Thou art so down upon the least disaster!
How wouldst thou ha' done, if I had not help'd thee out?

SUB. I thank thee, Face, for the angry boy, i' faith.

FACE. Who would ha' look'd[10] it should ha' been that rascal
Surly? He had dy'd his beard and all. Well, sir.
Here's damask come to make you a suit.

SUB.   Where's Drugger?

FACE. He is gone to borrow me a Spanish habit;
I'll be the count now.

SUB.   But where's the widow?

FACE. Within, with my lord's sister; Madam Dol
Is entertaining her.

SUB.   By you favour, Face,
Now she is honest, I will stand again.

FACE. You will not offer it?

SUB.   Why?

FACE. .   Stand to your word,
Or—here comes Dol. She knows——

SUB.   You're tyrannous still.

[*Enter* DOL *hastily*]

FACE.—Strict for my right.—How now, Dol! Hast told
    her,
The Spanish count will come?

DOL.   Yes; but another is come,
You little looked for!

FACE.   Who's that?

DOL.   Your master;

10 Expected.

The master of the house.

SUB.   How, Dol!

FACE.   She lies,
This is some trick. Come, leave your quiblins,[11] Dorothy.

DOL. Look out and see. [FACE *goes to the window.*]

SUB.   Art thou in earnest?

DOL.   'Slight,
Forty o' the neighbours are about him, talking.

FACE. 'Tis he, by this good day.

DOL.   'Twill prove ill day
For some on us.

FACE.   We are undone, and taken.

DOL. Lost, I'm afraid.

SUB.   You said he would not come,
While there died one a week within the liberties.[12]

FACE. No: 'twas within the walls.

SUB.   Was't so! cry you mercy
I thought the liberties. What shall we do now, Face?

FACE. Be silent: not a word, if he call or knock.
I'll into mine old shape again and meet him,
Of Jeremy, the butler. I' the meantime,
Do you two pack up all the goods and purchase[13]
That we can carry i' the two trunks. I'll keep him
Off for to-day, if I cannot longer: and then
At night, I'll ship you both away to Ratcliff,
Where we will meet to-morrow, and there we'll share.
Let Mammon's brass and pewter keep the cellar;
We'll have another time for that. But, Dol,
Prithee go heat a little water quickly;
Subtle must shave me. All my captain's beard
Must off, to make me appear smooth Jeremy.
You'll do it?

SUB.   Yes, I'll shave you as well as I can.

FACE. And not cut my throat, but trim me?

SUB.   You shall see, sir. [*Exeunt.*]

[11] Quibbles.
[12] The district outside the walls subject to the city authorities.
[13] Stolen goods, booty.

THE ALCHEMIST

ACT V

Scene I[1]

[*Enter*] Lovewit, [*with several of the*] Neighbours

Love. Has there been such resort, say you?

1 Nei.   Daily, sir.

2 Nei. And nightly, too.

3 Nei.   Ay, some as brave as lords.

4 Nei. Ladies and gentlewomen.

5 Nei.   Citizens' wives.

1 Nei. And knights.

6 Nei.   In coaches.

2 Nei.   Yes, and oyster-women.

1 Nei. Beside other gallants.

3 Nei.   Sailors' wives.

4 Nei.   Tobacco men.

5 Nei. Another Pimlico![2]

Love.   What should my knave advance,
To draw this company? He hung out no banners
Of a strange calf with five legs to be seen,
Or a huge lobster with six claws?

6 Nei.   No, sir.

3 Nei. We had gone in then, sir.

Love.   He has no gift
Of teaching i' the nose[3] that e'er I knew of.
You saw no bills set up that promis'd cure
Of agues, or the tooth-ache?

2 Nei.   No such thing, sir!

Love. Nor heard a drum struck for baboons or puppets?

5 Nei. Neither, sir.

Love.   What device should he bring forth now?
I love a teeming wit as I love my nourishment:
'Pray God he have not kept such open house,
That he hath sold my hangings, and my bedding!
I left him nothing else. If he have eat 'em,
A plague o' the moth, say I! Sure he has got
Some bawdy pictures to call all this ging;[4]

---

[1] Before Lovewit's door.
[2] A summer resort, where the citizens had cakes and ale.
[3] Like a Puritan preacher.   [4] Gang.

The Friar and the Nun; or the new motion[a]
Of the knight's courser and the parson's mare;
Or 't may be, he has the fleas that run at tilt
Upon a table, or some dog to dance.
When saw you him?

1 NEI.   Who, sir, Jeremy?

2 NEI.   Jeremy butler?
We saw him not this month.

LOVE.   How!

4 NEI.   Not these five weeks, sir.

6 NEI. These six weeks at the least.

LOVE.   You amaze me, neighbours!

5 NEI. Sure, if your worship know not where he is,
He's slipt away.

6 NEI.   Pray God he be not made away.

LOVE. Ha! it's no time to question, then.

           (*Knocks at the door.*)

6 NEI.   About
Some three weeks since I heard a doleful cry,
As I sat up a mending my wife's stockings.

LOVE. 'Tis strange that none will answer! Did'st thou hear
A cry, sayst thou?

6 NEI.   Yes, sir, like unto a man
That had been strangled an hour, and could not speak.

2 NEI. I heard it too, just this day three weeks, at two
   o'clock
Next morning.

LOVE.   These be miracles, or you make 'em so!
A man an hour strangled, and could not speak,
And both you heard him cry?

3 NEI.   Yes, downward, sir.

LOVE. Thou art a wise fellow. Give me thy hand, I pray
   thee.
What trade art thou on?

3 NEI.   A smith, an't please your worship.

LOVE. A smith! Then lend me thy help to get this door open.

3 NEI. That I will presently, sir, but fetch my tools—

             [*Exit.*]

1 NEI. Sir, best to knock again afore you break it.

      [a] Puppet show.

SCENE II[1]

LOVEWIT, Neighbours

LOVE. [*knocks again.*] I will.

[*Enter* FACE *in his butler's livery*]

FACE.   What mean you sir?

1, 2, 4 NEI.   O, here's Jeremy!

FACE. Good sir, come from the door.

LOVE.   Why, what's the matter?

FACE. Yet farther, you are too near yet.

LOVE.   In the name of wonder,
What means the fellow!

FACE.   The house, sir, has been visited.

LOVE. What, with the plague? Stand thou then farther.

FACE.   No, sir,
I had it not.

LOVE.   Who had it then? I left
None else but thee i' the house.

FACE.   Yes, sir, my fellow,
The cat that kept the buttery, had it on her
A week before I spied it; but I got her
Convey'd away i' the night: and so I shut
The house up for a month——

LOVE.   How!

FACE.   Purposing then, sir,
To have burnt rose-vinegar, treacle, and tar,
And have made it sweet, that you should ne'er ha' known it;
Because I knew the news would but afflict you, sir.

LOVE. Breathe less, and farther off! Why this is stranger:
The neighbours tell me all here that the doors
Have still been open——

FACE.   How, sir!

LOVE.   Gallants, men and women,
And of all sorts, tag-rag, been seen to flock here
In threaves,[2] these ten weeks, as to a second Hogsden,
In days of Pimlico and Eye-bright.[3]

FACE.   Sir,

[1] The same.   [2] Lit., two dozen sheaves; droves.
[3] A suburban tavern, eclipsed as a resort by Pimlico.

Their wisdoms will not say so.

LOVE.   To-day they speak
Of coaches and gallants; one in a French hood
Went in, they tell me; and another was seen
In a velvet gown at the window: divers more
Pass in and out.

FACE.   They did pass through the doors then,
Or walls, I assure their eye-sights, and their spectacles;
For here, sir, are the keys, and here have been,
In this my pocket, now above twenty days!
And for before, I kept the fort alone there.
But that 'tis yet not deep i' the afternoon,
I should believe my neighbours had seen double
Through the black pot,[*] and made these apparitions!
For, on my faith to your worship, for these three weeks
And upwards, the door has not been open'd.

LOVE.   Strange!

1 NEI. Good faith, I think I saw a coach.

2 NEI.   And I too,
I'd ha' been sworn.

LOVE.   Do you but think it now?
And but one coach?

4 NEI.   We cannot tell, sir: Jeremy
Is a very honest fellow.

FACE.   Did you see me at all?

1 NEI. No; that we are sure on.

2 NEI.   I'll be sworn o' that.

LOVE. Fine rogues to have your testimonies built on!

[Re-enter third Neighbour, with his tools]

3 NEI. Is Jeremy come!

1 NEI.   O yes; you may leave your tools:
We were deceiv'd, he says.

2 NEI.   He has had the keys;
And the door has been shut these three weeks.

3 NEI.   Like enough

LOVE. Peace, and get hence, you changelings.

                    [*] With drinking.

[*Enter* SURLY *and* MAMMON]

FACE.   [*Aside.*] Surly come!
And Mammon made acquainted! They'll tell all.
How shall I beat them off? What shall I do?
Nothing's more wretched than a guilty conscience.

SCENE III[1]

SURLY, MAMMON, LOVEWIT, FACE, Neighbours

SUR. No, sir, he was a great physician. This,
It was no bawdy-house, but a mere chancel!
You knew the lord and his sister.
MAM.   Nay, good Surly.——
SUR. The happy word, BE RICH——
MAM.   Play not the tyrant.—
SUR. Should be to-day pronounc'd to all your friends.
And where be your andirons now? And your brass pots,
That should have been golden flagons, and great wedges?
MAM. Let me but breathe. What, they have shut their
       doors,
Methinks!   (*He and* SURLY *knock.*)
SUR.   Ay, now 'tis holiday with them.
MAM.   Rogues,
Cozeners, impostors, bawds!
FACE.   What mean you, sir?
MAM. To enter if we can.
FACE.   Another man's house!
Here is the owner, sir; turn you to him,
And speak your business.
MAM.   Are you, sir, the owner?
LOVE. Yes, sir.
MAM.   And are those knaves within your cheaters!
LOVE. What knaves, what cheaters?
MAM.   Subtle and his Lungs.
FACE. The gentleman is distracted, sir! No lungs
Nor lights ha' been seen here these three weeks, sir,
Within these doors, upon my word.
SUR.   Your word,

                         [1] The same.

Groom arrogant!

FACE.   Yes, sir, I am the housekeeper,
And know the keys have not been out o' my hands.

SUR. This is a new Face.

FACE.   You do mistake the house, sir:
What sign was't at?

SUR.   You rascal! This is one
Of the confederacy. Come, let's get officers,
And force the door.

LOVE.   Pray you stay, gentlemen.

SUR. No, sir, we'll come with warrant.

MAM.   Ay, and then
We shall ha' your doors open.   [*Exeunt* MAM. *and* SUR.]

LOVE.   What means this?

FACE. I cannot tell, sir.

1 NEI.   These are two o' the gallants
That we do think we saw.

FACE.   Two o' the fools!
You talk as idly as they. Good faith, sir,
I think the moon has craz'd 'em all.—[*Aside.*] O me,

[*Enter* KASTRIL]

The angry boy come too! He'll make a noise,
And ne'er away till he have betray'd us all.

KAS. (*knocking.*) What rogues, bawds, slaves, you'll open
    the door, anon!
Punk, cockatrice, my suster! By this light
I'll fetch the marshal to you.

FACE.   Who would you speak with, sir?

KAS. The bawdy doctor, and the cozening captain,
And puss my suster.

LOVE.   This is something, sure.

FACE. Upon my trust, the doors were never open, sir.

KAS. I have heard all their tricks told me twice over,
By the fat knight and the lean gentleman.

LOVE. Here comes another.

[*Enter* ANANIAS *and* TRIBULATION]

FACE.   Ananias too!
And his pastor!

TRI. (*beating at the door.*)   The doors are shut against us.

ANA. Come forth, you seed of sulphur, sons of fire!
Your stench it is broke forth; abomination
Is in the house.

KAS.   Ay, my suster's there.

ANA.   The place,
It is become a cage of unclean birds.

KAS. Yes, I will fetch the scavenger, and the constable.

TRI. You shall do well.

ANA.   We'll join to weed them out.

KAS. You will not come then, punk devise,[2] my suster!

ANA. Call her not sister; she's a harlot verily.

KAS. I'll raise the street.

LOVE.   Good gentleman, a word.

ANA. Satan avoid, and hinder not our zeal!

          [*Exeunt* ANA., TRIB., *and* KAST.]

LOVE. The world's turned Bethlem.

FACE.   These are all broke loose,
Out of St. Katherine's, where they use to keep
The better sort of mad-folks.

1 NEI.   All these persons
We saw go in and out here.

2 NEI.   Yes, indeed, sir.

3 NEI. These were the parties.

FACE.   Peace, you drunkards! Sir,
I wonder at it. Please you to give me leave
To touch the door; I'll try an the lock be chang'd.

LOVE. It mazes me!

FACE. [*goes to the door.*] Good faith, sir, I believe
There's no such thing: 'tis all *deceptio visus.*[3]—
[*Aside.*] Would I could get him away.

DAP. [*within.*] Master captain! Master doctor!

LOVE. Who's that?

FACE. [*Aside.*] Our clerk within, that I forgot!—I know
     not, sir.

          [2] Perfect harlot.   [3] Optical illusion.

DAP. [*within.*] For God's sake, when will her grace be at
    leisure?

FACE.   Ha!

Illusions, some spirit o' the air!—[*Aside.*] His gag is melted,
And now he sets out the throat.

DAP.   [*within.*] I am almost stifled——

FACE. [*Aside.*] Would you were together.

LOVE.   'Tis in the house.
Ha! list.

FACE. Believe it, sir, i' the air.

LOVE.   Peace, you.

DAP. [*within.*] Mine aunt's grace does not use me well.

SUB.   [*within*] You fool,
Peace, you'll mar all.

FACE. [*speaks through the keyhole, while* LOVEWIT *ad-
    vances to the door unobserved.*] Or you will else,
    you rogue.

LOVE. O, is it so? Then you converse with spirits!—
Come, sir. No more of your tricks, good Jeremy.
The truth, the shortest way.

FACE.   Dismiss this rabble, sir.—
[*Aside.*] What shall I do? I am catch'd.

LOVE.   Good neighbours,
I thank you all. You may depart. [*Exeunt* Neighbours.]—
    Come, sir,
You know that I am an indulgent master;
And therefore conceal nothing. What's your medicine,
To draw so many several sorts of wild fowl?

FACE. Sir, you were wont to affect mirth and wit—
But here's no place to talk on't i' the street.
Give me but leave to make the best of my fortune,
And only pardon me th' abuse of your house:
It's all I beg. I'll help you to a widow,
In recompense, that you shall give me thanks for,
Will make you seven years younger, and a rich one.
'Tis but your putting on a Spanish cloak:
I have her within. You need not fear the house;
It was not visited.

LOVE.   But by me, who came
Sooner than you expected.

FACE.   It is true, sir.
'Pray you forgive me.

LOVE.   Well: let's see your widow. [*Exeunt.*]

SCENE IV[1]

[*Enter*] SUBTLE, [*leading in*] DAPPER, [*with his eyes bound as before*]

SUB. How! have you eaten your gag?

DAP.   Yes, faith, it crumbled
Away in my mouth.

SUB. You ha' spoil'd all then.

DAP.   No!
I hope my aunt of Fairy will forgive me.

SUB. Your aunt's a gracious lady; but in troth
You were to blame.

DAP.   The fume did overcome me,
And I did do't to stay my stomach. 'Pray you
So satisfy her grace.

[*Enter* FACE *in his uniform*]
           Hear comes the captain.

FACE. How now! Is his mouth down?

SUB.   Ay, he has spoken!

FACE. A pox, I heard him, and you too. He's undone
    then.—
[*Aside to* SUBTLE.] I have been fain to say, the house is
    haunted
With spirits, to keep churl back.

SUB.   And hast thou done it?

FACE. Sure, for this night.

SUB.   Why, then triumph and sing
Of Face so famous, the precious king
Of present wits.

FACE.   Did you not hear the coil
About the door?

SUB.   Yes, and I dwindled[2] with it.

---

[1] A room in the same.   [2] Shrank with fear.

FACE. Show him his aunt, and let him be dispatch'd:
I'll send her to you.   [*Exit* FACE.]
    SUB.   Well, sir, your aunt her grace
Will give you audience presently, on my suit,
And the captain's word that you did not eat your gag
In any contempt of her highness.   [*Unbinds his eyes.*]
    DAP.   Not I, in troth, sir.

        [*Enter*] DOL *like the Queen of Fairy*

    SUB. Here she is come. Down o' your knees and wriggle:
She has a stately presence. [DAPPER *kneels and shuffles
        towards her.*] Good! Yet nearer,
And bid, God save you!
    DAP.   Madam!
    SUB.   And your aunt.
    DAP. And my most gracious aunt, God save your grace.
    DOL. Nephew, we thought to have been angry with you;
But that sweet face of yours hath turn'd the tide,
And made it flow with joy, that ebb'd of love.
Arise, and touch our velvet gown.
    SUB.   The skirts,
And kiss 'em. So!
    DOL. Let me now stroke that head.
*Much, nephew, shalt thou win, much shalt thou spend;
Much shalt thou give away, much shalt thou lend.*
    SUB. [*Aside.*] Ay, much! indeed.—Why do you not thank
        her grace?
    DAP. I cannot speak for joy.
    SUB.   See, the kind wretch!
Your grace's kinsman right.
    DOL.   Give me the bird.
Here is your fly in a purse, about your neck, cousin;
Wear it, and feed it about this day sev'n-night,
On your right wrist——
    SUB.   Open a vein with a pin,
And let it suck but once a week; till then,
You must not look on't.
    DOL.   No: and, kinsman,
Bear yourself worthy of the blood you come on.

SUB. Her grace would ha' you eat no more Woolsack[3] pies,
Nor Dagger[3] frumety.[4]

DOL. Nor break his fast
In Heaven[3] and Hell.[3]

SUB. She's with you everywhere!
Nor play with costermongers, at mumchance,[5] traytrip,[5]
God-make-you-rich[5] (when as your aunt has done it); but keep
The gallant'st company, and the best games——

DAP. Yes, sir.

SUB. Gleek[5] and primero;[5] and what you get, be true to us.

DAP. By this hand, I will.

SUB. You may bring's a thousand pound
Before to-morrow night, if but three thousand
Be stirring, an you will.

DAP. I swear I will then.

SUB. Your fly will learn you all games.

FACE. [within.] Ha' you done there?

SUB. Your grace will command him no more duties?

DOL. No:
But come, and see me often. I may chance
To leave him three or four hundred chests of treasure,
And some twelve thousand acres of fairy land,
If he game well and comely with good gamesters.

SUB. There's a kind aunt: kiss her departing part.—
But you must sell your forty mark a year now.

DAP. Ay, sir, I mean.

SUB. Or, give 't away; pox on't!

DAP. I'll give 't mine aunt. I'll go and fetch the writings. [Exit.]

SUB. 'Tis well; away.

[Re-enter FACE]

FACE. Where's Subtle?

SUB. Here: what news?

FACE. Drugger is at the door, go take his suit,
And bid him fetch a parson presently.
Say he shall marry the widow. Thou shalt spend

---

[3] Names of taverns.   [4] Wheat boiled in milk.   [5] Games of chance.

A hundred pound by the service! [*Exit* SUBTLE.]   Now,
    Queen Dol,
Have you pack'd up all?
    DOL.   Yes.
    FACE.   And how do you like
The Lady Pliant?
    DOL.   A good dull innocent.

[*Re-enter* SUBTLE]

    SUB. Here's your Hieronimo's cloak and hat.
    FACE.   Give me 'em.
    SUB. And the ruff too?
    FACE.   Yes; I'll come to you presently.   [*Exit.*]
    SUB. Now he is gone about his project, Dol,
I told you of, for the widow.
    DOL.   'Tis direct
Against our articles.
    SUB.   Well, we will fit him, wench.
Hast thou gull'd her of her jewels or her bracelets?
    DOL. No; but I will do 't.
    SUB.   Soon at night, my Dolly,
When we are shipp'd, and all our goods aboard,
Eastward for Ratcliff, we will turn our course
To Brainford, westward, if thou sayst the word,
And take our leaves of this o'erweening rascal,
This peremptory Face.
    DOL.   Content; I'm weary of him.
    SUB. Thou'st cause, when the slave will run a wiving, Dol,
Against the instrument that was drawn between us.
    DOL. I'll pluck his bird as bare as I can.
    SUB.   Yes, tell her
She must by any means address some present
To the cunning man, make him amends for wronging
His art with her suspicion; send a ring,
Or chain of pearl; she will be tortur'd else
Extremely in her sleep, say, and have strange things
Come to her. Wilt thou?
    DOL.   Yes.
    SUB.   My fine flitter-mouse,[e]

* Bat.

My bird o' the night! We'll tickle it at the Pigeons,[7]
When we have all, and may unlock the trunks,
And say, this 's mine, and thine; and thine, and mine.

They kiss.

Re-enter FACE

FACE. What now! a billing?
SUB.   Yes, a little exalted
In the good passage of our stock-affairs.
FACE. Drugger has brought his parson; take him in,
    Subtle,
And send Nab back again to wash his face.
SUB. I will: and shave himself?   *[Exit.]*
FACE.   If you can get him.
DOL. You are hot upon it, Face, whate'er it is!
FACE. A trick that Dol shall spend ten pound a month by.

[Re-enter SUBTLE]

Is he gone?
SUB.   The chaplain waits you in the hall, sir.
FACE. I'll go bestow him.   *[Exit.]*
DOL.   He'll now marry her instantly.
SUB. He cannot yet, he is not ready. Dear Dol,
Cozen her of all thou canst. To deceive him
Is no deceit, but justice, that would break
Such an inextricable tie as ours was.
DOL. Let me alone to fit him.

[Re-enter FACE]

FACE.   Come, my venturers,
You ha' pack'd up all? Where be the trunks? Bring forth.
SUB. Here.
FACE.   Let us see 'em. Where's the money?
SUB.   Here,
In this.
FACE. Mammon's ten pound; eight score before:
The brethren's money this. Drugger's and Dapper's.
What paper's that?
DOL.   The jewel of the waiting maid's,

[7] An inn at Brentford.

That stole it from her lady, to know certain——

FACE. If she should have precedence of her mistress.

DOL.   Yes.

FACE. What box is that?

SUB.   The fish-wives' rings, I think,
And th' ale-wives' single money.[8] Is't not, Dol?

DOL. Yes; and the whistle that the sailor's wife
Brought you to know an her husband were with Ward.[9]

FACE. We'll wet it to-morrow; and our silver beakers
And tavern cups. Where be the French petticoats
And girdles and hangers?

SUB.   Here, i' the trunk,
And the bolts of lawn.

FACE.   Is Drugger's damask there,
And the tobacco?

SUB.   Yes.

FACE.   Give me the keys.

DOL. Why you the keys?

SUB.   No matter, Dol; because
We shall not open them before he comes.

FACE. 'Tis true, you shall not open them, indeed;
Nor have 'em forth, do you see? Not forth, Dol.

DOL.   No!

FACE. No, my smock-rampant. The right is, my master
Knows all, has pardon'd me, and he will keep 'em.
Doctor, 'tis true—you look—for all your figures:
I sent for him, indeed. Wherefore, good partners,
Both he and she be satisfied; for here
Determines[10] the indenture tripartite
'Twixt Subtle, Dol, and Face. All I can do
Is to help you over the wall, o' the back-side,
Or lend you a sheet to save your velvet gown, Dol.
Here will be officers presently, bethink you
Of some course suddenly to scape the dock;
For thither you will come else. (*Some knock.*) Hark you,
          thunder.

SUB. You are a precious fiend!

OFFI.   [*without.*] Open the door.

FACE. Dol, I am sorry for thee i' faith; but hear'st thou?

[8] Small change.   [9] A famous pirate.   [10] Ends.

It shall go hard but I will place thee somewhere:
Thou shalt ha' my letter to Mistress Amo——

DOL. Hang you!

FACE. Or Madam Cæsarean.

DOL. Pox upon you, rogue,
Would I had but time to beat thee!

FACE. Subtle,
Let's know where you set up next; I will send you
A customer now and then, for old acquaintance.
What new course have you?

SUB. Rogue, I'll hang myself;
That I may walk a greater devil than thou,
And haunt thee i' the flock-bed and the buttery. [*Exeunt.*]

SCENE V[1]

[*Enter*] LOVEWIT [*in the Spanish dress, with the* Parson.
Loud knocking at the door]

LOVE. What do you mean, my masters?

MAM. [*without.*] Open your door,
Cheaters, bawds, conjurers.

OFFI. [*without.*] Or we will break it open.

LOVE. What warrant have you?

OFFI. [*without.*] Warrant enough, sir, doubt not,
If you'll not open it.

LOVE. Is there an officer there?

OFFI. [*without.*] Yes, two or three for failing.[2]

LOVE. Have but patience,
And I will open it straight.

[*Enter* FACE, *as butler*]

FACE. Sir, ha' you done?
Is it a marriage? Perfect?

LOVE. Yes, my brain.

FACE. Off with your ruff and cloak then; be yourself, sir.

SUR. [*without.*] Down with the door.

KAS. [*without.*] 'Slight, ding[3] it open.

---

[1] An outer room in the same. [2] For fear of failing. [3] Break.

LOVE.   [*opening the door.*] Hold,
Hold, gentlemen, what means this violence?

[MAMMON, SURLY, KASTRIL, ANANIAS, TRIBULATION, *and*
                    Officers *rush in*]

MAM. Where is this collier?
SUR.   And my Captain Face?
MAM. These day owls.
SUR.   That are birding[4] in men's purses.
MAM. Madam Suppository.
KAS.   Doxy, my suster.
ANA.   Locusts
Of the foul pit.
TRI.   Profane as Bel and the Dragon.
ANA. Worse than the grasshoppers, or the lice of Egypt.
LOVE. Good gentlemen, hear me. Are you officers,
And cannot stay this violence?
1 OFFI.   Keep the peace.
LOVE. Gentlemen, what is the matter? Whom do you seek?
MAM. The chemical cozener.
SUR.   And the captain pander.
KAS. The nun my suster.
MAM.   Madam Rabbi.
ANA.   Scorpions,
And caterpillars.
LOVE.   Fewer at once, I pray you.
1 OFFI. One after another, gentlemen, I charge you,
By virtue of my staff.
ANA.   They are the vessels
Of pride, lust, and the cart.
LOVE.   Good zeal, lie still
A little while.
TRI.   Peace, Deacon Ananias.
LOVE. The house is mine here, and the doors are open;
If there be any such persons as you seek for,
Use your authority, search on o' God's name.
I am but newly come to town, and finding
This tumult 'bout my door, to tell you true,
It somewhat maz'd me; till my man here, fearing

                    [4] Stealing.

My more displeasure, told me he had done
Somewhat an insolent part, let out my house
(Belike presuming on my known aversion
From any air o' the town while there was sickness),
To a doctor and a captain: who, what they are
Or where they be, he knows not.

    MAM.   Are they gone?

    LOVE. You may go in and search, sir. [MAMMON, ANA.,
        and TRIB. *go in.*] Here, I find
The empty walls worse than I left 'em, smok'd,
A few crack'd pots, and glasses, and a furnace;
The ceiling fill'd with poesies of the candle,
And " Madam with a dildo "[5] writ o' the walls.
Only one gentlewoman I met here
That is within, that said she was a widow——

    KAS. Ay, that's my suster; I'll go thump her. Where
      is she?   [*Goes in.*]

    LOVE. And should ha' married a Spanish count, but he,
When he came to't, neglected her so grossly,
That I, a widower, am gone through with her.

    SUR. How! have I lost her then?

    LOVE.   Were you the don, sir?
Good faith, now she does blame you extremely, and says
You swore, and told her you had taken the pains
To dye your beard, and umber o'er your face,
Borrowed a suit, and ruff, all for her love:
And then did nothing. What an oversight
And want of putting forward, sir, was this!
Well fare an old harquebusier[6] yet,
Could prime his powder, and give fire, and hit,
All in a twinkling!

Re-enter MAMMON

    MAM.   The whole nest are fled!

    LOVE. What sort of birds were they?

    MAM.   A kind of choughs,[7]
Or thievish daws, sir, that have pick'd my purse
Of eight score and ten pounds within these five weeks,

[5] Probably a fragment of a song.   [6] Musketeer.   [7] Crow.

Beside my first materials; and my goods,
That lie i' the cellar, which I am glad they ha' left,
I may have home yet.

 LOVE.   Think you so, sir?

 MAM.   Ay.

 LOVE. By order of law, sir, but not otherwise.

 MAM. Not mine own stuff!

 LOVE.   Sir, I can take no knowledge
That they are yours, but by public means.
If you can bring certificate that you were gull'd of 'em,
Or any formal writ out of a court,
That you did cozen yourself, I will not hold them.

 MAM. I'll rather lose 'em.

 LOVE.   That you shall not, sir,
By me, in troth; upon these terms, they are yours.
What, should they ha' been, sir, turn'd into gold, all?

 MAM.   No.
I cannot tell.—It may be they should.—What then?

 LOVE. What a great loss in hope have you sustain'd!

 MAM. Not I, the commonwealth has.

 FACE.   Ay, he would ha' built
The city new; and made a ditch about it
Of silver, should have run with cream from Hogsden;
That every Sunday in Moorfields the younkers,
And tits[*] and tom-boys should have fed on, gratis.

 MAM. I will go mount a turnip-cart, and preach
The end of the world within these two months. Surly,
What! in a dream?

 SUR.   Must I needs cheat myself,
With that same foolish vice of honesty!
Come, let us go and hearken out the rogues:
That Face I'll mark for mine, if e'er I meet him.

 FACE. If I can hear of him, sir, I'll bring you word
Unto your lodging; for in troth, they were strangers
To me; I thought 'em honest as myself, sir.

       [*Exeunt* MAM. *and* SUR.]

    [*] Wenches.

[Re-enter ANANIAS *and* TRIBULATION]

TRI. 'Tis well, the saints shall not lose all yet. Go
And get some carts——

LOVE.   For what, my zealous friends?

ANA. To bear away the portion of the righteous
Out of this den of thieves.

LOVE.   What is that portion?

ANA. The goods sometimes the orphans', that the brethren
Bought with their silver pence.

LOVE.   What, those i' the cellar,
The knight Sir Mammon claims?

ANA.   I do defy
The wicked Mammon, so do all the brethren,
Thou profane man! I ask thee with what conscience
Thou canst advance that idol against us,
That have the seal?[8] Were not the shillings numb'red
That made the pounds; were not the pounds told out
Upon the second day of the fourth week,
In the eighth month, upon the table dormant,
The year of the last patience of the saints,
Six hundred and ten?

LOVE.   Mine earnest vehement botcher,
And deacon also, I cannot dispute with you:
But if you get you not away the sooner,
I shall confute you with a cudgel.

ANA.   Sir!

TRI. Be patient, Ananias.

ANA.   I am strong,
And will stand up, well girt, against an host
That threaten Gad in exile.

LOVE.   I shall send you
To Amsterdam, to your cellar.

ANA.   I will pray there,
Against thy house. May dogs defile thy walls,
And wasps and hornets breed beneath thy roof,
This seat of falsehood, and this cave of coz'nage!

                    [*Exeunt* ANA. *and* TRIB.

---

[8] That are sealed as God's people.

Enter DRUGGER

LOVE. Another too?

DRUG. Not I, sir, I am no brother.

LOVE. (*beats him.*) Away, you Harry Nicholas![10] do you
talk? [*Exit* DRUG.

FACE. No, this was Abel Drugger. Good sir, go,
(*To the* Parson.)
And satisfy him; tell him all is done:
He staid too long a washing of his face.
The doctor, he shall hear of him at Westchester;
And of the captain, tell him, at Yarmouth, or
Some good port-town else, lying for a wind. [*Exit* Parson.]
If you can get off the angry child now, sir——

[*Enter* KASTRIL, *dragging in his sister*]

KAS. Come on, you ewe, you have match'd most sweetly,
have you not?
Did not I say, I would never ha' you tupp'd
But by a dubb'd boy,[11] to make you a lady-tom?
'Slight, you are a mammet![12] O, I could touse you now.
Death, mun[13] you marry with a pox!

LOVE. You lie, boy;
As sound as you; and I'm aforehand with you.

KAS. Anon!

LOVE. Come, will you quarrel? I will feize[14] you, sirrah;
Why do you not buckle to your tools?

KAS. Od's light,
This is a fine old boy as e'er I saw!

LOVE. What, do you change your copy now? Proceed;
Here stands my dove: stoop[15] at her if you dare.

KAS. 'Slight, I must love him! I cannot choose, i' faith,
An I should be hang'd for't! Suster, I protest,
I honour thee for this match.

LOVE. O, do you so, sir?

KAS. Yes, an thou canst take tobacco and drink, old boy,

[10] The founder of the fanatical sect called "The Family of Love."
[11] Knight.   [12] Puppet.   [13] Must.   [14] Beat.
[15] A term of falconry: used in punning allusion to the name Kastril,
which means hawk.

I'll give her five hundred pound more to her marriage,
Than her own state.

    LOVE.   Fill a pipe full, Jeremy.

    FACE. Yes; but go in and take it, sir.

    LOVE.   We will.

I will be rul'd by thee in anything, Jeremy.

    KAS. 'Slight, thou art not hide-bound, thou art a jovy[16] boy!
Come, let us in, I pray thee, and take our whiffs.

    LOVE. Whiff in with your sister, brother boy. [*Exeunt* KAS.
        and Dame P.] That master
That had receiv'd such happiness by a servant,
In such a widow, and with so much wealth,
Were very ungrateful, if he would not be
A little indulgent to that servant's wit,
And help his fortune, though with some small strain
Of his own candour.[17] [*advancing.*] Therefore, gentlemen,
And kind spectators, if I have outstript
An old man's gravity, or strict canon, think
What a young wife and a good brain may do;
Stretch age's truth sometimes, and crack it too.
Speak for thyself, knave.

    FACE. So I will, sir. [*advancing to the front of the stage.*]
        Gentlemen,
My part a little fell in this last scene,
Yet 'twas decorum.[18] And though I am clean
Got off from Subtle, Surly, Mammon, Dol,
Hot Ananias, Dapper, Drugger, all
With whom I traded; yet I put myself
On you, that are my country:[19] and this pelf,
Which I have got, if you do quit me, rests
To feast you often, and invite new guests.   [*Exeunt.*]

    [16] Jovial.   [17] Fair reputation.   [18] Dramatic propriety.   [19] Jury.

PHILASTER

OR

LOVE LIES A-BLEEDING

BY

FRANCIS BEAUMONT AND JOHN FLETCHER

INTRODUCTORY NOTE

THE men who laid the foundations of the Elizabethan drama were generally of obscure origin; and though some of them had been educated at the universities, they were all poor. Beaumont and Fletcher are the first recruits to the profession of play-writing who came of distinguished families and habitually moved in wealthy circles; and this social environment was early suggested as an explanation of their power of representing naturally the conversation of high-born ladies and gentlemen.

Francis Beaumont, son of Sir Francis Beaumont, was born about 1585, and died in 1616. He was educated at Oxford and studied law at the Inner Temple; and though his career as a writer was short he won a high reputation as a poet and was buried in Westminster Abbey.

John Fletcher, son of the Bishop of London, was born in 1579, and died in 1625. He was a graduate of Cambridge, and appears to have been much more a professional man of letters than Beaumont. He wrote many plays by himself, and, after Beaumont ceased to write, worked in collaboration with several other men, including Shakespeare.

"Philaster" is an excellent typical example of their plays, which are thus admirably characterized by Thorndike:

"Their plots, largely invented, are ingenious and complicated. They deal with royal or noble persons, with heroic actions, and are placed in foreign localities. The conquests, usurpations, and passions that ruin kingdoms are their themes, there are no battles or pageants, and the action is usually confined to the rooms of the palace or its immediate neighborhood. Usually contrasting a story of gross sensual passion with one of idyllic love, they introduce a great variety of incidents, and aim at constant but varied excitement. . . . The plays depend for interest not on their observation or revelation of human nature, or the development of character, but on the variety of situations, the clever construction that holds the interest through one suspense to another up to the unravelling at the very end, and on the naturalness, felicity, and vigor of the poetry."

PHILASTER

[DRAMATIS PERSONÆ]

KING.
PHILASTER, Heir to the Crown of Sicily.
PHARAMOND, Prince of Spain.
DION, a Lord.
CLEREMONT, } Noble Gentlemen,
THRASILINE, } his associates.
An Old Captain.
Five Citizens.
A Country Fellow.
Two Woodmen.

The King's Guard and Train.

ARETHUSA, Daughter of the King.
EUPHRASIA, Daughter of DION, but disguised like a Page and called BELLARIO.
MEGRA, a lascivious Lady.
GALATEA, a wise modest Lady attending the Princess.
Two other Ladies.

SCENE.—[*Messina and its neighborhood*]

ACT THE FIRST

SCENE I[1]

Enter DION, CLEREMONT, *and* THRASILINE

Cleremont

HERE'S nor lords nor ladies.

DION. Credit me, gentlemen, I wonder at it. They receiv'd strict charge from the King to attend here; besides, it was boldly published that no officer should forbid any gentleman that desired to attend and hear.

CLE. Can you guess the cause?

DION. Sir, it is plain, about the Spanish Prince, that's come to marry our kingdom's heir and be our sovereign.

THRA. Many that will seem to know much say she looks not on him like a maid in love.

DION. Faith, sir, the multitude, that seldom know any thing but their own opinions, speak that they would have; but the prince, before his own approach, receiv'd so many

[1] The presence chamber in the palace.

confident messages from the state, that I think she's resolv'd to be rul'd.

CLE. Sir, it is thought, with her he shall enjoy both these kingdoms of Sicily and Calabria.

DION. Sir, it is without controversy so meant. But 'twill be a troublesome labour for him to enjoy both these kingdoms with safety, the right heir to one of them living, and living so virtuously; especially, the people admiring the bravery of his mind and lamenting his injuries.

CLE. Who, Philaster?

DION. Yes; whose father, we all know, was by our late King of Calabria unrighteously deposed from his fruitful Sicily. Myself drew some blood in those wars, which I would give my hand to be washed from.

CLE. Sir, my ignorance in state-policy will not let me know why, Philaster being heir to one of these kingdoms, the King should suffer him to walk abroad with such free liberty.

DION. Sir, it seems your nature is more constant than to inquire after state-news. But the King, of late, made a hazard of both the kingdoms, of Sicily and his own, with offering but to imprison Philaster; at which the city was in arms, not to be charmed down by any state-order or proclamation, till they saw Philaster ride through the streets pleased and without a guard; at which they threw their hats and their arms from them; some to make bonfires, some to drink, all for his deliverance: which wise men say is the cause the King labours to bring in the power of a foreign nation to awe his own with.

Enter GALATEA, a Lady and MEGRA

THRA. See, the ladies! What's the first?

DION. A wise and modest gentlewoman that attends the princess.

CLE. The second?

DION. She is one that may stand still discreetly enough, and ill-favour'dly dance her measure; simper when she is courted by her friend, and slight her husband.

CLE. The last?

DION Faith, I think she is one whom the state keeps for

the agents of our confederate princes; she'll cog[2] and lie with a whole army, before the league shall break. Her name is common through the kingdom, and the trophies of her dishonour advanced beyond Hercules' Pillars. She loves to try the several constitutions of men's bodies; and, indeed, has destroyed the worth of her own body by making experiment upon it for the good of the commonwealth.

CLE. She's a profitable member.

MEG. Peace, if you love me! You shall see these gentlemen stand their ground and not court us.

GAL. What if they should?

LA. What if they should!

MEG. Nay, let her alone.—What if they should! Why, if they should, I say they were never abroad. What foreigner would do so? It writes them directly untravell'd.

GAL. Why, what if they be?

LA. What if they be!

MEG. Good madam, let her go on.—What if they be! Why, if they be, I will justify, they cannot maintain discourse with a judicious lady, nor make a leg[3] nor say "Excuse me."

GAL. Ha, ha, ha!

MEG Do you laugh, madam?

DION. Your desires upon you, ladies!

MEG. Then you must sit beside us.

DION. I shall sit near you then, lady.

MEG. Near me, perhaps; but there's a lady endures no stranger; and to me you appear a very strange fellow.

LA. Methinks he's not so strange; he would quickly be acquainted.

THRA. Peace, the King!

Enter KING, PHARAMOND, ARETHUSA, *and* Train

KING. To give a stronger testimony of love
Than sickly promises (which commonly
In princes find both birth and burial
In one breath) we have drawn you, worthy sir,
To make your fair endearments to our daughter,
And worthy services known to our subjects,

---

[2] *Cheat.*   [3] *Bow.*

Now lov'd and wondered at; next, our intent
To plant you deeply our immediate heir
Both to our blood and kingdoms. For this lady,
(The best part of your life, as you confirm me,
And I believe,) though her few years and sex
Yet teach her nothing but her fears and blushes,
Desires without desire, discourse and knowledge
Only of what herself is to herself,
Make her feel moderate health; and when she sleeps,
In making no ill day, knows no ill dreams.
Think not, dear sir, these undivided parts,
That must mould up a virgin, are put on
To show her so, as borrowed ornaments
To speak her perfect love to you, or add
An artificial shadow to her nature,—
No, sir; I boldly dare proclaim her yet
No woman. But woo her still, and think her modesty
A sweeter mistress than the offer'd language
Of any dame, were she a queen, whose eye
Speaks common loves and comforts to her servants.[4]
Last, noble son (for so I now must call you),
What I have done thus public, is not only
To add a comfort in particular
To you or me, but all; and to confirm
The nobles and the gentry of these kingdoms
By oath to your succession, which shall be
Within this month at most.

   THRA. This will be hardly done.

   CLE. It must be ill done, if it be done.

   DION. When 'tis at best, 'twill be but half done, whilst
So brave a gentleman is wrong'd and flung off.

   THRA. I fear.

   CLE. Who does not?

   DION. I fear not for myself, and yet I fear too.
Well, we shall see, we shall see. No more.

   PHA. Kissing your white hand, mistress, I take leave
To thank your royal father; and thus far
To be my own free trumpet. Understand,
Great King, and these your subjects, mine that must be,

      ⁴ Lovers.

(For so deserving you have spoke me, sir,
And so deserving I dare speak myself,)
To what a person, of what eminence,
Ripe expectation, of what faculties,
Manners and virtues, you would wed your kingdoms;
You in me have your wishes. Oh, this country!
By more than all the gods, I hold it happy;
Happy in their dear memories that have been
Kings great and good; happy in yours that is;
And from you (as a chronicle to keep
Your noble name from eating age) do I
Opine myself most happy. Gentlemen,
Believe me in a word, a prince's word,
There shall be nothing to make up a kingdom
Mighty and flourishing, defenced, fear'd,
Equal to be commanded and obeyed,
But through the travails of my life I'll find it,
And tie it to this country. By all the gods,
My reign shall be so easy to the subject,
That every man shall be his prince himself,
And his own law—yet I his prince and law.
And, dearest lady, to your dearest self
(Dear in the choice of him whose name and lustre
Must make you more and mightier) let me say,
You are the blessed'st living; for, sweet princess,
You shall enjoy a man of men to be
Your servant; you shall make him yours, for whom
Great queens must die.

    THRA. Miraculous!

    CLE. This speech calls him Spaniard, being nothing but
a large inventory of his own commendations.

    DION. I wonder what's his price; for certainly
He'll sell himself, he has so prais'd his shape.

Enter PHILASTER

But here comes one more worthy those large speeches,
Than the large speaker of them.
Let me be swallowed quick, if I can find,
In all the anatomy of yon man's virtues,
One sinew sound enough to promise for him,

He shall be constable. By this sun,
He'll ne'er make king unless it be for trifles,
In my poor judgment.

PHI. [*kneeling.*] Right noble sir, as low as my obedience,
And with a heart as loyal as my knee,
I beg your favour.

KING.   Rise; you have it, sir. [PHILASTER *rises.*]

DION. Mark but the King, how pale he looks! He
        fears!
Oh, this same whorson conscience, how it jades us!

KING. Speak your intents, sir.

PHI.   Shall I speak 'em freely?
Be still my royal sovereign.

KING.   As a subject,
We give you freedom.

DION.   Now it heats.

PHI.   Then thus I turn
My language to you, prince; you, foreign man!
Ne'er stare nor put on wonder, for you must
Endure me, and you shall. This earth you tread upon
(A dowry, as you hope, with this fair princess),
By my dead father (oh, I had a father,
Whose memory I bow to!) was not left
To your inheritance, and I up and living—
Having myself about me and my sword,
The souls of all my name and memories,
These arms and some few friends beside the gods—
To part so calmly with it, and sit still
And say, "I might have been." I tell thee, Pharamond,
When thou art king, look I be dead and rotten,
And my name ashes: for, hear me, Pharamond!
This very ground thou goest on, this fat earth,
My father's friends made fertile with their faiths,
Before that day of shame shall gape and swallow
Thee and thy nation, like a hungry grave,
Into her hidden bowels. Prince, it shall;
By the just gods, it shall!

PHA.   He's mad; beyond cure, mad.

DION. Here is a fellow has some fire in's veins:
The outlandish prince looks like a tooth-drawer.

PHI. Sir prince of popinjays,[5] I'll make it well
Appear to you I am not mad.

KING.   You displease us:
You are too bold.

PHI.   No, sir, I am too tame,
Too much a turtle, a thing born without passion,
A faint shadow, that every drunken cloud
Sails over, and makes nothing.

KING.   I do not fancy this.
Call our physicians; sure, he's somewhat tainted.[6]

THRA. I do not think 'twill prove so.

DION. H'as given him a general purge already,
For all the right he has; and now he means
To let him blood. Be constant, gentlemen:
By heaven, I'll run his hazard,
Although I run my name out of the kingdom!

CLE. Peace, we are all one soul.

PHA. What you have seen in me to stir offence
I cannot find, unless it be this lady,
Offer'd into mine arms with the succession;
Which I must keep, (though it hath pleas'd your fury
To mutiny within you,) without disputing
Your genealogies, or taking knowledge
Whose branch you are. The King will leave it me,
And I dare make it mine. You have your answer.

PHI. If thou wert sole inheritor to him
That made the world his,[7] and couldst see no sun
Shine upon any thing but thine; were Pharamond
As truly valiant as I feel him cold,
And ring'd among the choicest of his friends
(Such as would blush to talk such serious follies,
Or back such bellied commendations),
And from this presence, spite of all these bugs,[8]
You should hear further from me.

KING. Sir, you wrong the prince; I gave you not this
        freedom
To brave our best friends. You deserve our frown.
Go to; be better temper'd.

---

[5] *Parrots.*   [6] *Unbalanced in mind.*
[7] *I. e., Alexander the Great.*   [8] *Bugbears.*

PHI. It must be, sir, when I am nobler us'd.

GAL. Ladies,
This would have been a pattern of succession,
Had he ne'er met this mischief. By my life,
He is the worthiest the true name of man
This day within my knowledge.

MEG. I cannot tell what you may call your knowledge;
But the other is the man set in mine eye.
Oh, 'tis a prince of wax![9]

GAL.   A dog it is.[10]

KING. Philaster, tell me
The injuries you aim at in your riddles.

PHI. If you had my eyes, sir, and sufferance,
My griefs upon you, and my broken fortunes,
My wants great, and now nought but hopes and fears,
My wrongs would make ill riddles to be laugh'd at.
Dare you be still my king, and right me not?

KING. Give me your wrongs in private.

PHI.   Take them,
And ease me of a load would bow strong Atlas.

They whisper.

CLE. He dares not stand the shock.

DION. I cannot blame him; there's danger in't.
Every man in this age has not a soul of crystal, for all
men to read their actions through: men's hearts and faces
are so far asunder, that they hold no intelligence. Do
but view yon stranger well, and you shall see a fever
through all his bravery, and feel him shake like a true
tenant.[11] If he give not back his crown again upon the
report of an elder-gun, I have no augury.

KING. Go to;
Be more yourself, as you respect our favour;
You'll stir us else. Sir, I must have you know,
That you are, and shall be, at our pleasure, what
Fashion we will put upon you. Smooth your brow,
Or by the gods——

---

[9] *A model prince.*
[10] *The phrase, a dog of wax, is used elsewhere in a contemptuous sense, but has not been explained.*
[11] *Probably corrupt.* Q1. truant. *Mod. edd.* tyrant, recreant, in a true tertian.

PHI. I am dead, sir; you're my fate. It was not I
Said, I was wrong'd; I carry all about me
My weak stars lead me to, all my weak fortunes.
Who dares in all this presence speak, (that is
But man of flesh, and may be mortal,) tell me
I do not most entirely love this prince,
And honour his full virtues!

KING.   Sure, he's possess'd.

PHI. Yes, with my father's spirit. It's here, O King,
A dangerous spirit! Now he tells me, King,
I was a king's heir, bids me be a king,
And whispers to me, these are all my subjects.
'Tis strange he will not let me sleep, but dives
Into my fancy, and there gives me shapes
That kneel and do me service, cry me king:
But I'll suppress him; he's a factious spirit,
And will undo me.—[*To* PHAR.] Noble sir, your hand;
I am your servant.

KING.   Away! I do not like this:
I'll make you tamer, or I'll dispossess you
Both of your life and spirit. For this time
I pardon your wild speech, without so much
As your imprisonment.

    Exeunt KING, PHARAMOND, ARETHUSA, *and* Attendants.

DION. I thank you, sir; you dare not for the people.

GAL. Ladies, what think you now of this brave fellow?

MEG. A pretty talking fellow, hot at hand. But eye yon
stranger: is he not a fine complete gentleman? Oh, these
strangers, I do affect them strangely! They do the rarest
home-things, and please the fullest! As I live, I could love
all the nation over and over for his sake.

GAL. Gods comfort your poor head-piece, lady! 'Tis a
weak one, and had need of a night-cap.   *Exeunt* Ladies.

DION. See, how his fancy labours! Has he not
Spoke home and bravely? What a dangerous train
Did he give fire to! How he shook the King,
Made his soul melt within him, and his blood
Run into whey! It stood upon his brow
Like a cold winter-dew.

PHI.   Gentlemen,

You have no suit to me? I am no minion.
You stand, methinks, like men that would be courtiers,
If I[12] could well be flatter'd at a price
Not to undo your children. You're all honest:
Go, get you home again, and make your country
A virtuous court, to which your great ones may,
In their diseased age, retire and live recluse.

 CLE. How do you, worthy sir?
 PHI.   Well, very well;
And so well that, if the King please, I find
I may live many years.

 DION.   The King must please,
Whilst we know what you are and who you are,
Your wrongs and virtues.[13] Shrink not, worthy sir,
But add your father to you; in whose name
We'll waken all the gods, and conjure up
The rods of vengeance, the abused people,
Who, like to raging torrents, shall swell high,
And so begirt the dens of these male-dragons,
That, through the strongest safety, they shall beg
For mercy at your sword's point.

 PHI.   Friends, no more;
Our ears may be corrupted; tis an age
We dare not trust our wills to. Do you love me?

 THRA. Do we love Heaven and honour?

 PHI. My Lord Dion, you had
A virtuous gentlewoman call'd you father;
Is she yet alive?

 DION.   Most honour'd sir, she is;
And, for the penance but of an idle dream,
Has undertook a tedious pilgrimage.

Enter a Lady

 PHI. Is it to me, or any of these gentlemen, you come?

 LADY. To you, brave lord; the princess would entreat
Your present company.

 PHI. The princess send for me! You are mistaken.

 LADY. If you be called Philaster, 'tis to you.

---

[12] *Mason conj. Qq. F.* you. *If I could be induced not to ruin your families by antagonizing the king.* [13] *Q*₁. *Other edd.* injuries.

PHI. Kiss her fair hand, and say I will attend her.

[*Exit* Lady.]

DION. Do you know what you do?

PHI. Yes; go to see a woman.

CLE. But do you weigh the danger you are in?

PHI. Danger in a sweet face!
By Jupiter, I must not fear a woman!

THRA. But are you sure it was the princess sent?
It may be some foul train[14] to catch your life.

PHI. I do not think it, gentlemen; she's noble.
Her eye may shoot me dead, or those true red
And white friends in her cheeks may steal my soul out;
There's all the danger in't. But, be what may,
Her single name hath armed me.   *Exit*.

DION.   Go on,
And be as truly happy as thou'rt fearless!—
Come, gentlemen, let's make our friends acquainted,
Lest the King prove false.   *Exeunt*.

[SCENE II[1]]

Enter ARETHUSA *and a* Lady

ARE. Comes he not?

LADY.   Madam?

ARE.   Will Philaster come?

LADY. Dear madam, you were wont to credit me
At first.

ARE. But didst thou tell me so?
I am forgetful, and my woman's strength
Is so o'ercharg'd with dangers like to grow
About my marriage, that these under-things
Dare not abide in such a troubled sea.
How look'd he when he told thee he would come?

LADY. Why, well.

ARE. And not a little fearful?

LADY. Fear, madam! Sure, he knows not what it is.

ARE. You all are of his faction; the whole court
Is bold in praise of him; whilst I

---

[14] *Plot.*
[1] *Arethusa's apartment in the palace.*

May live neglected, and do noble things,
As fools in strife throw gold into the sea,
Drown'd in the doing. But, I know he fears.

LADY. Fear, madam! Methought, his looks hid more
Of love than fear.

ARE.   Of love! To whom? To you?
Did you deliver those plain words I sent,
With such a winning gesture and quick look
That you have caught him?

LADY.   Madam, I mean to you.

ARE. Of love to me! alas, thy ignorance
Lets thee not see the crosses of our births!
Nature, that loves not to be questioned
Why she did this or that, but has her ends,
And knows she does well, never gave the world
Two things so opposite, so contrary,
As he and I am: if a bowl of blood
Drawn from this arm of mine would poison thee,
A draught of his would cure thee. Of love to me!

LADY. Madam, I think I hear him.

ARE.   Bring him in. [*Exit* Lady.]
You gods, that would not have your dooms withstood,
Whose holy wisdoms at this time it is
To make the passion of a feeble maid
The way unto your justice, I obey.

[*Re*]-*enter* [Lady *with*] PHILASTER

LADY. Here is my Lord Philaster.

ARE.   Oh, 'tis well.
Withdraw yourself.   [*Exit* Lady.]

PHI.   Madam, your messenger
Made me believe you wish'd to speak with me.

ARE. 'Tis true, Philaster; but the words are such
I have to say, and do so ill beseem
The mouth of woman, that I wish them said,
And yet am loath to speak them. Have you known
That I have aught detracted from your worth?
Have I in person wrong'd you, or have set
My baser instruments to throw disgrace
Upon your virtues?

PHI.   Never, madam, you.

ARE. Why, then, should you, in such a public place,
Injure a princess, and a scandal lay
Upon my fortunes, fam'd to be so great,
Calling a great part of my dowry in question?

PHI. Madam, this truth which I shall speak will be
Foolish: but, for your fair and virtuous self,
I could afford myself to have no right
To any thing you wish'd.

ARE.   Philaster, know,
I must enjoy these kingdoms.

PHI.   Madam, both?

ARE. Both, or I die: by heaven, I die, Philaster,
If I not calmly may enjoy them both.

PHI. I would do much to save that noble life;
Yet would be loath to have posterity
Find in our stories, that Philaster gave
His right unto a sceptre and a crown
To save a lady's longing.

ARE.   Nay, then, hear:
I must and will have them, and more——

PHI.   What more?

ARE. Or lose that little life the gods prepared
To trouble this poor piece of earth withal.

PHI. Madam, what more?

ARE.   Turn, then, away thy face.

PHI. No.

ARE. Do.

PHI. I can endure it. Turn away my face!
I never yet saw enemy that look'd
So dreadfully, but that I thought myself
As great a basilisk[2] as he; or spake
So horrible, but that I thought my tongue
Bore thunder underneath, as much as his;
Nor beast that I could turn from. Shall I then
Begin to fear sweet sounds? A lady's voice,
Whom I do love? Say you would have my life;
Why, I will give it you; for 'tis of me
A thing so loath'd, and unto you that ask

[2] *A fabulous serpent that killed with a glance.*

Of so poor use, that I shall make no price:
If you entreat, I will unmov'dly hear.

ARE. Yet, for my sake, a little bend thy looks.

PHI. I do.

ARE.   Then know, I must have them and thee.

PHI. And me?

ARE.   Thy love; without which, all the land
Discovered yet will serve me for no use
But to be buried in.

PHI.   Is't possible?

ARE. With it, it were too little to bestow
On thee. Now, though thy breath do strike me dead,
(Which, know, it may,) I have unript my breast.

PHI. Madam, you are too full of noble thoughts,
To lay a train for this contemned life,
Which you may have for asking. To suspect
Were base, where I deserve no ill. Love you!
By all my hopes, I do, above my life!
But how this passion should proceed from you
So violently, would amaze a man
That would be jealous.[3]

ARE. Another soul into my body shot
Could not have fill'd me with more strength and spirit
Than this thy breath. But spend not hasty time
In seeking how I came thus: 'tis the gods,
The gods, that make me so; and, sure, our love
Will be the nobler and the better blest,
In that the secret justice of the gods
Is mingled with it. Let us leave, and kiss;
Lest some unwelcome guest should fall betwixt us,
And we should part without it.

PHI.   'Twill be ill
I should abide here long.

ARE.   'Tis true; and worse
You should come often. How shall we devise
To hold intelligence, that our true loves,
On any new occasion, may agree
What path is best to tread?

PHI.   I have a boy,

------

[3] *Suspicious.*

Sent by the gods, I hope, to this intent
Not yet seen in the court. Hunting the buck,
I found him sitting by a fountain's side,
Of which he borrow'd some to quench his thirst,
And paid the nymph again as much in tears.
A garland lay him by, made by himself,
Of many several flowers bred in the vale,
Stuck in that mystic order that the rareness
Delighted me: but ever when he turn'd
His tender eyes upon 'em, he would weep,
As if he meant to make 'em grow again.
Seeing such pretty helpless innocence
Dwell in his face, I ask'd him all his story.
He told me that his parents gentle died,
Leaving him to the mercy of the fields,
Which gave him roots; and of the crystal springs,
Which did not stop their courses; and the sun,
Which still, he thank'd him, yielded him his light.
Then took he up his garland, and did show
What every flower, as country-people hold,
Did signify, and how all, ordered thus,
Express'd his grief; and, to my thoughts, did read
The prettiest lecture of his country-art
That could be wish'd: so that methought I could
Have studied it. I gladly entertain'd
Him, who was glad to follow; and have got
The trustiest, loving'st, and the gentlest boy
That ever master kept. Him will I send
To wait on you, and bear our hidden love.

    ARE. 'Tis well; no more.

Re-enter Lady

    LADY. Madam, the prince is come to do his service.
    ARE. What will you do, Philaster, with yourself?
    PHI. Why, that which all the gods have pointed out for
    me.
    ARE. Dear, hide thyself.—
Bring in the prince.   [*Exit* Lady.]
    PHI.   Hide me from Pharamond!
When thunder speaks, which is the voice of God,

Though I do reverence, yet I hide me not;
And shall a stranger-prince have leave to brag
Unto a foreign nation, that he made
Philaster hide himself?

ARE.   He cannot know it.

PHI. Though it should sleep for ever to the world,
It is a simple sin to hide myself,
Which will for ever on my conscience lie.

ARE. Then, good Philaster, give him scope and way
In what he says; for he is apt to speak
What you are loath to hear. For my sake, do.

PHI. I will.

Re-enter [Lady *with*] PHARAMOND

PHA. My princely mistress, as true lovers ought,
I come to kiss these fair hands, and to show,   [*Exit* Lady.]
In outward ceremonies, the dear love
Writ in my heart.

PHI. If I shall have an answer no directlier,
I am gone.

PHA. To what would he have answer?

ARE. To his claim unto the kingdom.

PHA. Sirrah, I forbare you before the King—

PHI. Good sir, do so still; I would not talk with you.

PHA. But now the time is fitter. Do but offer
To make mention of right to any kingdom,
Though it be scarce habitable——

PHI.   Good sir, let me go.

PHA. And by the gods—

PHI.   Peace, Pharamond! if thou——

ARE. Leave us, Philaster.

PHI.   I have done.   [*Going.*]

PHA. You are gone! by Heaven I'll fetch you back.

PHI. You shall not need.   [*Returning.*]

PHA.   What now?

PHI.   Know, Pharamond,
I loathe to brawl with such a blast as thou,
Who art nought but a valiant voice; but if
Thou shalt provoke me further, men shall say,
" Thou wert," and not lament it.

PHA.   Do you slight
My greatness so, and in the chamber of
The princess?

PHI. It is a place to which I must confess
I owe a reverence; but were't the church,
Ay, at the altar, there's no place so safe,
Where thou dar'st injure me, but I dare kill thee.
And for your greatness, know, sir, I can grasp
You and your greatness thus, thus into nothing.
Give not a word, not a word back! Farewell.   *Exit.*

PHA. 'Tis an odd fellow, madam; we must stop
His mouth with some office when we are married.

ARE. You were best make him your controller.

PHA. I think he would discharge it well. But, madam,
I hope our hearts are knit; but yet so slow
The ceremonies of state are, that 'twill be long
Before our hands be so. If then you please,
Being agreed in heart, let us not wait
For dreaming form, but take a little stolen
Delights, and so prevent[4] our joys to come.

ARE. If you dare speak such thoughts,
I must withdraw in honour.   *Exit.*

PHA. The constitution of my body will never hold out till
the wedding; I must seek elsewhere.   *Exit.*

ACT THE SECOND

SCENE I[1]

Enter PHILASTER *and* BELLARIO

PHI. And thou shalt find her honourable, boy;
Full of regard unto thy tender youth,
For thine own modesty; and, for my sake,
Apter to give than thou wilt be to ask,
Ay, or deserve.

BEL.   Sir, you did take me up
When I was nothing; and only yet am something
By being yours. You trusted me unknown;

* *Anticipate.*
[1] *An apartment in the palace.*

And that which you were apt to conster[2]
A simple innocence in me, perhaps
Might have been craft, the cunning of a boy
Hard'ned in lies and theft: yet ventur'd you
To part my miseries and me; for which,
I never can expect to serve a lady
That bears more honour in her breast than you.

PHI. But, boy, it will prefer[3] thee. Thou art young,
And bear'st a childish overflowing love
To them that clap thy cheeks and speak thee fair yet;
But when thy judgment comes to rule those passions,
Thou wilt remember best those careful friends
That plac'd thee in the noblest way of life.
She is a princess I prefer thee to.

BEL. In that small time that I have seen the world,
I never knew a man hasty to part
With a servant he thought trusty. I remember,
My father would prefer the boys he kept
To greater men than he; but did it not
Till they were grown too saucy for himself.

PHI. Why, gentle boy, I find no fault at all
In thy behaviour.

BEL.   Sir, if I have made
A fault in ignorance, instruct my youth:
I shall be willing, if not apt, to learn;
Age and experience will adorn my mind
With larger knowledge; and if I have done
A wilful fault, think me not past all hope
For once. What master holds so strict a hand
Over his boy, that he will part with him
Without one warning? Let me be corrected
To break my stubbornness, if it be so,
Rather than turn me off; and I shall mend.

PHI. Thy love doth plead so prettily to stay,
That, trust me, I could weep to part with thee.
Alas, I do not turn thee off! Thou knowest
It is my business that doth call thee hence;
And when thou art with her, thou dwell'st with me.
Think so, and 'tis so; and when time is full,

---

[2] Construe, interpret.   [3] Advance.

That thou hast well discharg'd this heavy trust,
Laid on so weak a one, I will again
With joy receive thee; as I live, I will!
Nay, weep not, gentle boy. 'Tis more than time
Thou didst attend the princess.

BEL.   I am gone.
But since I am to part with you, my lord,
And none knows whether I shall live to do
More service for you, take this little prayer:
Heaven bless your loves, your fights, all your designs!
May sick men, if they have your wish, be well;
And Heaven hate those you curse, though I be one! *Exit.*

PHI. The love of boys unto their lords is strange;
I have read wonders of it: yet this boy
For my sake (if a man may judge by looks
And speech) would out-do story. I may see
A day to pay him for his loyalty.   *Exit.*

[SCENE II[1]]

Enter PHARAMOND

PHA. Why should these ladies stay so long? They must
come this way. I know the queen employs 'em not; for the
reverend mother[2] sent me word, they would all be for the
garden. If they should all prove honest[3] now, I were in a
fair taking; I was never so long without sport in my life,
and, in my conscience, 'tis not my fault. Oh, for our country ladies!

Enter GALATEA

Here's one bolted; I'll hound at her.—Madam!

GAL. Your grace!

PHA. Shall I not be a trouble?

GAL.   Not to me, sir.

PHA. Nay, nay, you are too quick. By this sweet
hand——

GAL. You'll be forsworn, sir; 'tis but an old glove.
If you will talk at distance, I am for you:

---

[1] *A gallery in the palace.*   [2] *In charge of the maids of honor.*
[3] *Chaste.*

But, good prince, be not bawdy, nor do not brag;
These two I bar;
And then, I think, I shall have sense enough
To answer all the weighty apophthegms
Your royal blood shall manage.

PHA. Dear lady, can you love?

GAL. Dear prince! how dear? I ne'er cost you a coach
yet, nor put you to the dear repentance of a banquet. Here's
no scarlet, sir, to blush the sin out it was given for. This
wire mine own hair covers; and this face has been so far
from being dear to any, that it ne'er cost penny painting;
and, for the rest of my poor wardrobe, such as you see, it
leaves no hand[4] behind it, to make the jealous mercer's wife
curse our good doings.

PHA. You mistake me, lady.

GAL. Lord, I do so; would you or I could help it!

PHA. You're very dangerous bitter, like a potion.

GAL. No, sir, I do not mean to purge you, though
I mean to purge a little time on you.

PHA. Do ladies of this country use to give
No more respect to men of my full being?

GAL. Full being! I understand you not, unless your grace
means growing to fatness; and then your only remedy (upon
my knowledge, prince) is, in a morning, a cup of neat white
wine brew'd with carduus,[5] then fast till supper; about eight
you may eat; use exercise, and keep a sparrow-hawk; you can
shoot in a tiller:[6] but, of all, your grace must fly phlebotomy,[7]
fresh pork, conger,[8] and clarified whey; they are all duller
of the vital spirits.

PHA. Lady, you talk of nothing all this while.

GAL. 'Tis very true, sir; I talk of you.

PHA. [*Aside.*] This is a crafty wench; I like her wit well;
'twill be rare to stir up a leaden appetite. She's a Danaë,
and must be courted in a shower of gold.—Madam, look
here; all these, and more than——

GAL. What have you there, my lord? Gold! now, as I
live, 'tis fair gold! You would have silver for it, to play
with the pages. You could not have taken me in a worse

---

[4] *Note of indebtedness.*   [5] *A kind of thistle used as a medicine.*
[6] *Cross bow.*   [7] *Blood letting.*   [8] *Cucumber.*

time; but, if you have present use, my lord, I'll send my man
with silver and keep your gold for you.

PHA. Lady, lady!

GAL. She's coming, sir, behind, will take white money.—
[*Aside.*] Yet for all this I'll match ye.

Exit behind the hangings.

PHA. If there be but two such more in this kingdom, and
near the court, we may even hang up our harps. Ten such
camphire⁹ constitutions as this would call the golden age
again in question, and teach the old way for every ill-fac'd
husband to get his own children; and what a mischief that
would breed, let all consider!

Enter MEGRA

Here's another: if she be of the same last, the devil shall
pluck her on.—Many fair mornings, lady!

MEG. As many mornings bring as many days,
Fair, sweet and hopeful to your grace!

PHA. [*Aside.*] She gives good words yet; sure this wench
          is free.—
If your more serious business do not call you,
Let me hold quarter with you; we will talk
An hour out quickly.

MEG.   What would your grace talk of?

PHA. Of some such pretty subject as yourself:
I'll go no further than your eye, or lip;
There's theme enough for one man for an age.

MEG. Sir, they stand right, and my lips are yet even,
Smooth, young enough, ripe enough, and red enough,
Or my glass wrongs me.

PHA. Oh, they are two twinn'd cherries dy'd in blushes
Which those fair suns above with their bright beams
Reflect upon and ripen. Sweetest beauty,
Bow down those branches, that the longing taste
Of the faint looker-on may meet those blessings,
And taste and live.   *They kiss.*

MEG. [*Aside.*]   Oh, delicate sweet prince!
She that hath snow enough about her heart
To take the wanton spring of ten such lines off,

⁹ *I. e., cold.*

May be a nun without probation.—Sir,
You have in such neat poetry gathered a kiss,
That if I had but five lines of that number,
Such pretty begging blanks,[10] I should commend
Your forehead or your cheeks, and kiss you too.

PHA. Do it in prose; you cannot miss it, madam.

MEG. I shall, I shall.

PHA.   By my life, but you shall not;
I'll prompt you first. [*Kisses her.*] Can you do it now?

MEG. Methinks 'tis easy, now you ha' done't before me;
But yet I should stick at it.   [*Kisses him.*]

PHA.   Stick till to-morrow;
I'll ne'er part you, sweetest. But we lose time:
Can you love me?

MEG. Love you, my lord! How would you have me love
    you?

PHA. I'll teach you in a short sentence, 'cause I will not
load your memory.

MEG. Why, prince, you have a lady of your own
That yet wants teaching.

PHA. I'll sooner teach a mare the old measures[11] than
teach her anything.

MEG. By mine honour, that's a foul fault, indeed;
But time and your good help will wear it out, sir.
Has your grace seen the court-star, Galatea?

PHA. Out upon her! She's as cold of her favour as an
apoplex; she sailed by but now.

MEG. And how do you hold her wit, sir?

PHA. I hold her wit? The strength of all the guard cannot hold it, if they were tied to it; she would blow 'em out of
the kingdom. They talk of Jupiter; he's but a squib-cracker
to her: look well about you, and you may find a tongue-bolt.
But speak, sweet lady, shall I be freely welcome? If you
mistrust my faith, you do me the unnoblest wrong.

MEG. I dare not, prince, I dare not.

PHA. Make your own conditions, my purse shall seal 'em;
and what you dare imagine you can want, I'll furnish you
withal. Give two hours to your thoughts every morning
about it. Come, I know you are bashful;

---

[10] *Blank verses.*   [11] *Stately dances.*

Speak in my ear, will you be mine? Keep this,
And with it me: soon I will visit you.

MEG. My lord, my chamber's most unsafe; but when 'tis
    night,
I'll find some means to slip into your lodging;
Till when——

PHA. Till when, this and my heart go with thee!

Exeunt several ways.

Re-enter GALATEA *from behind the hangings*

GAL. Oh, thou pernicious petticoat prince! are these your
virtues? Well, if I do not lay a train to blow your sport up,
I am no woman: and, Lady Towsabel, I'll fit you for't. *Exit.*

[SCENE III¹]

Enter ARETHUSA *and a* Lady

ARE. Where's the boy?
LADY. Within, madam.
ARE. Gave you him gold to buy him clothes?
LADY. I did.
ARE. And has he done't?
LADY. Yes, madam.
ARE. 'Tis a pretty sad-talking boy, is it not?
Asked you his name?
LADY. No, madam.

Enter GALATEA

ARE. Oh, you are welcome. What good news?
GAL. As good as any one can tell your grace,
That says she has done that you would have wish'd.
ARE. Hast thou discovered?
GAL. I have strain'd a point of modesty for you.
ARE. I prithee, how?
GAL. In list'ning after bawdry. I see, let a lady live never
so modestly, she shall be sure to find a lawful time to hearken
after bawdry. Your prince, brave Pharamond, was so hot
on't!

<hr>

¹ *Arethusa's apartment in the palace.*

Are. With whom?

Gal. Why, with the lady I suspected. I can tell the time and place.

Are. Oh, when, and where?

Gal. To-night, his lodging.

Are. Run thyself into the presence; mingle there again
With other ladies; leave the rest to me.   [*Exit* Galatea.]
If destiny (to whom we dare not say,
"Why didst thou this?") have not decreed it so,
In lasting leaves (whose smallest characters
Were never alter'd yet), this match shall break.—
Where's the boy?

Lady. Here, madam.

Enter Bellario

Are. Sir, you are sad to change your service; is't not so?

Bel. Madam, I have not chang'd; I wait on you,
To do him service.

Are.   Thou disclaim'st in me.
Tell me thy name.

Bel. Bellario.

Are. Thou canst sing and play?

Bel. If grief will give me leave, madam, I can.

Are. Alas, what kind of grief can thy years know?
Hadst thou a curst master when thou went'st to school?
Thou art not capable of other grief;
Thy brows and cheeks are smooth as waters be
When no breath troubles them. Believe me, boy,
Care seeks out wrinkled brows and hollow eyes,
And builds himself caves, to abide in them.
Come, sir, tell me truly, doth your lord love me?

Bel. Love, madam! I know not what it is.

Are. Canst thou know grief, and never yet knew'st love?
Thou art deceiv'd, boy. Does he speak of me
As if he wish'd me well?

Bel.   If it be love
To forget all respect of his own friends
With thinking of your face; if it be love
To sit cross-arm'd and sigh away the day,
Mingled with starts, crying your name as loud

And hastily as men i' the streets do fire;
If it be love to weep himself away
When he but hears of any lady dead
Or kill'd, because it might have been your chance;
If, when he goes to rest (which will not be),
'Twixt every prayer he says, to name you once,
As others drop a bead, be to be in love,
Then, madam, I dare swear he loves you.

  ARE. Oh you're a cunning boy, and taught to lie
For your lord's credit! But thou know'st a lie
That bears this sound is welcomer to me
Than any truth that says he loves me not.
Lead the way, boy.—[*to Lady.*] Do you attend me too.—
'Tis thy lord's business hastes me thus. Away!   *Exeunt.*

[SCENE IV[1]]

Enter DION, CLEREMONT, THRASILINE, MEGRA, *and*
GALATEA

  DION. Come, ladies, shall we talk a round? As men
Do walk a mile, women should talk an hour
After supper: 'tis their exercise.

  GAL. 'Tis late.

  MEG. 'Tis all
My eyes will do to lead me to my bed.

  GAL. I fear, they are so heavy, you'll scarce find
The way to your own lodging with 'em to-night.

Enter PHARAMOND

  THRA. The prince!

  PHA. Not a-bed, ladies? You're good sitters-up.
What think you of a pleasant dream, to last
Till morning?

  MEG. I should choose, my lord, a pleasing wake before it.

Enter ARETHUSA *and* BELLARIO

  ARE. 'Tis well, my lord; you're courting of these ladies.—
Is't not late, gentlemen?

  CLE. Yes, madam.

       [1] *Before Pharamond's lodging in the court of the palace.*

ARE. Wait you there.   *Exit.*

MEG. [*Aside.*] She's jealous, as I live.—Look you, my lord,
The princess has a Hylas, an Adonis.

PHA. His form is angel-like.

MEG. Why, this is he that must, when you are wed,
Sit by your pillow, like young Apollo, with
His hand and voice binding your thoughts in sleep;
The princess does provide him for you and for herself.

PHA. I find no music in these boys.

MEG.   Nor I:
They can do little, and that small they do,
They have not wit to hide.

DION.   Serves he the princess?

THRA. Yes.

DION.   'Tis a sweet boy: how brave² she keeps him!

PHA. Ladies all, good rest; I mean to kill a buck
To-morrow morning ere you've done your dreams.

MEG. All happiness attend your grace! [*Exit* PHARA-
MOND.] Gentlemen, good rest.—Come, shall we go to bed?

GAL. Yes.—All good night.

DION. May your dreams be true to you!—

                              Exeunt GALATEA *and* MEGRA.

What shall we do, gallants? 'tis late. The King
Is up still: see, he comes; a guard along
With him.

                    Enter KING, ARETHUSA, *and* Guard

KING.   Look your intelligence be true.

ARE. Upon my life, it is; and I do hope
Your highness will not tie me to a man
That in the heat of wooing throws me off,
And takes another.

DION.   What should this mean?

KING. If it be true,
That lady had been better have embrac'd
Cureless diseases. Get you to your rest:
You shall be righted.   *Exeunt* ARETHUSA *and* BELLARIO.
                              —Gentlemen, draw near;
We shall employ you. Is young Pharamond
Come to his lodging?

                    ² *Finely dressed.*

DION.   I saw him enter there.

KING. Haste, some of you, and cunningly discover
If Megra be in her lodging.   [*Exit* DION.]

CLE. Sir,
She parted hence but now, with other ladies.

KING. If she be there, we shall not need to make
A vain discovery of our suspicion.
[*Aside.*] You gods, I see that who unrighteously
Holds wealth or state from others shall be curs'd
In that which meaner men are blest withal:
Ages to come shall know no male of him
Left to inherit, and his name shall be
Blotted from earth; if he have any child,
It shall be crossly match'd; the gods themselves
Shall sow wild strife betwixt her lord and her.
Yet, if it be your wills, forgive the sin
I have committed; let it not fall
Upon this understanding child of mine!
She has not broke your laws. But how can I
Look to be heard of gods that must be just,
Praying upon the ground I hold by wrong?

Re-enter DION

DION. Sir, I have asked, and her women swear she is
within; but they, I think, are bawds. I told 'em, I must
speak with her; they laugh'd, and said, their lady lay speech-
less. I said, my business was important; they said, their lady
was about it. I grew hot, and cried, my business was a
matter that concern'd life and death; they answered, so was
sleeping, at which their lady was. I urg'd again, she had
scarce time to be so since last I saw her: they smil'd again,
and seem'd to instruct me that sleeping was nothing but
lying down and winking.* Answers more direct I could not
get: in short, sir, I think she is not there.

KING. 'Tis then no time to dally.—You o' the guard,
Wait at the back door of the prince's lodging,
And see that none pass thence, upon your lives.
                           [*Exeunt* Guards.]

Closing the eyes.

Knock, gentlemen; knock loud; louder yet.

> [DION, CLER., &c. *knock at the door of*
> PHARAMOND'S *Lodging.*]

What, has their pleasure taken off their hearing?—
I'll break your meditations.—Knock again.—
Not yet? I do not think he sleeps, having this
Larum by him.—Once more.—Pharamond! prince!

> PHARAMOND [*appears*] *above.*

PHA. What saucy groom knocks at this dead of night?
Where be our waiters? By my vexed soul,
He meets his death that meets me, for this boldness.

KING. Prince, prince, you wrong your thoughts; we are
    your friends:
Come down.

PHA.   The King!

KING.   The same, sir. Come down, sir:
We have cause of present counsel with you.

PHA. If your grace please
To use me, I'll attend you to your chamber.

Enter PHARAMOND *below.*

KING. No, 'tis too late, prince; I'll make bold with yours.

PHA. I have some private reasons to myself
Make me unmannerly, and say you cannot.—

> *They press to come in.*

Nay, press not forward, gentlemen; he must
Come through my life that comes here.

KING. Sir, be resolv'd[4] I must and will come.—Enter.

PHA. I will not be dishonour'd.
He that enters, enters upon his death.
Sir, 'tis a sign you make no stranger of me,
To bring these renegadoes to my chamber
At these unseasoned hours.

KING.   Why do you
Chafe yourself so? You are not wronged nor shall be;
Only I'll search your lodging, for some cause
To ourself known.—Enter, I say.

PHA.   I say, no.   MEGRA *above.*

MEG. Let 'em enter, prince, let 'em enter;

---

[4] *Convinced.*

I am up and ready:[5] I know their business;
'Tis the poor breaking of a lady's honour
They hunt so hotly after; let 'em enjoy it.—
You have your business, gentlemen; I lay here.
Oh, my lord the King, this is not noble in you
To make public the weakness of a woman!

KING. Come down.

MEG. I dare, my lord. Your hootings and your clamours,
Your private whispers and your broad fleerings,
Can no more vex my soul than this base carriage.
But I have vengeance yet in store for some
Shall, in the most contempt you can have of me,
Be joy and nourishment.

KING. Will you come down?

MEG. Yes, to laugh at your worst; but I shall wring you,
If my skill fail me not.   [Exit above.]

KING. Sir, I must dearly chide you for this looseness;
You have wrong'd a worthy lady; but, no more.—
Conduct him to my lodging and to bed.

[Exeunt PHARAMOND and Attendants.]

CLE. Get him another wench, and you bring him to bed
indeed.

DION. 'Tis strange a man cannot ride a stage
Or two, to breathe himself, without a warrant.
If his gear hold, that lodgings be search'd thus,
Pray God we may lie with our own wives in safety,
That they be not by some trick of state mistaken!

Enter [Attendants] with MEGRA [below]

KING. Now, lady of honour, where's your honour now?
No man can fit your palate but the prince.
Thou most ill-shrouded rottenness, thou piece
Made by a painter and a 'pothecary,
Thou troubled sea of lust, thou wilderness
Inhabited by wild thoughts, thou swoln cloud
Of infection, thou ripe mine of all diseases,
Thou all-sin, all-hell, and last all-devils, tell me,
Had you none to pull on with your courtesies
But he that must be mine, and wrong my daughter?

* Dressed.

By all the gods, all these, and all the pages,
And all the court, shall hoot thee through the court,
Fling rotten oranges, make ribald rhymes,
And sear thy name with candles upon walls!
Do you laugh, Lady Venus?

MEG. Faith, sir, you must pardon me;
I cannot choose but laugh to see you merry.
If you do this, O King! nay, if you dare do it,
By all those gods you swore by, and as many
More of my own, I will have fellows, and such
Fellows in it, as shall make noble mirth!
The princess, your dear daughter, shall stand by me
On walls, and sung in ballads, any thing.
Urge me no more; I know her and her haunts,
Her lays, leaps, and outlays, and will discover all;
Nay, will dishonour her. I know the boy
She keeps; a handsome boy, about eighteen;
Know what she does with him, where, and when.
Come, sir, you put me to a woman's madness,
The glory of a fury; and if I do not
Do't to the height——

KING.   What boy is this she raves at?

MEG. Alas! good-minded prince, you know not these
      things!
I am loath to reveal 'em. Keep this fault,
As you would keep your health from the hot air
Of the corrupted people, or, by Heaven,
I will not fall alone. What I have known
Shall be as public as a print; all tongues
Shall speak it as they do the language they
Are born in, as free and commonly; I'll set it,
Like a prodigious⁶ star, for all to gaze at,
And so high and glowing, that other kingdoms far and
      foreign
Shall read it there, nay, travel with it, till they find
No tongue to make it more, nor no more people;
And then behold the fall of your fair princess!

KING. Has she a boy?

CLE. So please your grace, I have seen a boy wait

* *Portentous, ominous.*

On her,
A fair boy.

KING.   Go, get you to your quarter:
For this time I will study to forget you.

MEG. Do you study to forget me, and I'll study
To forget you.   *Exeunt* KING, MEGRA, *and Guard*.

CLE. Why, here's a male spirit fit for Hercules. If ever
there be Nine Worthies of women, this wench shall ride
astride and be their captain.

DION. Sure, she has a garrison of devils in her tongue, she
uttered such balls of wild-fire. She has so nettled the King, that
all the doctors in the country will scarce cure him. That boy
was a strange-found-out antidote to cure her infection; that
boy, that princess' boy; that brave, chaste, virtuous lady's
boy; and a fair boy, a well-spoken boy! All these considered,
can make nothing else—but there I leave you, gentlemen.

THRA. Nay, we'll go wander with you.   *Exeunt*.

ACT THE THIRD

SCENE I[1]

Enter DION, CLEREMONT, *and* THRASILINE

CLE. Nay, doubtless, 'tis true.

DION. Ay; and 'tis the gods
That rais'd this punishment, to scourge the King
With his own issue. Is it not a shame
For us that should write noble in the land,
For us that should be freemen, to behold
A man that is the bravery of his age,
Philaster, press'd down from his royal right
By this regardless King? and only look
And see the sceptre ready to be cast
Into the hands of that lascivious lady
That lives in lust with a smooth boy, now to be married
To yon strange prince, who, but that people please
To let him be a prince, is born a slave
In that which should be his most noble part,
His mind?

[1] *The court of the palace.*

THRA.   That man that would not stir with you
To aid Philaster, let the gods forget
That such a creature walks upon the earth!
    CLE. Philaster is too backward in 't himself.
The gentry do await it, and the people,
Against their nature, are all bent for him,
And like a field of standing corn, that's moved
With a stiff gale, their heads bow all one way.
    DION. The only cause that draws Philaster back
From this attempt is the fair princess' love,
Which he admires, and we can now confute.
    THRA. Perhaps he'll not believe it.
    DION. Why, gentlemen, 'tis without question so.
    CLE. Ay, 'tis past speech, she lives dishonestly.
But how shall we, if he be curious,[2] work
Upon his faith?
    THRA. We all are satisfied within ourselves.
    DION. Since it is true, and tends to his own good,
I'll make this new report to be my knowledge;
I'll say I know it; nay, I'll swear I saw it.
    CLE. It will be best.
    THRA.   'Twill move him.

Enter PHILASTER.

DION.   Here he comes.
Good morrow to your honour: we have spent
Some time in seeking you.
    PHI.   My worthy friends,
You that can keep your memories to know
Your friend in miseries, and cannot frown
On men disgrac'd for virtue, a good day
Attend you all! What service may I do
Worthy your acceptation?
    DION.   My good lord,
We come to urge that virtue, which we know
Lives in your breast, forth. Rise, and make a head:[3]
The nobles and the people are all dulled
With this usurping king; and not a man,
That ever heard the word, or knew such a thing

----

[2] *Scrupulous.*   [3] *Raise an armed force.*

As virtue, but will second your attempts.

PHI. How honourable is this love in you
To me that have deserv'd none! Know, my friends,
(You, that were born to shame your poor Philaster
With too much courtesy,) I could afford
To melt myself in thanks: but my designs
Are not yet ripe. Suffice it, that ere long
I shall employ your loves; but yet the time
Is short of what I would.

DION. The time is fuller, sir, than you expect;
That which hereafter will not, perhaps, be reach'd
By violence, may now be caught. As for the King,
You know the people have long hated him;
But now the princess, whom they lov'd——

PHI. Why, what of her?

DION.   Is loathed as much as he.

PHI. By what strange means?

DION.   She's known a whore.

PHI.   Thou liest.

DION. My lord——

PHI. Thou liest,   *Offers to draw and is held.*
And thou shalt feel it! I had thought thy mind
Had been of honour. Thus to rob a lady
Of her good name, is an infectious sin
Not to be pardon'd. Be it false as hell,
'Twill never be redeem'd, if it be sown
Amongst the people, fruitful to increase
All evil they shall hear. Let me alone
That I may cut off falsehood whilst it springs!
Set hills on hills betwixt me and the man
That utters this, and I will scale them all,
And from the utmost top fall on his neck,
Like thunder from a cloud.

DION.   This is most strange:
Sure, he does love her.

PHI.   I do love fair truth.
She is my mistress, and who injures her
Draws vengeance from me. Sirs, let go my arms.

THRA. Nay, good my lord, be patient.

CLE. Sir, remember this is your honour'd friend,

That comes to do his service, and will show you
Why he utter'd this.

PHI.   I ask you pardon, sir;
My zeal to truth made me unmannerly:
Should I have heard dishonour spoke of you,
Behind your back, untruly, I had been
As much distemper'd and enrag'd as now.

DION. But this, my lord, is truth.

PHI.   Oh, say not so!
Good sir, forbear to say so; 'tis then truth,
That womankind is false: urge it no more;
It is impossible. Why should you think
The princess light?

DION.   Why, she was taken at it.

PHI. 'Tis false! by Heaven, 'tis false! It cannot be!
Can it? Speak, gentlemen; for God's love, speak! Is't
possible? Can women all be damn'd?

DION. Why, no, my lord.

PHI.   Why, then, it cannot be.

DION. And she was taken with her boy.

PHI.   What boy?

DION. A page, a boy that serves her.

PHI.   Oh, good gods!
A little boy?

DION.   Ay; know you him, my lord?

PHI. [*Aside.*] Hell and sin know him!—Sir, you are de-
    ceiv'd;
I'll reason it a little coldly with you.
If she were lustful, would she take a boy,
That knows not yet desire? She would have one
Should meet her thoughts and know the sin he acts,
Which is the great delight of wickedness.
You are abus'd,' and so is she, and I.

DION. How you, my lord?

PHI.   Why, all the world's abused
In an unjust report.

DION.   Oh, noble sir, your virtues
Cannot look into the subtle thoughts of woman!
In short, my lord, I took them; I myself.

              ' *Deceived.*

PHI. Now, all the devils, thou didst! Fly from my rage!
Would thou hadst ta'en devils engend'ring plagues,
When thou did'st take them! Hide thee from mine eyes!
Would thou hadst taken thunder on thy breast,
When thou didst take them; or been strucken dumb
For ever; that this foul deed might have slept
In silence!

THRA.   Have you known him so ill-tempered?
CLE. Never before.
PHI.   The winds, that are let loose
From the four several corners of the earth,
And spread themselves all over sea and land,
Kiss not a chaste one. What friend bears a sword
To run me thorough?
DION.   Why, my lord, are you
So moved at this?
PHI.   When any fall from virtue,
I am distract; I have an interest in 't.

DION. But, good my lord, recall yourself, and think
What's best to be done.
PHI.   I thank you; I will do it.
Please you to leave me; I'll consider of it.
To-morrow I will find your lodging forth,
And give you answer.
DION.   All the gods direct you
The readiest way!
THRA.   He was extreme impatient.
CLE. It was his virtue and his noble mind.

[*Exeunt* DION, CLEREMONT, *and* THRASILINE.

PHI. I had forgot to ask him where he took them;
I'll follow him. Oh, that I had a sea
Within my breast, to quench the fire I feel!
More circumstances will but fan this fire:
It more afflicts me now, to know by whom
This deed is done, than simply that 'tis done;
And he that tells me this is honourable,
As far from lies as she is far from truth.
Oh, that, like beasts, we could not grieve ourselves
With that we see not! Bulls and rams will fight
To keep their females, standing in their sight;

But take 'em from them, and you take at once
Their spleens away; and they will fall again
Unto their pastures, growing fresh and fat;
And taste the waters of the springs as sweet
As 'twas before, finding no start in sleep;
But miserable man——

Enter BELLARIO

            See, see, you gods,
He walks still; and the face you let him wear
When he was innocent is still the same,
Not blasted! Is this justice? Do you mean
To intrap mortality, that you allow
Treason so smooth a brow? I cannot now
Think he is guilty.

BEL.   Health to you, my lord!
The princess doth commend her love, her life,
And this, unto you.   *Gives a letter.*

PHI.   Oh, Bellario,
Now I perceive she loves me; she does show it
In loving thee, my boy; she has made thee brave.

BEL. My lord, she has attir'd me past my wish,
Past my desert; more fit for her attendant,
Though far unfit for me who do attend.

PHI. Thou art grown courtly, boy.—Oh, let all women,
That love black deeds, learn to dissemble here,
Here, by this paper! She does write to me
As if her heart were mines of adamant
To all the world besides; but, unto me,
A maiden-snow that melted with my looks.—
Tell me, my boy, how doth the princess use thee?
For I shall guess her love to me by that.

BEL. Scarce like her servant, but as if I were
Something allied to her, or had preserv'd
Her life three times by my fidelity;
As mothers fond do use their only sons,
As I'd use one that's left unto my trust,
For whom my life should pay if he met harm,
So she does use me.

PHI.   Why, this is wondrous well:

But what kind language does she feed thee with?

BEL. Why, she does tell me she will trust my youth
With all her loving secrets, and does call me
Her pretty servant; bids me weep no more
For leaving you; she'll see my services
Regarded: and such words of that soft strain,
That I am nearer weeping when she ends
Than ere she spake.

PHI.   This is much better still.

BEL. Are you not ill, my lord?

PHI.   Ill? No, Bellario.

BEL.   Methinks your words
Fall not from off your tongue so evenly,
Nor is there in your looks that quietness
That I was wont to see.

PHI.   Thou art deceiv'd, boy:
And she strokes thy head?

BEL.   Yes.

PHI. And she does clap thy cheeks?

BEL.   She does, my lord.

PHI. And she does kiss thee, boy? ha!

BEL.   How, my lord?

PHI. She kisses thee?

BEL.   Never, my lord, by heaven.

PHI. That's strange; I know she does.

BEL.   No, by my life.

PHI. Why then she does not love me. Come, she does.
I bade her do it; I charg'd her, by all charms
Of love between us, by the hope of peace
We should enjoy, to yield thee all delights
Naked as to her bed; I took her oath
Thou should'st enjoy her. Tell me, gentle boy,
Is she not parallelless? Is not her breath
Sweet as Arabian winds when fruits are ripe?
Are not her breasts two liquid ivory balls?
Is she not all a lasting mine of joy?

BEL. Ay, now I see why my disturbed thoughts
Were so perplex'd. When first I went to her,
My heart held augury. You are abus'd;
Some villain has abus'd you; I do see

Whereto you tend. Fall rocks upon his head
That put this to you! 'Tis some subtle train
To bring that noble frame of yours to nought.

PHI. Thou think'st I will be angry with thee. Come,
Thou shalt know all my drift. I hate her more
Than I love happiness, and placed thee there
To pry with narrow eyes into her deeds.
Hast thou discovered? Is she fallen to lust,
As I would wish her? Speak some comfort to me.

BEL. My lord, you did mistake the boy you sent.
Had she the lust of sparrows or of goats,
Had she a sin that way, hid from the world,
Beyond the name of lust, I would not aid
Her base desires; but what I came to know
As servant to her, I would not reveal,
To make my life last ages.

PHI.   Oh, my heart!
This is a salve worse than the main disease.—
Tell me thy thoughts; for I will know the least
That dwells within thee, or will rip thy heart
To know it. I will see thy thoughts as plain
As I do now thy face.

BEL.   Why, so you do.
She is (for aught I know) by all the gods,
As chaste as ice! But were she foul as hell,
And I did know it thus, the breath of kings,
The points of swords, tortures, nor bulls of brass,
Should draw it from me.

PHI.   Then it is no time
To dally with thee; I will take thy life,
For I do hate thee. I could curse thee now.

BEL. If you do hate, you could not curse me worse;
The gods have not a punishment in store
Greater for me than is your hate.

PHI.   Fie, fie,
So young and so dissembling! Tell me when
And where thou didst enjoy her, or let plagues
Fall on me, if I destroy thee not!   *He draws his sword.*

BEL. By heaven, I never did; and when I lie
To save my life, may I live long and loath'd!

Hew me asunder, and, whilst I can think,
I'll love those pieces you have cut away
Better than those that grow, and kiss those limbs
Because you made 'em so.

Phi.   Fear'st thou not death?
Can boys contemn that?

Bel.   Oh, what boy is he
Can be content to live to be a man,
That sees the best of men thus passionate,
Thus without reason?

Phi.   Oh, but thou dost not know
What 'tis to die.

Bel.   Yes, I do know, my lord:
'Tis less than to be born; a lasting sleep;
A quiet resting from all jealousy,
A thing we all pursue. I know, besides,
It is but giving over of a game
That must be lost.

Phi.   But there are pains, false boy,
For perjur'd souls. Think but on those, and then
Thy heart will melt, and thou wilt utter all.

Bel. May they fall all upon me whilst I live,
If I be perjur'd, or have ever thought
Of that you charge me with! If I be false,
Send me to suffer in those punishments
You speak of; kill me!

Phi.   Oh, what should I do?
Why, who can but believe him? He does swear
So earnestly, that if it were not true,
The gods would not endure him. Rise, Bellario:
Thy protestations are so deep, and thou
Dost look so truly when thou utter'st them,
That, though I know 'em false as were my hopes,
I cannot urge thee further. But thou wert
To blame to injure me, for I must love
Thy honest looks, and take no revenge upon
Thy tender youth. A love from me to thee
Is firm, whate'er thou dost; it troubles me
That I have call'd the blood out of thy cheeks,
That did so well become thee. But, good boy,

Let me not see thee more: something is done
That will distract me, that will make me mad,
If I behold thee. If thou tender'st me,
Let me not see thee.

BEL.   I will fly as far
As there is morning, ere I give distaste
To that most honour'd mind. But through these tears,
Shed at my hopeless parting, I can see
A world of treason practis'd upon you,
And her, and me. Farewell for evermore!
If you shall hear that sorrow struck me dead,
And after find me loyal, let there be
A tear shed from you in my memory,
And I shall rest at peace.   *Exit.*

PHI.   Blessing be with thee,
Whatever thou deserv'st! Oh, where shall I
Go bathe this body? Nature too unkind;
That made no medicine for a troubled mind!   *Exit.*

[SCENE II[1]]

Enter ARETHUSA

ARE. I marvel my boy comes not back again:
But that I know my love will question him
Over and over,—how I slept, wak'd, talk'd,
How I rememb'red him when his dear name
Was last spoke, and how when I sigh'd, wept, sung,
And ten thousand such,—I should be angry at his stay.

Enter KING

KING. What, at your meditations! Who attends you?
ARE. None but my single self. I need no guard;
I do no wrong, nor fear none.
KING. Tell me, have you not a boy?
ARE.   Yes, sir.
KING. What kind of boy?
ARE.   A page, a waiting-boy.
KING. A handsome boy?

---

[1] *Arethusa's apartment in the palace.*

ARE.   I think he be not ugly:
Well qualified and dutiful I know him;
I took him not for beauty.
    KING. He speaks and sings and plays?
    ARE.   Yes, sir.
    KING. About eighteen?
    ARE.   I never ask'd his age.
    KING. Is he full of service?
    ARE. By your pardon, why do you ask?
    KING. Put him away.
    ARE.   Sir!
    KING. Put him away, I say.
H'as done you that good service shames me to speak of.
    ARE. Good sir, let me understand you.
    KING.   If you fear me,
Show it in duty; put away that boy.
    ARE. Let me have reason for it, sir, and then
Your will is my command.
    KING. Do not you blush to ask it? Cast him off,
Or I shall do the same to you. You're one
Shame with me, and so near unto myself,
That, by my life, I dare not tell myself
What you, myself, have done.
    ARE. What have I done, my lord?
    KING. 'Tis a new language, that all love to learn:
The common people speak it well already;
They need no grammar. Understand me well;
There be foul whispers stirring. Cast him off,
And suddenly. Do it! Farewell.   *Exit.*
    ARE. Where may a maiden live securely free,
Keeping her honour fair? Not with the living.
They feed upon opinions, errors, dreams,
And make 'em truths; they draw a nourishment
Out of defamings, grow upon disgraces,
And, when they see a virtue fortified
Strongly above the battery of their tongues,
Oh, how they cast to sink it! and, defeated,
(Soul-sick with poison) strike the monuments
Where noble names lie sleeping, till they sweat,
And the cold marble melt.

Enter PHILASTER

PHI. Peace to your fairest thoughts, dearest mistress!

ARE. Oh, my dearest servant,[2] I have a war within me!

PHI. He must be more than man that makes these crystals
Run into rivers. Sweetest fair, the cause?
And, as I am your slave, tied to your goodness,
Your creature, made again from what I was
And newly-spirited, I'll right your honour.

ARE. Oh, my best love, that boy!

PHI.   What boy?

ARE. The pretty boy you gave me——

PHI.   What of him?

ARE. Must be no more mine.

PHI.   Why?

ARE.   They are jealous of him.

PHI. Jealous! Who?

ARE.   The King.

PHI.   [*Aside.*] Oh, my misfortune!
Then 'tis no idle jealousy.—Let him go.

ARE. Oh, cruel!
Are you hard-hearted too? Who shall now tell you
How much I lov'd you? Who shall swear it to you,
And weep the tears I send? Who shall now bring you
Letters, rings, bracelets? Lose his health in service?
Wake tedious nights in stories of your praise?
Who shall now sing your crying elegies,
And strike a sad soul into senseless pictures,
And make them mourn? Who shall take up his lute,
And touch it till he crown a silent sleep
Upon my eye-lids, making me dream, and cry,
" Oh, my dear, dear Philaster! "

PHI.   [*Aside.*] Oh, my heart!
Would he had broken thee, that made me know
This lady was not loyal!—Mistress,
Forget the boy; I'll get thee a far better.

ARE. Oh, never, never such a boy again
As my Bellario!

PHI.   'Tis but your fond affection.

[2] *Lover.*

ARE. With thee, my boy, farewell for ever
All secrecy in servants! Farewell faith,
And all desire to do well for itself!
Let all that shall succeed thee for thy wrongs
Sell and betray chaste love!

PHI. And all this passion for a boy?

ARE. He was your boy, and you put him to me,
And the loss of such must have a mourning for.

PHI. Oh, thou forgetful woman!

ARE.   How, my lord?

PHI. False Arethusa!
Hast thou a medicine to restore my wits,
When I have lost 'em? If not, leave to talk,
And do thus.

ARE.   Do what, sir? Would you sleep?

PHI. For ever, Arethusa. Oh, you gods,
Give me a worthy patience! Have I stood
Naked, alone, the shock of many fortunes?
Have I seen mischiefs numberless and mighty
Grow like a sea upon me? Have I taken
Danger as stern as death into my bosom,
And laugh'd upon it, made it but a mirth,
And flung it by? Do I live now like him,
Under this tyrant King, that languishing
Hears his sad bell and sees his mourners? Do I
Bear all this bravely, and must sink at length
Under a woman's falsehood? Oh, that boy,
That cursed boy! None but a villain boy
To ease your lust?

ARE.   Nay, then, I am betrayed:
I feel the plot cast for my overthrow.
Oh, I am wretched!

PHI. Now you may take that little right I have
To this poor kingdom. Give it to your joy;
For I have no joy in it. Some far place,
Where never womankind durst set her foot
For[a] bursting with her poisons, must I seek,
And live to curse you;
There dig a cave, and preach to birds and beasts

[a] *For fear of.*

What woman is, and help to save them from you;
How heaven is in your eyes, but in your hearts
More hell than hell has; how your tongues, like scorpions,
Both heal and poison;[4] how your thoughts are woven
With thousand changes in one subtle web,
And worn so by you; how that foolish man,
That reads the story of a woman's face
And dies believing it, is lost for ever;
How all the good you have is but a shadow,
I' the morning with you, and at night behind you,
Past and forgotten; how your vows are frosts,
Fast for a night, and with the next sun gone;
How you are, being taken all together,
A mere confusion, and so dead a chaos,
That love cannot distinguish. These sad texts,
Till my last hour, I am bound to utter of you.
So, farewell all my woe, all my delight!   *Exit.*

    ARE. Be merciful, ye gods, and strike me dead!
What way have I deserv'd this? Make my breast
Transparent as pure crystal, that the world,
Jealous of me, may see the foulest thought
My heart holds. Where shall a woman turn her eyes,
To find out constancy?

Enter BELLARIO

               Save me, how black
And guiltily, methinks, that boy looks now!
Oh, thou dissembler, that, before thou spak'st,
Wert in thy cradle false, sent to make lies
And betray innocents! Thy lord and thou
May glory in the ashes of a maid
Fool'd by her passion; but the conquest is
Nothing so great as wicked. Fly away!
Let my command force thee to that which shame
Would do without it. If thou understood'st
The loathed office thou hast undergone,
Why, thou wouldst hide thee under heaps of hills,
Lest men should dig and find thee.

    BEL.   Oh, what god,

---

[4] *It was believed that scorpions, applied to the wound they made, cured it.*

Angry with men, hath sent this strange disease
Into the noblest minds! Madam, this grief
You add unto me is no more than drops
To seas, for which they are not seen to swell.
My lord hath struck his anger through my heart,
And let out all the hope of future joys.
You need not bid me fly; I came to part,
To take my latest leave. Farewell for ever!
I durst not run away in honesty
From such a lady, like a boy that stole
Or made some grievous fault. The power of gods
Assist you in your sufferings! Hasty time
Reveal the truth to your abused lord
And mine, that he may know your worth; whilst I
Go seek out some forgotten place to die! *Exit.*

ARE. Peace guide thee! Thou hast overthrown me once;
Yet, if I had another Troy to lose,
Thou, or another villain with thy looks,
Might talk me out of it, and send me naked,
My hair dishevell'd, through the fiery streets.

Enter a Lady

LADY. Madam, the King would hunt, and calls for you
With earnestness.

ARE.   I am in tune to hunt!
Diana, if thou canst rage with a maid
As with a man,[5] let me discover thee
Bathing, and turn me to a fearful hind,
That I may die pursued by cruel hounds,
And have my story written in my wounds! *Exeunt.*

              [5] *Actæon.*

ACT THE FOURTH

Scene I[1]

Enter KING, PHARAMOND, ARETHUSA, GALATEA, MEGRA,
DION, CLEREMONT, THRASILINE, *and* Attendants

KING. What, are the hounds before and all the woodmen,
Our horses ready and our bows bent?

DION. All, sir.

KING [*to* PHARAMOND.] You are cloudy, sir. Come, we
have forgotten
Your venial trespass; let not that sit heavy
Upon your spirit; here's none dare utter it.

DION. He looks like an old surfeited stallion, dull as a
dormouse. See how he sinks!

THRA. He needs no teaching, he strikes sure enough. His
greatest fault is, he hunts too much in the purlieus; would
he would leave off poaching!

DION. And for his horn, h'as left it at the lodge where he
lay late. Oh, he's a precious limehound![2] Turn him loose
upon the pursuit of a lady, and if he lose her, hang him up
i' the slip. When my fox-bitch Beauty grows proud, I'll
borrow him.

KING. Is your boy turn'd away?

ARE. You did command, sir, and I obey'd you.

KING. 'Tis well done. Hark ye further. [*They talk apart.*]

CLE. Is't possible this fellow should repent? Methinks,
that were not noble in him; and yet he looks like a mortified member, as if he had a sick man's salve[3] in's mouth.
If a worse man had done this fault now, some physical[4]
justice or other would presently (without the help of an
almanack[5]) have opened the obstructions of his liver, and
let him blood with a dog-whip.

DION. See, see how modestly yon lady looks, as if she
came from churching with her neighbour! Why, what a
devil can a man see in her face but that she's honest![6]

---

[1] *Before the palace.*   [2] *A hunting dog.* Lyme=*leash.*
[3] *An allusion to a religious work, Thomas Bacon's "The Sicke Man's
Salve," 1561.*   [4] *Acting as a doctor.*
[5] *Almanacs gave the proper seasons for blood-letting.*   [6] *Chaste.*

THRA. Faith, no great matter to speak of; a foolish twinkling with the eye, that spoils her coat;[7] but he must be a cunning herald that finds it.

DION. See how they muster one another! Oh, there's a rank regiment where the devil carries the colours and his dam drum-major! Now the world and the flesh come behind with the carriage.[8]

CLE. Sure this lady has a good turn done her against her will; before she was common talk, now none dare say cantharides[9] can stir her. Her face looks like a warrant, willing and commanding all tongues, as they will answer it, to be tied up and bolted when this lady means to let herself loose. As I live, she has got her a goodly protection and a gracious; and may use her body discreetly for her health's sake, once a week, excepting Lent and dog-days. Oh, if they were to be got for money, what a great sum would come out of the city for these licences!

KING. To horse, to horse! we lose the morning, gentlemen.

Exeunt.

[SCENE II[1]]

Enter two Woodmen

1ST WOOD. What, have you lodged the deer?

2ND WOOD. Yes, they are ready for the bow.

1ST WOOD. Who shoots?

2ND WOOD. The princess.

1ST WOOD. No, she'll hunt.

2ND WOOD. She'll take a stand, I say.

1ST WOOD. Who else?

2ND WOOD. Why, the young stranger-prince.

1ST WOOD. He shall shoot in a stone-bow[2] for me. I never lov'd his beyond-sea-ship since he forsook the say,[3] for paying ten shillings. He was there at the fall of a deer, and would needs (out of his mightiness) give ten groats for the

---

[7] *Coat of arms. Mason explains that the reference is to the introduction of stars into a coat of arms, denoting a younger branch.*
[8] *Baggage.* [9] *Spanish fly, used as a provocative.*
[1] *A forest* [2] *With a cross-bow for shooting stones.*
[3] *The assay or slitting of the deer, in order to test the quality of the flesh, which involved a fee of ten shillings to the keeper.*

dowcets; marry, his steward would have the velvet-head[4]
into the bargain, to turf[5] his hat withal. I think he should
love venery; he is an old Sir Tristrem; for, if you be rememb'red, he forsook the stag once to strike a rascal[6] mich-
ing[7] in a meadow, and her he killed in the eye. Who shoots
else?

2ND WOOD. The Lady Galatea.

1ST WOOD. That's a good wench. She's liberal, and, by the
Gods, they say she's honest, and whether that be a fault, I
have nothing to do. There's all.

2ND WOOD. No, one more; Megra.

1ST WOOD. That's a firker,[8] i'faith, boy. There's a wench
will ride her haunches as hard after a kennel of hounds as
a hunting saddle, and when she comes home, get 'em clapt,
and all is well again. I have known her lose herself three
times in one afternoon (if the woods have been answer-
able)[9], and it has been work enough for one man to find
her, and he has sweat for it. She rides well and she pays
well. Hark! let's go.   *Exeunt.*

Enter PHILASTER

PHI. Oh, that I had been nourish'd in these woods
With milk of goats and acorns, and not known
The right of crowns nor the dissembling trains
Of women's looks; but digg'd myself a cave,
Where I, my fire, my cattle, and my bed,
Might have been shut together in one shed;
And then had taken me some mountain-girl,
Beaten with winds, chaste as the hard'ned rocks
Whereon she dwelt, that might have strewed my bed
With leaves and reeds, and with the skins of beasts,
Our neighbours, and have borne at her big breasts
My large coarse issue! This had been a life
Free from vexation.

Enter BELLARIO

BEL.   Oh, wicked men!
An innocent may walk safe among beasts;

[4] *The hart's horns, which are covered with velvet pile when new.*
[5] *Re-cover.*   [6] *A lean doe.*   [7] *Creeping stealthily.*   [8] *A fast one.*
[9] *Suitable.*

Nothing assaults me here. See, my griev'd lord
Sits as his soul were searching out a way
To leave his body!—Pardon me, that must
Break thy last commandment; for I must speak.
You that are griev'd can pity; hear, my lord!

PHI. Is there a creature yet so miserable,
That I can pity?

BEL.　　　　　Oh, my noble lord,
View my strange fortune, and bestow on me,
According to your bounty (if my service
Can merit nothing), so much as may serve
To keep that little piece I hold of life
From cold and hunger!

PHI.　　　　　Is it thou? Be gone!
Go, sell those misbeseeming clothes thou wear'st,
And feed thyself with them.

BEL. Alas, my lord, I can get nothing for them!
The silly country-people think 'tis treason
To touch such gay things.

PHI.　　　　　Now, by the gods, this is
Unkindly done, to vex me with thy sight.
Thou'rt fallen again to thy dissembling trade;
How shouldst thou think to cozen me again?
Remains there yet a plague untried for me?
Even so thou wept'st, and looked'st, and spok'st when first
I took thee up.
Curse on the time! If thy commanding tears
Can work on any other, use thy art;
I'll not betray it. Which way wilt thou take,
That I may shun thee, for thine eyes are poison
To mine, and I am loath to grow in rage;
This way, or that way?

BEL. Any will serve; but I will choose to have
That path in chase that leads unto my grave.

Exeunt severally.

Enter [on one side] DION, *and [on the other] the two*
Woodmen

DION. This is the strangest sudden chance!—You, woodmen!
1ST WOOD. My lord Dion?

DION. Saw you a lady come this way on a sable horse
    studded with stars of white?

2ND WOOD. Was she not young and tall?

DION. Yes. Rode she to the wood or to the plain?

2ND WOOD. Faith my lord, we saw none.

                               Exeunt Woodmen.

DION. Pox of your questions then!

Enter CLEREMONT

                                What, is she found?

CLE. Nor will be, I think.

DION. Let him seek his daughter himself. She cannot
stray about a little necessary natural business, but the whole
court must be in arms. When she has done, we shall have
peace.

CLE. There's already a thousand fatherless tales amongst
us. Some say, her horse ran away with her; some, a wolf
pursued her; others, 't was a plot to kill her, and that arm'd
men were seen in the wood: but questionless she rode away
willingly.

Enter KING, *and* THRASILINE

KING. Where is she?

CLE.   Sir, I cannot tell.

KING.   How's that?
Answer me so again!

CLE.   Sir, shall I lie?

KING. Yes, lie and damn, rather than tell me that.
I say again, where is she? Mutter not!—
Sir, speak you; where is she?

DION.   Sir, I do not know.

KING. Speak that again so boldly, and, by Heaven,
It is thy last!—You, fellows, answer me;
Where is she? Mark me, all; I am your King:
I wish to see my daughter; show her me;
I do command you all, as you are subjects,
To show her me! What! am I not your King?
If ay, then am I not to be obeyed?

DION. Yes, if you command things possible and honest

KING. Things possible and honest! Hear me, thou,—
Thou traitor, that dar'st confine thy King to things

Possible and honest! Show her me,
Or, let me perish, if I cover not
All Sicily with blood!

DION.   Faith, I cannot,
Unless you tell me where she is.

KING. You have betray'd me; you have let me lose
The jewel of my life. Go, bring her to me,
And set her here before me. 'Tis the King
Will have it so; whose breath can still the winds,
Uncloud the sun, charm down the swelling sea,
And stop the floods of heaven. Speak, can it not?

DION. No.

KING.   No! cannot the breath of kings do this?

DION. No; nor smell sweet itself, if once the lungs
Be but corrupted.

KING.   Is it so? Take heed!

DION. Sir, take you heed how you dare the powers
That must be just.

KING.   Alas! what are we kings!
Why do you gods place us above the rest,
To be serv'd, flatter'd, and ador'd, till we
Believe we hold within our hands your thunder?
And when we come to try the power we have,
There's not a leaf shakes at our threatenings.
I have sinn'd, 'tis true, and here stand to be punish'd;
Yet would not thus be punish'd. Let me choose
My way, and lay it on!

DION. [*Aside.*] He articles with the gods. Would somebody would draw bonds for the performance of covenants
betwixt them!

Enter PHARAMOND, GALATEA, *and* MEGRA

KING. What, is she found?

PHA.   No; we have ta'en her horse:
He gallop'd empty by. There is some treason.
You, Galatea, rode with her into the wood;
Why left you her?

GAL.   She did command me.

KING. Command! you should not.

GAL. 'Twould ill become my fortunes and my birth

To disobey the daughter of my King.

KING. You're all cunning to obey us for our hurt;
But I will have her.

PHA.   If I have her not,
By this hand, there shall be no more Sicily.

DION. [*Aside.*] What, will he carry it to Spain in's
  pocket?

PHA. I will not leave one man alive, but the King,
A cook, and a tailor.

KING. [*Aside.*] I see the injuries I have done must be
  reveng'd.

DION. Sir, this is not the way to find her out.

KING. Run all, disperse yourselves. The man that finds
  her,
Or (if she be kill'd) the traitor, I'll make him great.

DION. I know some would give five thousand pounds to
  find her.

PHA. Come, let us seek.

KING. Each man a several way; here I myself.

DION. Come, gentlemen, we here.

CLE. Lady, you must go search too.

MEG. I had rather be search'd myself.   *Exeunt severally.*

[SCENE III[1]]

Enter ARETHUSA

ARE. Where am I now? Feet, find me out a way,
Without the counsel of my troubled head.
I'll follow you boldly about these woods,
O'er mountains, thorough brambles, pits, and floods.
Heaven, I hope, will ease me: I am sick.   *Sits down.*

Enter BELLARIO

BEL. Yonder's my lady. God knows I want nothing,
Because I do not wish to live; yet I
Will try her charity. [*Aside.*]—Oh hear, you that have
  plenty!

---
[1] *Another part of the forest.*

From that flowing store drop some on dry ground.—
    See,
The lively red is gone to guard her heart!
I fear she faints.—Madam, look up!—She breathes not.—
Open once more those rosy twins, and send
Unto my lord your latest farewell!—Oh, she stirs.—
How is it, madam? speak comfort.

    ARE.   'Tis not gently done,
To put me in a miserable life,
And hold me there. I prithee, let me go;
I shall do best without thee; I am well.

               Enter PHILASTER

    PHI. I am to blame to be so much in rage.
I'll tell her coolly when and where I heard
This killing truth. I will be temperate
In speaking, and as just in hearing.——
Oh, monstrous! Tempt me not, you gods! good gods,
Tempt not a frail man! What's he, that has a heart,
But he must ease it here!

    BEL. My lord, help, help! The princess!

    ARE. I am well: forbear.

    PHI. [*Aside.*] Let me love lightning, let me be em-
        brac'd
And kiss'd by scorpions, or adore the eyes
Of basilisks, rather than trust the tongues
Of hell-bred women! Some good god look down,
And shrink these veins up! Stick me here a stone,
Lasting to ages in the memory
Of this damn'd act!

                —Hear me, you wicked ones!
You have put hills of fire into this breast,
Not to be quench'd with tears; for which may guilt
Sit on your bosoms! At your meals and beds
Despair await you! What, before my face?
Poison of asps between your lips! Diseases
Be your best issues! Nature make a curse,
And throw it on you!

    ARE.   Dear Philaster, leave

To be enrag'd, and hear me.

PHI.   I have done;
Forgive my passion. Not the calmed sea,
When Æolus locks up his windy brood,
Is less disturb'd than I. I'll make you know 't.
Dear Arethusa, do but take this sword,

                      Offers his drawn sword.

And search how temperate a heart I have;
Then you and this your boy may live and reign
In lust without control.—Wilt thou, Bellario?
I prithee kill me; thou art poor, and may'st
Nourish ambitious thoughts; when I am dead,
Thy way were freer. Am I raging now?
If I were mad, I should desire to live.
Sirs,[2] feel my pulse, whether you have known
A man in a more equal tune to die.

     BEL. Alas, my lord, your pulse keeps madman's time!
So does your tongue.

PHI.   You will not kill me, then?

ARE. Kill you!

BEL.   Not for the world.

PHI.   I blame not thee,
Bellario; thou hast done but that which gods
Would have transform'd themselves to do. Be gone,
Leave me without reply; this is the last
Of all our meetings—(*Exit* BELLARIO.) Kill me with this
     sword;
Be wise, or worse will follow: we are two
Earth cannot bear at once. Resolve to do,
Or suffer.

     ARE. If my fortune be so good to let me fall
Upon thy hand, I shall have peace in death.
Yet tell me this, will there be no slanders,
No jealousy in the other world; no ill there?

     PHI. No.

     ARE.   Show me, then, the way.

     PHI. Then guide my feeble hand,
You that have power to do it, for I must
Perform a piece of justice!—If your youth

              [2] *Formerly used to women as well as to men.*

Have any way offended Heaven, let prayers
Short and effectual reconcile you to it.

ARE. I am prepared.

Enter a Country Fellow

C. FELL. I'll see the King, if he be in the forest; I have
hunted him these two hours. If I should come home and not
see him, my sisters would laugh at me. I can see nothing
but people better hors'd than myself, that out-ride me; I
can hear nothing but shouting. These kings had need of
good brains; this whooping is able to put a mean man out of
his wits. There's a courtier with his sword drawn; by this
hand, upon a woman, I think!

PHI. Are you at peace?

ARE.   With heaven and earth.

PHI. May they divide thy soul and body!   *Wounds her.*

C. FELL. Hold, dastard! strike a woman! Thou'rt a
craven, I warrant thee; thou wouldst be loth to play half a
dozen venies[8] at wasters[4] with a good fellow for a broken
head.

PHI. Leave us, good friend.

ARE. What ill-bred man art thou, to intrude thyself
Upon our private sports, our recreations?

C. FELL. God 'uds[5] me, I understand you not; but
I know the rogue has hurt you.

PHI. Pursue thy own affairs: it will be ill
To multiply blood upon my head; which thou
Wilt force me to.

C. FELL. I know not your rhetoric; but I can lay it on, if
you touch the woman.

PHI. Slave, take what thou deservest!   *They fight.*

ARE.   Heavens guard my lord!

C. FELL. Oh, do you breathe?

PHI. I hear the tread of people. I am hurt.
The gods take part against me: could this boor
Have held me thus else? I must shift for life,
Though I do loathe it. I would find a course
To lose it rather by my will than force.   *Exit.*

[8] *Bouts.*   [4] *Cudgels.*   [5] *God judge.*

C. FELL. I cannot follow the rogue. I pray thee, wench, come and kiss me now.

Enter PHARAMOND, DION, CLEREMONT, THRASILINE, *and* Woodmen

PHA. What art thou?

C. FELL. Almost kill'd I am for a foolish woman; a knave has hurt her.

PHA. The princess, gentlemen!—Where's the wound, madam!
Is it dangerous?

ARE. He has not hurt me.

C. FELL. By God, she lies; h'as hurt her in the breast; look else.

PHA. O, sacred spring of innocent blood!

DION. 'Tis above wonder! Who should dare this?

ARE. I felt it not.

PHA. Speak, villain, who has hurt the princess?

C. FELL. Is it the princess?

DION. Ay.

C. FELL. Then I have seen something yet.

PHA. But who has hurt her?

C. FELL. I told you, a rogue; I ne'er saw him before, I.

PHA. Madam, who did it?

ARE.   Some dishonest wretch;
Alas, I know him not, and do forgive him!

C. FELL. He's hurt too; he cannot go far; I made my father's old fox[6] fly about his ears.

PHA. How will you have me kill him?

ARE. Not at all; 'tis some distracted fellow.

PHA. By this hand, I'll leave ne'er a piece of him bigger than a nut, and bring him all to you in my hat.

ARE. Nay, good sir,
If you do take him, bring him quick[7] to me,
And I will study for a punishment
Great as his fault.

PHA. I will.

ARE.   But swear.

_____

[6] *Broad sword.*   [7] *Alive.*

Pha.   By all my love, I will.——
Woodmen, conduct the princess to the King,
And bear that wounded fellow to dressing.——
Come, gentlemen, we'll follow the chase close.
Exeunt [on one side] Pharamond, Dion, Cleremont, *and*
        Thrasiline; *[exit on the other]* Arethusa *[attended
        by the]* First Woodman
C. Fell. I pray you, friend, let me see the King.
2nd Wood. That you shall, and receive thanks.
C. Fell. If I get clear with this, I'll go see no more gay
sights.   *Exeunt.*

[Scene IV¹]

Enter Bellario

Bel. A heaviness near death sits on my brow,
And I must sleep. Bear me, thou gentle bank,
For ever, if thou wilt. You sweet ones all,   [*Lies down.*]
Let me unworthy press you; I could wish
I rather were a corse strew'd o'er with you
Than quick above you. Dulness² shuts mine eyes,
And I am giddy: oh, that I could take
So sound a sleep that I might never wake!   [*Sleeps.*]

Enter Philaster

Phi. I have done ill; my conscience calls me false,
To strike at her that would not strike at me.
When I did fight, methought I heard her pray
The gods to guard me. She may be abus'd,
And I a loathed villain; if she be,
She will conceal who hurt her. He has wounds
And cannot follow; neither knows he me.
Who's this? Bellario sleeping! If thou be'st
Guilty, there is no justice that thy sleep
Should be so sound, and mine, whom thou hast wrong'd,
So broken. (*Cry within.*) Hark! I am pursued. You
    gods

---

¹ *Another part of the forest.*   ² *Sleepiness.*

I'll take this offer'd means of my escape.
They have no mark to know me but my blood,
If she be true; if false, let mischief light
On all the world at once! Sword, print my wounds
Upon this sleeping boy! I ha' none, I think,
Are mortal, nor would I lay greater on thee.

Wounds BELLARIO.

BEL. Oh, death, I hope, is come! Blest be that hand!
It meant me well. Again, for pity's sake!

PHI. I have caught myself;   *Falls.*
The loss of blood hath stay'd my flight. Here, here,
Is he that struck thee: take thy full revenge;
Use me, as I did mean thee, worse than death;
I'll teach thee to revenge. This luckless hand
Wounded the princess; tell my followers[3]
Thou didst receive these hurts in staying me,
And I will second thee; get a reward.

BEL. Fly, fly, my lord, and save yourself!

PHI.   How's this?
Wouldst thou I should be safe?

BEL.   Else were it vain
For me to live. These little wounds I have
Ha' not bled much. Reach me that noble hand;
I'll help to cover you.

PHI.   Art thou then true to me?

BEL. Or let me perish loath'd! Come, my good lord,
Creep in amongst those bushes; who does know
But that the gods may save your much-lov'd breath?

PHI. Then I shall die for grief, if not for this,
That I have wounded thee. What wilt thou do?

BEL. Shift for myself well. Peace! I hear 'em come.

[PHILASTER *creeps into a bush.*]

[*Voices*] *within.* Follow, follow, follow! that way they
went.

BEL. With my own wounds I'll bloody my own sword.
I need not counterfeit to fall; Heaven knows
That I can stand no longer.   *Falls.*

[3] *Pursuers.*

Enter PHARAMOND, DION, CLEREMONT, *and* THRASILINE

PHA. To this place we have track'd him by his blood.

CLE. Yonder, my lord, creeps one away.

DION. Stay, sir! what are you?

BEL. A wretched creature, wounded in these woods
By beasts. Relieve me, if your names be men,
Or I shall perish.

DION.   This is he, my lord,
Upon my soul, that hurt her. 'Tis the boy,
That wicked boy, that serv'd her.

PHA.   Oh, thou damn'd
In thy creation! What cause couldst thou shape
To hurt the princess?

BEL.   Then I am betrayed.

DION. Betrayed! No, apprehended.

BEL.   I confess,
(Urge it no more) that, big with evil thoughts
I set upon her, and did take my aim,
Her death. For charity let fall at once
The punishment you mean, and do not load
This weary flesh with tortures.

PHA.   I will know
Who hir'd thee to this deed.

BEL.   Mine own revenge.

PHA. Revenge! for what?

BEL.   It pleas'd her to receive
Me as her page, and, when my fortunes ebb'd,
That men strid o'er them careless, she did shower
Her welcome graces on me, and did swell
My fortunes till they overflow'd their banks,
Threat'ning the men that crossed 'em; when, as swift
As storms arise at sea, she turn'd her eyes
To burning suns upon me, and did dry
The streams she had bestow'd, leaving me worse
And more contemn'd than other little brooks,
Because I had been great. In short, I knew
I could not live, and therefore did desire
To die reveng'd.

PHA.   If tortures can be found

Long as thy natural life, resolve to feel
The utmost rigour.

CLE.   Help to lead him hence.

            PHILASTER *creeps out of the bush.*

PHI. Turn back, you ravishers of innocence!
Know ye the price of that you bear away
So rudely?

PHA.   Who's that?

DION.   'Tis the Lord Philaster.

PHI. 'Tis not the treasure of all kings in one,
The wealth of Tagus, nor the rocks of pearl
That pave the court of Neptune, can weigh down
That virtue. It was I that hurt the princess.
Place me, some god, upon a pyramis[4]
Higher than hills of earth, and lend a voice
Loud as your thunder to me, that from thence
I may discourse to all the under-world
The worth that dwells in him!

PHA.   How's this?

BEL.   My lord, some man
Weary of life, that would be glad to die.

PHI. Leave these untimely courtesies, Bellario.

BEL. Alas, he's mad! Come, will you lead me on?

PHI. By all the oaths that men ought most to keep,
And gods to punish most when men do break,
He touch'd her not.—Take heed, Bellario,
How thou dost drown the virtues thou hast shown
With perjury.—By all that's good, 'twas I!
You know she stood betwixt me and my right.

PHA. Thy own tongue be thy judge!

CLE.   It was Philaster.

DION. Is't not a brave boy?
Well, sirs, I fear me we were all deceived.

PHI. Have I no friend here?

DION.   Yes.

PHI.   Then show it: some
Good body lend a hand to draw us nearer.
Would you have tears shed for you when you die?
Then lay me gently on his neck, that there

            [4] *Pyramid.*

I may weep floods and breathe forth my spirit.
'Tis not the wealth of Plutus, nor the gold [*Embraces* BEL.]
Lock'd in the heart of earth, can buy away
This arm-full from me; this had been a ransom
To have redeemed the Great Augustus Cæsar,
Had he been taken. You hard-hearted men,
More stony than these mountains, can you see
Such clear pure blood drop, and not cut your flesh
To stop his life, to bind whose bitter wounds,
Queens ought to tear their hair, and with their tears
Bathe 'em?—Forgive me, thou that art the wealth
Of poor Philaster!

Enter KING, ARETHUSA, *and* Guard

KING.   Is the villain ta'en?
PHA. Sir, here be two confess the deed; but sure
It was Philaster.
PHI.   Question it no more;
It was.
KING. The fellow that did fight with him,
Will tell us that.
ARE.   Aye me! I know he will.
KING. Did not you know him?
ARE.   Sir, if it was he,
He was disguis'd.
PHI.   I was so. Oh, my stars,
That I should live still.   *Aside.*
KING.   Thou ambitious fool,
Thou that hast laid a train for thy own life!—
Now I do mean to do, I'll leave to talk.
Bear them to prison.
ARE. Sir, they did plot together to take hence
This harmless life; should it pass unreveng'd,
I should to earth go weeping. Grant me, then,
By all the love a father bears his child,
Their custodies, and that I may appoint
Their tortures and their deaths.
DION. Death! Soft; our law will not reach that for this
fault.

KING. 'Tis granted; take 'em to you with a guard.—
Come, princely Pharamond, this business past,
We may with more security go on
To your intended match.
[*Exeunt all except* DION, CLEREMONT, *and* THRASILINE.]
CLE. I pray that this action lose not Philaster the hearts
of the people.
DION. Fear it not; their over-wise heads will think it but
a trick.   *Exeunt.*

ACT THE FIFTH

SCENE I[1]

Enter DION, CLEREMONT, *and* THRASILINE

THRA. Has the King sent for him to death?
DION. Yes; but the King must know 'tis not in his power
to war with Heaven.
CLE. We linger time; the King sent for Philaster and the
headsman an hour ago.
THRA. Are all his wounds well?
DION. All; they were but scratches; but the loss of blood
made him faint.
CLE. We dally, gentlemen.
THRA. Away!
DION. We'll scuffle hard before he perish.   *Exeunt.*

[SCENE II[1]]

Enter PHILASTER, ARETHUSA, *and* BELLARIO

ARE. Nay, dear Philaster, grieve not; we are well.
BEL. Nay, good my lord, forbear; we are wondrous well.
PHI. Oh, Arethusa, oh, Bellario,
Leave to be kind!
I shall be shut from Heaven, as now from earth,
If you continue so. I am a man
False to a pair of the most trusty ones

---
[1] *Before the palace.*
[1] *A prison.*

That ever earth bore; can it bear us all?
Forgive, and leave me. But the King hath sent
To call me to my death: oh, shew it me,
And then forget me! And for thee, my boy,
I shall deliver words will mollify
The hearts of beasts to spare thy innocence.

BEL. Alas, my lord, my life is not a thing
Worthy your noble thoughts! 'Tis not a life,
'Tis but a piece of childhood thrown away.
Should I outlive you, I should then outlive
Virtue and honour; and when that day comes,
If ever I shall close these eyes but once,
May I live spotted for my perjury,
And waste my limbs to nothing!

ARE. And I (the woful'st maid that ever was,
Forc'd with my hands to bring my lord to death)
Do by the honour of a virgin swear
To tell no hours beyond it!

PHI.   Make me not hated so.

ARE. Come from this prison all joyful to our deaths!

PHI. People will tear me, when they find you true
To such a wretch as I; I shall die loath'd.
Enjoy your kingdoms peaceably, whilst I
For ever sleep forgotten with my faults.
Every just servant, every maid in love,
Will have a piece of me, if you be true.

ARE. My dear lord, say not so.

BEL.   A piece of you!
He was not born of woman that can cut
It and look on.

PHI. Take me in tears betwixt you, for my heart
Will break with shame and sorrow.

ARE.   Why, 'tis well.

BEL. Lament no more.

PHI.   Why, what would you have done
If you had wrong'd me basely, and had found
Your² life no price compared to mine?² For love, sirs,
Deal with me truly.

BEL.   'Twas mistaken, sir.

² *Mason conj. Qq. F.* my . . . yours.

PHI. Why, if it were?

BEL.   Then, sir, we would have ask'd
You pardon.

PHI.   And have hope to enjoy it?

ARE. Enjoy it! ay.

PHI.   Would you indeed? be plain.

BEL. We would, my lord.

PHI.   Forgive me, then.

ARE.   So, so.

BEL. 'Tis as it should be now.

PHI.   Lead to my death. *Exeunt.*

[SCENE III[1]]

Enter KING, DION, CLEREMONT, THRASILINE, *and*
Attendants

KING. Gentlemen, who saw the prince?

CLE. So please you, sir, he's gone to see the city
And the new platform, with some gentlemen
Attending on him.

KING.   Is the princess ready
To bring her prisoner out?

THRA.   She waits your grace.

KING. Tell her we stay.   *Exit* THRASILINE.

DION.   [*Aside.*] King, yóu may be deceiv'd yet.
The head you aim at cost more setting on
Than to be lost so lightly. If it must off,—
Like a wild overflow, that swoops before him
A golden stack, and with it shakes down bridges,
Cracks the strong hearts of pines, whose cable-roots
Held out a thousand storms, a thousand thunders,
And, so made mightier, takes whole villages
Upon his back, and in that heat of pride
Charges strong towns, towers, castles, palaces,
And lays them desolate; so shall thy head,
Thy noble head, bury the lives of thousands,
That must bleed with thee like a sacrifice,
In thy red ruins.

[1] *A state-room in the palace.*

Enter ARETHUSA, PHILASTER, BELLARIO *in a robe and garland,* [*and* THRASILINE]

KING. How now? What masque is this?

BEL. Right royal sir, I should
Sing you an epithalamion of these lovers,
But having lost my best airs with my fortunes,
And wanting a celestial harp to strike
This blessed union on, thus in glad story
I give you all. These two fair cedar-branches
The noblest of the mountain where they grew,
Straightest and tallest, under whose still shades
The worthier beasts have made their lairs, and slept
Free from the fervour of the Sirian star
And the fell thunder-stroke, free from the clouds,
When they were big with humour, and deliver'd,
In thousand spouts their issues to the earth;
Oh, there was none but silent quiet there!
Till never-pleased Fortune shot up shrubs,
Base under-brambles, to divorce these branches;
And for a while they did so, and did reign
Over the mountain, and choke up his beauty
With brakes, rude thorns and thistles, till the sun
Scorch'd them even to the roots and dried them there.
And now a gentle gale hath blown again,
That made these branches meet and twine together,
Never to be divided. The god that sings
His holy numbers over marriage-beds
Hath knit their noble hearts; and here they stand
Your children, mighty King: and I have done.

KING. How, how?

ARE.   Sir, if you love it in plain truth,
(For now there is no masquing in't,) this gentleman,
The prisoner that you gave me, is become
My keeper, and through all the bitter throes
Your jealousies and his ill fate have wrought him,
Thus nobly hath he struggled, and at length
Arrived here my dear husband.

KING.   Your dear husband!—
Call in the Captain of the Citadel.—

There you shall keep your wedding. I'll provide
A masque shall make your Hymen turn his saffron
Into a sullen coat, and sing sad requiems
To your departing souls.
Blood shall put out your torches; and, instead
Of gaudy flowers about your wanton necks,
An axe shall hang, like a prodigious meteor,
Ready to crop your loves' sweets. Hear, you gods!
From this time do I shake all title off
Of father to this woman, this base woman;
And what there is of vengeance in a lion
Chaf'd among dogs or robb'd of his dear young,
The same, enforc'd more terrible, more mighty,
Expect from me!

   Are. Sir, by that little life I have left to swear by,
There's nothing that can stir me from myself.
What I have done, I have done without repentance,
For death can be no bugbear unto me,
So long as Pharamond is not my headsman.

   Dion. [*Aside.*] Sweet peace upon thy soul, thou worthy
      maid,
Whene'er thou diest! For this time I'll excuse thee,
Or be thy prologue.

   Phi.   Sir, let me speak next;
And let my dying words be better with you
Than my dull living actions. If you aim
At the dear life of this sweet innocent,
You are a tyrant and a savage monster,
That feeds upon the blood you gave a life to;
Your memory shall be as foul behind you,
As you are living; all your better deeds
Shall be in water writ, but this in marble;
No chronicle shall speak you, though your own,
But for the shame of men. No monument,
Though high and big as Pelion, shall be able
To cover this base murder: make it rich
With brass, with purest gold and shining jasper,
Like the Pyramides; lay on epitaphs
Such as make great men gods; my little marble
That only clothes my ashes, not my faults,

Shall far outshine it. And for after-issues,
Think not so madly of the heavenly wisdoms,
That they will give you more for your mad rage
To cut off, unless it be some snake, or something
Like yourself, that in his birth shall strangle you.
Remember my father, King! There was a fault,
But I forgive it. Let that sin persuade you
To love this lady; if you have a soul,
Think, save her, and be saved. For myself,
I have so long expected this glad hour,
So languish'd under you, and daily withered,
That, Heaven knows, it is a joy to die;
I find a recreation in't.

Enter a Messenger

MESS. Where is the King?
KING.   Here.
MESS.   Get you to your strength,
And rescue the Prince Pharamond from danger;
He's taken prisoner by the citizens,
Fearing² the Lord Philaster.
    DION.   [*Aside.*]   Oh, brave followers!
Mutiny, my fine dear countrymen, mutiny!
Now, my brave valiant foremen, shew your weapons
In honour of your mistresses!   [*Aside.*]

Enter a Second Messenger

2ND MESS. Arm, arm, arm, arm!
KING. A thousand devils take 'em!
DION. [*Aside.*] A thousand blessings on 'em!
    2ND MESS. Arm, O King! The city is in mutiny,
Led by an old grey ruffian, who comes on
In rescue of the Lord Philaster.
    KING. Away to the citadel! I'll see them safe,
And then cope with these burghers. Let the guard
And all the gentlemen give strong attendance.
    Exeunt all except DION, CLEREMONT, *and* THRASILINE

² *i. e., fearing for.*

CLE. The city up! this was above our wishes.

DION. Ay, and the marriage too. By my life,
This noble lady has deceiv'd us all.
A plague upon myself, a thousand plagues,
For having such unworthy thoughts of her dear honour!
Oh, I could beat myself! Or do you beat me,
And I'll beat you; for we had all one thought.

CLE. No, no, 'twill but lose time.

DION. You say true. Are your swords sharp?—Well, my
dear countrymen What-ye-lacks,[3] if you continue, and fall
not back upon the first broken skin, I'll have you chronicled
and chronicled, and cut and chronicled, and all-to-be-prais'd
and sung in sonnets, and bawled in new brave ballads, that
all tongues shall troll you in *sæcula sæculorum,* my kind
can-carriers.

THRA. What, if a toy[4] take 'em i' the heels now, and they
run all away, and cry, "the devil take the hindmost?"

DION. Then the same devil take the foremost too, and
souse him for his breakfast! If they all prove cowards, my
curses fly amongst them, and be speeding! May they have
murrains reign to keep the gentlemen at home unbound in
easy frieze! May the moths branch[5] their velvets, and their
silks only to be worn before sore eyes! May their false
lights undo 'em, and discover presses,[6] holes, stains, and old-
ness in their stuffs, and make them shop-rid! May they
keep whores and horses, and break; and live mewed up
with necks of beef and turnips! May they have many children, and none like the father! May they know no language
but that gibberish they prattle to their parcels, unless it be
the goatish Latin they write in their bonds—and may they
write that false, and lose their debts!

Re-enter KING

KING. Now the vengeance of all the gods confound them!
How they swarm together! What a hum they raise!—
Devils choke your wild throats! If a man had need to use
their valours, he must pay a brokage for it, and then bring
'em on, and they will fight like sheep. 'Tis Philaster, none

---

[3] *I. e., shopkeepers, who were in the habit of thus addressing passers-by.*
[4] *Trifle, whim.* [5] *Eat patterns on.* [6] *Creases.*

but Philaster, must allay this heat. They will not hear me
speak, but fling dirt at me and call me tyrant. Oh, run,
dear friend, and bring the Lord Philaster! Speak him fair;
call him prince; do him all the courtesy you can; commend
me to him. Oh, my wits, my wits! *Exit* CLEREMONT.

DION. [*Aside.*] Oh, my brave countrymen! as I live,
I will not buy a pin out of your walls for this. Nay,
you shall cozen me, and I'll thank you, and send you
brawn and bacon, and soil[7] you every long vacation a
brace of foremen,[8] that at Michaelmas shall come up
fat and kicking.

KING. What they will do with this poor prince, the gods
know, and I fear.

DION. [*Aside.*] Why, sir, they'll flay him, and make
church-buckets on's skin, to quench rebellion; then clap a
rivet in's sconce, and hang him up for a sign.

Enter CLEREMONT *with* PHILASTER

KING. Oh, worthy sir, forgive me! Do not make
Your miseries and my faults meet together,
To bring a greater danger. Be yourself,
Still sound amongst diseases. I have wrong'd you;
And though I find it last, and beaten to it,
Let first your goodness know it. Calm the people,
And be what you were born to. Take your love,
And with her my repentance, all my wishes,
And all my prayers. By the gods, my heart speaks this;
And if the least fall from me not perform'd,
May I be struck with thunder!

PHI.   Mighty sir,
I will not do your greatness so much wrong,
As not to make your word truth. Free the princess
And the poor boy, and let me stand the shock
Of this mad sea-breach, which I'll either turn,
Or perish with it.

KING.   Let your own word free them.

PHI. Then thus I take my leave, kissing your hand,
And hanging on your royal word. Be kingly,
And be not moved, sir. I shall bring you peace

[7] *Fatten.*   [8] *Geese.*

Or never bring myself back.

KING.   All the gods go with thee. *Exeunt.*

[SCENE IV[1]]

Enter an old Captain *and* Citizens *with* PHARAMOND

CAP. Come, my brave myrmidons, let us fall on.
Let your caps swarm, my boys, and your nimble tongues
Forget your mother-gibberish of " what do you lack,"
And set your mouths ope, children, till your palates
Fall frighted half a fathom past the cure
Of bay-salt and gross pepper, and then cry
" Philaster, brave Philaster ! " Let Philaster
Be deeper in request, my ding-dongs,[2]
My pairs of dear indentures,[2] kings of clubs,[3]
Than your cold water-camlets,[4] or your paintings
Spitted with copper.[5] Let not your hasty silks,
Or your branch'd cloth of bodkin,[6] or your tissues,
Dearly beloved of spiced cake and custard,
Your Robin Hoods, Scarlets, and Johns, tie your affections
In darkness to your shops. No, dainty duckers[7]
Up with your three-piled spirits, your wrought valours;[8]
And let your uncut cholers[9] make the King feel
The measure of your mightiness. Philaster !
Cry, my rose-nobles,[10] cry !

ALL.   Philaster ! Philaster !

CAP. How do you like this, my lord-prince ?
These are mad boys, I tell you; these are things
That will not strike their top-sails to a foist,[11]
And let a man of war, an argosy,
Hull[12] and cry cockles.[13]

PHA. Why, you rude slave, do you know what you do ?

CAP. My pretty prince of puppets, we do know;
And give your greatness warning that you talk

---

[1] *A street.*   [2] *Darlings.*   [3] *Apprentices, who were bound by indentures,
and whose usual weapons were clubs.   Throughout these scenes, it is, of
course, London citizens who are in view.*
   [4] *A cloth, made of wool, sometimes mixed with silk, with a watered
surface.*   [5] *Colored cloth interwoven with copper.*   [6] *Embroidered cloth,
originally of gold and silk.*   [7] *Cringers (?), duck-hunters (?).*
   [8] *A pun on velour.*   [9] *A pun on collars.*   [10] *Another pun. Rose-nobles
were gold coins.*   [11] *A small vessel.*   [12] *Float idly.*   [13] *Crow over them.*

No more such bug's-words,[14] or that solder'd crown
Shall be scratch'd with a musket.[15] Dear prince Pippin,
Down with your noble blood, or, as I live,
I'll have you coddled.[16]—Let him loose, my spirits:
Make us a round ring with your bills, my Hectors,
And let us see what this trim man dares do.
Now, sir, have at you! here I lie;
And with this swashing blow (do you see, sweet prince?)
I could hulk[17] your grace, and hang you up cross-legg'd,
Like a hare at a poulter's, and do this with this wiper.[18]

PHA. You will not see me murder'd, wicked villains?

1ST CIT. Yes, indeed, will we, sir; we have not seen one
For a great while.

CAP.   He would have weapons, would he?
Give him a broadside, my brave boys, with your pikes;
Branch[19] me his skin in flowers like a satin,
And between every flower a mortal cut.—
Your royalty shall ravel!—Jag him, gentlemen;
I'll have him cut to the kell,[20] then down the seams.
O for a whip to make him galloon-laces![21]
I'll have a coach-whip.

PHA.   Oh, spare me, gentlemen!

CAP. Hold, hold;
The man begins to fear and know himself.
He shall for this time only be seel'd up,[22]
With a feather through his nose, that he may only
See heaven, and think whither he is going.
Nay, my beyond-sea sir, we will proclaim you:
You would be king!
Thou tender heir apparent to a church-ale,[23]
Thou slight prince of single sarcenet,[24]
Thou royal ring-tail,[25] fit to fly at nothing
But poor men's poultry, and have every boy
Beat thee from that too with his bread and butter!

PHA. Gods keep me from these hell-hounds!

1ST CIT. I'll have a leg, that's certain.

[14] *Swaggering words.*   [15] *A male sparrow-hawk, with a pun on the weapon.*
[16] *Stewed.*   [17] *Disembowel.*   [18] *Instrument for cleaning a gun.*
[19] *Embroider.*   [20] *The caul about the hart's paunch.*   [21] *Ribbons, tape.*
[22] *Have his eyelids sewed together like a hawk's.*
[23] *I. e., a bastard, one born after the convivialities of a church feast.*
[24] *Thin silk.*   [25] *A sort of kite.*

2ND CIT.   I'll have an arm.

3RD CIT. I'll have his nose, and at mine own charge build
A college and clap't upon the gate.[26]

4TH CIT. I'll have his little gut to string a kit[27] with;
For certainly a royal gut will sound like silver.

PHA. Would they were in thy belly, and I past
My pain once!

5TH CIT. Good captain, let me have his liver to feed
ferrets.

CAP. Who will have parcels else? Speak.

PHA. Good gods, consider me! I shall be tortur'd.

1ST CIT. Captain, I'll give you the trimming of your two-
hand sword,
And let me have his skin to make false scabbards.

2ND CIT. He had no horns, sir, had he?

CAP. No, sir, he's a pollard.[28]
What wouldst thou do with horns?

2ND CIT.   Oh, if he had had,
I would have made rare hafts and whistles of 'em;
But his shin-bones, if they be sound, shall serve me.

Enter PHILASTER

ALL. Long live Philaster, the brave Prince Philaster!

PHI. I thank you, gentlemen. But why are these
Rude weapons brought abroad, to teach your hands
Uncivil trades?

CAP.   My royal Rosicleer,[29]
We are thy myrmidons, thy guard, thy roarers;[30]
And when thy noble body is in durance,
Thus do we clap our musty murrions[31] on,
And trace the streets in terror. Is it peace,
Thou Mars of men? Is the King sociable,
And bids thee live? Art thou above thy foemen,
And free as Phœbus? Speak. If not, this stand[32]
Of royal blood shall be abroach, a-tilt,
And run even to the lees of honour.

[26] *In allusion to Brazen Nose College, Oxford.*
[27] *Cittern.*   [28] *Hornless animal.*
[29] *A hero in " The Mirrour of Knighthood," a romance from the Spanish*
See *" The Knight of the Burning Castle."*   [30] *Roistering blades.*
[31] *Steel caps.*   [32] *Cask.*

Phi. Hold, and be satisfied. I am myself;
Free as my thoughts are; by the gods, I am!

Cap. Art thou the dainty darling of the King?
Art thou the Hylas to our Hercules?
Do the lords bow, and the regarded scarlets[33]
Kiss their gummed golls,[34] and cry, " We are your servants? "
Is the court navigable, and the presence stuck
With flags of friendship? If not, we are thy castle,
And this man sleeps.

Phi. I am what I desire to be, your friend;
I am what I was born to be, your prince.

Pha. Sir, there is some humanity in you;
You have a noble soul. Forget my name,
And know my misery; set me safe aboard
From these wild cannibals, and, as I live,
I'll quit this land for ever. There is nothing,—
Perpetual prisonment, cold, hunger, sickness
Of all sorts, of all dangers, and all together,
The worst company of the worst men, madness, age,
To be as many creatures as a woman,
And do as all they do, nay, to despair,—
But I would rather make it a new nature,
And live with all these, than endure one hour
Amongst these wild dogs.

Phi. I do pity you.—Friends, discharge your fears;
Deliver me the prince. I'll warrant you
I shall be old enough to find my safety.

3rd Cit. Good sir, take heed he does not hurt you;
He is a fierce man, I can tell you, sir.

Cap. Prince, by your leave, I'll have a surcingle,[35]
And make[36] you like a hawk.   [Phar.] *strives*.

Phi. Away, away, there is no danger in him:
Alas, he had rather sleep to shake his fit off!
Look you, friends, how gently he leads! Upon my word,
He's tame enough, he needs no further watching.
Good my friends, go to your houses,
And by me have your pardons and my love;
And know there shall be nothing in my power
You may deserve, but you shall have your wishes.

[33] *Courtiers clad in scarlet.*   [34] *Perfumed hands.*   [35] *Band.*   [36] *Train*

To give you more thanks, were to flatter you.
Continue still your love; and, for an earnest,
Drink this.   [*Gives money.*]

   ALL. Long mayst thou live, brave prince, brave prince,
      brave prince!   *Exeunt* PHIL. *and* PHAR.

   CAP. Go thy ways, thou art the king of courtesy!
Fall off again, my sweet youths. Come,
And every man trace to his house again,
And hang his pewter up; then to the tavern,
And bring your wives in muffs. We will have music;
And the red grape shall make us dance and rise, boys.

                        Exeunt.

[SCENE V[1]]

Enter KING, ARETHUSA, GALATEA, MEGRA, DION, CLERE-
   MONT, THRASILINE, BELLARIO, *and* Attendants

   KING. Is it appeas'd?
   DION. Sir, all is quiet as this dead of night,
As peaceable as sleep. My lord Philaster
Brings on the prince himself.
   KING.   Kind gentleman!
I will not break the least word I have given
In promise to him. I have heap'd a world
Of grief upon his head, which yet I hope
To wash away.

Enter PHILASTER *and* PHARAMOND

   CLE.   My lord is come.
   KING.   My son!
Blest be the time that I have leave to call
Such virtue mine! Now thou art in mine arms,
Methinks I have a salve unto my breast
For all the stings that dwell there. Streams of grief
That I have wrong'd thee, and as much of joy
That I repent it, issue from mine eyes;
Let them appease thee. Take thy right; take her;
She is thy right too; and forget to urge
My vexed soul with that I did before.

           [1] *An apartment in the palace.*

PHI. Sir, it is blotted from my memory,
Past and forgotten.—For you, prince of Spain,
Whom I have thus redeem'd, you have full leave
To make an honourable voyage home.
And if you would go furnish'd to your realm
With fair provision, I do see a lady,
Methinks, would gladly bear you company.
How like you this piece?
    MEG.   Sir, he likes it well,
I know your meaning. I am not the first
That nature taught to seek a fellow forth;
Can shame remain perpetually in me,
And not in others? Or have princes salves
To cure ill names, that meaner people want?
    PHI. What mean you?
    MEG.   You must get another ship,
To bear the princess and her boy together.
    DION. How now!
    MEG. Others took me, and I took her and him.
Ship us all four, my lord; we can endure
Weather and wind alike.
    KING. Clear thou thyself, or know not me for father.
    ARE. This earth, how false it is! What means is left
        for me
To clear myself? It lies in your belief.
My lords, believe me; and let all things else
Struggle together to dishonour me.
    BEL. Oh, stop your ears, great King, that I may speak
As freedom would! Then I will call this lady
As base as are her actions. Hear me, sir;
Believe your heated blood when it rebels
Against your reason, sooner than this lady.
    MEG. By this good light, he bears it handsomely.
    PHI. This lady! I will sooner trust the wind
With feathers, or the troubled sea with pearl,
Than her with any thing. Believe her not.
Why, think you, if I did believe her words,
I would outlive 'em? Honour cannot take
Revenge on you; then what were to be known
But death?

KING.   Forget her, sir, since all is knit
Between us.   But I must request of you
One favour, and will sadly[2] be denied.

PHI. Command, whate'er it be.

KING.   Swear to be true
To what you promise.

PHI.   By the powers above,
Let it not be the death of her or him,
And it is granted!

KING.   Bear away that boy
To torture; I will have her clear'd or buried.

PHI. Oh, let me call my word back, worthy sir!
Ask something else: bury my life and right
In one poor grave; but do not take away
My life and fame at once.

KING. Away with him!   It stands irrevocable.

PHI. Turn all your eyes on me.   Here stands a man,
The falsest and the basest of this world.
Set swords against this breast, some honest man,
For I have liv'd till I am pitied!
My former deeds were hateful; but this last
Is pitiful, for I unwillingly
Have given the dear preserver of my life
Unto his torture.   Is it in the power
Of flesh and blood to carry this, and live?

                              Offers to stab himself.

ARE. Dear sir, be patient yet!   Oh, stay that hand!

KING. Sirs, strip that boy.

DION.   Come, sir; your tender flesh
Will try your constancy.

BEL.   Oh, kill me, gentlemen!

DION. No.—Help, sirs.

BEL.   Will you torture me?

KING.   Haste there;
Why stay you?

BEL.   Then I shall not break my vow,
You know, just gods, though I discover all.

KING. How's that?   Will he confess?

DION.   Sir, so he says.

                    [2] *Shall be sorry to be denied.*

KING. Speak then.

BEL.   Great King, if you command
This lord to talk with me alone, my tongue,
Urg'd by my heart, shall utter all the thoughts
My youth hath known; and stranger things than these
You hear not often.

KING.   Walk aside with him.
                [DION *and* BELLARIO *walk apart.*]

DION. Why speak'st thou not?

BEL.   Know you this face, my lord?

DION. No.

BEL.   Have you not seen it, nor the like?

DION. Yes, I have seen the like, but readily
I know not where.

BEL.   I have been often told
In court of one Euphrasia, a lady,
And daughter to you; betwixt whom and me
They that would flatter my bad face would swear
There was such strange resemblance, that we two
Could not be known asunder, drest alike.

DION. By Heaven, and so there is!

BEL.   For her fair sake,
Who now doth spend the spring-time of her life
In holy pilgrimage, move to the King,
That I may scape this torture.

DION.   But thou speak'st
As like Euphrasia as thou dost look.
How came it to thy knowledge that she lives
In pilgrimage?

BEL.   I know it not, my lord;
But I have heard it, and do scarce believe it.

DION. Oh, my shame! is it possible? Draw near,
That I may gaze upon thee. Art thou she,
Or else her murderer?[3] Where wert thou born?

BEL. In Syracusa.

DION.   What's thy name?

BEL.   Euphrasia.

DION. Oh, 'tis just, 'tis she!

---

[3] *In some barbarous countries, it was believed that the murderer inherited the form and qualities of his victim.*—Mason.

Now I do know thee. Oh, that thou hadst died,
And I had never seen thee nor my shame!
How shall I own thee? Shall this tongue of mine
E'er call thee daughter more?

    BEL. Would I had died indeed! I wish it too;
And so I must have done by vow, ere publish'd
What I have told, but that there was no means
To hide it longer. Yet I joy in this,
The princess is all clear.

    KING.   What, have you done?

    DION. All is discovered.

    PHI.   Why then hold you me?
All is discovered! Pray you, let me go. *Offers to stab himself.*

    KING. Stay him.

    ARE.   What is discovered?

    DION.   Why, my shame.
It is a woman: let her speak the rest.

    PHI. How? That again!

    DION.   It is a woman.

    PHI. Blessed be you powers that favour innocence!

    KING. Lay hold upon that lady.   [MEGRA *is seized.*]

    PHI. It is a woman, sir!—Hark, gentlemen,
It is a woman!—Arethusa, take
My soul into thy breast, that would be gone
With joy. It is a woman! Thou art fair,
And virtuous still to ages, in despite
Of malice.

    KING. Speak you, where lies his shame?

    BEL.   I am his daughter.

    PHI. The gods are just.

    DION. I dare accuse none; but, before you two,
The virtue of our age, I bend my knee
For mercy.   [*Kneels.*]

    PHI. [*raising him*] Take it freely; for I know,
Though what thou didst were undiscreetly done,
'Twas meant well.

    ARE.   And for me,
I have a power to pardon sins, as oft
As any man has power to wrong me.

    CLE. Noble and worthy!

PHI.   But, Bellario,
(For I must call thee still so,) tell me why
Thou didst conceal thy sex. It was a fault,
A fault, Bellario, though thy other deeds
Of truth outweigh'd it: all these jealousies
Had flown to nothing, if thou hadst discovered
What now we know.

BEL.   My father oft would speak
Your worth and virtue; and, as I did grow
More and more apprehensive,[*] I did thirst
To see the man so prais'd. But yet all this
Was but a maiden-longing, to be lost
As soon as found; till, sitting in my window,
Printing my thoughts in lawn, I saw a god,
I thought, (but it was you,) enter our gates.
My blood flew out and back again, as fast
As I had puff'd it forth and suck'd it in
Like breath. Then was I called away in haste
To entertain you. Never was a man,
Heav'd from a sheep-cote to a sceptre, rais'd
So high in thoughts as I. You left a kiss
Upon these lips then, which I mean to keep
From you for ever. I did hear you talk,
Far above singing. After you were gone,
I grew acquainted with my heart, and search'd
What stirred it so: alas, I found it love!
Yet far from lust; for, could I but have liv'd
In presence of you, I had had my end.
For this I did delude my noble father
With a feign'd pilgrimage, and dress'd myself
In habit of a boy; and, for I knew
My birth no match for you, I was past hope
Of having you; and, understanding well
That when I made discovery of my sex
I could not stay with you, I made a vow,
By all the most religious things a maid
Could call together, never to be known,
Whilst there was hope to hide me from men's eyes,
For other than I seem'd, that I might ever

[*] *Quick to understand.*

Abide with you. Then sat I by the fount,
Where first you took me up.

KING.   Search out a match
Within our kingdom, where and when thou wilt,
And I will pay thy dowry; and thyself
Wilt well deserve him.

BEL.   Never, sir, will I
Marry; it is a thing within my vow:
But, if I may have leave to serve the princess,
To see the virtues of her lord and her,
I shall have hope to live.

ARE.   I, Philaster,
Cannot be jealous, though you had a lady
Drest like a page to serve you; nor will I
Suspect her living here.—Come, live with me;
Live free as I do. She that loves my lord,
Curs'd be the wife that hates her!

PHI. I grieve such virtue should be laid in earth
Without an heir.—Hear me, my royal father:
Wrong not the freedom of our souls so much,
To think to take revenge of that base woman;
Her malice cannot hurt us. Set her free
As she was born, saving from shame and sin.

KING. Set her at liberty.—But leave the court;
This is no place for such.—You, Pharamond,
Shall have free passage, and a conduct home
Worthy so great a prince. When you come there,
Remember 'twas your faults that lost you her,
And not my purpos'd will.

PHA.   I do confess,
Renowned sir.

KING. Last, join your hands in one. Enjoy, Philaster,
This kingdom, which is yours, and, after me,
Whatever I call mine. My blessing on you!
All happy hours be at your marriage-joys,
That you may grow yourselves over all lands,
And live to see your plenteous branches spring
Wherever there is sun! Let princes learn
By this to rule the passions of their blood;
For what Heaven wills can never be withstood.   *Exeunt.*

THE DUCHESS OF MALFI

BY
JOHN WEBSTER

INTRODUCTORY NOTE

OF *John Webster's* life almost nothing is known. The dates *1580-1625* given for his birth and death are conjectural inferences, about which the best that can be said is that no known facts contradict them.

The first notice of Webster so far discovered shows that he was collaborating in the production of plays for the theatrical manager, Henslowe, in *1602*, and of such collaboration he seems to have done a considerable amount. Four plays exist which he wrote alone, "The White Devil," "The Duchess of Malfi," "The Devil's Law-Case," and "Appius and Virginia."

"The Duchess of Malfi" was published in *1623*, but the date of writing may have been as early as *1611*. It is based on a story in Painter's "Palace of Pleasure," translated from the Italian novelist, Bandello; and it is entirely possible that it has a foundation in fact. In any case, it portrays with a terrible vividness one side of the court life of the Italian Renaissance; and its picture of the fierce quest of pleasure, the recklessness of crime, and the worldliness of the great princes of the Church finds only too ready corroboration in the annals of the time.

Webster's tragedies come toward the close of the great series of tragedies of blood and revenge, in which "The Spanish Tragedy" and "Hamlet" are landmarks, but before decadence can fairly be said to have set in. He, indeed, loads his scene with horrors almost past the point which modern taste can bear; but the intensity of his dramatic situations, and his superb power of flashing in a single line a light into the recesses of the human heart at the crises of supreme emotion, redeems him from mere sensationalism, and places his best things in the first rank of dramatic writing.

THE DUCHESS OF MALFI

DRAMATIS PERSONÆ

FERDINAND [Duke of Calabria],
CARDINAL [his brother].
ANTONIO [BOLOGNA, Steward of
the Household to the Duch-
ess].
DELIO [his friend].
DANIEL DE BOSOLA [Gentleman of
the Horse to the Duchess].
[CASTRUCCIO, an old Lord].
MARQUIS OF PESCARA.
[COUNT] MALATESTI.

RODERIGO,
SILVIO, }[Lords].
GRISOLAN,
DOCTOR.
The Several Madmen.

DUCHESS [OF MALFI].
CARIOLA [her woman].
[JULIA, Castruccio's wife, and]
the Cardinal's mistress.
[Old Lady].

Ladies, Three Young Children, Two Pilgrims, Executioners,
Court Officers, and Attendants.

ACT I

SCENE I[1]

[*Enter*] ANTONIO *and* DELIO

Delio

YOU are welcome to your country, dear Antonio;
You have been long in France, and you return
A very formal Frenchman in your habit:
How do you like the French court?
   ANT.   I admire it:
In seeking to reduce both state and people
To a fix'd order, their judicious king
Begins at home; quits first his royal palace
Of flattering sycophants, of dissolute
And infamous persons,—which he sweetly terms
His master's master-piece, the work of heaven;
Considering duly that a prince's court

[1] Malfi. The presence-chamber in the palace of the Duchess.

721

Is like a common fountain, whence should flow
Pure silver drops in general, but if 't chance
Some curs'd example poison 't near the head,
Death and diseases through the whole land spread.
And what is 't makes this blessed government
But a most provident council, who dare freely
Inform him the corruption of the times?
Though some o' the court hold it presumption
To instruct princes what they ought to do,
It is a noble duty to inform them
What they ought to foresee.[2]—Here comes Bosola,
The only court-gall; yet I observe his railing
Is not for simple love of piety:
Indeed, he rails at those things which he wants;
Would be as lecherous, covetous, or proud,
Bloody, or envious, as any man,
If he had means to be so.—Here's the cardinal.

[*Enter* CARDINAL *and* BOSOLA]

BOS. I do haunt you still.

CARD. So.

BOS. I have done you better service than to be slighted
thus. Miserable age, where only the reward of doing well
is the doing of it!

CARD. You enforce your merit too much.

BOS. I fell into the galleys in your service; where, for
two years together, I wore two towels instead of a shirt, with
a knot on the shoulder, after the fashion of a Roman mantle.
Slighted thus! I will thrive some way. Black-birds fatten
best in hard weather; why not I in these dog-days?

CARD. Would you could become honest!

BOS. With all your divinity do but direct me the way to
it. I have known many travel far for it, and yet return
as arrant knaves as they went forth, because they carried
themselves always along with them. [*Exit* CARDINAL.] Are
you gone? Some fellows, they say, are possessed with the
devil, but this great fellow were able to possess the greatest
devil, and make him worse.

ANT. He hath denied thee some suit?

[2] Prevent.

Bos. He and his brother are like plum-trees that grow crooked over standing-pools; they are rich and o'erladen with fruit, but none but crows, pies, and caterpillars feed on them. Could I be one of their flattering panders, I would hang on their ears like a horseleech, till I were full, and then drop off. I pray, leave me. Who would rely upon these miserable dependencies, in expectation to be advanc'd to-morrow? What creature ever fed worse than hoping Tantalus? Nor ever died any man more fearfully than he that hoped for a pardon. There are rewards for hawks and dogs when they have done us service; but for a soldier that hazards his limbs in a battle, nothing but a kind of geometry is his last supportation.

Delio. Geometry?

Bos. Ay, to hang in a fair pair of slings, take his latter swing in the world upon an honourable pair of crutches, from hospital to hospital. Fare ye well, sir: and yet do not you scorn us; for places in the court are but like beds in the hospital, where this man's head lies at that man's foot, and so lower and lower. [*Exit.*]

Del. I knew this fellow seven years in the galleys
For a notorious murder; and 'twas thought
The cardinal suborn'd it: he was releas'd
By the French general, Gaston de Foix,
When he recover'd Naples.

Ant. 				'Tis great pity
He should be thus neglected: I have heard
He 's very valiant. This foul melancholy
Will poison all his goodness; for, I 'll tell you,
If too immoderate sleep be truly said
To be an inward rust unto the soul,
It then doth follow want of action
Breeds all black malcontents; and their close rearing,
Like moths in cloth, do hurt for want of wearing.

Scene II[1]

Antonio, Delio, [*Enter* Silvio, Castruccio, Julia, Roderigo *and* Grisolan]

Delio. The presence 'gins to fill: you promis'd me
To make me the partaker of the natures
Of some of your great courtiers.
    Ant.   The lord cardinal's
And other strangers' that are now in court?
I shall.—Here comes the great Calabrian duke.

[*Enter* Ferdinand *and Attendants*]

Ferd. Who took the ring oftenest?[2]
Sil. Antonio Bologna, my lord.
Ferd. Our sister duchess' great-master of her household?
Give him the jewel.—When shall we leave this sportive
action, and fall to action indeed?

Cast. Methinks, my lord, you should not desire to go to
war in person.

Ferd. Now for some gravity.—Why, my lord?

Cast. It is fitting a soldier arise to be a prince, but not
necessary a prince descend to be a captain.

Ferd. No.

Cast. No, my lord; he were far better do it by a deputy.

Ferd. Why should he not as well sleep or eat by a
deputy? This might take idle, offensive, and base office
from him, whereas the other deprives him of honour.

Cast. Believe my experience, that realm is never long in
quiet where the ruler is a soldier.

Ferd. Thou toldest me thy wife could not endure fighting.

Cast. True, my lord.

Ferd. And of a jest she broke of[3] a captain she met full
of wounds: I have forgot it.

Cast. She told him, my lord, he was a pitiful fellow, to
lie, like the children of Ismael, all in tents.[4]

Ferd. Why, there's a wit were able to undo all the chirur-
geons[5] o' the city; for although gallants should quarrel,

---

[1] The same.
[2] The reference is to the knightly sport of riding at the ring.
[3] At the expense of. [4] Rolls of lint used to dress wounds. [5] Surgeons.

and had drawn their weapons, and were ready to go to it, yet her persuasions would make them put up.

CAST. That she would, my lord.—How do you like my Spanish gennet?[6]

ROD. He is all fire.

FERD. I am of Pliny's opinion, I think he was begot by the wind; he runs as if he were ballass'd[7] with quicksilver.

SIL. True, my lord, he reels from the tilt often.

ROD. GRIS. Ha, ha, ha!

FERD. Why do you laugh? Methinks you that are courtiers should be my touch-wood, take fire when I give fire; that is, laugh when I laugh, were the subject never so witty.

CAST. True, my lord: I myself have heard a very good jest, and have scorn'd to seem to have so silly a wit as to understand it.

FERD. But I can laugh at your fool, my lord.

CAST. He cannot speak, you know, but he makes faces; my lady cannot abide him.

FERD. No?

CAST. Nor endure to be in merry company; for she says too much laughing, and too much company, fills her too full of the wrinkle.

FERD. I would, then, have a mathematical instrument made for her face, that she might not laugh out of compass.—I shall shortly visit you at Milan, Lord Silvio.

SIL. Your grace shall arrive most welcome.

FERD. You are a good horseman, Antonio: you have excellent riders in France: what do you think of good horsemanship?

ANT. Nobly, my lord: as out of the Grecian horse issued many famous princes, so out of brave horsemanship arise the first sparks of growing resolution, that raise the mind to noble action.

FERD. You have bespoke it worthily.

SIL. Your brother, the lord cardinal, and sister duchess.

[6] A small horse. [7] Ballasted.

[*Enter* CARDINAL, *with* DUCHESS, *and* CARIOLA]

CARD. Are the galleys come about?

GRIS.   They are, my lord.

FERD. Here 's the Lord Silvio is come to take his
    leave.

DELIO. Now, sir, your promise: what 's that cardinal?
I mean his temper? They say he 's a brave fellow,
Will play his five thousand crowns at tennis, dance,
Court ladies, and one that hath fought single combats.

ANT. Some such flashes superficially hang on him for
form; but observe his inward character: he is a melancholy
churchman. The spring in his face is nothing but the engend'ring of toads; where he is jealous of any man, he lays
worse plots for them than ever was impos'd on Hercules, for
he strews in his way flatterers, panders, intelligencers, atheists, and a thousand such political monsters. He should have
been Pope; but instead of coming to it by the primitive
decency of the church, he did bestow bribes so largely and
so impudently as if he would have carried it away without
heaven's knowledge. Some good he hath done——

DELIO. You have given too much of him. What 's his
    brother?

ANT. The duke there? A most perverse and turbulent na-
    ture.
What appears in him mirth is merely outside;
If he laught heartily, it is to laugh
All honesty out of fashion.

DELIO.   Twins?

ANT.   In quality.
He speaks with others' tongues, and hears men's suits
With others' ears; will seem to sleep o' the bench
Only to entrap offenders in their answers;
Dooms men to death by information;
Rewards by hearsay.

DELIO.   Then the law to him
Is like a foul, black cobweb to a spider,—
He makes it his dwelling and a prison
To entangle those shall feed him.

ANT.   Most true:

He never pays debts unless they be shrewd turns,
And those he will confess that he doth owe.
Last, for his brother there, the cardinal,
They that do flatter him most say oracles
Hang at his lips; and verily I believe them,
For the devil speaks in them.
But for their sister, the right noble duchess,
You never fix'd your eye on three fair medals
Cast in one figure, of so different temper.
For her discourse, it is so full of rapture,
You only will begin then to be sorry
When she doth end her speech, and wish, in wonder,
She held it less vain-glory to talk much,
Than your penance to hear her. Whilst she speaks,
She throws upon a man so sweet a look
That it were able to raise one to a galliard.⁸
That lay in a dead palsy, and to dote
On that sweet countenance; but in that look
There speaketh so divine a continence
As cuts off all lascivious and vain hope.
Her days are practis'd in such noble virtue,
That sure her nights, nay, more, her very sleeps,
Are more in heaven than other ladies' shrifts.
Let all sweet ladies break their flatt'ring glasses,
And dress themselves in her.

DELIO.   Fie, Antonio,
You play the wire-drawer with her commendations.

ANT. I 'll case the picture up: only thus much;
All her particular worth grows to this sum,—
She stains⁹ the time past, lights the time to come.

CARI. You must attend my lady in the gallery,
Some half an hour hence.

ANT.   I shall. [*Exeunt* ANTONIO *and* DELIO.]

FERD. Sister, I have a suit to you.

DUCH.   To me, sir?

FERD. A gentleman here, Daniel de Bosola,
One that was in the galleys——

DUCH.   Yes, I know him.

FERD. A worthy fellow he is: pray, let me entreat for

⁸ A lively dance.   ⁹ Throws into the shade.

The provisorship of your horse.

DUCH.   Your knowledge of him
Commends him and prefers him.

FERD.   Call him hither.   [*Exit Attendant.*]
We [are] now upon[10] parting. Good Lord Silvio,
Do us commend to all our noble friends
At the leaguer.

SIL.   Sir, I shall.

[DUCH.]   You are for Milan?

SIL. I am.

DUCH.   Bring the caroches.[11]—We 'll bring you down
To the haven.

        [*Exeunt* DUCHESS, SILVIO, CASTRUCCIO, RODERIGO,
            GRISOLAN, CARIOLA, JULIA, *and Attendants.*]

CARD.   Be sure you entertain that Bosola
For your intelligence.[12] I would not be seen in 't;
And therefore many times I have slighted him
When he did court our furtherance, as this morning.

FERD. Antonio, the great-master of her household,
Had been far fitter.

CARD.   You are deceiv'd in him.
His nature is too honest for such business.—
He comes: I 'll leave you.   [*Exit.*]

        [*Re-enter* BOSOLA]

BOS.   I was lur'd to you.

FERD. My brother, here, the cardinal, could never
Abide you.

BOS.   Never since he was in my debt.

FERD. May be some oblique character in your face
Made him suspect you.

BOS.   Doth he study physiognomy?
There 's no more credit to be given to the face
Than to a sick man's urine, which some call
The physician's whore, because she cozens[13] him.
He did suspect me wrongfully.

FERD.   For that

        [10] At the point of.   [11] Coaches.   [12] Spy.   [13] Cheats.

You must give great men leave to take their times.
Distrust doth cause us seldom be deceiv'd.
You see the oft shaking of the cedar-tree
Fastens it more at root.

   Bos.   Yet take heed;
For to suspect a friend unworthily
Instructs him the next way to suspect you,
And prompts him to deceive you.

   Ferd.   There 's gold.

   Bos.   So:
What follows? [*Aside.*] Never rain'd such showers as these
Without thunderbolts i' the tail of them.—Whose throat must
     I cut?

   Ferd. Your inclination to shed blood rides post
Before my occasion to use you. I give you that
To live i' the court here, and observe the duchess;
To note all the particulars of her haviour,
What suitors do solicit her for marriage,
And whom she best affects. She 's a young widow:
I would not have her marry again.

   Bos.   No, sir?

   Ferd. Do not you ask the reason; but be satisfied.
I say I would not.

   Bos.   It seems you would create me
One of your familiars.

   Ferd.   Familiar! What 's that?

   Bos. Why, a very quaint invisible devil in flesh,—
An intelligencer.[24]

   Ferd   Such a kind of thriving thing
I would wish thee; and ere long thou mayst arrive
At a higher place by 't.

   Bos.   Take your devils,
Which hell calls angels! These curs'd gifts would make
You a corrupter, me an impudent traitor;
And should I take these, they'd take me [to] hell.

   Ferd. Sir, I 'll take nothing from you that I have given.
There is a place that I procur'd for you
This morning, the provisorship o' the horse;
Have you heard on 't?

<hr>

   24 Spy.

Bos. No.

Ferd. 'Tis yours: is 't not worth thanks?

Bos. I would have you curse yourself now, that your bounty
(Which makes men truly noble) e'er should make me
A villain. O, that to avoid ingratitude
For the good deed you have done me, I must do
All the ill man can invent! Thus the devil
Candies all sins o'er; and what heaven terms vile,
That names he complimental.

Ferd. Be yourself;
Keep your old garb of melancholy; 'twill express
You envy those that stand above your reach,
Yet strive not to come near 'em. This will gain
Access to private lodgings, where yourself
May, like a politic dormouse——

Bos. As I have seen some
Feed in a lord's dish, half asleep, not seeming
To listen to any talk; and yet these rogues
Have cut his throat in a dream. What's my place?
The provisorship o' the horse? Say, then, my corruption
Grew out of horse-dung: I am your creature.

Ferd. Away! [Exit.]

Bos. Let good men, for good deeds, covet good fame,
Since place and riches oft are bribes of shame.
Sometimes the devil doth preach. Exit.

[Scene III[1]]

[Enter Ferdinand, Duchess, Cardinal, and Cariola]

Card. We are to part from you; and your own discretion
Must now be your director.

Ferd. You are a widow:
You know already what man is; and therefore
Let not youth, high promotion, eloquence——

Card. No,
Nor anything without the addition, honour,
Sway your high blood.

Ferd. Marry! they are most luxurious[2]
Will wed twice.

[1] Malfi. Gallery in the Duchess's palace. [2] Lustful.

CARD.   O, fie!

FERD.   Their livers are more spotted
Than Laban's sheep.[3]

DUCH.   Diamonds are of most value,
They say, that have pass'd through most jewellers' hands.

FERD. Whores by that rule are precious.

DUCH.   .   Will you hear me?
I 'll never marry.

CARD.   So most widows say;
But commonly that motion lasts no longer
Than the turning of an hour-glass: the funeral sermon
And it end both together.

FERD.   Now hear me:
You live in a rank pasture, here, i' the court;
There is a kind of honey-dew that 's deadly;
'Twill poison your fame; look to 't. Be not cunning;
For they whose faces do belie their hearts
Are witches ere they arrive at twenty years,
Ay, and give the devil suck.

DUCH. This is terrible good counsel.

FERD. Hypocrisy is woven of a fine small thread,
Subtler than Vulcan's engine:[4] yet, believe 't,
Your darkest actions, nay, your privat'st thoughts,
Will come to light.

CARD.   You may flatter yourself,
And take your own choice; privately be married
Under the eaves of night——

FERD.   Think 't the best voyage
That e'er you made; like the irregular crab,
Which, though 't goes backward, thinks that it goes right
Because it goes its own way: but observe,
Such weddings may more properly be said
To be executed than celebrated.

CARD.   The marriage night
Is the entrance into some prison.

FERD.   And those joys,
Those lustful pleasures, are like heavy sleeps
Which do fore-run man's mischief.

CARD.   Fare you well.

---

[3] Genesis xxxi., 31-42.   [4] The net in which he caught Venus and Mars.

Wisdom begins at the end: remember it.   [*Exit.*]

DUCH. I think this speech between you both was studied,
It came so roundly off.

FERD.   You are my sister;
This was my father's poniard, do you see?
I 'd be loth to see 't look rusty, 'cause 'twas his.
I would have you give o'er these chargeable revels:
A visor and a mask are whispering-rooms
That were never built for goodness,—fare ye well—
And women like variety of courtship.
What cannot a neat knave with a smooth tale
Make a woman believe? Farewell, lusty widow.   [*Exit.*]

DUCH. Shall this move me? If all my royal kindred
Lay in my way unto this marriage,
I 'd make them my low footsteps. And even now,
Even in this hate, as men in some great battles,
By apprehending danger, have achiev'd
Almost impossible actions (I have heard soldiers say so),
So I through frights and threatenings will assay
This dangerous venture. Let old wives report
I wink'd and chose a husband.—Cariola,
To thy known secrecy I have given up
More than my life,—my fame.

CARI.   Both shall be safe;
For I 'll conceal this secret from the world
As warily as those that trade in poison
Keep poison from their children.

DUCH.   Thy protestation
Is ingenious and hearty; I believe it.
Is Antonio come?

CARI.   He attends you.

DUCH.   Good dear soul,
Leave me; but place thyself behind the arras,
Where thou mayst overhear us. Wish me good speed;
For I am going into a wilderness,
Where I shall find nor path nor friendly clue
To be my guide.   [CARIOLA *goes behind the arras.*]

[*Enter* ANTONIO]

I sent for you: sit down;
Take pen and ink, and write: are you ready?

ANT.   Yes.

DUCH. What did I say?

ANT. That I should write somewhat.

DUCH.   O, I remember.
After these triumphs and this large expense
It 's fit, like thrifty husbands,[5] we inquire
What 's laid up for to-morrow.

ANT. So please your beauteous excellence.

DUCH.   Beauteous!
Indeed, I thank you. I look young for your sake;
You have ta'en my cares upon you.

ANT.   I 'll fetch your grace
The particulars of your revenue and expense.

DUCH. O, you are
An upright treasurer: but you mistook;
For when I said I meant to make inquiry
What 's laid up for to-morrow, I did mean
What 's laid up yonder for me.

ANT.   Where?

DUCH.   In heaven.
I am making my will (as 'tis fit princes should,
In perfect memory), and, I pray, sir, tell me,
Were not one better make it smiling, thus,
Than in deep groans and terrible ghastly looks,
As if the gifts we parted with procur'd[6]
That violent distraction?

ANT.   O, much better.

DUCH. If I had a husband now, this care were quit:
But I intend to make you overseer.
What good deed shall we first remember? Say.

ANT. Begin with that first good deed began i' the world
After man's creation, the sacrament of marriage;
I 'd have you first provide for a good husband;
Give him all.

DUCH.   All!

[5] Housekeepers.   [6] Produced.

ANT.   Yes, your excellent self.

DUCH. In a winding-sheet?

ANT.   In a couple.

DUCH. Saint Winifred, that were a strange will!

ANT. 'Twere stranger[7] if there were no will in you
To marry again.

DUCH.   What do you think of marriage?

ANT. I take 't, as those that deny purgatory,
It locally contains or heaven or hell;
There 's no third place in 't.

DUCH.   How do you affect it?

ANT. My banishment, feeding my melancholy,
Would often reason thus.

DUCH.   Pray, let 's hear it.

ANT. Say a man never marry, nor have children,
What takes that from him? Only the bare name
Of being a father, or the weak delight
To see the little wanton ride a-cock-horse
Upon a painted stick, or hear him chatter
Like a taught starling.

DUCH.   Fie, fie, what 's all this?
One of your eyes is blood-shot; use my ring to 't.
They say 'tis very sovereign. 'Twas my wedding-ring,
And I did vow never to part with it
But to my second husband.

ANT. You have parted with it now.

DUCH. Yes, to help your eye-sight.

ANT. You have made me stark blind.

DUCH. How?

ANT. There is a saucy and ambitious devil
Is dancing in this circle.

DUCH.   Remove him.

ANT. How?

DUCH. There needs small conjuration, when your finger
May do it: thus. Is it fit?

          [*She puts the ring upon his finger*]: *he kneels.*

ANT.   What said you?

DUCH.   Sir,
This goodly roof of yours is too low built;

                    7 Qq. read *strange.*

I cannot stand upright in 't nor discourse,
Without I raise it higher. Raise yourself;
Or, if you please, my hand to help you: so.   [*Raises him.*]

ANT. Ambition, madam, is a great man's madness,
That is not kept in chains and close-pent rooms,
But in fair lightsome lodgings, and is girt
With the wild noise of prattling visitants,
Which makes it lunatic beyond all cure.
Conceive not I am so stupid but I aim[s]
Whereto your favours tend: but he 's a fool
That, being a-cold, would thrust his hands i' the fire
To warm them.

DUCH.   So, now the ground 's broke,
You may discover what a wealthy mine
I make you lord of.

ANT.   O my unworthiness!

DUCH. You were ill to sell yourself:
This dark'ning of your worth is not like that
Which tradesmen use i' the city; their false lights
Are to rid bad wares off: and I must tell you,
If you will know where breathes a cómplete man
(I speak it without flattery), turn your eyes,
And progress through yourself.

ANT. Were there nor heaven nor hell,
I should be honest: I have long serv'd virtue,
And ne'er ta'en wages of her.

DUCH.   Now she pays it.
The misery of us that are born great!
We are forc'd to woo, because none dare woo us;
And as a tyrant doubles with his words,
And fearfully equivocates, so we
Are forc'd to express our violent passions
In riddles and in dreams, and leave the path
Of simple virtue, which was never made
To seem the thing it is not. Go, go brag
You have left me heartless; mine is in your bosom:
I hope 'twill multiply love there. You do tremble:
Make not your heart so dead a piece of flesh,
To fear more than to love me. Sir, be confident:

[s] Guess.

What is 't distracts you? This is flesh and blood, sir;
'Tis not the figure cut in alabaster
Kneels at my husband's tomb. Awake, awake, man!
I do here put off all vain ceremony,
And only do appear to you a young widow
That claims you for her husband, and, like a widow,
I use but half a blush in 't.

ANT.   Truth speak for me;
I will remain the constant sanctuary
Of your good name.

DUCH.   I thank you, gentle love:
And 'cause you shall not come to me in debt,
Being now my steward, here upon your lips
I sign your *Quietus est.*[9] This you should have begg'd
    now.
I have seen children oft eat sweetmeats thus,
As fearful to devour them too soon.

ANT. But for your brothers?

DUCH.   Do not think of them:
All discord without this circumference
Is only to be pitied, and not fear'd:
Yet, should they know it, time will easily
Scatter the tempest.

ANT.   These words should be mine,
And all the parts you have spoke, if some part of it
Would not have savour'd flattery.

DUCH. Kneel. [CARIOLA *comes from behind the arras.*]
ANT.   Ha!

DUCH. Be not amaz'd; this woman 's of my counsel:
I have heard lawyers say, a contract in a chamber
Per verba [*de*] *presenti*[10] is absolute marriage.

                            [*She and* ANTONIO *kneel.*]
Bless, heaven, this sacred gordian[11] which let violence
Never untwine!

ANT. And may our sweet affections, like the spheres,
Be still in motion!

DUCH.   Quickening, and make

----

[9] The phrase used to indicate that accounts had been examined and
found correct.
[10] Using words of present time; *i. e.*, "I take," not "I will take."
[11] Knot.

The like soft music!

ANT. That we may imitate the loving palms,
Best emblem of a peaceful marriage,
That never bore fruit, divided!

DUCH. What can the church force more?

ANT. That fortune may not know an accident,
Either of joy or sorrow, to divide
Our fixed wishes!

DUCH.   How can the church build faster?[12]
We now are man and wife, and 'tis the church
That must but echo this.—Maid, stand apart:
I now am blind.

ANT.   What 's your conceit in this?

DUCH. I would have you lead your fortune by the hand
Unto your marriage-bed:
(You speak in me this, for we now are one:)
We 'll only lie and talk together, and plot
To appease my humorous[13] kindred; and if you please,
Like the old tale in *Alexander and Lodowick,*
Lay a naked sword between us, keep us chaste.
O, let me shroud my blushes in your bosom,
Since 'tis the treasury of all my secrets!

                    [*Exeunt* DUCHESS *and* ANTONIO.]

CARI. Whether the spirit of greatness or of woman
Reign most in her, I know not; but it shows
A fearful madness. I owe her much of pity.   *Exit.*

ACT II

SCENE I[1]

[*Enter*] BOSOLA *and* CASTRUCCIO

BOS. You say you would fain be taken for an eminent
    courtier?

CAST. 'Tis the very main[2] of my ambition.

BOS. Let me see: you have a reasonable good face for 't
already, and your night-cap expresses your ears sufficient

---

[12] More firmly.   [13] Of difficult disposition.
[1] Malfi.   An apartment in the palace of the Duchess.
[2] Chief part.

largely. I would have you learn to twirl the strings of your band with a good grace, and in a set speech, at th' end of every sentence, to hum three or four times, or blow your nose till it smart again, to recover your memory. When you come to be a president in criminal causes, if you smile upon a prisoner, hang him; but if you frown upon him and threaten him, let him be sure to scape the gallows.

CAST. I would be a very merry president.

BOS. Do not sup o' nights; 'twill beget you an admirable wit.

CAST. Rather it would make me have a good stomach to quarrel; for they say, your roaring boys eat meat seldom, and that makes them so valiant. But how shall I know whether the people take me for an eminent fellow?

BOS. I will teach a trick to know it: give out you lie a-dying, and if you hear the common people curse you, be sure you are taken for one of the prime night-caps.[3]

[Enter an Old Lady]

You come from painting now.

OLD LADY. From what?

BOS. Why, from your scurvy face-physic. To behold thee not painted inclines somewhat near a miracle. These in thy face here were deep ruts and foul sloughs the last progress.[4] There was a lady in France that, having had the small-pox, flayed the skin off her face to make it more level; and whereas before she looked like a nutmeg-grater, after she resembled an abortive hedge-hog.

OLD LADY. Do you call this painting?

BOS. No, no, but you call [it] careening[5] of an old morphewed[6] lady, to make her disembogue[7] again: there 's roughcast phrase to your plastic.[8]

OLD LADY. It seems you are well acquainted with my closet.

BOS. One would suspect it for a shop of witchcraft, to find in it the fat of serpents, spawn of snakes, Jews' spittle, and their young children's ordure; and all these for the face.

---

[3] Bullies (Hazlitt); lawyers (Vaughan).   [4] Royal journey.
[5] Turning a boat on its side for repairs.   [6] Scabbed.   [7] Empty.
[8] Face-modeling (Sampson).   "There's a plain statement of your prac-
tises."

I would sooner eat a dead pigeon taken from the soles of
the feet of one sick of the plague, than kiss one of you
fasting. Here are two of you, whose sin of your youth is
the very patrimony of the physician; makes him renew his
foot-cloth with the spring, and change his high-pric'd
courtezan with the fall of the leaf. I do wonder you do not
loathe yourselves. Observe my meditation now.
What thing is in this outward form of man
To be belov'd? We account it ominous,
If nature do produce a colt, or lamb,
A fawn, or goat, in any limb resembling
A man, and fly from 't as a prodigy:
Man stands amaz'd to see his deformity
In any other creature but himself.
But in our own flesh though we bear diseases
Which have their true names only ta'en from beasts,—
As the most ulcerous wolf and swinish measle,—
Though we are eaten up of lice and worms,
And though continually we bear about us
A rotten and dead body, we delight
To hide it in rich tissue: all our fear,
Nay, all our terror, is, lest our physician
Should put us in the ground to be made sweet.—
Your wife 's gone to Rome: you two couple, and get you to
the wells at Lucca to recover your aches. I have other
work on foot.   [*Exeunt* CASTRUCCIO *and Old Lady*]
I observe our duchess
Is sick a-days, she pukes, her stomach seethes,
The fins of her eye-lids look most teeming blue,[9]
She wanes i' the cheek, and waxes fat i' the flank,
And, contrary to our Italian fashion,
Wears a loose-bodied gown: there 's somewhat in 't,
I have a trick may chance discover it,
A pretty one; I have bought some apricocks,
The first our spring yields.

[9] Blue like those of a woman with child.

[*Enter* ANTONIO *and* DELIO, *talking together apart*]

DELIO.   And so long since married?
You amaze me.

ANT.   Let me seal your lips for ever:
For, did I think that anything but th' air
Could carry these words from you, I should wish
You had no breath at all.—Now, sir, in your contemplation?
You are studying to become a great wise fellow.

BOS. O, sir, the opinion of wisdom is a foul tetter[10] that
runs all over a man's body: if simplicity direct us to have no
evil, it directs us to a happy being; for the subtlest folly
proceeds from the subtlest wisdom: let me be simply honest.

ANT. I do understand your inside.

BOS.   Do you so?

ANT. Because you would not seem to appear to th' world
Puff'd up with your preferment, you continue
This out-of-fashion melancholy: leave it, leave it.

BOS. Give me leave to be honest in any phrase, in any
compliment whatsoever. Shall I confess myself to you?
I look no higher than I can reach: they are the gods that
must ride on winged horses. A lawyer's mule of a slow
pace will both suit my disposition and business; for, mark
me, when a man's mind rides faster than his horse can
gallop, they quickly both tire.

ANT. You would look up to heaven, but I think
The devil, that rules i' th' air, stands in your light.

BOS. O, sir, you are lord of the ascendant,[11] chief man with
the duchess: a duke was your cousin-german remov'd. Say
you were lineally descended from King Pepin, or he himself, what of this? Search the heads of the greatest rivers
in the world, you shall find them but bubbles of water.
Some would think the souls of princes were brought forth
by some more weighty cause than those of meaner persons:
they are deceiv'd, there 's the same hand to them; the like
passions sway them; the same reason that makes a vicar go
to law for a tithe-pig, and undo his neighbours, makes them
spoil a whole province, and batter down goodly cities with
the cannon.

[10] Scurf.   [11] Person of highest influence.

[*Enter* DUCHESS *and Ladies*]

DUCH. Your arm, Antonio: do I not grow fat?
I am exceeding short-winded.—Bosola,
I would have you, sir, provide for me a litter;
Such a one as the Duchess of Florence rode in.

BOS. The duchess us'd one when she was great with child.

DUCH. I think she did.—Come hither, mend my ruff:
Here, when? thou art such a tedious lady; and
Thy breath smells of lemon-pills: would thou hadst done!
Shall I swoon under thy fingers? I am
So troubled with the mother![12]

BOS.   [*aside*.] I fear too much.

DUCH. I have heard you say that the French courtiers
Wear their hats on 'fore the king.

ANT. I have seen it.

DUCH.   In the presence?

ANT.   Yes.

DUCH. Why should not we bring up that fashion?
'Tis ceremony more than duty that consists
In the removing of a piece of felt.
Be you the example to the rest o' th' court;
Put on your hat first.

ANT.   You must pardon me:
I have seen, in colder countries than in France,
Nobles stand bare to th' prince; and the distinction
Methought show'd reverently.

BOS. I have a present for your grace.

DUCH.   For me, sir?

BOS. Apricocks, madam.

DUCH.   O, sir, where are they?
I have heard of none to-year[13]

BOS.   [*aside*.] Good; her colour rises.

DUCH. Indeed, I thank you: they are wondrous fair ones.
What an unskilful fellow is our gardener!
We shall have none this month.

BOS. Will not your grace pare them?

DUCH. No: they taste of musk, methinks; indeed they do.

BOS. I know not: yet I wish your grace had par'd 'em.

[12] Hysteria.   [13] This year.

Duch. Why?

Bos.   I forget to tell you, the knave gardener,
Only to raise his profit by them the sooner,
Did ripen them in horse-dung.

Duch.   O, you jest.—
You shall judge: pray, taste one.

Ant.   Indeed, madam,
I do not love the fruit.

Duch.   Sir, you are loth
To rob us of our dainties. 'Tis a delicate fruit;
They say they are restorative.

Bos.   'Tis a pretty art,
This grafting.

Duch. 'Tis so; a bettering of nature.

Bos. To make a pippin grow upon a crab,
A damson on a black-thorn.—[*Aside.*] How greedily she
    eats them!
A whirlwind strike off these bawd farthingales!
For, but for that and the loose-bodied gown,
I should have discover'd apparently[14]
The young springal[15] cutting a caper in her belly.

Duch. I thank you, Bosola: they were right good ones,
If they do not make me sick.

Ant.   How now, madam!

Duch. This green fruit and my stomach are not friends:
How they swell me!

Bos.   [*aside.*] Nay, you are too much swell'd already.

Duch. O, I am in an extreme cold sweat!

Bos.   I am very sorry. [*Exit.*]

Duch. Lights to my chamber!—O good Antonio,
I fear I am undone!

Delio.   Lights there, lights!
                    Exeunt Duchess [*and Ladies.*]

Ant. O my most trusty Delio, we are lost!
I fear she 's fall'n in labour; and there 's left
No time for her remove.

Delio.   Have you prepar'd
Those ladies to attend her; and procur'd
That politic safe conveyance for the midwife

----

[14] Clearly.   [15] Youngster.

Your duchess plotted?

ANT.   I have.

DELIO. Make use, then, of this forc'd occasion.
Give out that Bosola hath poison'd her
With these apricocks; that will give some colour
For her keeping close.

ANT.   Fie, fie, the physicians
Will then flock to her.

DELIO. For that you may pretend
She'll use some prepar'd antidote of her own,
Lest the physicians should re-poison her.

ANT. I am lost in amazement: I know not what to think
on 't.   *Exeunt.*

SCENE II[1]

[*Enter*] BOSOLA *and Old Lady*

BOS. So, so, there 's no question but her techiness[2] and
most vulturous eating of the apricocks are apparent signs
of breeding, now?

OLD LADY. I am in haste, sir.

BOS. There was a young waiting-woman had a monstrous
desire to see the glass-house——

OLD LADY. Nay, pray, let me go. I will hear no more of
the glass-house. You are still[3] abusing women!

BOS. Who, I? No; only, by the way now and then, mention your frailties. The orange-tree bears ripe and green
fruit and blossoms all together; and some of you give entertainment for pure love, but more for more precious
reward. The lusty spring smells well; but drooping autumn
tastes well. If we have the same golden showers that
rained in the time of Jupiter the thunderer, you have the
same Danäes still, to hold up their laps to receive them.
Didst thou never study the mathematics?

OLD LADY. What 's that, sir?

BOS. Why, to know the trick how to make a many lines
meet in one centre. Go, go, give your foster-daughters
good counsel: tell them, that the devil takes delight to
hang at a woman's girdle, like a false rusty watch, that
she cannot discern how the time passes. [*Exit Old Lady.*]

---

[1] A hall in the same palace.   [2] Crossness.   [3] Always.

[*Enter* ANTONIO, RODERIGO, *and* GRISOLAN]

ANT. Shut up the court-gates.

ROD.   Why, sir? What's the danger?

ANT. Shut up the posterns presently, and call
All the officers o' th' court.

GRIS.   I shall instantly.   [*Exit.*]

ANT. Who keeps the key o' th' park-gate?

ROD.   Forobosco.

ANT. Let him bring 't presently.

[*Re-enter* GRISOLAN *with Servants*]

FIRST SERV. O, gentleman o' th' court, the foulest treason!

BOS. [*aside.*] If that these apricocks should be poison'd
        now,
Without my knowledge?

FIRST SERV. There was taken even now a Switzer in the
        duchess' bed-chamber——

SECOND SERV. A Switzer!

FIRST SERV. With a pistol——

SECOND SERV. There was a cunning traitor!

FIRST SERV. And all the moulds of his buttons were leaden
bullets.

SECOND SERV. O wicked cannibal!

FIRST SERV. 'Twas a French plot, upon my life.

SECOND SERV. To see what the devil can do!

ANT. [Are] all the officers here?

SERVANTS. We are.

ANT. Gentlemen,
We have lost much plate, you know; and but this evening
Jewels, to the value of four thousand ducats,
Are missing in the duchess' cabinet.
Are the gates shut?

SERV.   Yes.

ANT.   'Tis the duchess' pleasure
Each officer be lock'd into his chamber
Till the sun-rising; and to send the keys
Of all their chests and of their outward doors
Into her bed-chamber. She is very sick.

ROD. At her pleasure.

ANT. She entreats you take 't not ill: the innocent
Shall be the more approv'd by it.

BOS. Gentlemen o' the wood-yard, where 's your Switzer
now?

FIRST SERV. By this hand, 'twas credibly reported by one o'
the black guard.⁴   [*Exeunt all except* ANTONIO *and* DELIO.]

DELIO. How fares it with the duchess?

ANT.   She 's expos'd
Unto the worst of torture, pain, and fear.

DELIO. Speak to her all happy comfort.

ANT. How I do play the fool with mine own danger!
You are this night, dear friend, to post to Rome:
My life lies in your service.

DELIO.   Do not doubt me.

ANT. O, 'tis far from me: and yet fear presents me
Somewhat that looks like danger.

DELIO.   Believe it,
'Tis but the shadow of your fear, no more:
How superstitiously we mind our evils!
The throwing down salt, or crossing of a hare,
Bleeding at nose, the stumbling of a horse,
Or singing of a cricket, are of power
To daunt whole man in us. Sir, fare you well:
I wish you all the joys of a bless'd father;
And, for my faith, lay this unto your breast,—
Old friends, like old swords, still are trusted best.   [*Exit.*]

[Enter CARIOLA*]*

CARI. Sir, you are the happy father of a son:
Your wife commends him to you.

ANT.   Blessèd comfort!—
For heaven' sake, tend her well: I 'll presently⁵
Go set a figure for 's nativity.⁶   *Exeunt.*

⁴ The meaner servants.   ⁵ At once.   ⁶ Cast his horoscope.

Scene III[1]

[Enter Bosola, *with a dark lantern]*

Bos. Sure I did hear a woman shriek: list, ha!
And the sound came, if I receiv'd it right,
From the duchess' lodgings. There 's some stratagem
In the confining all our courtiers
To their several wards: I must have part of it;
My intelligence will freeze else. List, again!
It may be 'twas the melancholy bird,
Best friend of silence and of solitariness,
The owl, that screamed so.—Ha! Antonio!

[Enter Antonio *with a candle, his sword drawn]*

Ant. I heard some noise.—Who 's there? What art thou?
　　Speak.

Bos. Antonio, put not your face nor body
To such a forc'd expression of fear;
I am Bosola, your friend.

Ant. 　　　　　　Bosola!—
[Aside.] This mole does undermine me.—Heard you not
A noise even now?

Bos. 　　　　From whence?

Ant. 　　　　　　　　From the duchess' lodging.

Bos. Not I: did you?

Ant. 　　　　I did, or else I dream'd.

Bos. Let 's walk towards it.

Ant. 　　　　　　No: it may be 'twas
But the rising of the wind.

Bos. 　　　　　Very likely.
Methinks 'tis very cold, and yet you sweat:
You look wildly.

Ant. 　　　I have been setting a figure[2]
For the duchess' jewels.

Bos. 　　　　Ah, and how falls your question?
Do you find it radical?[3]

Ant. 　　　　What 's that to you?
'Tis rather to be question'd what design,

---

[1] The court of the same palace.　[2] Making an astrological calculation.
[3] Going to the root of the matter.

When all men were commanded to their lodgings,
Makes you a night-walker.

Bos.   In sooth, I 'll tell you:
Now all the court 's asleep, I thought the devil
Had least to do here; I came to say my prayers;
And if it do offend you I do so,
You are a fine courtier.

ANT.   [*aside.*] This fellow will undo me.—
You gave the duchess apricocks to-day:
Pray heaven they were not poison'd!

Bos. Poison'd! a Spanish fig
For the imputation!

ANT.   Traitors are ever confident
Till they are discover'd. There were jewels stol'n too:
In my conceit, none are to be suspected
More than yourself.

Bos.   You are a false steward.

ANT. Saucy slave, I 'll pull thee up by the roots.

Bos. May be the ruin will crush you to pieces.

ANT. You are an impudent snake indeed, sir:
Are you scarce warm, and do you show your sting?
You libel[4] well, sir?

Bos.   No, sir: copy it out,
And I will set my hand to 't.

ANT.   [*aside.*] My nose bleeds.
One that were superstitious would count
This ominous, when it merely comes by chance.
Two letters, that are wrought here for my name,[5]
Are drown'd in blood!
Mere accident.—For you, sir, I 'll take order
I' the morn you shall be safe.—[*Aside.*] 'Tis that must
     colour
Her lying-in.—Sir, this door you pass not:
I do not hold it fit that you come near
The duchess' lodgings, till you have quit yourself.—
[*Aside.*] The great are like the base, nay, they are the same,
When they seek shameful ways to avoid shame.   *Exit.*

Bos. Antonio hereabout did drop a paper:—
Some of your help, false friend.[6]—O, here it is.

---

[4] Write.   [5] *I. e.*, on his handkerchief.   [6] Addressing the lantern.

What 's here? a child's nativity calculated!   [*Reads.*]
'*The duchess was deliver'd of a son, 'tween the hours
twelve and one in the night, Anno Dom.* 1504,'—that 's this
year—'*decimo nono Decembris,*'—that 's this night—'*taken
according to the meridian of Malfi,*'—that 's our duchess:
happy discovery!—'*The lord of the first house being com-
bust in the ascendant, signifies short life; and Mars being in
a human sign, joined to the tail of the Dragon, in the eighth
house, doth threaten a violent death. Cætera non scrutantur.*'[7]
Why, now 'tis most apparent; this precise fellow
Is the duchess' bawd:—I have it to my wish!
This is a parcel of intelligency[8]
Our courtiers were cas'd up for: it needs must follow
That I must be committed on pretence
Of poisoning her; which I 'll endure, and laugh at.
If one could find the father now! but that
Time will discover. Old Castruccio
I' th' morning posts to Rome: by him I 'll send
A letter that shall make her brothers' galls
O'erflow their livers. This was a thrifty[9] way!
Though lust do mask in ne'er so strange disguise,
She 's oft found witty, but is never wise.   [*Exit.*]

SCENE IV[1]

[*Enter*] CARDINAL *and* JULIA

CARD. Sit: thou art my best of wishes. Prithee, tell me
What trick didst thou invent to come to Rome
Without thy husband?

JULIA.   Why, my lord, I told him
I came to visit an old anchorite[2]
Here for devotion.

CARD.   Thou art a witty false one,—
I mean, to him.

JULIA. You have prevail'd with me
Beyond my strongest thoughts; I would not now

[7] "The rest not considered."   [8] A piece of news.   [9] Cleverly contrived.
[1] Rome. An apartment in the palace of the Cardinal.
[2] Religious recluse.

Find you inconstant.

CARD.   Do not put thyself
To such a voluntary torture, which proceeds
Out of your own guilt.

JULIA.   How, my lord!

CARD.   You fear
My constancy, because you have approv'd[3]
Those giddy and wild turnings in yourself.

JULIA. Did you e'er find them?

CARD.   Sooth, generally for women,
A man might strive to make glass malleable,
Ere he should make them fixed.

JULIA.   So, my lord.

CARD. We had need go borrow that fantastic glass
Invented by Galileo the Florentine
To view another spacious world i' th' moon,
And look to find a constant woman there.

JULIA. This is very well, my lord.

CARD.   Why do you weep?
Are tears your justification? The self-same tears
Will fall into your husband's bosom, lady,
With a loud protestation that you love him
Above the world. Come, I 'll love you wisely,
That 's jealously; since I am very certain
You cannot make me cuckold.

JULIA.   I 'll go home
To my husband.

CARD.   You may thank me, lady,
I have taken you off your melancholy perch,
Bore you upon my fist, and show'd you game,
And let you fly at it.—I pray thee, kiss me.—
When thou wast with thy husband, thou wast watch'd
Like a tame elephant:—still you are to thank me:—
Thou hadst only kisses from him and high feeding;
But what delight was that? 'Twas just like one
That hath a little fing'ring on the lute,
Yet cannot tune it:—still you are to thank me.

JULIA. You told me of a piteous wound i' th' heart,
And a sick liver, when you woo'd me first,

[3] Experienced.

And spake like one in physic.[a]

CARD.   Who 's that?——

[Enter Servant]

Rest firm, for my affection to thee,
Lightning moves slow to 't.

SERV.   Madam, a gentleman,
That 's come post from Malfi, desires to see you.

CARD. Let him enter: I 'll withdraw.   *Exit.*

SERV.   He says
Your husband, old Castruccio, is come to Rome,
Most pitifully tir'd with riding post.   *[Exit.]*

[Enter DELIO*]*

JULIA. *[aside.]* Signior Delio! 'tis one of my old suitors.

DELIO. I was bold to come and see you.

JULIA.   Sir, you are welcome.

DELIO. Do you lie here?

JULIA.   Sure, your own experience
Will satisfy you no: our Roman prelates
Do not keep lodging for ladies.

DELIO.   Very well:
I have brought you no commendations from your husband,
For I know none by him.

JULIA.   I hear he 's come to Rome.

DELIO. I never knew man and beast, of a horse and a
    knight,
So weary of each other. If he had had a good back,
He would have undertook to have borne his horse,
His breech was so pitifully sore.

JULIA.   Your laughter
Is my pity.

DELIO. Lady, I know not whether
You want money, but I have brought you some.

JULIA. From my husband?

DELIO.   No, from mine own allowance.

JULIA. I must hear the condition, ere I be bound to take it

DELIO. Look on 't, 'tis gold; hath it not a fine colour?

JULIA. I have a bird more beautiful.

[a] Sick.

DELIO.   Try the sound on 't.
JULIA. A lute-string far exceeds it.
It hath no smell, like cassia or civet;
Nor is it physical,[5] though some fond doctors
Persuade us seethe 't in cullises.[6] I 'll tell you,
This is a creature bred by——

[Re-enter Servant]

SERV.   Your husband 's come,
Hath deliver'd a letter to the Duke of Calabria
That, to my thinking, hath put him out of his wits. [*Exit.*]
JULIA. Sir, you hear:
Pray, let me know your business and your suit
As briefly as can be.
DELIO. With good speed: I would wish you,
At such time as you are non-resident
With your husband, my mistress.
JULIA. Sir, I 'll go ask my husband if I shall,
And straight return your answer.   *Exit.*
DELIO.   Very fine!
Is this her wit, or honesty, that speaks thus?
I heard one say the duke was highly mov'd
With a letter sent from Malfi. I do fear
Antonio is betray'd. How fearfully
Shows his ambition now! Unfortunate fortune!
They pass through whirl-pools, and deep woes do shun,
Who the event weigh ere the action 's done.   *Exit.*

SCENE V[1]

[Enter] CARDINAL *and* FERDINAND *with a letter*

FERD. I have this night digg'd up a mandrake.[2]
CARD.   Say you?
FERD. And I am grown mad with 't.
CARD.   What 's the prodigy
FERD. Read there,—a sister damn'd: she 's loose i' the hilts;[3]
Grown a notorious strumpet.
CARD.   Speak lower.

[5] Medicinal.   [6] Strong broth.
[1] Another apartment in the same palace.
[2] The mandrake was supposed to give forth shrieks when uprooted, which
drove the hearer mad.   [3] Unchaste.

FERD. Lower!

Rogues do not whisper 't now, but seek to publish 't
(As servants do the bounty of their lords)
Aloud; and with a covetous searching eye,
To mark who note them. O, confusion seize her!
She hath had most cunning bawds to serve her turn,
And more secure conveyances for lust
Than towns of garrison for service.

CARD. Is 't possible?

Can this be certain?

FERD. Rhubarb, O, for rhubarb
To purge this choler! Here 's the cursèd day
To prompt my memory; and here 't shall stick
Till of her bleeding heart I make a sponge
To wipe it out.

CARD. Why do you make yourself
So wild a tempest?

FERD. Would I could be one,
That I might toss her palace 'bout her ears,
Root up her goodly forests, blast her meads,
And lay her general territory as waste
As she hath done her honours.

CARD. Shall our blood,
The royal blood of Arragon and Castile,
Be thus attainted?

FERD. Apply desperate physic:
We must not now use balsamum, but fire,
The smarting cupping-glass, for that 's the mean
To purge infected blood, such blood as hers.
There is a kind of pity in mine eye,—
I 'll give it to my handkercher; and now 'tis here,
I 'll bequeath this to her bastard.

CARD. What to do?

FERD. Why, to make soft lint for his mother's wounds,
When I have hew'd her to pieces.

CARD. Curs'd creature!
Unequal nature, to place women's hearts
So far upon the left side!⁴

FERD. Foolish men,

⁴ Supposed to be a sign of folly.

That e'er will trust their honour in a bark
Made of so slight weak bulrush as is woman,
Apt every minute to sink it!

CARD. Thus ignorance, when it hath purchas'd honour,
It cannot wield it.

FERD.   Methinks I see her laughing,—
Excellent hyena! Talk to me somewhat quickly,
Or my imagination will carry me
To see her in the shameful act of sin.

CARD. With whom?

FERD.   Happily with some strong-thigh'd bargeman,
Or one o' th' wood-yard that can quoit the sledge*
Or toss the bar, or else some lovely squire
That carries coals up to her privy lodgings.

CARD. You fly beyond your reason.

FERD.   Go to, mistress!
'Tis not your whore's milk that shall quench my wild-fire,
But your whore's blood.

CARD. How idly shows this rage, which carries you,
As men convey'd by witches through the air,
On violent whirlwinds! This intemperate noise
Fitly resembles deaf men's shrill discourse,
Who talk aloud, thinking all other men
To have their imperfection.

FERD.   Have not you
My palsy?

CARD.   Yes, [but] I can be angry
Without this rupture. There is not in nature
A thing that makes man so deform'd, so beastly,
As doth intemperate anger. Chide yourself.
You have divers men who never yet express'd
Their strong desire of rest but by unrest,
By vexing of themselves. Come, put yourself
In tune.

FERD. So I will only study to seem
The thing I am not. I could kill her now,
In you, or in myself; for I do think
It is some sin in us heaven doth revenge
By her.

<hr>

*Throw the hammer.

CARD. Are you stark mad?

FERD.   I would have their bodies
Burnt in a coal-pit with the ventage stopp'd,
That their curs'd smoke might not ascend to heaven;
Or dip the sheets they lie in in pitch or sulphur,
Wrap them in 't, and then light them like a match;
Or else to-boil⁶ their bastard to a cullis,
And give 't his lecherous father to renew
The sin of his back.

CARD.   I 'll leave you.

FERD.   Nay, I have done.
I am confident, had I been damn'd in hell,
And should have heard of this, it would have put me
Into a cold sweat. In, in; I 'll go sleep.
Till I know who [loves] my sister, I 'll not stir:
That known, I 'll find scorpions to string my whips,
And fix her in a general eclipse.   *Exeunt.*

ACT III

SCENE I¹

[*Enter*] ANTONIO *and* DELIO

ANT. Our noble friend, my most beloved Delio!
Ʊ, you have been a stranger long at court:
Came you along with the Lord Ferdinand?

DELIO. I did, sir: and how fares your noble duchess?

ANT. Right fortunately well: she 's an excellent
Feeder of pedigrees; since you last saw her,
She hath had two children more, a son and daughter.

DELIO. Methinks 'twas yesterday. Let me but wink,
And not behold your face, which to mine eye
Is somewhat leaner, verily I should dream
It were within this half hour.

ANT. You have not been in law, friend Delio,
Nor in prison, nor a suitor at the court,
Nor begg'd the reversion of some great man's place,
Nor troubled with an old wife, which doth make

⁶ Boil to shreds. (Dyce.) Qq. *to boil.*
¹ Malfi. An apartment in the palace of the Duchess.

Your time so insensibly hasten.

DELIO.   Pray, sir, tell me,
Hath not this news arriv'd yet to the ear
Of the lord cardinal?

ANT.   I fear it hath:
The Lord Ferdinand, that 's newly come to court,
Doth bear himself right dangerously.

DELIO.   Pray, why?

ANT. He is so quiet that he seems to sleep
The tempest out, as dormice do in winter.
Those houses that are haunted are most still
Till the devil be up.

DELIO.   What say the common people?

ANT. The common rabble do directly say
She is a strumpet.

DELIO.   And your graver heads
Which would be politic, what censure they?

ANT. They do observe I grow to infinite purchase,[2]
The left hand way; and all suppose the duchess
Would amend it, if she could; for, say they,
Great princes, though they grudge their officers
Should have such large and unconfined means
To get wealth under them, will not complain,
Lest thereby they should make them odious
Unto the people. For other obligation
Of love or marriage between her and me
They never dream of.

DELIO.   The Lord Ferdinand
Is going to bed.

[*Enter* DUCHESS, FERDINAND, *and Attendants*]

FERD.   I 'll instantly to bed,
For I am weary.—I am to bespeak
A husband for you.

DUCH.   For me, sir! Pray, who is 't?

FERD. The great Count Malatesti.

DUCH.   Fie upon him!
A count! He 's a mere stick of sugar-candy;
You may look quite through him. When I choose

          [2] Wealth.

A husband, I will marry for your honour.

    FERD. You shall do well in 't.—How is 't, worthy Antonio?

    DUCH. But, sir, I am to have private conference with
        you

About a scandalous report is spread

Touching mine honour.

    FERD.   Let me be ever deaf to 't:

One of Pasquil's paper-bullets,[3] court-calumny,

A pestilent air, which princes' palaces

Are seldom purg'd of. Yet, say that it were true,

I pour it in your bosom, my fix'd love

Would strongly excuse, extenuate, nay, deny

Faults, were they apparent in you. Go, be safe

In your own innocency.

    DUCH.   [*aside.*] O bless'd comfort!

This deadly air is purg'd.

       Exeunt [DUCHESS, ANTONIO, DELIO, *and Attendants.*]

    FERD.   Her guilt treads on

Hot-burning coulters.[4]

Enter BOSOLA

            Now, Bosola,

How thrives our intelligence?[5]

    BOS.   Sir, uncertainly:

'Tis rumour'd she hath had three bastards, but

By whom we may go read i' the stars.

    FERD.   Why, some

Hold opinion all things are written there.

    BOS. Yes, if we could find spectacles to read them.

I do suspect there hath been some sorcery

Us'd on the duchess.

    FERD.   Sorcery! to what purpose?

    BOS. To make her dote on some desertless fellow

She shames to acknowledge.

    FERD.   Can your faith give way

To think there 's power in potions or in charms,

To make us love whether we will or no?

    BOS. Most certainly.

    FERD. Away! these are mere gulleries,[6] horrid things,

       [3] Lampoons.   [4] Plowshares.   [5] Spying.   [6] Deceptions.

Invented by some cheating mountebanks
To abuse us. Do you think that herbs or charms
Can force the will? Some trials have been made
In this foolish practice, but the ingredients
Were lenitive[7] poisons, such as are of force
To make the patient mad; and straight the witch
Swears by equivocation they are in love.
The witch-craft lies in her rank blood. This night
I will force confession from her. You told me
You had got, within these two days, a false key
Into her bed-chamber.

Bos.   I have.

Ferd.   As I would wish.

Bos. What do you intend to do?

Ferd.   Can you guess?

Bos.   No.

Ferd. Do not ask, then:
He that can compass me, and know my drifts,
May say he hath put a girdle 'bout the world,
And sounded all her quick-sands.

Bos.   I do not
Think so.

Ferd.   What do you think, then, pray?

Bos.   That you
Are your own chronicle too much, and grossly
Flatter yourself.

Ferd.   Give me thy hand; I thank thee:
I never gave pension but to flatterers,
Till I entertained thee. Farewell.
That friend a great man's ruin strongly checks,
Who rails into his belief all his defects.   *Exeunt.*

SCENE II[1]

[*Enter*] DUCHESS, ANTONIO, *and* CARIOLA

Duch. Bring me the casket hither, and the glass.—
You get no lodging here to-night, my lord.

Ant. Indeed, I must persuade one.

---

[7] Soothing.
[1] The bed-chamber of the Duchess in the same.

DUCH.   Very good:
I hope in time 'twill grow into a custom,
That noblemen shall come with cap and knee
To purchase a night's lodging of their wives.

   ANT. I must lie here.

   DUCH.   Must! You are a lord of mis-rule.

   ANT. Indeed, my rule is only in the night.

   DUCH. I 'll stop your mouth.   [*Kisses him.*]

   ANT. Nay, that 's but one; Venus had two soft doves
To draw her chariot; I must have another.—

                        [*She kisses him again.*]
When wilt thou marry, Cariola?

   CARI.   Never, my lord.

   ANT. O, fie upon this single life! forgo it.
We read how Daphne, for her peevish [flight,][2]
Became a fruitless bay-tree; Syrinx turn'd
To the pale empty reed; Anaxarete
Was frozen into marble: whereas those
Which married, or prov'd kind unto their friends,
Were by a gracious influence transhap'd
Into the olive, pomegranate, mulberry,
Became flowers, precious stones, or eminent stars.

   CARI. This is a vain poetry: but I pray you, tell me,
If there were propos'd me, wisdom, riches, and beauty,
In three several young men, which should I choose?

   ANT. 'Tis a hard question. This was Paris' case,
And he was blind in 't, and there was a great cause;
For how was 't possible he could judge right,
Having three amorous goddesses in view,
And they stark naked? 'Twas a motion
Were able to benight the apprehension
Of the severest counsellor of Europe.
Now I look on both your faces so well form'd,
It puts me in mind of a question I would ask.

   CARI. What is 't?

   ANT.   I do wonder why hard-favour'd ladies,
For the most part, keep worse-favour'd waiting-women
To attend them, and cannot endure fair ones.

   DUCH. O, that 's soon answer'd.

              [2] Qq. read *slight.*

Did you ever in your life know an ill painter
Desire to have his dwelling next door to the shop
Of an excellent picture-maker? 'Twould disgrace
His face-making, and undo him. I prithee,
When were we so merry?—My hair tangles.

    ANT. Pray thee, Cariola, let 's steal forth the room,
And let her talk to herself: I have divers times
Serv'd her the like, when she hath chaf'd extremely.
I love to see her angry. Softly, Cariola.

               Exeunt [ANTONIO *and* CARIOLA.]

    DUCH. Doth not the colour of my hair 'gin to change?
When I wax gray, I shall have all the court
Powder their hair with arras,[a] to be like me.
You have cause to love me; I ent'red you into my heart

[*Enter* FERDINAND *unseen*]

Before you would vouchsafe to call for the keys.
We shall one day have my brothers take you napping.
Methinks his presence, being now in court,
Should make you keep your own bed; but you 'll say
Love mix'd with fear is sweetest. I 'll assure you,
You shall get no more children till my brothers
Consent to be your gossips. Have you lost your tongue?
'Tis welcome:
For know, whether I am doom'd to live or die,
I can do both like a prince.

    FERD.   Die, then, quickly! *Giving her a poniard.*
Virtue, where art thou hid? What hideous thing
Is it that doth eclipse thee?

    DUCH.   Pray, sir, hear me.

    FERD. Or is it true thou art but a bare name,
And no essential thing?

    DUCH.   Sir——

    FERD.   Do not speak.

    DUCH. No, sir:
I will plant my soul in mine ears, to hear you.

    FERD. O most imperfect light of human reason,
That mak'st [us] so unhappy to foresee
What we can least prevent! Pursue thy wishes,

         [a] Powder of orris-root.

And glory in them: there 's in shame no comfort
But to be past all bounds and sense of shame.

    DUCH. I pray, sir, hear me: I am married.

    FERD.   So!

    DUCH. Happily, not to your liking: but for that,
Alas, your shears do come untimely now
To clip the bird's wings that 's already flown!
Will you see my husband?

    FERD.   Yes, if I could change
Eyes with a basilisk.

    DUCH.   Sure, you came hither
By his confederacy.

    FERD.   The howling of a wolf
Is music to thee, screech-owl: prithee, peace.—
Whate'er thou art that hast enjoy'd my sister,
For I am sure thou hear'st me, for thine own sake
Let me not know thee. I came hither prepar'd
To work thy discovery; yet am now persuaded
It would beget such violent effects
As would damn us both. I would not for ten millions
I had beheld thee: therefore use all means
I never may have knowledge of thy name;
Enjoy thy lust still, and a wretched life,
On that condition.—And for thee, vile woman,
If thou do wish thy lecher may grow old
In thy embracements, I would have thee build
Such a room for him as our anchorites
To holier use inhabit. Let not the sun
Shine on him till he 's dead; let dogs and monkeys
Only converse with him, and such dumb things
To whom nature denies use to sound his name;
Do not keep a paraquito, lest she learn it;
If thou do love him, cut out thine own tongue,
Lest it bewray him.

    DUCH.   Why might not I marry?
I have not gone about in this to create
Any new world or custom.

    FERD.   Thou art undone;
And thou hast ta'en that massy sheet of lead
That hid thy husband's bones, and folded it

About my heart.

DUCH.   Mine bleeds for 't.

FERD.   Thine! thy heart!
What should I name 't unless a hollow bullet
Fill'd with unquenchable wild-fire?

DUCH.   You are in this
Too strict; and were you not my princely brother,
I would say, too wilful: my reputation
Is safe.

FERD. Dost thou know what reputation is?
I 'll tell thee,—to small purpose, since the instruction
Comes now too late.
Upon a time Reputation, Love, and Death,
Would travel o'er the world; and it was concluded
That they should part, and take three several ways.
Death told them, they should find him in great battles,
Or cities plagu'd with plagues: Love gives them counsel
To inquire for him 'mongst unambitious shepherds,
Where dowries were not talk'd of, and sometimes
'Mongst quiet kindred that had nothing left
By their dead parents: ' Stay,' quoth Reputation,
' Do not forsake me; for it is my nature,
If once I part from any man I meet,
I am never found again.' And so for you:
You have shook hands with Reputation,
And made him invisible. So, fare you well:
I will never see you more.

DUCH.   Why should only I,
Of all the other princes of the world,
Be cas'd up, like a holy relic? I have youth
And a little beauty.

FERD.   So you have some virgins
That are witches. I will never see thee more. *Exit.*

Re-enter ANTONIO *with a pistol,* [*and* CARIOLA]

DUCH. You saw this apparition?

ANT.   Yes: we are
Betray'd. How came he hither? I should turn
This to thee, for that.

CARI.   Pray, sir, do; and when

That you have cleft my heart, you shall read there
Mine innocence.
    DUCH.   That gallery gave him entrance.
    ANT. I would this terrible thing would come again,
That, standing on my guard, I might relate
My warrantable love.—   (*She shows the poniard.*)
                Ha! what means this?
    DUCH. He left this with me.
    ANT.   And it seems did wish
You would use it on yourself.
    DUCH.   His action seem'd
To intend so much.
    ANT.   This hath a handle to 't,
As well as a point: turn it towards him, and
So fasten the keen edge in his rank gall.
                     [*Knocking within.*]
How now! who knocks? More earthquakes?
    DUCH.   I stand
As if a mine beneath my feet were ready
To be blown up.
    CARI.   'Tis Bosola.
    DUCH.   Away!
O misery! methinks unjust actions
Should wear these masks and curtains, and not we.
You must instantly part hence: I have fashion'd it already.
                     Exit ANTONIO.

Enter BOSOLA

    BOS. The duke your brother is ta'en up in a whirlwind;
Hath took horse, and 's rid post to Rome.
    DUCH.   So late?
    BOS. He told me, as he mounted into the saddle,
You were undone.
    DUCH.   Indeed, I am very near it.
    BOS. What 's the matter?
    DUCH. Antonio, the master of our household,
Hath dealt so falsely with me in 's accounts.
My brother stood engag'd with me for money
Ta'en up of certain Neapolitan Jews,
And Antonio lets the bonds be forfeit.

Bos. Strange!—[*Aside.*] This is cunning.

Duch.   And hereupon
My brother's bills at Naples are protested
Against.—Call up our officers.

Bos.   I shall.   *Exit.*

[*Re-enter* ANTONIO]

Duch. The place that you must fly to is Ancona:
Hire a house there; I 'll send after you
My treasure and my jewels. Our weak safety
Runs upon enginous wheels:[4] short syllables
Must stand for periods. I must now accuse you
Of such a feigned crime as Tasso calls
Magnanima menzogna, a noble lie,
'Cause it must shield our honours.—Hark! they are coming.

[*Re-enter* BOSOLA *and Officers*]

Ant. Will your grace hear me?

Duch. I have got well by you; you have yielded me
A million of loss: I am like to inherit
The people's curses for your stewardship.
You had the trick in audit-time to be sick,
Till I had sign'd your quietus;[5] and that cur'd you
Without help of a doctor.—Gentlemen,
I would have this man be an example to you all;
So shall you hold my favour; I pray, let him;
For h'as done that, alas, you would not think of,
And, because I intend to be rid of him,
I mean not to publish.—Use your fortune elsewhere.

Ant. I am strongly arm'd to brook my overthrow,
As commonly men bear with a hard year.
I will not blame the cause on 't; but do think
The necessity of my malevolent star
Procures this, not her humour. O, the inconstant
And rotten ground of service! You may see,
'Tis even like him, that in a winter night,
Takes a long slumber o'er a dying fire,
A-loth to part from 't; yet parts thence as cold

<hr>

[4] Wheels of craft.
[5] Certificate that the books were found correct.

As when he first sat down.

DUCH.   We do confiscate,
Towards the satisfying of your accounts,
All that you have.

ANT.   I am all yours; and 'tis very fit
All mine should be so.

DUCH.   So, sir, you have your pass.

ANT. You may see, gentlemen, what 'tis to serve
A prince with body and soul.   *Exit.*

BOS. Here 's an example for extortion: what moisture is
drawn out of the sea, when foul weather comes, pours down,
and runs into the sea again.

DUCH. I would know what are your opinions
Of this Antonio.

SEC. OFF. He could not abide to see a pig's head gaping:
I thought your grace would find him a Jew.

THIRD OFF. I would you had been his officer, for your
own sake.

FOURTH OFF. You would have had more money.

FIRST OFF. He stopped his ears with black wool, and to
those came to him for money said he was thick of hearing.

SEC. OFF. Some said he was an hermaphrodite, for he
could not abide a woman.

FOURTH OFF. How scurvy proud he would look when the
treasury was full! Well, let him go.

FIRST OFF. Yes, and the chippings of the buttery fly after
him, to scour his gold chain.[6]

DUCH. Leave us.   *Exeunt [Officers.]*
What do you think of these?

BOS. That these are rogues that in 's prosperity,
But to have waited on his fortune, could have wish'd
His dirty stirrup riveted through their noses,
And follow'd after 's mule, like a bear in a ring;
Would have prostituted their daughters to his lust;
Made their first-born intelligencers;[7] thought none happy
But such as were born under his blest planet,
And wore his livery: and do these lice drop off now?
Well, never look to have the like again:
He hath left a sort[8] of flattering rogues behind him;

   [6] The badge of a steward.   [7] Spies.   [8] Lot.

Their doom must follow. Princes pay flatterers
In their own money: flatterers dissemble their vices,
And they dissemble their lies; that 's justice.
Alas, poor gentleman!

Duch. Poor! he hath amply fill'd his coffers.

Bos. Sure, he was too honest. Pluto,[9] the god of riches,
When he 's sent by Jupiter to any man,
He goes limping, to signify that wealth
That comes on God's name comes slowly; but when he's sent
On the devil's errand, he rides post and comes in by scuttles.[10]
Let me show you what a most unvalu'd jewel
You have in a wanton humour thrown away,
To bless the man shall find him. He was an excellent
Courtier and most faithful; a soldier that thought it
As beastly to know his own value too little
As devilish to acknowledge it too much.
Both his virtue and form deserv'd a far better fortune:
His discourse rather delighted to judge itself than show
      itself:
His breast was fill'd with all perfection,
And yet it seemed a private whisp'ring-room,
It made so little noise of 't.

Duch. But he was basely descended.

Bos. Will you make yourself a mercenary herald,
Rather to examine men's pedigrees than virtues?
You shall want[11] him:
For know an honest statesman to a prince
Is like a cedar planted by a spring;
The spring bathes the tree's root, the grateful tree
Rewards it with his shadow: you have not done so.
I would sooner swim to the Bermoothes on
Two politicians' rotten bladders, tied
Together with an intelligencer's heart-string,
Than depend on so changeable a prince's favour.
Fare thee well, Antonio! Since the malice of the world
Would needs down with thee, it cannot be said yet
That any ill happen'd unto thee, considering thy fall
Was accompanied with virtue.

[9] For *Plutus*.   [10] Quick steps.   [11] Miss.

DUCH. O, you render me excellent music!

BOS. Say you?

DUCH. This good one that you speak of is my husband.

BOS. Do I not dream? Can this ambitious age
Have so much goodness in 't as to prefer
A man merely for worth, without these shadows
Of wealth and painted honours? Possible?

DUCH. I have had three children by him.

BOS. Fortunate lady!
For you have made your private nuptial bed
The humble and fair seminary of peace,
No question but: many an unbenefic'd scholar
Shall pray for you for this deed, and rejoice
That some preferment in the world can yet
Arise from merit. The virgins of your land
That have no dowries shall hope your example
Will raise them to rich husbands. Should you want
Soldiers, 'twould make the very Turks and Moors
Turn Christians, and serve you for this act.
Last, the neglected poets of your time,
In honour of this trophy of a man,
Rais'd by that curious engine, your white hand,
Shall thank you, in your grave, for 't; and make that
More reverend than all the cabinets
Of living princes. For Antonio,
His fame shall likewise flow from many a pen,
When heralds shall want coats to sell to men.

DUCH. As I taste comfort in this friendly speech,
So would I find concealment.

BOS. O, the secret of my prince,
Which I will wear on th' inside of my heart!

DUCH. You shall take charge of all my coin and jewels,
And follow him; for he retires himself
To Ancona.

BOS. So.

DUCH. Whither, within few days,
I mean to follow thee.

BOS. Let me think:
I would wish your grace to feign a pilgrimage
To our Lady of Loretto, scarce seven leagues

From fair Ancona; so may you depart
Your country with more honour, and your flight
Will seem a princely progress, retaining
Your usual train about you.

    DUCH.   Sir, your direction
Shall lead me by the hand.

    CARI.   In my opinion,
She were better progress to the baths at Lucca,
Or go visit the Spa
In Germany; for, if you will believe me,
I do not like this jesting with religion,
This feigned pilgrimage.

    DUCH. Thou art a superstitious fool:
Prepare us instantly for our departure.
Past sorrows, let us moderately lament them,
For those to come, seek wisely to prevent them.

                  [*Exeunt* DUCHESS *and* CARIOLA.]

    BOS. A politician is the devil's quilted anvil;
He fashions all sins on him, and the blows
Are never heard: he may work in a lady's chamber,
As here for proof.   What rests[12] but I reveal
All to my lord?   O, this base quality[13]
Of intelligencer!   Why, every quality i' the world
Prefers but gain or commendation:
Now, for this act I am certain to be rais'd,
And men that paint weeds to the life are prais'd.   [*Exit.*

SCENE III[1]

[*Enter*] CARDINAL, FERDINAND, MALATESTI, PESCARA, DELIO,
                    and SILVIO

    CARD. Must we turn soldier, then?

    MAL.   The emperor,
Hearing your worth that way, ere you attain'd
This reverend garment, joins you in commission
With the right fortunate soldier the Marquis of Pescara,
And the famous Lannoy.

    CARD.   He that had the honour

---

[12] Remains.   [13] Profession.
[1] An apartment in the Cardinal's palace at Rome.

Of taking the French king prisoner?

MAL. The same.
Here 's a plot drawn for a new fortification
At Naples.

FERD. This great Count Malatesti, I perceive,
Hath got employment?

DELIO. No employment, my lord;
A marginal note in the muster-book, that he is
A voluntary lord.

FERD. He 's no soldier.

DELIO. He has worn gun-powder in 's hollow tooth for the
tooth-ache.

SIL. He comes to the leaguer with a full intent
To eat fresh beef and garlic, means to stay
Till the scent be gone, and straight return to court.

DELIO. He hath read all the late service
As the City-Chronicle relates it;
And keeps two pewterers going, only to express
Battles in model.

SIL. Then he 'll fight by the book.

DELIO. By the almanac, I think,
To choose good days and shun the critical;
That 's his mistress' scarf.

SIL. Yes, he protests
He would do much for that taffeta.

DELIO. I think he would run away from a battle,
To save it from taking prisoner.

SIL. He is horribly afraid
Gun-powder will spoil the perfume on 't.

DELIO. I saw a Dutchman break his pate once
For calling him pot-gun; he made his head
Have a bore in 't like a musket.

SIL. I would he had made a touch-hole to 't.
He is indeed a guarded sumpter-cloth,³
Only for the remove of the court.

³ A decorated horse-cloth, used only when the court is traveling.

[Enter Bosola]

Pes. Bosola arriv'd! What should be the business?
Some falling-out amongst the cardinals.
These factions amongst great men, they are like
Foxes, when their heads are divided,
They carry fire in their tails, and all the country
About them goes to wrack for 't.

Sil.   What 's that Bosola?

Delio. I knew him in Padua,—a fantastical scholar, like
such who study to know how many knots was in Hercules'
club, of what colour Achilles' beard was, or whether Hector
were not troubled with the tooth-ache. He hath studied himself half blear-eyed to know the true symmetry of Cæsar's
nose by a shoeing-horn; and this he did to gain the name of
a speculative man.

Pes. Mark Prince Ferdinand:
A very salamander lives in 's eye,
To mock the eager violence of fire.

Sil. That cardinal hath made more bad faces with his
oppression than ever Michael Angelo made good ones. He
lifts up 's nose, like a foul porpoise before a storm.

Pes. The Lord Ferdinand laughs.

Delio.   Like a deadly cannon
That lightens ere it smokes.

Pes. These are your true pangs of death,
The pangs of life, that struggle with great statesmen.

Delio. In such a deformed silence witches whisper their
        charms.

Card. Doth she make religion her riding-hood
To keep her from the sun and tempest?

Ferd. That, that damns her. Methinks her fault and
        beauty,
Blended together, show like leprosy,
The whiter, the fouler. I make it a question
Whether her beggarly brats were ever christ'ned.

Card. I will instantly solicit the state of Ancona
To have them banish'd.

Ferd.   You are for Loretto:
I shall not be at your ceremony; fare you well.—

Write to the Duke of Malfi, my young nephew
She had by her first husband, and acquaint him
With 's mother's honesty.

    Bos.   I will.

    FERD.   Antonio!
A slave that only smell'd of ink and counters,
And never in 's life look'd like a gentleman,
But in the audit-time.—Go, go presently,
Draw me out an hundred and fifty of our horse,
And meet me at the foot-bridge.   *Exeunt.*

SCENE IV

[*Enter*] *Two Pilgrims to the Shrine of our Lady of Loretto*

    FIRST PIL. I have not seen a goodlier shrine than this;
Yet I have visited many.

    SEC. PIL.   The Cardinal of Arragon
Is this day to resign his cardinal's hat:
His sister duchess likewise is arriv'd
To pay her vow of pilgrimage. I expect
A noble ceremony.

    FIRST PIL.   No question.—They come.

[*Here the ceremony of the Cardinal's instalment, in the habit
    of a soldier, perform'd in delivering up his cross, hat,
    robes, and ring, at the shrine, and investing him with
    sword, helmet, shield, and spurs; then* ANTONIO, *the*
    DUCHESS *and their children, having presented themselves
    at the shrine, are, by a form of banishment in dumb-
    show expressed towards them by the* CARDINAL *and the
    state of Ancona, banished: during all which ceremony,
    this ditty is sung, to very solemn music, by divers church-
    men: and then exeunt* [*all except the*] *Two Pilgrims.*

            Arms and honours deck thy story,
            To thy fame's eternal glory!
            Adverse fortune ever fly thee;
            No disastrous fate come nigh thee!

I alone will sing thy praises,
Whom to honour virtue raises,
And thy study, that divine is,
Bent to martial discipline is,
Lay aside all those robes lie by thee;
Crown thy arts with arms, they 'll beautify thee.

O worthy of worthiest name, adorn'd in this manner,
Lead bravely thy forces on under war's warlike banner!
O, mayst thou prove fortunate in all martial courses!
Guide thou still by skill in arts and forces!
Victory attend thee nigh, whilst fame sings loud thy
          powers;
Triumphant conquest crown thy head, and blessings
          pour down showers![1]

FIRST PIL. Here 's a strange turn of state! who would
          have thought
So great a lady would have match'd herself
Unto so mean a person? Yet the cardinal
Bears himself much too cruel.
    SEC. PIL.   They are banish'd.
    FIRST PIL. But I would ask what power hath this state
Of Ancona to determine of a free prince?
    SEC. PIL. They are a free state, sir, and her brother show'd
How that the Pope, fore-hearing of her looseness,
Hath seiz'd into th' protection of the church
The dukedom which she held as dowager.
    FIRST PIL. But by what justice?
    SEC. PIL.   Sure, I think by none,
Only her brother's instigation.
    FIRST PIL. What was it with such violence he took
Off from her finger?
    SEC. PIL.   'Twas her wedding-ring;
Which he vow'd shortly he would sacrifice
To his revenge.
    FIRST PIL.   Alas, Antonio!
If that a man be thrust into a well,
No matter who sets hand to 't, his own weight
Will bring him sooner to th' bottom. Come, let 's hence.

[1] The first quarto has in the margin: "The Author disclaims this Ditty to be his."

Fortune makes this conclusion general,
All things do help th' unhappy man to fall.   *Exeunt.*

SCENE V[1]

[*Enter*] DUCHESS, ANTONIO, *Children,* CARIOLA, *and Servants*

DUCH. Banish'd Ancona!

ANT.   Yes, you see what power
Lightens in great men's breath.

DUCH.   Is all our train
Shrunk to this poor remainder?

ANT.   These poor men
Which have got little in your service, vow
To take your fortune: but your wiser buntings,[2]
Now they are fledg'd, are gone.

DUCH.   They have done wisely.
This puts me in mind of death: physicians thus,
With their hands full of money, use to give o'er
Their patients.

ANT.   Right the fashion of the world:
From decay'd fortunes every flatterer shrinks;
Men cease to build where the foundation sinks.

DUCH. I had a very strange dream to-night.

ANT.   What was 't?

DUCH. Methought I wore my coronet of state,
And on a sudden all the diamonds
Were chang'd to pearls.

ANT.   My interpretation
Is, you 'll weep shortly; for to me the pearls
Do signify your tears.

DUCH.   The birds that live i' th' field
On the wild benefit of nature live
Happier than we; for they may choose their mates,
And carol their sweet pleasures to the spring.

[1] Near Loretto.   [2] Small birds.

[*Enter* BOSOLA *with a letter*]

BOS. You are happily o'erta'en.

DUCH.   From my brother?

BOS. Yes, from the Lord Ferdinand your brother
All love and safety.

DUCH.   Thou dost blanch mischief,
Would'st make it white. See, see, like to calm weather
At sea before a tempest, false hearts speak fair
To those they intend most mischief.   [*Reads.*]
'*Send Antonio to me; I want his head in a business.*'
A politic equivocation!
He doth not want your counsel, but your head;
That is, he cannot sleep till you be dead.
And here 's another pitfall that 's strew'd o'er
With roses; mark it, 'tis a cunning one: [*Reads.*]
'*I stand engaged for your husband for several debts at
Naples: let not that trouble him; I had rather have his heart
than his money*':—
And I believe so too.

BOS.   What do you believe?

DUCH. That he so much distrusts my husband's love,
He will by no means believe his heart is with him
Until he see it: the devil is not cunning enough
To circumvent us in riddles.

BOS. Will you reject that noble and free league
Of amity and love which I present you?

DUCH. Their league is like that of some politic kings,
Only to make themselves of strength and power
To be our after-ruin; tell them so.

BOS. And what from you?

ANT.   Thus tell him; I will not come.

BOS. And what of this?

ANT.   My brothers have dispers'd
Bloodhounds abroad; which till I hear are muzzl'd,
No truce, though hatch'd with ne'er such politic skill,
Is safe, that hangs upon our enemies' will.
I 'll not come at them.

BOS.   This proclaims your breeding.
Every small thing draws a base mind to fear,

As the adamant draws iron. Fare you well, sir;
You shall shortly hear from 's.　　　　　　　　*Exit.*

DUCH.　　　　　　　　I suspect some ambush;
Therefore by all my love I do conjure you
To take your eldest son, and fly towards Milan.
Let us not venture all this poor remainder
In one unlucky bottom.

ANT.　　　　　　　　You counsel safely.
Best of my life, farewell. Since we must part,
Heaven hath a hand in 't; but no otherwise
Than as some curious artist takes in sunder
A clock or watch, when it is out of frame,
To bring 't in better order.

DUCH. I know not which is best,
To see you dead, or part with you.—Farewell, boy:
Thou art happy that thou hast not understanding
To know thy misery; for all our wit
And reading brings us to a truer sense
Of sorrow.—In the eternal church, sir,
I do hope we shall not part thus.

ANT.　　　　　　　　O, be of comfort!
Make patience a noble fortitude,
And think not how unkindly we are us'd:
Man, like to cassia, is prov'd best, being bruis'd.

DUCH. Must I, like to slave-born Russian,
Account it praise to suffer tyranny?
And yet, O heaven, thy heavy hand is in 't!
I have seen my little boy oft scourge his top,
And compar'd myself to 't: naught made me e'er
Go right but heaven's scourge-stick.

ANT.　　　　　　　　Do not weep:
Heaven fashion'd us of nothing; and we strive
To bring ourselves to nothing.—Farewell, Cariola,
And thy sweet armful.—If I do never see thee more,
Be a good mother to your little ones,
And save them from the tiger: fare you well.

DUCH. Let me look upon you once more, for that speech
Came from a dying father. Your kiss is colder
Than that I have seen an holy anchorite
Give to a dead man's skull.

Ant. My heart is turn'd to a heavy lump of lead,
With which I sound my danger: fare you well.

> *Exeunt* [Antonio *and his son.*]

Duch. My laurel is all withered.

Cari. Look, madam, what a troop of armed men
Make toward us!

Re-enter Bosola [*visarded,*] *with a Guard*

Duch.   O, they are very welcome:
When Fortune's wheel is over-charg'd with princes,
The weight makes it move swift: I would have my ruin
Be sudden.—I am your adventure, am I not?

Bos. You are: you must see your husband no more.

Duch. What devil art thou that counterfeit'st heaven's
    thunder?

Bos. Is that terrible? I would have you tell me whether
Is that note worse that frights the silly birds
Out of the corn, or that which doth allure them
To the nets? You have heark'ned to the last too much.

Duch. O misery! like to a rusty o'ercharg'd cannon,
Shall I never fly in pieces?—Come, to what prison?

Bos. To none.

Duch.   Whither, then?

Bos.   To your palace.

Duch.   I have heard
That Charon's boat serves to convey all o'er
The dismal lake, but brings none back again.

Bos. Your brothers mean you safety and pity.

Duch.   Pity!
With such a pity men preserve alive
Pheasants and quails, when they are not fat enough
To be eaten.

Bos.   These are your children?

Duch.   Yes.

Bos.   Can they prattle?

Duch. No:
But I intend, since they were born accurs'd,
Curses shall be their first language.

Bos.   Fie, madam!
Forget this base, low fellow——

Duch.   Were I a man,
I 'd beat that counterfeit face[3] into thy other.
  Bos. One of no birth.
  Duch.   Say that he was born mean,
Man is most happy when 's own actions
Be arguments and examples of his virtue.
  Bos. A barren, beggarly virtue.
  Duch. I prithee, who is greatest? Can you tell?
Sad tales befit my woe: I 'll tell you one.
A salmon, as she swam unto the sea,
Met with a dog-fish, who encounters her
With this rough language; 'Why art thou so bold
To mix thyself with our high state of floods,
Being no eminent courtier, but one
That for the calmest and fresh time o' th' year
Dost live in shallow rivers, rank'st thyself
With silly smelts and shrimps? And darest thou
Pass by our dog-ship without reverence?'
'O,' quoth the salmon, 'sister, be at peace:
Thank Jupiter we both have pass'd the net!
Our value never can be truly known,
Till in the fisher's basket we be shown:
I' th' market then my price may be the higher,
Even when I am nearest to the cook and fire.'
So to great men the moral may be stretched;
Men oft are valu'd high, when they're most wretched.—
But come, whither you please. I am arm'd 'gainst misery;
Bent to all sways of the oppressor's will:
There 's no deep valley but near some great hill.   *Exeunt.*

ACT IV

Scene I[1]

[Enter] Ferdinand *and* Bosola

  Ferd. How doth our sister duchess bear herself
In her imprisonment?
  Bos.   Nobly: I 'll describe her.

        [3] His vizard.
        [1] Malfi. An apartment in the palace of the Duchess.

She 's sad as one long us'd to 't, and she seems
Rather to welcome the end of misery
Than shun it; a behaviour so noble
As gives a majesty to adversity:
You may discern the shape of loveliness
More perfect in her tears than in her smiles:
She will muse for hours together; and her silence,
Methinks, expresseth more than if she spake.

    FERD. Her melancholy seems to be fortified
With a strange disdain.

    Bos.   'Tis so; and this restraint,
Like English mastives that grow fierce with tying,
Makes her too passionately apprehend
Those pleasures she is kept from.

    FERD.   Curse upon her!
I will no longer study in the book
Of another's heart. Inform her what I told you.   *Exit.*

[Enter DUCHESS *and Attendants]*

    Bos. All comfort to your grace!

    DUCH.   I will have none.
Pray thee, why dost thou wrap thy poison'd pills
In gold and sugar?

    Bos. Your elder brother, the Lord Ferdinand,
Is come to visit you, and sends you word,
'Cause once he rashly made a solemn vow
Never to see you more, he comes i' th' night;
And prays you gently neither torch nor taper
Shine in your chamber. He will kiss your hand,
And reconcile himself; but for his vow
He dares not see you.

    DUCH.   At his pleasure.—
Take hence the lights.—He 's come.

                 [Exeunt Attendants with lights.]

[Enter FERDINAND*]*

    FERD.   Where are you?

    DUCH.   Here, sir.

    FERD. This darkness suits you well.

Duch.   I would ask you pardon.

Ferd. You have it;
For I account it the honorabl'st revenge,
Where I may kill, to pardon.—Where are your cubs?

 Duch. Whom?

 Ferd.   Call them your children;
For though our national law distinguish bastards
From true legitimate issue, compassionate nature
Makes them all equal.

 Duch.   Do you visit me for this?
You violate a sacrament o' th' church
Shall make you howl in hell for 't.

 Ferd.   It had been well,
Could you have liv'd thus always; for, indeed,
You were too much i' th' light:—but no more;
I come to seal my peace with you. Here 's a hand
          Gives her a dead man's hand.
To which you have vow'd much love; the ring upon 't
You gave.

 Duch. I affectionately kiss it.

 Ferd. Pray, do, and bury the print of it in your heart.
I will leave this ring with you for a love-token;
And the hand as sure as the ring; and do not doubt
But you shall have the heart too. When you need a friend,
Send it to him that ow'd it; you shall see
Whether he can aid you.

 Duch.   You are very cold:
I fear you are not well after your travel.—
Ha! lights!——O, horrible!

 Ferd.   Let her have lights enough. *Exit.*

 Duch. What witchcraft doth he practise, that he hath left
A dead man's hand here?

    [*Here is discovered, behind a traverse,*[2] *the artificial
     figures of* Antonio *and his children, appearing
     as if they were dead.*

 Bos. Look you, here 's the piece from which 'twas ta'en.
He doth present you this sad spectacle,
That, now you know directly they are dead,
Hereafter you may wisely cease to grieve

        [2] **Curtain.**

For that which cannot be recovered.

    Duch. There is not between heaven and earth one wish
I stay for after this. It wastes me more
Than were 't my picture, fashion'd out of wax,
Stuck with a magical needle, and then buried
In some foul dunghill; and yon 's an excellent property
For a tyrant, which I would account mercy.

    Bos.   What 's that?

    Duch. If they would bind me to that lifeless trunk,
And let me freeze to death.

    Bos.   Come, you must live.

    Duch. That 's the greatest torture souls feel in hell,
In hell, that they must live, and cannot die.
Portia,[3] I 'll new kindle thy coals again,
And revive the rare and almost dead example
Of a loving wife.

    Bos.   O, fie! despair? Remember
You are a Christian.

    Duch.   The church enjoins fasting:
I 'll starve myself to death.

    Bos.   Leave this vain sorrow.
Things being at the worst begin to mend: the bee
When he hath shot his sting into your hand,
May then play with your eye-lid.

    Duch.   Good comfortable fellow,
Persuade a wretch that 's broke upon the wheel
To have all his bones new set; entreat him live
To be executed again. Who must despatch me?
I account this world a tedious theatre,
For I do play a part in 't 'gainst my will.

    Bos. Come, be of comfort; I will save your life.

    Duch. Indeed, I have not leisure to tend so small a
        business.

    Bos. Now, by my life, I pity you.

    Duch.   Thou art a fool, then,
To waste thy pity on a thing so wretched
As cannot pity itself. I am full of daggers.
Puff, let me blow these vipers from me.

            [3] The wife of Brutus, who died by swallowing fire.

[Enter Servant]

What are you?

SERV. One that wishes you long life.

DUCH. I would thou wert hang'd for the horrible curse
Thou hast given me: I shall shortly grow one
Of the miracles of pity. I 'll go pray;— *[Exit Servant.]*
No, I 'll go curse.

BOS. O, fie!

DUCH. I could curse the stars.

BOS. O, fearful!

DUCH. And those three smiling seasons of the year
Into a Russian winter; nay, the world
To its first chaos.

BOS. Look you, the stars shine still

DUCH. O, but you must
Remember, my curse hath a great way to go.—
Plagues, that make lanes through largest families,
Consume them!—

BOS. Fie, lady!

DUCH. Let them, like tyrants,
Never be remembered but for the ill they have done;
Let all the zealous prayers of mortified
Churchmen forget them!—

BOS. O, uncharitable!

DUCH. Let heaven a little while cease crowning martyrs,
To punish them!—
Go, howl them this, and say, I long to bleed:
It is some mercy when men kill with speed. *Exit.*

[Re-enter FERDINAND]

FERD. Excellent, as I would wish; she's plagu'd in art.[a]
These presentations are but fram'd in wax
By the curious master in that quality,[b]
Vincentio Lauriola, and she takes them
For true substantial bodies.

BOS. Why do you do this?

FERD. To bring her to despair.

BOS. Faith, end here,

[a] By artificial means. [b] Profession.

And go no farther in your cruelty:
Send her a penitential garment to put on
Next to her delicate skin, and furnish her
With beads and prayer-books.

FERD.   Damn her! that body of hers,
While that my blood ran pure in 't, was more worth
Than that which thou wouldst comfort, call'd a soul.
I will send her masques of common courtezans,
Have her meat serv'd up by bawds and ruffians,
And, 'cause she 'll needs be mad, I am resolv'd
To move forth the common hospital
All the mad-folk, and place them near her lodging;
There let them practise together, sing and dance,
And act their gambols to the full o' th' moon:
If she can sleep the better for it, let her.
Your work is almost ended.

Bos.   Must I see her again?

FERD. Yes.

Bos.   Never.

FERD.   You must.

Bos.   Never in mine own shape;
That 's forfeited by my intelligence[6]
And this last cruel lie: when you send me next,
The business shall be comfort.

FERD.   Very likely;
Thy pity is nothing of kin to thee. Antonio
Lurks about Milan: thou shalt shortly thither,
To feed a fire as great as my revenge,
Which nev'r will slack till it hath spent his fuel:
Intemperate agues make physicians cruel.   *Exeunt.*

SCENE II[1]

[*Enter*] DUCHESS *and* CARIOLA

DUCH. What hideous noise was that?

CARI.   'Tis the wild consort[2]
Of madmen, lady, which your tyrant brother

---

[6] Spying.
[1] Another room in the lodging of the Duchess.   [2] Band.

Hath plac'd about your lodging. This tyranny,
I think, was never practis'd till this hour.

DUCH. Indeed, I thank him. Nothing but noise and folly
Can keep me in my right wits; whereas reason
And silence make me stark mad. Sit down;
Discourse to me some dismal tragedy.

CARI. O, 'twill increase your melancholy!

DUCH. Thou art deceiv'd:
To hear of greater grief would lessen mine.
This is a prison?

CARI. Yes, but you shall live
To shake this durance off.

DUCH. Thou art a fool:
The robin-red-breast and the nightingale
Never live long in cages.

CARI. Pray, dry your eyes.
What think you of, madam?

DUCH. Of nothing;
When I muse thus, I sleep.

CARI. Like a madman, with your eyes open?

DUCH. Dost thou think we shall know one another
In th' other world?

CARI. Yes, out of question.

DUCH. O, that it were possible we might
But hold some two days' conference with the dead!
From them I should learn somewhat, I am sure,
I never shall know here. I 'll tell thee a miracle:
I am not mad yet, to my cause of sorrow:
Th' heaven o'er my head seems made of molten brass,
The earth of flaming sulphur, yet I am not mad.
I am acquainted with sad misery
As the tann'd galley-slave is with his oar;
Necessity makes me suffer constantly,
And custom makes it easy. Who do I look like now?

CARI. Like to your picture in the gallery,
A deal of life in show, but none in practice;
Or rather like some reverend monument
Whose ruins are even pitied.

DUCH. Very proper;
And Fortune seems only to have her eye-sight

To behold my tragedy.—How now!
What noise is that?

[Enter Servant]

SERV.   I am come to tell you
Your brother hath intended you some sport.
A great physician, when the Pope was sick
Of a deep melancholy, presented him
With several sorts[3] of madmen, which wild object
Being full of change and sport, forc'd him to laugh,
And so the imposthume[4] broke: the self-same cure
The duke intends on you.

DUCH.   Let them come in.

SERV. There 's a mad lawyer; and a secular priest;
A doctor that hath forfeited his wits
By jealousy; an astrologian
That in his works said such a day o' the month
Should be the day of doom, and, failing of 't,
Ran mad; an English tailor craz'd i' the brain
With the study of new fashions; a gentleman-usher
Quite beside himself with care to keep in mind
The number of his lady's salutations
Or ' How do you,' she employ'd him in each morning;
A farmer, too, an excellent knave in grain,[5]
Mad 'cause he was hind'red transportation:[6]
And let one broker that 's mad loose to these,
You 'd think the devil were among them.

DUCH. Sit, Cariola.—Let them loose when you please
For I am chain'd to endure all your tyranny.

[Enter Madman]

*Here by a Madman this song is sung to a dismal
kind of music*

O, let us howl some heavy note,
    Some deadly dogged howl,
Sounding as from the threatening throat
    Of beasts and fatal fowl!

---

[3] Bands.   [4] Boil.
[5] Punning on the two senses of " dye " and " corn."[20]
[6] From exporting his grain.

As ravens, screech-owls, bulls, and bears,
 We 'll bell, and bawl our parts,
Till irksome noise have cloy'd your ears
 And corrosiv'd your hearts.
At last, whenas our choir wants breath,
 Our bodies being blest,
We 'll sing, like swans, to welcome death,
 And die in love and rest.

FIRST MADMAN. Doom's-day not come yet! I 'll draw it nearer by a perspective,[7] or make a glass that shall set all the world on fire upon an instant. I cannot sleep; my pillow is stuffed with a litter of porcupines.

SECOND MADMAN. Hell is a mere glass-house, where the devils are continually blowing up women's souls on hollow irons, and the fire never goes out.

FIRST MADMAN. I have skill in heraldry.

SECOND MADMAN. Hast?

FIRST MADMAN. You do give for your crest a woodcock's head with the brains picked out on 't; you are a very ancient gentleman.

THIRD MADMAN. Greek is turned Turk: we are only to be saved by the Helvetian translation.[8]

FIRST MADMAN. Come on, sir, I will lay the law to you.

SECOND MADMAN. O, rather lay a corrosive: the law will eat to the bone.

THIRD MADMAN. He that drinks but to satisfy nature is damn'd.

FOURTH MADMAN. If I had my glass here, I would show a sight should make all the women here call me mad doctor.

FIRST MADMAN. What 's he? a rope-maker?

SECOND MADMAN. No, no, no, a snuffling knave that, while he shows the tombs, will have his hand in a wench's placket.[9]

THIRD MADMAN. Woe to the caroche[10] that brought home my wife from the masque at three o'clock in the morning! It had a large feather-bed in it.

FOURTH MADMAN. I have pared the devil's nails forty

7 Optical glass. 8 The Geneva Bible. 9 Petticoat. 10 Coach.

times, roasted them in raven's eggs, and cured agues with them.

THIRD MADMAN. Get me three hundred milch-bats, to make possets[11] to procure sleep.

FOURTH MADMAN. All the college may throw their caps at me: I have made a soap-boiler costive; it was my masterpiece.

> *Here the dance, consisting of Eight Madmen, with music answerable thereunto; after which,* BOSOLA, *like an old man, enters.*

DUCH. Is he mad too?

SERV.   Pray, question him. I 'll leave you.
> [*Exeunt Servant and Madmen.*]

BOS. I am come to make thy tomb.

DUCH.   Ha! my tomb!
Thou speak'st as if I lay upon my death-bed,
Gasping for breath. Dost thou perceive me sick?

BOS. Yes, and the more dangerously, since thy sickness is insensible.

DUCH. Thou art not mad, sure: dost know me?

BOS.   Yes.

DUCH.   Who am I?

BOS. Thou art a box of worm-seed, at best but a salvatory[12] of green mummy.[13] What 's this flesh? a little crudded[14] milk, fantastical puff-paste. Our bodies are weaker than those paper-prisons boys use to keep flies in; more contemptible, since ours is to preserve earth-worms. Didst thou ever see a lark in a cage? Such is the soul in the body: this world is like her little turf of grass, and the heaven o'er our heads like her looking-glass, only gives us a miserable knowledge of the small compass of our prison.

DUCH. Am not I thy duchess?

BOS. Thou art some great woman, sure, for riot begins to sit on thy forehead (clad in gray hairs) twenty years sooner than on a merry milk-maid's. Thou sleepest worse than if a mouse should be forced to take up her lodging in a cat's ear: a little infant that breeds its teeth, should it lie

---

[11] A warm drink containing milk, wine, etc.
[12] Receptacle.   [13] A drug supposed to ooze from embalmed bodies.
[14] Curdled.

with thee, would cry out, as if thou wert the more unquiet
bedfellow.

Duch. I am Duchess of Malfi still.

Bos. That makes thy sleep so broken:
Glories, like glow-worms, afar off shine bright,
But, look'd to near, have neither heat nor light.

Duch. Thou art very plain.

Bos. My trade is to flatter the dead, not the living; I am
a tomb-maker.

Duch. And thou comest to make my tomb?

Bos. Yes.

Duch. Let me be a little merry:—of what stuff wilt thou
make it?

Bos. Nay, resolve me first, of what fashion?

Duch. Why, do we grow fantastical on our deathbed?
Do we affect fashion in the grave?

Bos. Most ambitiously. Princes' images on their tombs
do not lie, as they were wont, seeming to pray up to heaven;
but with their hands under their cheeks, as if they died of
the tooth-ache. They are not carved with their eyes fix'd
upon the stars, but as their minds were wholly bent upon the
world, the selfsame way they seem to turn their faces.

Duch. Let me know fully therefore the effect
Of this thy dismal preparation,
This talk fit for a charnel.

Bos.   Now I shall:—

[*Enter Executioners, with*] *a coffin, cords, and a bell*

Here is a present from your princely brothers;
And may it arrive welcome, for it brings
Last benefit, last sorrow.

Duch.   Let me see it:
I have so much obedience in my blood,
I wish it in their veins to do them good.

Bos. This is your last presence-chamber.

Cari. O my sweet lady!

Duch.   Peace; it affrights not **me.**

Bos. I am the common bellman
That usually is sent to condemn'd persons

The night before they suffer.

DUCH.   Even now thou said'st
Thou wast a tomb-maker.

BOS.   'Twas to bring you
By degrees to mortification.   Listen.

> Hark, now everything is still,
> The screech-owl and the whistler shrill
> Call upon our dame aloud,
> And bid her quickly don her shroud!
> Much you had of land and rent;
> Your length in clay 's now competent:
> A long war disturb'd your mind;
> Here your perfect peace is sign'd.
> Of what is 't fools make such vain keeping?
> Sin their conception, their birth weeping,
> Their life a general mist of error,
> Their death a hideous storm of terror.
> Strew your hair with powders sweet,
> Don clean linen, bathe your feet,
> And (the foul fiend more to check)
> A crucifix let bless your neck.
> 'Tis now full tide 'tween night and day;
> End your groan, and come away.

CARI. Hence, villains, tyrants, murderers! Alas!
What will you do with my lady?—Call for help!

DUCH. To whom? To our next neighbours? They are
mad-folks.

BOS. Remove that noise.

DUCH.   Farewell, Cariola.
In my last will I have not much to give:
A many hungry guests have fed upon me;
Thine will be a poor reversion.

CARI.   I will die with her.

DUCH. I pray thee, look thou giv'st my little boy
Some syrup for his cold, and let the girl
Say her prayers ere she sleep.

[CARIOLA *is forced out by the Executioners.*]
                          Now what you please:

What death?

Bos.   Strangling; here are your executioners.

Duch. I forgive them:

The apoplexy, catarrh, or cough o' th' lungs,

Would do as much as they do.

Bos. Doth not death fright you?

Duch.   Who would be afraid on 't,

Knowing to meet such excellent company

In th' other world?

Bos. Yet, methinks,

The manner of your death should much afflict you:

This cord should terrify you.

Duch.   Not a whit:

What would it pleasure me to have my throat cut

With diamonds? or to be smothered

With cassia? or to be shot to death with pearls?

I know death hath ten thousand several doors

For men to take their exits; and 'tis found

They go on such strange geometrical hinges,

You may open them both ways: any way, for heaven-sake,

So I were out of your whispering. Tell my brothers

That I perceive death, now I am well awake,

Best gift is they can give or I can take.

I would fain put off my last woman's-fault,

I 'd not be tedious to you.

First Execut.   We are ready.

Duch. Dispose my breath how please you; but my body

Bestow upon my women, will you?

First Execut.   Yes.

Duch. Pull, and pull strongly, for your able strength

Must pull down heaven upon me:—

Yet stay; heaven-gates are not so highly arch'd

As princes' palaces; they that enter there

Must go upon their knees [*Kneels*].—Come, violent death,

Serve for mandragora to make me sleep!—

Go tell my brothers, when I am laid out,

They then may feed in quiet.   *They strangle her.*

Bos. Where 's the waiting--woman??

Fetch her: some other strangle the children.

[*Enter* CARIOLA]

Look you, there sleeps your mistress.

CARI.   O, you are damn'd
Perpetually for this! My turn is next;
Is 't not so ordered?

Bos.   Yes, and I am glad
You are so well prepar'd for 't.

CARI.   You are deceiv'd, sir,
I am not prepar'd for 't, I will not die;
I will first come to my answer,[15] and know
How I have offended.

Bos.   Come, despatch her.—
You kept her counsel; now you shall keep ours.

CARI. I will not die, I must not; I am contracted
To a young gentleman.

FIRST EXECUT.   Here 's your wedding-ring.

CARI. Let me but speak with the duke. I 'll discover
Treason to his person.

Bos.   Delays:—throttle her.

FIRST EXECUT. She bites and scratches.

CARI.   If you kill me now,
I am damn'd; I have not been at confession
This two years.

Bos. [*To* EXECUTIONERS.] When?[16]

CARI.   I am quick with child.

Bos.   Why, then,
Your credit 's saved.   [*Executioners strangle* CARIOLA.]
                      Bear her into the next room;
Let these lie still.

     [*Exeunt the Executioners with the body of* CARIOLA.]

[*Enter* FERDINAND]

FERD.   Is she dead?

Bos.   She is what
You 'd have her. But here begin your pity:
                  Shows the Children strangled.
Alas, how have these offended?

FERD.   The death

---

[15] Trial.   [16] An exclamation of impatience.

Of young wolves is never to be pitied.

   Bos. Fix your eye here.

   Ferd.   Constantly.

   Bos.   Do you not weep?

Other sins only speak; murder shrieks out.

The element of water moistens the earth,

But blood flies upwards and bedews the heavens.

   Ferd. Cover her face; mine eyes dazzle: she died young.

   Bos. I think not so; her infelicity

Seem'd to have years too many.

   Ferd. She and I were twins;

And should I die this instant, I had liv'd

Her time to a minute.

   Bos.   It seems she was born first:

You have bloodily approv'd the ancient truth,

That kindred commonly do worse agree

Than remote strangers.

   Ferd.   Let me see her face

Again. Why didst thou not pity her? What

An excellent honest man mightst thou have been,

If thou hadst borne her to some sanctuary!

Or, bold in a good cause, oppos'd thyself,

With thy advanced sword above thy head,

Between her innocence and my revenge!

I bade thee, when I was distracted of my wits,

Go kill my dearest friend, and thou hast done 't.

For let me but examine well the cause:

What was the meanness of her match to me?

Only I must confess I had a hope,

Had she continu'd widow, to have gain'd

An infinite mass of treasure by her death:

And that was the main cause,—her marriage,

That drew a stream of gall quite through my heart.

For thee, as we observe in tragedies

That a good actor many times is curs'd

For playing a villain's part, I hate thee for 't,

And, for my sake, say, thou hast done much ill well.

   Bos. Let me quicken your memory, for I perceive

You are falling into ingratitude: I challenge

The reward due to my service.

FERD.   I 'll tell thee
What I 'll give thee.
  BOS.   Do.
  FERD.   I 'll give thee a pardon
For this murder.
  BOS.   Ha!
  FERD.   Yes, and 'tis
The largest bounty I can study to do thee.
By what authority didst thou execute
This bloody sentence?
  BOS.   By yours.
  FERD. Mine! was I her judge?
Did any ceremonial form of law
Doom her to not-being? Did a cómplete jury
Deliver her conviction up i' the court?
Where shalt thou find this judgment register'd,
Unless in hell? See, like a bloody fool,
Thou 'st forfeited thy life, and thou shalt die for 't.
  BOS. The office of justice is perverted quite
When one thief hangs another. Who shall dare
To reveal this?
  FERD.   O, I 'll tell thee;
The wolf shall find her grave, and scrape it up,
Not to devour the corpse, but to discover
The horrid murder.
  BOS.   You, not I, shall quake for 't.
  FERD. Leave me.
  BOS.   I will first receive my pension.
  FERD. You are a villain.
  BOS.   When your ingratitude
Is judge, I am so.
  FERD.   O horror,
That not the fear of him which binds the devils
Can prescribe man obedience!—
Never look upon me more.
  BOS.   Why, fare thee well.
Your brother and yourself are worthy men!
You have a pair of hearts are hollow graves,
Rotten, and rotting others; and your vengeance,
Like two chain'd-bullets, still goes arm in arm:

You may be brothers; for treason, like the plague,
Doth take much in a blood. I stand like one
That long hath ta'en a sweet and golden dream:
I am angry with myself, now that I wake.

FERD. Get thee into some unknown part o' the world,
That I may never see thee.

Bos.   Let me know
Wherefore I should be thus neglected. Sir,
I serv'd your tyranny, and rather strove
To satisfy yourself than all the world:
And though I loath'd the evil, yet I lov'd
You that did counsel it; and rather sought
To appear a true servant than an honest man.

FERD. I 'll go hunt the badger by owl-light:
'Tis a deed of darkness.   *Exit.*

Bos. He 's much distracted. Off, my painted honour!
While with vain hopes our faculties we tire,
We seem to sweat in ice and freeze in fire.
What would I do, were this to do again?
I would not change my peace of conscience
For all the wealth of Europe.—She stirs; here 's life:—
Return, fair soul, from darkness, and lead mine
Out of this sensible hell:—she 's warm, she breathes:—
Upon thy pale lips I will melt my heart,
To store them with fresh colour.—Who 's there?
Some cordial drink!—Alas! I dare not call:
So pity would destroy pity.—Her eye opes,
And heaven in it seems to ope, that late was shut,
To take me up to mercy.

DUCH. Antonio!

Bos.   Yes, madam, he is living;
The dead bodies you saw were but feign'd statues.
He 's reconcil'd to your brothers; the Pope hath wrought
The atonement.

DUCH.   Mercy!   *Dies*

Bos. O, she 's gone again! there the cords of life broke.
O sacred innocence, that sweetly sleeps
On turtles' feathers, whilst a guilty conscience
Is a black register wherein is writ
All our good deeds and bad, a perspective

That shows us hell! That we cannot be suffer'd
To do good when we have a mind to it!
This is manly sorrow;
These tears, I am very certain, never grew
In my mother's milk. My estate is sunk
Below the degree of fear: where were
These penitent fountains while she was living?
O, they were frozen up! Here is a sight
As direful to my soul as is the sword
Unto a wretch hath slain his father.
Come, I 'll bear thee hence,
And execute thy last will; that 's deliver
Thy body to the reverend dispose
Of some good women: that the cruel tyrant
Shall not deny me. Then I 'll post to Milan,
Where somewhat I will speedily enact
Worth my dejection.   *Exit [with the body].*

ACT V

Scene I[1]

[Enter] Antonio *and* Delio

ANT. What think you of my hope of reconcilement
To the Arragonian brethren?
    DELIO.   I misdoubt it;
For though they have sent their letters of safe-conduct
For your repair to Milan, they appear
But nets to entrap you. The Marquis of Pescara,
Under whom you hold certain land in cheat,[2]
Much 'gainst his noble nature hath been mov'd
To seize those lands; and some of his dependants
Are at this instant making it their suit
To be invested in your revenues.
I cannot think they mean well to your life
That do deprive you of your means of life,
Your living.
    ANT.   You are still an heretic[3]

---

[1] Milan. A public place.   [2] In escheat; here, in fee.   [3] Disbeliever.

To any safety I can shape myself.

DELIO. Here comes the marquis: I will make myself
Petitioner for some part of your land,
To know whither it is flying.

ANT.   I pray, do.   [*Withdraws.*]

[*Enter* PESCARA]

DELIO. Sir, I have a suit to you.

PES.   To me?

DELIO.   An easy one:
There is the Citadel of Saint Bennet,
With some demesnes, of late in the possession
Of Antonio Bologna,—please you bestow them on me.

PES. You are my friend; but this is such a suit,
Nor fit for me to give, nor you to take.

DELIO. No, sir?

PES.   I will give you ample reason for 't
Soon in private:—here 's the cardinal's mistress.

[*Enter* JULIA]

JULIA. My lord, I am grown your poor petitioner,
And should be an ill beggar, had I not
A great man's letter here, the cardinal's,
To court you in my favour.   [*Gives a letter.*]

PES.   He entreats for you
The Citadel of Saint Bennet, that belong'd
To the banish'd Bologna.

JULIA.   Yes.

PES. I could not have thought of a friend I could rather
Pleasure with it: 'tis yours.

JULIA.   Sir, I thank you;
And he shall know how doubly I am engag'd
Both in your gift, and speediness of giving
Which makes your grant the greater.   *Exit.*

ANT.   How they fortify
Themselves with my ruin!

DELIO.   Sir, I am
Little bound to you.

PES.   Why?

DELIO. Because you deni'd this suit to me, and gave 't
To such a creature.

PES.   Do you know what it was?
It was Antonio's land; not forfeited
By course of law, but ravish'd from his throat
By the cardinal's entreaty. It were not fit
I should bestow so main a piece of wrong
Upon my friend; 'tis a gratification
Only due to a strumpet, for it is injustice.
Shall I sprinkle the pure blood of innocents
To make those followers I call my friends
Look ruddier upon me? I am glad
This land, ta'en from the owner by such wrong,
Returns again unto so foul an use
As salary for his lust. Learn, good Delio,
To ask noble things of me, and you shall find
I 'll be a noble giver.

DELIO.   You instruct me well.

ANT. Why, here 's a man now would fright impudence
From sauciest beggars.

PES.   Prince Ferdinand 's come to Milan,
Sick, as they give out, of an apoplexy;
But some say 'tis a frenzy: I am going
To visit him.   *Exit*

ANT.   'Tis a noble old fellow.

DELIO. What course do you mean to take, Antonio?

ANT. This night I mean to venture all my fortune,
Which is no more than a poor ling'ring life,
To the cardinal's worst of malice. I have got
Private access to his chamber; and intend
To visit him about the mid of night,
As once his brother did our noble duchess.
It may be that the sudden apprehension
Of danger,—for I 'll go in mine own shape,—
When he shall see it fraught[4] with love and duty,
May draw the poison out of him, and work
A friendly reconcilement. If it fail,
Yet it shall rid me of this infamous calling;
For better fall once than be ever falling.

[4] Fraught.

DELIO. I 'll second you in all danger; and howe'er,
My life keeps rank with yours.

ANT. You are still my lov'd and best friend.　　　　*Exeunt*

SCENE II[1]

[Enter] PESCARA *and* DOCTOR

PES. Now, doctor, may I visit your patient?

DOC. If 't please your lordship; but he 's instantly
To take the air here in the gallery
By my direction.

PES.　　　　　　　Pray thee, what 's his disease?

DOC. A very pestilent disease, my lord,
They call lycanthropia.

PES.　　　　　　　What 's that?

I need a dictionary to 't.

DOC.　　　　　　　I 'll tell you.

In those that are possess'd with 't there o'erflows
Such melancholy humour they imagine
Themselves to be transformed into wolves;
Steal forth to church-yards in the dead of night,
And dig dead bodies up: as two nights since
One met the duke 'bout midnight in a lane
Behind Saint Mark's church, with the leg of a man
Upon his shoulder; and he howl'd fearfully;
Said he was a wolf, only the difference
Was, a wolf's skin was hairy on the outside,
His on the inside; bade them take their swords,
Rip up his flesh, and try.　Straight I was sent for,
And, having minister'd to him, found his grace
Very well recover'd.

PES. I am glad on 't.

DOC.　　　　　　　Yet not without some fear
Of a relapse.　If he grow to his fit again,
I 'll go a nearer way to work with him
Than ever Paracelsus dream'd of; if
They 'll give me leave, I' ll buffet his madness out of him.
Stand aside; he comes.

　　　　[1] A gallery in the residence of the Cardinal and Ferdinand.

[*Enter* FERDINAND, CARDINAL, MALATESTI, *and* BOSOLA]

FERD. Leave me.

MAL. Why doth your lordship love this solitariness?

FERD. Eagles commonly fly alone: they are crows, daws, and starlings that flock together. Look, what 's that follows me?

MAL. Nothing, my lord.

FERD. Yes.

MAL. 'Tis your shadow.

FERD. Stay it; let it not haunt me.

MAL. Impossible, if you move, and the sun shine.

FERD. I will throttle it.

[*Throws himself down on his shadow.*]

MAL. O, my lord, you are angry with nothing.

FERD. You are a fool: how is 't possible I should catch my shadow, unless I fall upon 't? When I go to hell, I mean to carry a bribe; for, look you, good gifts evermore make way for the worst persons.

PES. Rise, good my lord.

FERD. I am studying the art of patience.

PES. 'Tis a noble virtue.

FERD. To drive six snails before me from this town to Moscow; neither use goad nor whip to them, but let them take their own time;—the patient'st man i' th' world match me for an experiment:—an I 'll crawl after like a sheep-biter.²

CARD. Force him up.   [*They raise him.*]

FERD. Use me well, you were best. What I have done, I have done: I 'll confess nothing.

DOC. Now let me come to him.—Are you mad, my lord? are you out of your princely wits?

FERD.   What 's he?

PES.   Your doctor.

FERD. Let me have his beard saw'd off, and his eye-brows fil'd more civil.

DOC. I must do mad tricks with him, for that 's the only way on 't.—I have brought your grace a salamander's skin to keep you from sun-burning.

---

² A dog which worries sheep.

FERD. I have cruel sore eyes.

DOC. The white of a cockatrix's[3] egg is present remedy.

FERD. Let it be a new-laid one, you were best.
Hide me from him: physicians are like kings,—
They brook no contradiction.

DOC. Now he begins to fear me: now let me alone with him.

CARD. How now! put off your gown!

DOC. Let me have some forty urinals filled with rose-
water: he and I 'll go pelt one another with them.—Now he
begins to fear me.—Can you fetch a frisk,[4] sir?—Let him go,
let him go, upon my peril: I find by his eye he stands in awe
of me; I 'll make him as tame as a dormouse.

FERD. Can you fetch your frisks, sir!—I will stamp him
into a cullis,[5] flay off his skin to cover one of the anatomies[6]
this rogue hath set i' th' cold yonder in Barber-Chirurgeon's-
hall.—Hence, hence! you are all of you like beasts for sacrifice. [Throws the DOCTOR down and beats him.] There's
nothing left of you but tongue and belly, flattery and
lechery.   [Exit.]

PES. Doctor, he did not fear you throughly.

DOC. True; I was somewhat too forward.

BOS. Mercy upon me, what a fatal judgment
Hath fall'n upon this Ferdinand!

PES.   Knows your grace
What accident hath brought unto the prince
This strange distraction?

CARD. [aside.] I must feign somewhat.—Thus they say it
        grew.
You have heard it rumour'd, for these many years
None of our family dies but there is seen
The shape of an old woman, which is given
By tradition to us to have been murder'd
By her nephews for her riches. Such a figure
One night, as the prince sat up late at 's book,
Appear'd to him; when crying out for help,
The gentleman of 's chamber found his grace
All on a cold sweat, alter'd much in face
And language: since which apparition,

---

[3] A fabulous serpent that killed by its glance.
[4] Cut a caper.   [5] Broth.   [6] Skeletons.

He hath grown worse and worse, and I much fear
He cannot live.

Bos.   Sir, I would speak with you.

Pes. We 'll leave your grace,
Wishing to the sick prince, our noble lord,
All health of mind and body.

Card.   You are most welcome.

[*Exeunt* Pescara, Malatesti, *and* Doctor.]

Are you come? so.—[*Aside.*] This fellow must not know
By any means I had intelligence
In our duchess' death; for, though I counsell'd it,
The full of all th' engagement seem'd to grow
From Ferdinand.—Now, sir, how fares our sister?
I do not think but sorrow makes her look
Like to an oft-dy'd garment: she shall now
Take comfort from me. Why do you look so wildly?
O, the fortune of your master here the prince
Dejects you; but be you of happy comfort:
If you 'll do one thing for me I 'll entreat,
Though he had a cold tomb-stone o'er his bones,
I 'd make you what you would be.

Bos.   Any thing;
Give it me in a breath, and let me fly to 't.
They that think long small expedition win,
For musing much o' th' end cannot begin.

[*Enter* Julia]

Julia. Sir, will you come into supper?

Card.   I am busy; leave me

Julia [*aside.*] What an excellent shape hath that fellow!

Exit.

Card. 'Tis thus. Antonio lurks here in Milan:
Inquire him out, and kill him. While he lives,
Our sister cannot marry; and I have thought
Of an excellent match for her. Do this, and style me
Thy advancement.

Bos. But by what means shall I find him out?

Card. There is a gentleman call'd Delio
Here in the camp, that hath been long approv'd
His loyal friend. Set eye upon that fellow;

Follow him to mass; may be Antonio,
Although he do account religion
But a school-name, for fashion of the world
May accompany him; or else go inquire out
Delio's confessor, and see if you can bribe
Him to reveal it.   There are a thousand ways
A man might find to trace him; as to know
What fellows haunt the Jews for taking up
Great sums of money, for sure he 's in want;
Or else to go to the picture-makers, and learn
Who bought[7] her picture lately: some of these
Happily may take.

Bos.   Well, I 'll not freeze i' th' business:
I would see that wretched thing, Antonio,
Above all sights i' th' world.

Card.   Do, and be happy.   *Exit*

Bos. This fellow doth breed basilisks in 's eyes,
He 's nothing else but murder; yet he seems
Not to have notice of the duchess' death.
'Tis his cunning: I must follow his example;
There cannot be a surer way to trace
Than that of an old fox.

                [Re-enter Julia, *with a pistol]*

Julia. So sir, you are well met.
Bos.   How now!
Julia. Nay, the doors are fast enough:
Now, sir, I will make you confess your treachery.
Bos. Treachery!
Julia.   Yes, confess to me
Which of my women 'twas you hir'd to put
Love-powder into my drink?
Bos. Love-powder!
Julia.   Yes, when I was at Malfi.
Why should I fall in love with such a face else?
I have already suffer'd for thee so much pain,
The only remedy to do me good
Is to kill my longing.
Bos.   Sure, your pistol holds

                    [7] So Dyce. Qq. *brought.*

Nothing but perfumes or kissing-comfits.[3]
Excellent lady!
You have a pretty way on 't to discover
Your longing. Come, come, I 'll disarm you,
And arm you thus: yet this is wondrous strange.

JULIA. Compare thy form and my eyes together,
You 'll find my love no such great miracle.
Now you 'll say
I am wanton: this nice modesty in ladies
Is but a troublesome familiar
That haunts them.

Bos. Know you me, I am a blunt soldier.
JULIA.   The better:
Sure, there wants fire where there are no lively sparks
Of roughness.

Bos.   And I want compliment.
JULIA.   Why, ignorance
In courtship cannot make you do amiss,
If you have a heart to do well.

Bos.   You are very fair.
JULIA. Nay, if you lay beauty to my charge,
I must plead unguilty.

Bos.   Your bright eyes
Carry a quiver of darts in them sharper
Than sun-beams.

JULIA.   You will mar me with commendation,
Put yourself to the charge of courting me,
Whereas now I woo you.

Bos. [aside.] I have it, I will work upon this creature.—
Let us grow most amorously familiar:
If the great cardinal now should see me thus,
Would he not count me a villain?

JULIA. No; he might count me a wanton,
Not lay a scruple of offence on you;
For if I see and steal a diamond,
The fault is not i' th' stone, but in me the thief
That purloins it. I am sudden with you.
We that are great women of pleasure use to cut off
These uncertain wishes and unquiet longings,

                *Perfumed sweetmeats for the breath.

And in an instant join the sweet delight
And the pretty excuse together. Had you been i' th' street,
Under my chamber-window, even there
I should have courted you.

   Bos. O, you are an excellent lady!

   Julia. Bid me do somewhat for you presently
To express I love you.

   Bos.   I will; and if you love me,
Fail not to effect it.
The cardinal is grown wondrous melancholy;
Demand the cause, let him not put you off
With feign'd excuse; discover the main ground on 't.

   Julia. Why would you know this?

   Bos.   I have depended on him,
And I hear that he is fall'n in some disgrace
With the emperor: if he be, like the mice
That forsake falling houses, I would shift
To other dependance.

   Julia.   You shall not need
Follow the wars: I 'll be your maintenance.

   Bos. And I your loyal servant: but I cannot
Leave my calling.

   Julia.   Not leave an ungrateful
General for the love of a sweet lady!
You are like some cannot sleep in feather-beds,
But must have blocks for their pillows.

   Bos.   Will you do this?

   Julia. Cunningly.

   Bos. To-morrow I 'll expect th' intelligence.

   Julia. To-morrow! get you into my cabinet;
You shall have it with you. Do not delay me,
No more than I do you: I am like one
That is condemn'd; I have my pardon promis'd,
But I would see it seal'd. Go, get you in:
You shall see me wind my tongue about his heart
Like a skein of silk.   [*Exit* Bosola.]

        [*Re-enter* Cardinal]

Card.   Where are you?

[*Enter Servants.*]

SERVANTS.   Here.

CARD. Let none, upon your lives, have conference
With the Prince Ferdinand, unless I know it.—
[*Aside*] In this distraction he may reveal
The murder.   [*Exeunt Servants.*]
            Yond 's my lingering consumption:
I am weary of her, and by any means
Would be quit of.

JULIA.   How now, my lord! what ails you?

CARD. Nothing.

JULIA.   O, you are much alter'd:
Come, I must be your secretary, and remove
This lead from off your bosom: what 's the matter?

CARD. I may not tell you.

JULIA. Are you so far in love with sorrow
You cannot part with part of it? Or think you
I cannot love your grace when you are sad
As well as merry? Or do you suspect
I, that have a been a secret to your heart
These many winters, cannot be the same
Unto your tongue?

CARD.   Satisfy thy longing,—
The only way to make thee keep my counsel
Is, not to tell thee.

JULIA.   Tell your echo this,
Or flatterers, that like echoes still report
What they hear though most imperfect, and not me;
For if that you be true unto yourself,
I 'll know.

CARD.   Will you rack me?

JULIA.   No, judgment shall
Draw it from you: it is an equal fault,
To tell one's secrets unto all or none.

CARD. The first argues folly.

JULIA. But the last tyranny.

CARD. Very well: why, imagine I have committed
Some secret deed which I desire the world
May never hear of.

JULIA.   Therefore may not I know it?
You have conceal'd for me as great a sin
As adultery. Sir, never was occasion
For perfect trial of my constancy
Till now: sir, I beseech you——
    CARD.   You 'll repent it.
    JULIA. Never.
    CARD. It hurries thee to ruin: I 'll not tell thee.
Be well advis'd, and think what danger 'tis
To receive a prince's secrets. They that do,
Had need have their breasts hoop'd with adamant
To contain them. I pray thee, yet be satisfi'd;
Examine thine own frailty; 'tis more easy
To tie knots than unloose them. 'Tis a secret
That, like a ling'ring poison, may chance lie
Spread in thy veins, and kill thee seven year hence.
    JULIA. Now you dally with me.
    CARD.   No more; thou shalt know it.
By my appointment the great Duchess of Malfi
And two of her young children, four nights since,
Were strangl'd.
    JULIA.   O heaven! sir, what have you done!
    CARD. How now? How settles this? Think you your
        bosom
Will be a grave dark and obscure enough
For such a secret?
    JULIA.   You have undone yourself, sir.
    CARD. Why?
    JULIA.   It lies not in me to conceal it.
    CARD.   No?
Come, I will swear you to 't upon this book.
    JULIA. Most religiously.
    CARD.   Kiss it. [*She kisses the book.*]
Now you shall never utter it; thy curiosity
Hath undone thee; thou 'rt poison'd with that book.
Because I knew thou couldst not keep my counsel,
I have bound thee to 't by death.

[Re-enter Bosola]

Bos. For pity-sake, hold!

Card.   Ha, Bosola!

Julia.   I forgive you
This equal piece of justice you have done;
For I betray'd your counsel to that fellow.
He over-heard it; that was the cause I said
It lay not in me to conceal it.

Bos. O foolish woman,
Couldst not thou have poison'd him?

Julia.   'Tis weakness,
Too much to think what should have been done. I go,
I know not whither.   *[Dies]*

Card.   Wherefore com'st thou hither?

Bos. That I might find a great man like yourself,
Not out of his wits, as the Lord Ferdinand,
To remember my service.

Card. I 'll have thee hew'd in pieces.

Bos. Make not yourself such a promise of that life
Which is not yours to dispose of.

Card.   Who plac'd thee here?

Bos. Her lust, as she intended.

Card.   Very well:
Now you know me for your fellow-murderer.

Bos. And wherefore should you lay fair marble colours
Upon your rotten purposes to me?
Unless you imitate some that do plot great treasons,
And when they have done, go hide themselves i' th' grave
Of those were actors in 't?

Card.   No more; there is
A fortune attends thee.

Bos. Shall I go sue to Fortune any longer?
'Tis the fool's pilgrimage.

Card. I have honours in store for thee.

Bos. There are a many ways that conduct to seeming
Honour, and some of them very dirty ones.

Card. Throw to the devil
Thy melancholy. The fire burns well;
What need we keep a stirring of 't, and make

A greater smother?[9] Thou wilt kill Antonio?

Bos. Yes.

Card.　　　Take up that body.

Bos.　　　　　　　　　　I think I shall
Shortly grow the common bier for church-yards.

Card. I will allow thee some dozen of attendants
To aid thee in the murder.

Bos. O, by no means. Physicians that apply horse-leeches
to any rank swelling use to cut off their tails, that the blood
may run through them the faster: let me have no train
when I go to shed blood, less it make me have a greater
when I ride to the gallows.

Card. Come to me after midnight, to help to remove
That body to her own lodging. I 'll give out
She died o' th' plague; 'twill breed the less inquiry
After her death.

Bos. Where 's Castruccio her husband?

Card. He 's rode to Naples, to take possession
Of Antonio's citadel.

Bos. Believe me, you have done a very happy turn.

Card. Fail not to come. There is the master-key
Of our lodgings; and by that you may conceive
What trust I plant in you.

Bos.　　　　　You shall find me ready. *Exit* Cardinal.
O poor Antonio, though nothing be so needful
To thy estate as pity, yet I find
Nothing so dangerous! I must look to my footing:
In such slippery ice-pavements men had need
To be frost-nail'd well, they may break their necks else;
The precedent 's here afore me. How this man
Bears up in blood! seems fearless! Why, 'tis well;
Security some men call the suburbs of hell,
Only a dead wall between. Well, good Antonio,
I 'll seek thee out; and all my care shall be
To put thee into safety from the reach
Of these most cruel biters that have got
Some of thy blood already. It may be,
I 'll join with thee in a most just revenge.
The weakest arm is strong enough that strikes

　　　　　　　　　[9] Smoke.

With the sword of justice.   Still methinks the duchess
Haunts me: there, there!—'Tis nothing but my melancholy.
O Penitence, let me truly taste thy cup,
That throws men down only to raise them up!   *Exit.*

SCENE III[1]

[*Enter*] ANTONIO *and* DELIO.   *Echo (from the* DUCHESS'S
Grave)

DELIO. Yond 's the cardinal's window.   This fortification
Grew from the ruins of an ancient abbey;
And to yond side o' th' river lies a wall,
Piece of a cloister, which in my opinion
Gives the best echo that you ever heard,
So hollow and so dismal, and withal
So plain in the distinction of our words,
That many have suppos'd it is a spirit
That answers.

ANT.   I do love these ancient ruins.
We never tread upon them but we set
Our foot upon some reverend history;
And, questionless, here in this open court,
Which now lies naked to the injuries
Of stormy weather, some men lie interr'd
Lov'd the church so well, and gave so largely to 't,
They thought it should have canopied their bones
Till dooms-day.   But all things have their end;
Churches and cities, which have diseases like to men,
Must have like death that we have.

ECHO.   *Like death that we have.*

DELIO. Now the echo hath caught you.

ANT. It groan'd methought, and gave
A very deadly accent.

ECHO.   *Deadly accent.*

DELIO. I told you 'twas a pretty one.   You may make it
A huntsman, or a falconer, a musician,
Or a thing of sorrow.

ECHO.   *A thing of sorrow.*

[1] A fortification.

Ant. Ay, sure, that suits it best.

Echo.   *That suits it best.*

Ant. 'Tis very like my wife's voice.

Echo.   *Ay, wife's voice.*

Delio. Come, let us walk further from t.

I would not have you go to the cardinal's to-night:

Do not.

Echo. *Do not.*

Delio. Wisdom doth not more moderate wasting sorrow

Than time. Take time for 't; be mindful of thy safety.

Echo. *Be mindful of thy safety.*

Ant. Necessity compels me.

Make scrutiny through the passages

Of your own life, you 'll find it impossible

To fly your fate.

Echo.   *O, fly your fate!*

Delio. Hark! the dead stones seem to have pity on you,

And give you good counsel.

Ant. Echo, I will not talk with thee,

For thou art a dead thing.

Echo.   *Thou art a dead thing.*

Ant. My duchess is asleep now,

And her little ones, I hope sweetly. O heaven,

Shall I never see her more?

Echo.   *Never see her more.*

Ant. I mark'd not one repetition of the echo

But that; and on the sudden a clear light

Presented me a face folded in sorrow.

Delio. Your fancy merely.

Ant.   Come, I 'll be out of this ague,

For to live thus is not indeed to live;

It is a mockery and abuse of life.

I will not henceforth save myself by halves;

Lose all, or nothing.

Delio.   **Your own virtue save you!**

I 'll fetch your eldest son, and second you.

It may be that the sight of his own blood

Spread in so sweet a figure may beget

The more compassion. However, fare you well.

Though in our miseries Fortune have a part,

Yet in our noble sufferings she hath none.
Contempt of pain, that we may call our own.   *Exeunt.*

SCENE IV[1]

[*Enter*] CARDINAL, PESCARA, MALATESTI, RODERIGO, *and*
GRISOLAN

CARD. You shall not watch to-night by the sick prince;
His grace is very well recover'd.
MAL. Good my lord, suffer us.
CARD.   O, by no means;
The noise, and change of object in his eye,
Doth more distract him. I pray, all to bed;
And though you hear him in his violent fit,
Do not rise, I entreat you.
PES. So, sir; we shall not.
CARD.   Nay, I must have you promise
Upon your honours, for I was enjoin'd to 't
By himself; and he seem'd to urge it sensibly.
PES. Let our honours bind this trifle.
CARD. Nor any of your followers.
MAL. Neither.
CARD. It may be, to make trial of your promise,
When he 's asleep, myself will rise and feign
Some of his mad tricks, and cry out for help,
And feign myself in danger.
MAL. If your throat were cutting,
I 'd not come at you, now I have protested against it.
CARD. Why, I thank you.
GRIS.   'Twas a foul storm to-night.
ROD. The Lord Ferdinand's chamber shook like an osier.
MAL. 'Twas nothing but pure kindness in the devil
To rock his own child.   *Exeunt* [*all except the* CARDINAL.]
CARD. The reason why I would not suffer these
About my brother, is, because at midnight
I may with better privacy convey
Julia's body to her own lodging. O, my conscience!
I would pray now; but the devil takes away my heart

¹ Milan. An apartment in the residence of the Cardinal and Ferdinand.

For having any confidence in prayer.
About this hour I appointed Bosola
To fetch the body. When he hath serv'd my turn,
He dies.   *Exit.*

[*Enter* BOSOLA]

Bos. Ha! 'twas the cardinal's voice; I heard him name
Bosola and my death. Listen; I hear one's footing.

[*Enter* FERDINAND]

FERD. Strangling is a very quiet death.
Bos. [*aside.*] Nay, then, I see I must stand upon my guard.
FERD. What say to that? Whisper softly: do you agree
to 't? So; it must be done i' th' dark; the cardinal would
not for a thousand pounds the doctor should see it.   *Exit.*
Bos. My death is plotted; here 's the consequence of
        murder.
We value not desert nor Christian breath,
When we know black deeds must be cur'd with death.

[*Enter* ANTONIO *and Servant*]

SERV. Here stay, sir, and be confident, I pray;
I 'll fetch you a dark lantern.   *Exit.*
ANT. Could I take him at his prayers,
There were hope of pardon.
Bos. Fall right, my sword!—   [*Stabs him.*]
I 'll not give thee so much leisure as to pray.
ANT. O, I am gone! Thou hast ended a long suit
In a minute.
Bos.   What art thou?
ANT.   A most wretched thing,
That only have thy benefit in death,
To appear myself.

[*Re-enter Servant with a lantern*]

SERV. Where are you, sir?
ANT. Very near my home.—Bosola!
SERV. O, misfortune!
Bos. Smother thy pity, thou art dead else.—Antonio!
The man I would have sav'd 'bove mine own life!

We are merely the stars' tennis-balls, struck and banded
Which way please them.—O good Antonio,
I 'll whisper one thing in thy dying ear
Shall make thy heart break quickly! Thy fair duchess
And two sweet children——

ANT.   Their very names
Kindle a little life in me.

BOS.   Are murder'd.

ANT. Some men have wish'd to die
At the hearing of sad tidings; I am glad
That I shall do 't in sadness.[2] I would not now
Wish my wounds balm'd nor heal'd, for I have no use
To put my life to. In all our quest of greatness,
Like wanton boys whose pastime is their care,
We follow after bubbles blown in th' air.
Pleasure of life, what is 't? Only the good hours
Of an ague; merely a preparative to rest,
To endure vexation. I do not ask
The process of my death; only commend me
To Delio.

BOS.   Break, heart!

ANT. And let my son fly the courts of princes.   [Dies.]

BOS. Thou seem'st to have lov'd Antonio.

SERV. I brought him hither,
To have reconcil'd him to the cardinal.

BOS. I do not ask thee that.
Take him up, if thou tender thine own life,
And bear him where the lady Julia
Was wont to lodge.—O, my fate moves swift!
I have this cardinal in the forge already;
Now I 'll bring him to th' hammer. O direful misprision![3]
I will not imitate things glorious,
No more than base; I 'll be mine own example.—
On, on, and look thou represent, for silence,
The thing thou bear'st.[4]   Exeunt.

     [2] Reality.   [3] Mistake.   [4] I. e., the dead body.

Scene V[1]

[Enter] Cardinal, *with a book*

Card. I am puzzl'd in a question about hell;
He says, in hell there 's one material fire,
And yet it shall not burn all men alike.
Lay him by. How tedious is a guilty conscience!
When I look into the fish-ponds in my garden,
Methinks I see a thing arm'd with a rake,
That seems to strike at me.

[Enter Bosola, *and Servant bearing* Antonio's *body]*
       Now, art thou come?
Thou look'st ghastly;
There sits in thy face some great determination
Mix'd with some fear.
  Bos.   Thus it lightens into action:
I am come to kill thee.
  Card.   Ha!—Help! our guard!
  Bos. Thou art deceiv'd; they are out of thy howling.
  Card. Hold; and I will faithfully divide
Revenues with thee.
  Bos.   Thy prayers and proffers
Are both unseasonable.
  Card.   Raise the watch!
We are betray'd!
  Bos.   I have confin'd your flight:
I 'll suffer your retreat to Julia's chamber,
But no further.
  Card.   Help! we are betray'd!

[Enter, above, Pescara, Malatesti, Roderigo, *and*
Grisolan]

Mal. Listen.
Card. My dukedom for rescue!
Rod. Fie upon his counterfeiting!
Mal. Why, 'tis not the cardinal.
Rod. Yes, yes, 'tis he:

---

[1] Another apartment in the same.

But, I 'll see him hang'd ere I 'll go down to him.

CARD. Here 's a plot upon me; I am assaulted! I am lost,
Unless some rescue!

GRIS.   He doth this pretty well;
But it will not serve to laugh me out of mine honour.

CARD. The sword's at my throat!

ROD.   You would not bawl so loud then.

MAL. Come, come, let 's go to bed: he told us this much
aforehand.

PES. He wish'd you should not come at him; but, believe 't,
The accent of the voice sounds not in jest:
I 'll down to him, howsoever, and with engines
Force ope the doors.   [*Exit above.*]

ROD.   Let 's follow him aloof,
And note how the cardinal will laugh at him.

　　　[*Exeunt, above,* MALATESTI, RODERIGO, *and* GRISOLAN.]

BOS. There 's for you first,
'Cause you shall not unbarricade the door
To let in rescue.   *Kills the Servant.*

CARD. What cause hast thou to pursue my life?

BOS.   Look there.

CARD. Antonio!

BOS.   Slain by my hand unwittingly.
Pray, and be sudden. When thou kill'd'st thy sister,
Thou took'st from Justice her most equal balance,
And left her naught but her sword.

CARD.   O, mercy!

BOS. Now it seems thy greatness was only outward;
For thou fall'st faster of thyself than calamity
Can drive thee. I 'll not waste longer time; there!
                                    [*Stabs him.*]

CARD. Thou hast hurt me.

BOS.   Again!

CARD.   Shall I die like a leveret,
Without any resistance?—Help, help, help!
I am slain!

[*Enter* FERDINAND]

FERD.   Th' alarum! Give me a fresh horse;
Rally the vaunt-guard, or the day is lost,
Yield, yield! I give you the honour of arms
Shake my sword over you; will you yield?
    CARD. Help me; I am your brother!
    FERD.   The devil!
My brother fight upon the adverse party!

> *He wounds the* CARDINAL, *and, in the scuffle,*
>   *gives* BOSOLA *his death-wound.*

There flies your ransom.
    CARD. O justice!
I suffer now for what hath former bin:
Sorrow is held the eldest child of sin.
    FERD. Now you 're brave fellows. Cæsar's fortune was
harder than Pompey's; Cæsar died in the arms of prosperity,
Pompey at the feet of disgrace. You both died in the field.
The pain 's nothing; pain many times is taken away with the
apprehension of greater, as the tooth-ache with the sight of
a barber that comes to pull it out. There 's philosophy for you.
    BOS. Now my revenge is perfect.—Sink, thou main cause
                                        Kills FERDINAND.
Of my undoing!—The last part of my life
Hath done me best service.
    FERD. Give me some wet hay; I am broken-winded.
I do account this world but a dog-kennel:
I will vault credit and affect high pleasures
Beyond death.
    BOS.   He seems to come to himself,
Now he 's so near the bottom.
    FERD. My sister, O my sister! there 's the cause on 't.
Whether we fall by ambition, blood, or lust,
Like diamonds, we are cut with our own dust.   [*Dies.*]
    CARD. Thou hast thy payment too.
    BOS. Yes, I hold my weary soul in my teeth;
'Tis ready to part from me. I do glory
That thou, which stood'st like a huge pyramid
Begun upon a large and ample base,
Shalt end in a little point, a kind of nothing.

[*Enter, below,* PESCARA, MALATESTI, RODERIGO, *and*
GRISOLAN]

PES. How now, my lord!

MAL.   O sad disaster!

ROD.   How comes this?

BOS. Revenge for the Duchess of Malfi murdered
By the Arragonian brethren; for Antonio
Slain by this hand; for lustful Julia
Poison'd by this man; and lastly for myself,
That was an actor in the main of all
Much 'gainst mine own good nature, yet i' the end
Neglected.

PES.   How now, my lord!

CARD.   Look to my brother:
He gave us these large wounds, as we were struggling
Here i' th' rushes. And now, I pray, let me
Be laid by and never thought of.   [*Dies.*]

PES. How fatally, it seems, he did withstand
His own rescue!

MAL.   Thou wretched thing of blood,
How came Antonio by his death?

BOS. In a mist; I know not how:
Such a mistake as I have often seen
In a play. O, I am gone!
We are only like dead walls or vaulted graves,
That, ruin'd, yield no echo. Fare you well.
It may be pain, but no harm, to me to die
In so good a quarrel. O, this gloomy world!
In what a shadow, or deep pit of darkness,
Doth womanish and fearful mankind live!
Let worthy minds ne'er stagger in distrust
To suffer death or shame for what is just:
Mine is another voyage.   [*Dies.*]

PES. The noble Delio, as I came to th' palace,
Told me of Antonio's being here, and show'd me
A pretty gentleman, his son and heir.

[*Enter* DELIO, *and* ANTONIO's *Son*]

MAL. O sir, you come too late!

DELIO.   I heard so, and
Was arm'd for 't, ere I came.   Let us make noble use
Of this great ruin; and join all our force
To establish this young hopeful gentleman
In 's mother's right.   These wretched eminent things
Leave no more fame behind 'em, than should one
Fall in a frost, and leave his print in snow;
As soon as the sun shines, it ever melts,
Both form and matter.   I have ever thought
Nature doth nothing so great for great men
As when she 's pleas'd to make them lords of truth:
Integrity of life is fame's best friend,
Which nobly, beyond death, shall crown the end.   *Exeunt.*

A NEW WAY
TO PAY OLD DEBTS

BY

PHILIP MASSINGER

INTRODUCTORY NOTE

PHILIP MASSINGER *was born at Salisbury in 1584. Though the son of a Member of Parliament, he seems to have inherited no means, for the first notice we have of him after his leaving Oxford in 1606 is a petition addressed to Henslowe by him and two friends for a payment of five pounds on account, to get them out of prison.*

After Beaumont retired from play-writing, Massinger became Fletcher's chief partner, and there is evidence that there existed between them a warm friendship. All Massinger's relations with his fellow authors of which we have record seem to have been pleasant; and the impression of his personality which one derives from his work is that of a dignified, hard-working, and conscientious man. He seems to have been much interested in public affairs, and he at times came into collision with the authorities on account of the introduction into his plays of more or less veiled allusions to political personages and events. He died in 1640.

The best known of Massinger's works is "A New Way to Pay Old Debts," which was probably acted for the first time in 1625. The popularity of the play is chiefly due to the principal character, Sir Giles Overreach, a usurer and extortioner, drawn, however, on such magnificent lines as to rise far above the conventional miser of literature. Overreach is presented with great dramatic skill, the situations being chosen and elaborated so as to throw his figure into high relief; and though his villainy reaches the pitch of monstrosity, the illusion of life is preserved. Here, as elsewhere, Massinger's sympathies are on the side of wholesome morals; and it was probably the powerful didactic tendency of the play and its fine rhetoric which, united with the impressiveness of the main figure, enabled it to hold the stage into the nineteenth century.

A NEW WAY
TO PAY OLD DEBTS

DRAMATIS PERSONÆ

LORD LOVELL, an English Lord.
SIR GILES OVERREACH, a cruel extortioner.
[FRANK] WELLBORN, a Prodigal.
[TOM] ALLWORTH, a young Gentleman, Page to Lord Lovell.
GREEDY, a hungry Justice of Peace.
MARRALL, a Term-Driver; a creature of Sir Giles Overreach.
ORDER [Steward],
AMBLE [Usher],
FURNACE [Cook],   } Servants to Lady Allworth.
WATCHALL [Porter],
WILLDO, a Parson.
TAPWELL, an Alehouse Keeper.
Three Creditors, Servants, &c.

LADY ALLWORTH, a rich Widow.
MARGARET, Daughter of Sir Giles Overreach.
FROTH, Wife of Tapwell.
Chambermaid.
Waiting Woman.

[SCENE—*The Country near Nottingham*]

ACT I

SCENE I[1]

[*Enter*] WELLBORN [*in tattered apparel,*] TAPWELL *and* FROTH

Wellborn

NO BOUSE?[2] nor no tobacco?
    TAP.   Not a suck, sir;
  Nor the remainder of a single can
Left by a drunken porter, all night pall'd[3] too.
  FROTH. Not the dropping of the tap for your morning's
      draught, sir:
'Tis verity, I assure you.

               [1] Before Tapwell's house.   [2] Booze, drink.   [3] Staled.

WELL.   Verity, you brache![4]
The devil turn'd precisian![5] Rogue, what am I?

TAP. Troth, durst I trust you with a looking-glass,
To let you see your trim shape, you would quit me
And take the name yourself.

WELL.   How, dog!

TAP.   Even so, sir.
And I must tell you, if you but advance
Your Plymouth cloak[6] you shall be soon instructed
There dwells, and within call, if it please your worship,
A potent monarch call'd the constable,
That does command a citadel called the stocks;
Whose guards are certain files of rusty billmen
Such as with great dexterity will hale
Your tatter'd, lousy——

WELL.   Rascal! slave!

FROTH.   No rage, sir.

TAP. At his own peril. Do not put yourself
In too much heat, there being no water near
To quench your thirst; and sure, for other liquor,
As mighty ale, or beer, they are things, I take it,
You must no more remember; not in a dream, sir.

WELL. Why, thou unthankful villain, dar'st thou talk thus!
Is not thy house, and all thou hast, my gift?

TAP. I find it not in chalk; and Timothy Tapwell
Does keep no other register.

WELL.   Am not I he
Whose riots fed and cloth'd thee? Wert thou not
Born on my father's land, and proud to be
A drudge in his house?

TAP.   What I was, sir, it skills[7] not;
What you are, is apparent. Now, for a farewell,
Since you talk of father, in my hope it will torment you,
I'll briefly tell your story. Your dead father,
My quondam master, was a man of worship,
Old Sir John Wellborn, justice of peace and *quorum*,[8]
And stood fair to be *custos rotulorum*;[9]
Bore the whole sway of the shire, kept a great house,

---

[4] Hound.   [5] Puritan.   [6] Cudgel.   [7] Matters.
[8] A select number of the more learned justices, whose presence was necessary to constitute the bench.   [9] Keeper of the county records.

Reliev'd the poor, and so forth; but he dying,
And the twelve hundred a year coming to you,
Late Master Francis, but now forlorn Wellborn——
    WELL. Slave, stop! or I shall lose myself.
    FROTH.   Very hardly;
You cannot out of your way.
    TAP.   But to my story:
You were then a lord of acres, the prime gallant,
And I your under-butler. Note the change now;
You had a merry time of't; hawks and hounds,
With choice of running horses; mistresses
Of all sorts and all sizes, yet so hot,
As their embraces made your lordship melt;
Which your uncle, Sir Giles Overreach, observing,
(Resolving not to lose a drop of them,)
On foolish mortgages, statutes, and bonds,
For a while suppli'd your looseness, and then left you.
    WELL. Some curate hath penn'd this invective, mongrel,
And you have studied it.
    TAP.   I have not done yet.
Your land gone, and your credit not worth a token,
You grew a common borrower; no man scap'd
Your paper-pellets,[10] from the gentleman
To the beggars on highways, that sold you switches
In your gallantry.
    WELL.   I shall switch your brains out.
    TAP. Where poor Tim Tapwell, with a little stock,
Some forty pounds or so, bought a small cottage;
Humbled myself to marriage with my Froth here,
Gave entertainment——
    WELL.   Yes, to whores and canters,[11]
Clubbers by night.
    TAP.   True, but they brought in profit,
And had a gift to pay for what they call'd for,
And stuck not like your mastership. The poor income
I glean'd from them hath made me in my parish
Thought worthy to be scavenger, and in time
I may rise to be overseer of the poor;
Which if I do, on your petition, Wellborn,

    [10] Acknowledgments of indebtedness.   [11] Whining beggars.

I may allow you thirteen-pence a quarter.
And you shall thank my worship.

    WELL.   Thus, you dog-bolt,
  And thus——   *Beats and kicks him.*

    TAP. [*to his wife.*] Cry out for help!

    WELL.   Stir, and thou diest:
Your potent prince, the constable, shall not save you.
Hear me, ungrateful hell-hound! Did not I
Make purses for you? Then you lick'd my boots,
And thought your holiday cloak too coarse to clean them.
'Twas I that, when I heard thee swear if ever
Thou couldst arrive at forty pounds thou wouldst
Live like an emperor, 'twas I that gave it
In ready gold. Deny this, wretch!

    TAP.   I must, sir;
For, from the tavern to the taphouse, all,
On forfeiture of their licenses, stand bound
Ne'er to remember who their best guests were,
If they grew poor like you.

    WELL.   They are well rewarded
That beggar themselves to make such cuckolds rich.
Thou viper, thankless viper! impudent bawd!—
But since you are grown forgetful, I will help
Your memory, and tread you into mortar,
Nor leave one bone unbroken.   [*Beats him again.*]

    TAP.   Oh!

    FROTH.   Ask mercy.

Enter ALLWORTH

    WELL. 'Twill not be granted.

    ALL.   Hold—for my sake, hold.
Deny me, Frank? They are not worth your anger.

    WELL. For once thou hast redeem'd them from this
        sceptre;[12]
But let 'em vanish, creeping on their knees,
And, if they grumble, I revoke my pardon.

    FROTH. This comes of your prating, husband; you presum'd
On your ambling wit, and must use your glib tongue,
Though you are beaten lame for't.

[12] *I. e.,* his cudgel.

TAP.   Patience, Froth;
There's law to cure our bruises.

They go off on their hands and knees.

WELL.   Sent to your mother?
ALL. My lady, Frank, my patroness, my all!
She's such a mourner for my father's death,
And, in her love to him, so favours me,
That I cannot pay too much observance to her.
There are few such stepdames.

WELL.   'Tis a noble widow,
And keeps her reputation pure, and clear
From the least taint of infamy; her life,
With the splendour of her actions, leaves no tongue
To envy or detraction. Prithee tell me,
Has she no suitors?

ALL.   Even the best of the shire, Frank,
My lord excepted; such as sue and send,
And send and sue again, but to no purpose;
Their frequent visits have not gain'd her presence.
Yet she's so far from sullenness and pride,
That I dare undertake you shall meet from her
A liberal entertainment. I can give you
A catalogue of her suitors' names.

WELL.   Forbear it,
While I give you good counsel: I am bound to it.
Thy father was my friend, and that affection
I bore to him, in right descends to thee;
Thou art a handsome and a hopeful youth,
Nor will I have the least affront stick on thee,
If I with any danger can prevent it.

ALL. I thank your noble care; but, pray you, in what
Do I run the hazard?

WELL.   Art thou not in love?
Put it not off with wonder.

ALL.   In love, at my years!

WELL. You think you walk in clouds, but are transparent.
I have heard all, and the choice that you have made,
And, with my finger, can point out the north star
By which the loadstone of your folly's guided;
And, to confirm this true, what think you of

Fair Margaret, the only child and heir
Of Cormorant Overreach? Does it blush and start,
To hear her only nam'd? Blush at your want
Of wit and reason.

    ALL.   You are too bitter, sir.

    WELL. Wounds of this nature are not to be cur'd
With balms, but corrosives. I must be plain:
Art thou scarce manumis'd[13] from the porter's lodge[14]
And yet sworn servant to the pantofle,[15]
And dar'st thou dream of marriage? I fear
'Twill be concluded for impossible
That there is now, or e'er shall be hereafter,
A handsome page or player's boy of fourteen
But either loves a wench, or drabs love him;
Court-waiters not exempted.

    ALL.   This is madness.
Howe'er you have discover'd my intents,
You know my aims are lawful; and if ever
The queen of flowers, the glory of the spring,
The sweetest comfort to our smell, the rose,
Sprang from an envious briar, I may infer
There's such disparity in their conditions
Between the goodness of my soul, the daughter,
And the base churl her father.

    WELL.   Grant this true,
As I believe it, canst thou ever hope
To enjoy a quiet bed with her whose father
Ruin'd thy state?

    ALL.   And yours too.

    WELL.   I confess it;
True; I must tell you as a friend, and freely,
That, where impossibilities are apparent,
'Tis indiscretion to nourish hopes.
Canst thou imagine (let not self-love blind thee)
That Sir Giles Overreach, that, to make her great
In swelling titles, without touch of conscience
Will cut his neighbour's throat, and I hope his own too,
Will e'er consent to make her thine? Give o'er,
And think of some course suitable to thy rank,

---

[13] Freed.   [14] Where servants used to be punished.   [15] Slipper.

And prosper in it.

ALL.   You have well advis'd me.
But in the mean time you that are so studious
Of my affairs wholly neglect your own.
Remember yourself, and in what plight you are.

WELL. No matter, no matter.

ALL.   Yes, 'tis much material.
You know my fortune and my means; yet something
I can spare from myself to help your wants.

WELL.   How's this?

ALL. Nay, be not angry; there's eight pieces
To put you in better fashion.

WELL.   Money from thee!
From a boy! A stipendiary! One that lives
At the devotion of a stepmother
And the uncertain favour of a lord!
I'll eat my arms first. Howsoe'er blind Fortune
Hath spent the utmost of her malice on me—
Though I am vomited out of an alehouse,
And thus accoutred—know not where to eat,
Or drink, or sleep, but underneath this canopy[16]—
Although I thank thee, I despise thy offer;
And as I in my madness broke my state
Without th' assistance of another's brain,
In my right wits I'll piece it; at the worst,
Die thus and be forgotten.

ALL.   A strange humour! *Exeunt.*

SCENE II[1]

[*Enter*] ORDER, AMBLE, FURNACE, *and* WATCHALL

ORD. Set all things right, or, as my name is Order,
And by this staff of office that commands you,
This chain and double ruff, symbols of power,
Whoever misses in his function,
For one whole week makes forfeiture of his breakfast,
And privilege in the wine-cellar.

[16] *I. e.*, the sky.
[1] A room in Lady Allworth's house.

AMB.   You are merry,
Good master steward.

FURN.   Let him; I'll be angry.

AMB. Why, fellow Furnace, 'tis not twelve o'clock yet,
Nor dinner taking up; then, 'tis allow'd,
Cooks, by their places, may be choleric.

FURN. You think you have spoke wisely, goodman Amble,
My lady's go-before!

ORD.   Nay, nay, no wrangling.

FURN. Twit me with the authority of the kitchen!
At all hours, and all places, I'll be angry;
And thus provok'd, when I am at my prayers
I will be angry.

AMB.   There was no hurt meant.

FURN. I am friends with thee; and yet I will be angry.

ORD. With whom?

FURN.   No matter whom: yet, now I think on it,
I am angry with my lady.

WATCH.   Heaven forbid, man!

ORD. What cause has she given thee?   •

FURN.   Cause enough, master steward.
I was entertain'd by her to please her palate,
And, till she forswore eating, I perform'd it.
Now, since our master, noble Allworth, died,
Though I crack my brains to find out tempting sauces,
And raise fortifications in the pastry   •
Such as might serve for models in the Low Countries;
Which, if they had been practised at Breda,
Spinola might have thrown his cap at it, and ne'er took it[2]—

AMB. But you had wanted matter there to work on.

FURN. Matter! with six eggs, and a strike[3] of rye meal,
I had kept the town till doomsday, perhaps longer.

ORD. But what's this to your pet against my lady?

FURN. What's this? Marry this: when I am three parts
          roasted
And the fourth part parboil'd, to prepare her viands,
She keeps her chamber, dines with a panada[4]
Or water-gruel, my sweat never thought on.

---

[2] The siege of Breda by Spinola in 1624-5 was one of the great events of the time.   [3] Two bushels.   [4] Bread soaked in hot water and milk.

ORD. But your art is seen in the dining-room.
FURN.   By whom?
By such as pretend love to her, but come
To feed upon her. Yet, of all the harpies
That do devour her, I am out of charity
With none so much as the thin-gutted squire
That's stolen into commission.
ORD.   Justice Greedy?
FURN. The same, the same; meat's cast away upon him,
It never thrives; he holds this paradox,
Who eats not well, can ne'er do justice well.
His stomach's as insatiate as the grave,
Or strumpet's ravenous appetites.   *Knocking.*
WATCH.   One knocks.

Enter ALLWORTH

ORD. Our late young master!
AMB.   Welcome, sir.
FURN.   Your hand;
If you have a stomach, a cold bake-meat's ready.
ORD. His father's picture in little.
FURN.   We are all your servants.
AMB. In you he lives.
ALL.   At once, my thanks to all;
This is yet some comfort. Is my lady stirring?

Enter LADY ALLWORTH, *Waiting Woman, and
Chambermaid*

ORD. Her presence answers for us.
L. ALL.   Sort those silks well.
I'll take the air alone.
                Exeunt Waiting Woman and Chambermaid.
FURN.   You air and air;
But will you never taste but spoon-meat more?
To what use serve I?
L. ALL.   Prithee, be not angry;
I shall ere long: i' the mean time, there is gold
To buy thee aprons, and a summer suit.

FURN. I am appeas'd, and Furnace now grows cool.[2]

L. ALL. And, as I gave directions, if this morning
I am visited by any, entertain 'em
As heretofore; but say, in my excuse,
I am indispos'd.

ORD. I shall, madam.

L. ALL. Do, and leave them.
Nay, stay you, Allworth.

Exeunt ORDER, AMBLE, FURNACE, *and* WATCHALL.

ALL. I shall gladly grow here,
To wait on your commands.

L. ALL. So soon turn'd courtier!

ALL. Style not that courtship, madam, which is duty
Purchas'd on your part.

L. ALL. Well, you shall o'ercome;
I'll not contend in words. How is it with
Your noble master?

ALL. Ever like himself,
No scruple lessen'd in the full weight of honour.
He did command me, pardon my presumption,
As his unworthy deputy, to kiss
Your ladyship's fair hands.

L. ALL. I am honour'd in
His favour to me. Does he hold his purpose
For the Low Countries?

ALL. Constantly, good madam;
But he will in person first present his service.

L. ALL. And how approve you of his course? You are
yet
Like virgin parchment, capable of any
Inscription, vicious or honourable.
I will not force your will, but leave you free
To your own election.

ALL. Any form you please,
I will put on; but, might I make my choice,
With humble emulation I would follow
The path my lord marks to me.

L. ALL. 'Tis well answer'd,
And I commend your spirit. You had a father,

Blest be his memory! that some few hours
Before the will of Heaven took him from me,
Who did commend you, by the dearest ties
Of perfect love between us, to my charge;
And, therefore, what I speak, you are bound to hear
With such respect as if he liv'd in me.
He was my husband, and howe'er you are not
Son of my womb, you may be of my love,
Provided you deserve it.

ALL.   I have found you,
Most honour'd madam, the best mother to me;
And, with my utmost strengths of care and service,
Will labour that you never may repent
Your bounties shower'd upon me.

L. ALL.   I much hope it.
These were your father's words: "If e'er my son
Follow the war, tell him it is a school
Where all the principles tending to honour
Are taught, if truly followed: but for such
As repair thither as a place in which
They do presume they may with license practise
Their lusts and riots, they shall never merit
The noble name of soldiers. To dare boldly,
In a fair cause, and for their country's safety,
To run upon the cannon's mouth undaunted;
To obey their leaders, and shun mutinies;
To bear with patience the winter's cold
And summer's scorching heat, and not to faint,
When plenty of provision fails, with hunger;
Are the essential parts make up a soldier,
Not swearing, dice, or drinking."

ALL.   There's no syllable
You speak, but is to me an oracle,
Which but to doubt were impious.

L. ALL.   To conclude:
Beware ill company, for often men
Are like to those with whom they do converse;
And, from one man I warn* you, and that's Wellborn:
Not 'cause he's poor, that rather claims your pity;

* Q. *warn'a.*

But that he's in his manners so debauch'd,
And hath to vicious courses sold himself.
'Tis true, your father lov'd him, while he was
Worthy the loving; but if he had liv'd
To have seen him as he is, he had cast him off,
As you must do.

ALL.   I shall obey in all things.

L. ALL. Follow me to my chamber, you shall have gold
To furnish you like my son, and still supplied,
As I hear from you.

ALL.   I am still your creature.   *Exeunt.*

SCENE III[1]

[Enter] OVERREACH, GREEDY, ORDER, AMBLE, FURNACE
WATCHALL, *and* MARRALL

GREEDY. Not to be seen!

OVER.   Still cloistered up! Her reason,
I hope, assures her, though she make herself
Close prisoner ever for her husband's loss,
'Twill not recover him.

ORD.   Sir, it is her will,
Which we, that are her servants, ought to serve,
And not dispute. Howe'er, you are nobly welcome;
And, if you please to stay, that you may think so,
There came, not six days since, from Hull, a pipe
Of rich Canary, which shall spend itself
For my lady's honour.

GREEDY.   Is it of the right race?

ORD. Yes, Master Greedy.

AMB.   How his mouth runs o'er!

FURN. I'll make it run, and run. Save your good worship!

GREEDY. Honest Master Cook, thy hand; again, how I love
        thee!
Are the good dishes still in being? Speak, boy.

FURN. If you have a mind to feed, there is a chine[2]
Of beef, well seasoned.

------

[1] A hall in the same.
[2] Part of the back: ribs or sirloin.

GREEDY.   Good!

FURN.   A pheasant, larded.

GREEDY. That I might now give thanks for't!

FURN.   Other kickshaws.
Besides, there came last night, from the forest of Sher-
      wood,
The fattest stag I ever cook'd.

GREEDY.   A stag, man!

FURN. A stag, sir; part of it prepar'd for dinner,
And bak'd in puff-paste.

GREEDY.   Puff-paste too! Sir Giles,
A ponderous chine of beef! a pheasant larded!
And red deer too, Sir Giles, and bak'd in puff-paste!
All business set aside, let us give thanks here.

FURN. How the lean skeleton's rapt!

OVER.   You know we cannot.

MAR. Your worships are to sit on a commission,
And if you fail to come, you lose the cause.

GREEDY. Cause me no causes. I'll prove't, for such dinner,
We may put off a commission: you shall find it
Henrici decimo quarto.

OVER.   Fie, Master Greedy!
Will you lose me a thousand pounds for a dinner?
No more, for shame! We must forget the belly
When we think of profit.

GREEDY.   Well, you shall o'er-rule me;
I could ev'n cry now.—Do you hear, Master Cook,
Send but a corner of that immortal pasty,
And I, in thankfulness, will, by your boy,
Send you—a brace of three-pences.

FURN.   Will you be so prodigal?

Enter WELLBORN

OVER. Remember me to your lady. Who have we here?

WELL. You know me.

OVER.   I did once, but now I will not;
Thou art no blood of mine. Avaunt, thou beggar!
If ever thou presume to own me more,
I'll have thee cag'd and whipp'd.

GREEDY.   I'll grant the warrant.
Think of pie-corner, Furnace!
                    [*Exeunt* OVERREACH, GREEDY, *and* MARRALL.
WATCH.   Will you out, sir?
I wonder how you durst creep in.
ORD.   This is rudeness,
And saucy impudence.
AMB.   Cannot you stay
To be serv'd, among your fellows, from the basket,*
But you must needs press into the hall?
FURN.   Prithee, vanish
Into some outhouse, though it be the pigstye;
My scullion shall come to thee.

Enter ALLWORTH

WELL.   This is rare:
Oh, here's Tom Allworth.   Tom!
ALL.   We must be strangers;
Nor would I have you seen here for a million.   *Exit*
WELL. Better and better.   He contemns me too!

Enter Waiting Woman and Chambermaid

WOMAN. Foh, what a smell's here!   What thing's this?
CHAM.   A creature
Made out of the privy; let us hence, for love's sake,
Or I shall swoon.
WOMAN.   I begin to feel faint already.
                    [*Exeunt Waiting Woman and Chambermaid.*
WATCH. Will you know your way;
AMB.   Or shall we teach it you,
By the head and shoulders?
WELL.   No; I will not stir;
Do you mark, I will not: let me see the wretch
That dares attempt to force me.   Why, you slaves,
Created only to make legs,* and cringe;
To carry in a dish, and shift a trencher;
That have not souls only to hope a blessing

-----

* The basket of broken meats given in alms.   * Bow.

Beyond black-jacks⁵ or flagons; you, that were born
Only to consume meat and drink, and batten⁶
Upon reversions!—who advances? Who
Shews me the way?
    ORD.   My lady!

Enter LADY ALLWORTH, *Waiting Woman, and Chambermaia*
    CHAM.   Here's the monster.
    WOMAN. Sweet madam, keep your glove to your nose.
    CHAM.   Or let me
Fetch some perfumes may be predominant;
You wrong yourself else.
    WELL.   Madam, my designs
Bear me to you.
    L. ALL.   To me!
    WELL.   And though I have met with
But ragged entertainment from your grooms here,
I hope from you to receive that noble usage
As may become the true friend of your husband,
And then I shall forget these.
    L. ALL.   I am amaz'd
To see and hear this rudeness. Dar'st thou think,
Though sworn, that it can ever find belief,
That I, who to the best men of this country
Deni'd my presence since my husband's death,
Can fall so low as to change words with thee?
Thou son of infamy, forbear my house,
And know and keep the distance that's between us;
Or, though it be against my gentler temper,
I shall take order you no more shall be
An eyesore to me.
    WELL.   Scorn me not, good lady;
But, as in form you are angelical,
Imitate the heavenly natures, and vouchsafe
At the least awhile to hear me. You will grant
The blood that runs in this arm is as noble
As that which fills your veins; those costly jewels,
And those rich clothes you wear, your men's observance,

        ⁵ A leathern beer can.   ⁶ Feed.

And women's flattery, are in you no virtues,
Nor these rags, with my poverty, in me vices.
You have a fair fame, and, I know, deserve it;
Yet, lady, I must say, in nothing more
Than in the pious sorrow you have shewn
For your late noble husband.

 ORD.   How she starts!

 FURN. And hardly can keep finger from the eye,
To hear him nam'd.

 L. ALL.   Have you aught else to say?

 WELL. That husband, madam, was once in his fortune
Almost as low as I; want, debts, and quarrels
Lay heavy on him: let it not be thought
A boast in me, though I say, I reliev'd him.
'Twas I that gave him fashion; mine the sword,
That did on all occasions second his;
I brought him on and off with honour, lady;
And when in all men's judgments he was sunk,
And, in his own hopes, not to be buoy'd[7] up,
I stepp'd unto him, took him by the hand,
And set him upright.

 FURN.   Are not we base rogues,
That could forget this?

 WELL.   I confess, you made him
Master of your estate; nor could your friends,
Though he brought no wealth with him, blame you for it;
For he had a shape, and to that shape a mind
Made up of all parts, either great or noble;
So winning a behaviour, not to be
Resisted, madam.

 L. ALL.   'Tis most true, he had.

 WELL. For his sake, then, in that I was his friend,
Do not contemn me.

 L. ALL.   For what's past excuse me,
I will redeem it. Order, give the gentleman
A hundred pounds.

 WELL.   No, madam, on no terms:
I will nor beg nor borrow sixpence of you,
But be suppli'd elsewhere, or want thus ever.

      [7] Q. *bung'd.*

Only one suit I make, which you deny not
To strangers; and 'tis this.   *Whispers to her.*

    L. ALL.   Fie! nothing else?

    WELL. Nothing, unless you please to charge your servants
To throw away a little respect upon me.

    L. ALL. What you demand is yours.

    WELL.   I thank you, lady.
Now what can be wrought out of such a suit
Is yet in supposition: I have said all;
When you please, you may retire.—   [*Exit* LADY ALL.]
Nay, all's forgotten; [*To the Servants.*]
And, for a lucky omen to my project,
Shake hands, and end all quarrels in the cellar.

    ORD. Agreed, agreed.

    FURN.   Still merry Master Wellborn.   *Exeunt.*

ACT II

SCENE I[1]

Enter OVERREACH *and* MARRALL

    OVER. He's gone, I warrant thee; this commission crush'd
      him.

    MAR. Your worships have the way on't, and ne'er miss
To squeeze these unthrifts into air; and yet,
The chapfallen[2] justice did his part, returning
For your advantage the certificate,
Against his conscience, and his knowledge too,
With your good favour, to the utter ruin
Of the poor farmer.

    OVER.   'Twas for these good ends
I made him a justice; he that bribes his belly,
Is certain to command his soul.

    MAR.   I wonder,
Still with your license, why, your worship having
The power to put this thin-gut in commission,
You are not in't yourself?

    OVER.   Thou art a fool;

---

[1] A room in Overreach's house.   [2] Hollow-cheeked.

In being out of office I am out of danger;
Where, if I were a justice, besides the trouble,
I might or out of wilfulness or error
Run myself finely into a *premunire*,[*]
And so become a prey to the informer.
No, I'll have none of't; 'tis enough I keep
Greedy at my devotion; so he serve
My purposes, let him hang or damn, I care not;
Friendship is but a word.

MAR.   You are all wisdom.

OVER. I would be worldly wise; for the other wisdom,
That does prescribe us a well govern'd life,
And to do right to others as ourselves,
I value not an atom.

MAR.   What course take you,
With your good patience, to hedge in the manor
Of your neighbour, Master Frugal? as 'tis said
He will nor sell, nor borrow, nor exchange;
And his land, lying in the midst of your many lordships,
Is a foul blemish.

OVER.   I have thought on't, Marrall,
And it shall take. I must have all men sellers,
And I the only purchaser.

MAR.   'Tis most fit, sir.

OVER. I'll therefore buy some cottage near his manor,
Which done, I'll make my men break ope his fences,
Ride o'er his standing corn, and in the night
Set fire on his barns, or break his cattle's legs.
These trespasses draw on suits, and suits' expenses,
Which I can spare, but will soon beggar him.
When I have harried him thus two or three year,
Though he sue *in forma pauperis*, in spite
Of all his thrift and care, he'll grow behindhand.

MAR. The best I ever heard! I could adore you.

OVER. Then, with the favour of my man of law,
I will pretend some title. Want will force him
To put it to arbitrement; then, if he sell
For half the value, he shall have ready money,

---

[*] A writ issued for the offense of acknowledging foreign authority within the realm, or some offense with the same penalties.

And I possess his land.

MAR.   'Tis above wonder!
Wellborn was apt to sell, and needed not
These fine arts, sir, to hook him in.

OVER.   Well thought on.
This varlet, Marrall, lives too long, to upbraid me
With my close cheat put upon him. Will nor cold
Nor hunger kill him?

MAR.   I know not what to think on't.
I have us'd all means; and the last night I caus'd
His host, the tapster, to turn him out of doors;
And have been since with all you friends and tenants,
And, on the forfeit of your favour, charg'd them,
Though a crust of mouldy bread would keep him from
        starving,
Yet they should not relieve him. This is done, sir.

OVER. That was something, Marrall; but thou must go
        further,
And suddenly, Marrall.

MAR.   Where, and when you please, sir.

OVER. I would have thee seek him out, and, if thou canst,
Persuade him that 'tis better steal than beg;
Then, if I prove he has but robb'd a henroost,
Not all the world shall save him from the gallows.
Do any thing to work him to despair;
And 'tis thy masterpiece.

MAR.   I will do my best, sir.

OVER. I am now on my main work with the Lord Lovell,
The gallant-minded, popular Lord Lovell,
The minion of the people's love. I hear
He's come into the country, and my aims are
To insinuate myself into his knowledge,
And then invite him to my house.

MAR.   I have you;
This points at my young mistress.

OVER.   She must part with
That humble title, and write honourable,
Right honourable, Marrall, my right honourable daughter,
If all I have, or e'er shall get, will do it.
I'll have her well attended; there are ladies

Of errant knights decay'd and brought so low,
That for cast clothes and meat will gladly serve her.
And 'tis my glory, though I come from the city,
To have their issue whom I have undone,
To kneel to mine as bondslaves.

MAR.   'Tis fit state, sir.

OVER. And therefore, I'll not have a chambermaid
That ties her shoes, or any meaner office,
But such whose fathers were right worshipful.
'Tis a rich man's pride! there having ever been
More than a feud, a strange antipathy,
Between us and true gentry.

Enter WELLBORN

MAR.   See, who's here, sir.

OVER. Hence, monster! prodigy!

WELL.   Sir, your wife's nephew.

OVER. Avoid my sight! thy breath's infectious, rogue!
I shun thee as a leprosy, or the plague.
Come hither, Marrall [*Aside.*]—this is the time to work him.
                                                   Exit.

MAR. I warrant you, sir.

WELL.   By this light I think he's mad.

MAR. Mad! had you ta'en compassion on yourself,
You long since had been mad.

WELL.   You have ta'en a course,
Between you and my venerable uncle,
To make me so.

MAR.   The more pale-spirited you.
That would not be instructed. I swear deeply——

WELL. By what?

MAR.   By my religion.

WELL.   Thy religion!
The devil's creed:—but what would you have done?

MAR. Had there been but one tree in all the shire,
Nor any hope to compass a penny halter,
Before, like you, I had outliv'd my fortunes,
A withe had serv'd my turn to hang myself.
I am zealous in your cause; pray you hang yourself,

And presently,[4] as you love your credit.

WELL.   I thank you.

MAR. Will you stay till you die in a ditch, or lice devour
    you?——

Or, if you dare not do the feat yourself,
But that you'll put the state to charge and trouble,
Is there no purse to be cut, house to be broken,
Or market-woman with eggs, that you may murder,
And so dispatch the business?

WELL.   Here's variety,
I must confess; but I'll accept of none
Of all your gentle offers, I assure you.

MAR. Why, have you hope ever to eat again,
Or drink? or be the master of three farthings?
If you like not hanging, drown yourself! Take some course
For your reputation.

WELL.   'Twill not do, dear tempter,
With all the rhetoric the fiend hath taught you.
I am as far as thou art from despair;
Nay, I have confidence, which is more than hope,
To live, and suddenly, better than ever.

MAR. Ha! ha! these castles you build in the air
Will not persuade me to give or lend
A token to you.

WELL.   I'll be more kind to thee:
Come, thou shalt dine with me.

MAR.   With you!

WELL.   Nay more, dine gratis.

MAR. Under what hedge, I pray you? or at whose cost?
Are they padders[5] or abram-men[6] that are your consorts?

WELL. Thou art incredulous; but thou shalt dine
Not alone at her house, but with a gallant lady;
With me, and with a lady.

MAR.   Lady! what lady?
With the Lady of the Lake, or queen of fairies?
For I know it must be an enchanted dinner.

WELL. With the Lady Allworth, knave.

MAR.   Nay, now there's hope
Thy brain is crack'd.

---

[4] At once.   [5] Footpads.   [6] Beggars pretending lunacy.

WELL.   Mark there, with what respect
I am entertain'd.
MAR.   With choice, no doubt, of dog-whips.
Why, dost thou ever hope to pass her porter?
WELL. 'Tis not far off, go with me; trust thine own eyes.
MAR. Troth, in my hope, or my assurance rather,
To see thee curvet[7] and mount like a dog in a blanket,
If ever thou presume to cross her threshold,
I will endure thy company.
WELL.   Come along then.   *Exeunt.*

SCENE II[1]

[*Enter*] ALLWORTH, *Waiting Woman, Chambermaid,* ORDER,
AMBLE, FURNACE, *and* WATCHALL

WOMAN. Could you not command your leisure one hour
    longer?
CHAM. Or half an hour?
ALL.   I have told you what my haste is:
Besides, being now another's, not mine own,
Howe'er I much desire to enjoy you longer,
My duty suffers, if, to please myself,
I should neglect my lord.
WOMAN.   Pray you do me the favour
To put these few quince-cakes into your pocket;
They are of mine own preserving.
CHAM.   And this marmalade;
Tis comfortable for your stomach.
WOMAN.   And, at parting,
Excuse me if I beg a farewell from you.
CHAM. You are still before me. I move the same suit, sir.
                [ALLWORTH] *kisses them severally.*
FURN. How greedy these chamberers are of a beardless
    chin!
I think the tits[2] will ravish him.
ALL.   My service
To both.

_____
[7] Bound. The reference is to the game of tossing in a blanket.
[1] A room in Lady Allworth's house.   [2] Wenches.

WOMAN.   Ours waits on you.

CHAM.   And shall do ever.

ORD. You are my lady's charge, be therefore careful
That you sustain your parts.

WOMAN.   We can bear, I warrant you.

Exeunt Waiting Woman and Chambermaid.

FURN. Here, drink it off; the ingredients are cordial,
And this the true elixir; it hath boil'd
Since midnight for you. 'Tis the quintessence
Of five cocks of the game, ten dozen of sparrows,
Knuckles of veal, potatoe-roots and marrow,
Coral and ambergris. Were you two years older,
And I had a wife, or gamesome mistress,
I durst trust you with neither. You need not bait
After this, I warrant you, though your journey's long;
You may ride on the strength of this till to-morrow morning.

ALL. Your courtesies overwhelm me: I much grieve
To part from such true friends; and yet find comfort,
My attendance on my honourable lord,
Whose resolution holds to visit my lady,
Will speedily bring me back.   *Knocking at the gate.*

MAR.   (*within.*) Dar'st thou venture further?

WELL. (*within.*) Yes, yes, and knock again.

ORD.   'Tis he; disperse!

AMB. Perform it bravely.

FURN.   I know my cue, ne'er doubt me.

Exeunt [all but ALLWORTH.]

[*Enter WATCHALL, ceremoniously introducing WELLBORN
and MARRALL*]

WATCH. Beast that I was, to make you stay! Most
    welcome;
You were long since expected.

WELL.   Say so much
To my friend, I pray you.

WATCH.   For your sake, I will, sir.

MAR. For his sake!

WELL.   Mum; this is nothing.

MAR.   More than ever

I would have believ'd, though I had found it in my primer.
ALL. When I have given you reasons for my late harshness,
You'll pardon and excuse me; for, believe me,
Though now I part abruptly, in my service
I will deserve it.
MAR.   Service! with a vengeance!
WELL. I am satisfied: farewell, Tom.
ALL.   All joy stay with you! *Exit.*

Re-enter AMBLE

AMB. You are happily encounter'd; I yet never
Presented one so welcome as I know
You will be to my lady.
MAR.   This is some vision,
Or, sure, these men are mad, to worship a dunghill;
It cannot be a truth.
WELL.   Be still a pagan,
An unbelieving infidel; be so, miscreant,
And meditate on " blankets, and on dog-whips!"

Re-enter FURNACE

FURN. I am glad you are come; until I know your pleasure
I knew not how to serve up my lady's dinner.
MAR. His pleasure! is it possible?
WELL.   What's thy will?
FURN. Marry, sir, I have some grouse, and turkey chicken,
Some rails* and quails, and my lady will'd me ask you,
What kind of sauces best affect your palate,
That I may use my utmost skill to please it.
MAR. [*Aside.*] The devil's enter'd this cook. Sauce for
    his palate!
That, on my knowledge, for almost this twelvemonth,
Durst wish but cheese-parings and brown bread on Sundays.
WELL. That way I like 'em best.
FURN.   It shall be done, sir. *Exit.*
WELL. What think you of "the hedge we shall dine
    under?"

* Marsh birds.

Shall we feed gratis?

MAR.   I know not what to think;
Pray you make me not mad.

Re-enter ORDER

ORD.   This place becomes you not;
Pray you walk, sir, to the dining room.

WELL.   I am well here,
Till her ladyship quits her chamber.

MAR.   Well here, say you?
'Tis a rare change! But yesterday you thought
Yourself well in a barn, wrapp'd up in peas-straw.

Re-enter Waiting Woman and Chambermaid

WOMAN. O! sir, you are wish'd for.

CHAM.   My lady dreamt, sir, of you.

WOMAN. And the first command she gave, after she rose,
Was (her devotions done) to give her notice
When you approach'd here.

CHAM.   Which is done, on my virtue.

MAR. I shall be converted; I begin to grow
Into a new belief, which saints nor angels
Could have won me to have faith in.

WOMAN.   Sir, my lady!

Enter LADY ALLWORTH

L. ALL. I come to meet you, and languish'd till I saw you.
This first kiss is for form; I allow a second
To such a friend.   [*Kisses* WELLBORN.]

MAR.   To such a friend! Heaven bless me!

WELL. I am wholly yours; yet, madam, if you please
To grace this gentleman with a salute——

MAR. Salute me at his bidding!

WELL.   I shall receive it
As a most high favour.

L. ALL.   Sir, you may command me.
         [*Advances to kiss* MARRALL, *who retires.*]

WELL. Run backward from a lady! and such a lady!

MAR. To kiss her foot is, to poor me, a favour
I am unworthy of.   *Offers to kiss her foot.*

L. ALL.   Nay, pray you rise;
And since you are so humble, I'll exalt you.
You shall dine with me to-day, at mine own table.

MAR. Your ladyship's table! I am not good enough
To sit at your steward's board.

L. ALL.   You are too modest;
I will not be deni'd.

Re-enter FURNACE

FURN.   Will you still be babbling
Till your meat freeze on the table? The old trick still;
My art ne'er thought on!

L. ALL.   Your arm, Master Wellborn:——
Nay, keep us company.   [*To* MARRALL.]

MAR.   I was ne'er so graced.

> *Exeunt* WELLBORN, LADY ALLWORTH, AMBLE,
> MARRALL, *Waiting Woman,* [*and Cham-
> bermaid.*]

ORD. So! we have play'd our parts, and are come off well;
But if I know the mystery, why my lady
Consented to it, or why Master Wellborn
Desir'd it, may I perish!

FURN.   Would I had
The roasting of his heart that cheated him,
And forces the poor gentleman to these shifts!
By fire! for cooks are Persians, and swear by it,
Of all the griping and extorting tyrants
I ever heard or read of, I ne'er met
A match to Sir Giles Overreach.

WATCH.   What will you take
To tell him so, fellow Furnace?

FURN.   Just as much
As my throat is worth, for that would be the price on't.
To have a usurer that starves himself,
And wears a cloak of one and twenty years
On a suit of fourteen groats, bought of the hangman,

To grow rich, and then purchase, is too common;
But this Sir Giles feeds high, keeps many servants,
Who must at his command do any outrage;
Rich in his habit, vast in his expenses;
Yet he to admiration[4] still increases
In wealth and lordships.

 ORD.   He frights men out of their estates,
And breaks through all law-nets, made to curb ill men,
As they were cobwebs. No man dares reprove him.
Such a spirit to dare and power to do were never
Lodg'd so unluckily.

     Re-enter AMBLE [*laughing*]

 AMB.   Ha! ha! I shall burst.
 ORD. Contain thyself, man.
 FURN.   Or make us partakers
Of your sudden mirth.
 AMB.   Ha! ha! my lady has got
Such a guest at her table!—this term-driver, Marrall,
This snip of an attorney——
 FURN.   What of him, man?
 AMB. The knave thinks still he's at the cook's shop in
  Ram Alley,[5]
Where the clerks divide, and the elder is to choose;
And feeds so slovenly!
 FURN.   Is this all?
 AMB.   My lady
Drank to him for fashion sake, or to please Master Well-
  born;
As I live, he rises, and takes up a dish
In which there were some remnants of a boil'd capon,
And pledges her in white broth!
 FURN.   Nay, 'tis like
The rest of his tribe.
 AMB.   And when I brought him wine,
He leaves his stool, and, after a leg or two,
Most humbly thanks my worship.

  [4] Marvellously. [5] Off Fleet Street, famous for its restaurants.

ORD.   Risen already!
AMB. I shall be chid.

Re-enter LADY ALLWORTH, WELLBORN, *and* MARRALL

FURN.   My lady frowns.
L. ALL.   You wait well! [*To* AMBLE.]
Let me have no more of this; I observ'd your jeering:
Sirrah, I'll have you know, whom I think worthy
To sit at my table, be he ne'er so mean,
When I am present, is not your companion.
ORD. Nay, she'll preserve what's due to her.
FURN.   This refreshing
Follows your flux of laughter.
L. ALL.   [*To* WELLBORN.] You are master
Of your own will. I know so much of manners,
As not to inquire your purposes; in a word,
To me you are ever welcome, as to a house
That is your own.
WELL. [*Aside to* MARRALL.] Mark that.
MAR.   With reverence, sir,
An it like your worship.
WELL.   Trouble yourself no further,
Dear madam; my heart's full of zeal and service,
However in my language I am sparing.
Come, Master Marrall.
MAR.   I attend your worship.
                    Exeunt WELLBORN *and* MARRALL.
  L. ALL. I see in your looks you are sorry, and you know
    me
An easy mistress. Be merry; I have forgot all.
Order and Furnace, come with me; I must give you
Further directions.
ORD.   What you please.
FURN.   We are ready. *Exeunt.*

Scene III[1]

[*Enter*] WELLBORN, *and* MARRALL [*bare-headed*]

WELL. I think I am in a good way.

MAR.   Good! sir; the best way,
The certain best way.

WELL.   There are casualties
That men are subject to.

MAR.   You are above 'em;
And as you are already worshipful,
I hope ere long you will increase in worship,
And be right worshipful.

WELL.   Prithee do not flout me:
What I shall be, I shall be. Is't for your ease,
You keep your hat off?

MAR.   Ease! an it like your worship!
I hope Jack Marrall shall not live so long,
To prove himself such an unmannerly beast,
Though it hail hazel-nuts, as to be cover'd
When your worship's present.

WELL.   (*Aside.*) Is not this a true rogue,
That, out of mere hope of a future coz'nage,[2]
Can turn thus suddenly? 'Tis rank already.

MAR. I know your worship's wise, and needs no counsel,
Yet if, in my desire to do you service,
I humbly offer my advice, (but still
Under correction,) I hope I shall not
Incur your high displeasure.

WELL.   No; speak freely.

MAR. Then, in my judgment, sir, my simple judgment,
(Still with your worship's favour,) I could wish you
A better habit, for this cannot be
But much distasteful to the noble lady
(I say no more) that loves you; for, this morning,
To me, and I am but a swine to her,
Before the assurance of her wealth perfum'd you,
You savour'd not of amber.[3]

---

[1] The country near Lady Allworth's house.   [2] Cheating.
[3] Ambergris, a fashionable perfume.

WELL.   I do now then!

MAR. This your batoon hath got a touch of it.——

Kisses the end of his cudgel

Yet, if you please, for change, I have twenty pounds here,
Which, out of my true love, I'll presently
Lay down at your worship's feet; 'twill serve to buy you
A riding suit.

WELL.   But where's the horse?

MAR.   My gelding
Is at your service; nay, you shall ride me,
Before your worship shall be put to the trouble
To walk afoot. Alas, when you are lord
Of this lady's manor, as I know you will be,
You may with the lease of glebe land, called Knave's-acre,
A place I would manure,[4] requite your vassal.

WELL. I thank thy love, but must make no use of it;
What's twenty pounds?

MAR.   'Tis all that I can make, sir.

WELL. Dost thou think, though I want clothes, I could
        not have them,
For one word to my lady?

MAR.   As I know not that!

WELL. Come, I will tell thee a secret, and so leave thee.
I will not give her the advantage, though she be
A gallant-minded lady, after we are married,
(There being no woman but is sometimes froward,)
To hit me in the teeth, and say, she was forc'd
To buy my wedding-clothes, and took me on
With a plain riding-suit, and an ambling nag.
No, I'll be furnish'd something like myself,
And so farewell: for thy suit touching Knave's-acre.
When it is mine, 'tis thine.

MAR.   I thank your worship. *Exit* WELL.
How was I cozen'd[5] in the calculation
Of this man's fortune! My master cozen'd too,
Whose pupil I am in the art of undoing men;
For that is our profession! Well, well, Master Wellborn,
You are of a sweet nature, and fit again to be cheated:
Which, if the Fates please, when you are possess'd

4 Cultivate.   5 Cheated.

Of the land and lady, you, sans question, shall be.
I'll presently think of the means.   *Walks by, musing.*

Enter Overreach, [*speaking to a Servant within*]

Over.   Sirrah, take my horse.
I'll walk to get me an appetite; 'tis but a mile,
And exercise will keep me from being pursy.°
Ha! Marrall! Is he conjuring? Perhaps
The knave has wrought the prodigal to do
Some outrage on himself, and now he feels
Compunction in his conscience for't: no matter,
So it be done. Marrall!
  Mar.   Sir.
  Over.   How succeed we
In our plot on Wellborn?
  Mar.   Never better, sir.
  Over. Has he hang'd or drown'd himself?
  Mar.   No, sir, he lives;
Lives once more to be made a prey to you,
A greater prey than ever.
  Over.   Art thou in thy wits?
If thou art, reveal this miracle, and briefly.
  Mar. A lady, sir, is fall'n in love with him.
  Over. With him? What lady?
  Mar.   The rich Lady Allworth.
  Over. Thou dolt! how dar'st thou speak this?
  Mar.   I speak truth.
And I do so but once a year, unless
It be to you, sir. We din'd with her ladyship,
I thank his worship.
  Over.   His worship!
  Mar.   As I live, sir,
I din'd with him, at the great lady's table,
Simple as I stand here; and saw when she kiss'd him,
And would, at his request, have kiss'd me too:
But I was not so audacious as some youths are,
That dare do anything, be it ne'er so absurd,
And sad after performance.

      ° Fat and short-winded.

Over.   Why, thou rascal!
To tell me these impossibilities.
Dine at her table! and kiss him! or thee!——
Impudent varlet, have not I myself,
To whom great countesses' doors have oft flew open,
Ten times attempted, since her husband's death,
In vain, to see her, though I came—a suitor?
And yet your good solicitorship, and rogue Wellborn,
Were brought into her presence, feasted with her!——
But that I know thee a dog that cannot blush,
This most incredible lie would call up one
On thy buttermilk cheeks.
      Mar.   Shall I not trust my eyes, sir,
Or taste? I feel her good cheer in my belly.
      Over. You shall feel me, if you give not over, sirrah:
Recover your brains again, and be no more gull'd
With a beggar's plot, assisted by the aids
Of serving-men and chambermaids, for beyond these
Thou never saw'st a woman, or I'll quit you
From my employments.
      Mar.   Will you credit this yet?
On my confidence of their marriage, I offer'd Wellborn——
(*Aside.*) I would give a crown now I durst say "his wor-
            ship"——
My nag and twenty pounds.
      Over.   Did you so, idiot! *Strikes him down.*
Was this the way to work him to despair,
Or rather to cross me?
      Mar.   Will your worship kill me?
      Over. No, no; but drive the lying spirit out of you.
      Mar. He's gone.
      Over.   I have done then: now, forgetting
Your late imaginary feast and lady,
Know, my Lord Lovell dines with me to-morrow.
Be careful nought be wanting to receive him;
And bid my daughter's women trim her up,
Though they paint her, so she catch the lord, I'll thank them
There's a piece for my late blows.
      Mar.   (*Aside.*) I must yet suffer:
But there may be a time——

OVER. Do you grumble?

MAR. No, sir. [*Exeunt.*]

ACT III

SCENE I[1]

[*Enter*] LORD LOVELL, ALLWORTH, *and Servants*

LOV. Walk the horses down the hill: something in private
I must impart to Allworth. *Exeunt Servants.*

ALL. O, my lord,
What a sacrifice of reverence, duty, watching,
Although I could put off the use of sleep,
And ever wait on your commands to serve them;
What dangers, though in ne'er so horrid shapes,
Nay death itself, though I should run to meet it,
Can I, and with a thankful willingness suffer!
But still the retribution will fall short
Of your bounties shower'd upon me.

LOV. Loving youth,
Till what I purpose be put into act,
Do not o'erprize it; since you have trusted me
With your soul's nearest, nay, her dearest secret,
Rest confident 'tis in a cabinet lock'd
Treachery shall never open. I have found you
(For so much to your face I must profess,
Howe'er you guard your modesty with a blush for't)
More zealous in your love and service to me
Than I have been in my rewards.

ALL. Still great ones,
Above my merit.

LOV. Such your gratitude calls 'em;
Nor am I of that harsh and rugged temper
As some great men are tax'd with, who imagine
They part from the respect due to their honours
If they use not all such as follow 'em,
Without distinction of their births, like slaves.
I am not so condition'd; I can make

---

[1] The country near Overreach's house.

A fitting difference between my footboy
And a gentleman by want compell'd to serve me.
    ALL. 'Tis thankfully acknowledg'd; you have been
More like a father to me than a master.
Pray you, pardon the comparison.
    Lov.   I allow it:
And, to give you assurance I am pleas'd in't,
My carriage and demeanour to your mistress,
Fair Margaret, shall truly witness for me
I can command my passions.
    ALL.   'Tis a conquest
Few lords can boast of when they are tempted—Oh!
    Lov. Why do you sigh? Can you be doubtful of me?
By that fair name I in the wars have purchas'd,
And all my actions, hitherto untainted,
I will not be more true to mine own honour
Than to my Allworth!
    ALL.   As you are the brave Lord Lovell,
Your bare word only given is an assurance
Of more validity and weight to me
Than all the oaths, bound up with imprecations,
Which, when they would deceive, most courtiers practise;
Yet being a man, (for, sure, to style you more
Would relish of gross flattery,) I am forc'd,
Against my confidence of your worth and virtues,
To doubt, nay more, to fear.
    Lov.   So young, and jealous!
    ALL. Were you to encounter with a single foe,
The victory were certain; but to stand
The charge of two such potent enemies,
At once assaulting you, as wealth and beauty,
And those too seconded with power, is odds
Too great for Hercules.
    Lov.   Speak your doubts and fears,
Since you will nourish them, in plainer language,
That I may understand them.
    ALL.   What's your will,
Though I lend arms against myself, (provided
They may advantage you,) must be obeyed.
My much-lov'd lord, were Margaret only fair,

The cannon of her more than earthly form,
Though mounted high, commanding all beneath it,
And ramm'd with bullets of her sparkling eyes,
Of all the bulwarks that defend your senses
Could batter none, but that which guards your sight.
But when the well-tun'd accents of her tongue
Make music to you, and with numerous[2] sounds
Assault your hearing, (such as if Ulysses,
Now liv'd again, howe'er he stood the Syrens,
Could not resist,) the combat must grow doubtful
Between your reason and rebellious passions.
Add this too; when you feel her touch, and breath
Like a soft western wind when it glides o'er
Arabia, creating gums and spices;
And, in the van, the nectar of her lips,
Which you must taste, bring the battalia on,
Well arm'd, and strongly lin'd[3] with her discourse,
And knowing manners, to give entertainment;—
Hippolytus himself would leave Diana,
To follow such a Venus.

Lov.   Love hath made you
Poetical, Allworth.

ALL.   Grant all these beat off,
Which if it be in man to do, you'll do it,
Mammon, in Sir Giles Overreach, steps in
With heaps of ill-got gold, and so much land,
To make her more remarkable, as would tire
A falcon's wings in one day to fly over.
O my good lord! these powerful aids, which would
Make a mis-shapen negro beautiful,
(Yet are but ornaments to give her lustre,
That in herself is all perfection,) must
Prevail for her. I here release your trust;
'Tis happiness enough for me to serve you
And sometimes, with chaste eyes, to look upon her.

Lov. Why, shall I swear?

ALL.   O, by no means, my lord;
And wrong not so your judgment to the world
As from your food indulgence to a boy,

[2] Rhythmical.   [3] Reinforced.

Your page, your servant, to refuse a blessing
Divers great men are rivals for.
  Lov.   Suspend
Your judgment till the trial. How far is it
To Overreach's house?
    All.   At the most, some half hour's riding;
You'll soon be there.
    Lov.   And you the sooner freed
From your jealous fears.
    All.   O that I durst but hope it ! *Exeunt.*

SCENE II[1]

    •   [*Enter*] OVERREACH, GREEDY, *and* MARRALL

  Over. Spare for no cost; let my dressers crack with the
      weight
Of curious viands.
    Greedy.   " Store indeed's no sore," sir.
  Over. That proverb fits your stomach, Master Greedy.
And let no plate be seen but what's pure gold,
Or such whose workmanship exceeds the matter
That it is made of; let my choicest linen
Perfume the room, and, when we wash, the water,
With precious powders mix'd, so please my lord,
That he may with envy wish to bathe so ever.
    Mar. 'Twill be very chargeable.
    Over.   Avaunt, you drudge!
Now all my labour'd ends are at the stake,
Is't a time to think of thrift? Call in my daughter.
                      [*Exit* MARRALL.]
And, Master Justice, since you love choice dishes,
And plenty of them——
    Greedy.   As I do, indeed, sir,
Almost as much as to give thanks for 'em.
  Over. I do confer that providence,[2] with my power
Of absolute command to have abundance,
To your best care.
    Greedy.   I'll punctually discharge it,
And give the best directions. Now am I,

       [1] A room in Overreach' house.   [2] Responsibility for providing.

In mine own conceit, a monarch; at the least,
Arch-president of the boil'd, the roast, the bak'd;
For which I will eat often, and give thanks
When my belly's brac'd up like a drum, and that's pure
    justice.   *Exit.*

OVER. It must be so. Should the foolish girl prove modest,
She may spoil all; she had it not from me,
But from her mother; I was ever forward,
As she must be, and therefore I'll prepare her.

[*Enter*] MARGARET

Alone—and let your women wait without.

MARG. Your pleasure, sir?

OVER.   Ha! this is a neat dressing!
These orient pearls and diamonds well plac'd too!
The gown affects me not, it should have been
Embroider'd o'er and o'er with flowers of gold;
But these rich jewels and quaint fashion help it.
And how below? since oft the wanton eye,
The face observ'd, descends unto the foot,
Which being well proportion'd, as yours is,
Invites as much as perfect white and red,
Though without art. How like you your new woman,
The Lady Downfall'n?

MARG.   Well, for a companion;
Not as a servant.

OVER.   Is she humble, Meg,
And careful too, her ladyship forgotten?

MARG. I pity her fortune.

OVER.   Pity her! trample on her.
I took her up in an old tamin* gown,
(Even starv'd for want of twopenny chops,) to serve thee;
And if I understand she but repines
To do thee any duty, though ne'er so servile,
I'll pack her to her knight, where I have lodg'd him,
Into the Counter,* and there let them howl together.

MARG. You know your own ways; but for me, I blush

---

        * A coarse cloth.   * One of the London prisons.

When I command her, that was once attended
With persons not inferior to myself
In birth.

OVER. In birth! why, art thou not my daughter,
The blest child of my industry and wealth?
Why, foolish girl, was't not to make thee great
That I have run, and still pursue, those ways
That hale down curses on me, which I mind not?
Part with these humble thoughts, and apt[5] thyself
To the noble state I labour to advance thee;
Or, by my hopes to see thee honourable,
I will adopt a stranger to my heir,
And throw thee from my care. Do not provoke me.

MARG. I will not, sir; mould me which way you please.

Re-enter GREEDY

OVER. How! interrupted!

GREEDY. 'Tis matter of importance.
The cook, sir, is self-will'd, and will not learn
From my experience. There's a fawn brought in, sir,
And, for my life, I cannot make him roast it
With a Norfolk dumpling in the belly of it;
And, sir, we wise men know, without the dumpling
'Tis not worth three-pence.

OVER. Would it were whole in thy belly,
To stuff it out! Cook it any way; prithee, leave me.

GREEDY. Without order for the dumpling?

OVER. Let it be dumpl'd
Which way thou wilt; or tell him, I will scald him
In his own caldron.

GREEDY. I had lost my stomach
Had I lost my mistress dumpling; I'll give thanks for't.

[*Exit.*]

OVER. But to our business, Meg; you have heard who
dines here?

MARG. I have, sir.

OVER. 'Tis an honourable man;
A lord, Meg, and commands a regiment

---

[5] Fit.

Of soldiers, and, what's rare, is one himself,
A bold and understanding one; and to be
A lord, and a good leader, in one volume,
Is granted unto few but such as rise up
The kingdom's glory.

Re-enter GREEDY

GREEDY.   I'll resign my office,
If I be not better obey'd.
   OVER.   'Slight, art thou frantic?
   GREEDY. Frantic! 'Twould make me frantic, and stark
     mad,
Were I not a justice of peace and quorum too,
Which this rebellious cook cares not a straw for.
There are a dozen of woodcocks——
   OVER.   Make thyself
Thirteen, the baker's dozen.
   GREEDY.   I am contented,
So they may be dress'd to my mind; he has found out
A new device for sauce, and will not dish 'em
With toasts and butter. My father was a tailor,
And my name, though a justice, Greedy Woodcock;
And, ere I'll see my lineage so abus'd,
I'll give up my commission.
   OVER.   [*loudly.*] Cook!—Rogue, obey him!
I have given the word, pray you now remove yourself
To a collar of brawn,[6] and trouble me no further.
   GREEDY. I will, and meditate what to eat at dinner. *Exit*
   OVER. And as I said, Meg, when this gull[7] disturb'd us,
This honourable lord, this colonel,
I would have thy husband.
   MARG.   There's too much disparity
Between his quality and mine, to hope it.
   OVER. I more than hope't, and doubt not to effect it.
Be thou no enemy to thyself, my wealth
Shall weigh his titles down, and make you equals.
Now for the means to assure him thine, observe me:
Remember he's a courtier, and a soldier,

        6 Neck of a boar.   7 Fool.

And not to be trifled with; and, therefore, when
He comes to woo you, see you do not coy it:
This mincing modesty has spoil'd many a match
By a first refusal, in vain after hop'd for.

MARG. You'll have me, sir, preserve the distance that
Confines a virgin?

OVER.   Virgin me no virgins!
I must have you lose that name, or you lose me.
I will have you private—start not—I say, private;
If thou art my true daughter, not a bastard,
Thou wilt venture alone with one man, though he came
Like Jupiter to Semele, and come off, too;
And therefore, when he kisses you, kiss close.

MARG. I have heard this is the strumpet's fashion, sir,
Which I must never learn.

OVER.   Learn any thing,
And from any creature that may make thee great;
From the devil himself.

MARG.   [Aside.] This is but devilish doctrine!

OVER. Or, if his blood grow hot, suppose he offer
Beyond this, do not you stay till it cool,
But meet his ardour; if a couch be near,
Sit down on't, and invite him.

MARG.   In your house,
Your own house, sir! For Heaven's sake, what are you
    then?
Or what shall I be, sir?

OVER.   Stand not on form;
Words are no substances.

MARG.   Though you could dispense
With your own honour, cast aside religion,
The hopes of Heaven, or fear of hell, excuse me,
In worldly policy, this is not the way
To make me his wife; his whore, I grant it may do.
My maiden honour so soon yielded up,
Nay, prostituted, cannot but assure him
I, that am light to him, will not hold weight
Whene'er⁸ tempted by others; so, in judgment,
When to his lust I have given up my honour,

⁸ So Gifford. Q. *when he is.*

He must and will forsake me.

OVER.   How! forsake thee!
Do I wear a sword for fashion? or is this arm
Shrunk up or wither'd? Does there live a man
Of that large list I have encounter'd with
Can truly say I e'er gave inch of ground
Not purchas'd with his blood that did oppose me?
Forsake thee when the thing is done! He dares not.
Give me but proof he has enjoy'd thy person,
Though all his captains, echoes to his will,
Stood arm'd by his side to justify the wrong,
And he himself in the head of his bold troop,
Spite of his lordship, and his colonelship,
Or the judge's favour, I will make him render
A bloody and a strict account, and force him,
By marrying thee, to cure thy wounded honour!
I have said it.

Re-enter MARRALL

MAR.   Sir, the man of honour's come,
Newly alighted.

OVER.   In, without reply;
And do as I command, or thou art lost.   *Exit* MARGARET.
Is the loud music I gave order for
Ready to receive him?

MAR.   'Tis, sir.

OVER.   Let them sound
A princely welcome. [*Exit* MARRALL.] Roughness awhile
        leave me;
For fawning now, a stranger to my nature,
Must make way for me.

Loud music. Enter LORD LOVELL, GREEDY, ALLWORTH,
                and MARRALL

LOV.   Sir, you meet your trouble.

OVER. What you are pleas'd to style so is an honour
Above my worth and fortunes.

ALL.   [*Aside.*] Strange, so humble.

OVER. A justice of peace, my lord.

                          Presents GREEDY *to him.*

Lov.   Your hand, good sir.
Greedy. [*Aside.*] This is a lord, and some think this a
        favour;
But I had rather have my hand in my dumpling.
    Over. Room for my lord.
    Lov.   I miss, sir, your fair daughter
To crown my welcome.
    Over.   May it please my lord
To taste a glass of Greek wine first, and suddenly
She shall attend my lord
    Lov. You'll be obey'd, sir.   *Exeunt all but* Overreach.
    Over. 'Tis to my wish: as soon as come, ask for her!
Why, Meg! Meg Overreach.—

                    [*Re-enter* Margaret]
                                How! tears in your eyes!
Hah! dry 'em quickly, or I'll dig 'em out.
Is this a time to whimper? Meet that greatness
That flies into thy bosom, think what 'tis
For me to say, " My honourable daughter;"
And thou, when I stand bare, to say, " Put on;"
Or, " Father, you forget yourself." No more:
But be instructed, or expect——he comes.

Re-enter Lord Lovell, Greedy, Allworth, *and* Marrall
A black-brow'd girl, my lord,
    Lov.   As I live, a rare one. *They salute.*
    All. [*Aside.*] He's ta'en already: I am lost.
    Over.   [*Aside.*] That kiss
Came twangling off, I like it.—Quit the room.
        [*Exeunt all but* Overreach, Lovell, *and* Margaret.
A little bashful, my good lord, but you,
I hope, will teach her boldness.
    Lov.   \   I am happy
In such a scholar: but——
    Over.   I am past learning,
And therefore leave you to yourselves.—Remember.
                        Aside to Margaret *and exit.*
    Lov. You see, fair lady, your father is solicitous,

To have you change the barren name of virgin
Into a hopeful wife.

MARG.   His haste, my lord,
Holds no power o'er my will.

Lov.   But o'er your duty.

MARG. Which forc'd too much, may break.

Lov.   Bend rather, sweetest:
Think of your years.

MARG.   Too few to match with yours:
And choicest fruits too soon pluck'd, rot and wither.

Lov. Do you think I am old?

MARG.   I am sure I am too young.

Lov. I can advance you.

MARG.   To a hill of sorrow,
Where every hour I may expect to fall,
But never hope firm footing. You are noble,
I of a low descent, however rich;
And tissues match'd with scarlet[9] suit but ill.
O, my good lord, I could say more, but that
I dare not trust these walls.

Lov.   Pray you, trust my ear then.

Re-enter OVERREACH [*behind,*] *listening*

OVER. Close at it! whispering! this is excellent!
And, by their postures, a consent on both parts.

Re-enter GREEDY *behind*

GREEDY. Sir Giles, Sir Giles!

OVER.   The great fiend stop that clapper!

GREEDY. It must ring out, sir, when my belly rings noon.
The bak'd-meats are run out, the roasts turn'd powder.

OVER. I shall powder you.

GREEDY.   Beat me to dust, I care not;
In such a cause as this, I'll die a martyr.

OVER. Marry, and shall, you barathrum[10] of the shambles!
                    Strikes him.

GREEDY. How! strike a justice of peace! 'Tis petty
    treason,

---

[9] Silks matched with woolen.   [10] Gulf: here, insatiable glutton.

Edwardi quinto: but that you are my friend,
I would commit you without bail or mainprize.[11]

OVER. Leave your bawling, sir, or I shall commit you
Where you shall not dine to-day. Disturb my lord,
When he is in discourse!

GREEDY.   Is't a time to talk
When we should be munching!

LOV.   Hah! I heard some noise.

OVER. Mum, villain; vanish! Shall we break a bargain
Almost made up?   *Thrusts* GREEDY *off.*

LOV.   Lady, I understand you,
And rest most happy in your choice, believe it;
I'll be a careful pilot to direct
Your yet uncertain bark to a port of safety.

MARG. So shall your honour save two lives, and bind us
Your slaves for ever.

LOV.   I am in the act rewarded,
Since it is good; howe'er, you must put on
An amorous carriage towards me to delude
Your subtle father.

MARG.   I am prone to that.

LOV. Now break we off our conference.—Sir Giles!
Where is Sir Giles??   [OVERREACH *comes forward.*]

Re-enter ALLWORTH, MARRALL, *and* GREEDY

OVER.   My noble lord; and how
Does your lordship find her?

LOV.   Apt, Sir Giles, and coming;
And I like her the better.

OVER.   So do I too.

LOV. Yet should we take forts at the first assault,
'Twere poor in the defendant; I must confirm her
With a love-letter or two, which I must have
Deliver'd by my page, and you give way to't.

OVER. With all my soul:—a towardly gentleman!
Your hand, good Master Allworth; know my house
Is ever open to you.

ALL.   (*Aside.*) 'Twas shut till now.

---

[11] A writ commanding the sheriff to take bail.

OVER. Well done, well done, my honourable daughter!
Thou'rt so already. Know this gentle youth,
And cherish him, my honourable daughter.

    MARG. I shall, with my best care.

                      Noise within, as of a coach.

    OVER.   A coach!

    GREEDY.   More stops
Before we go to dinner! O my guts!

        Enter LADY ALLWORTH *and* WELLBORN

    L. ALL.   If I find welcome,
You share in it; if not, I'll back again,
Now I know your ends; for I come arm'd for all
Can be objected.

    LOV.   How! the Lady Allworth!

    OVER. And thus attended!

       LOVELL *salutes* LADY ALLWORTH, LADY ALLWORTH
       salutes MARGARET.

    MAR.   No, "I am a dolt!
The spirit of lies had ent'red me!"

    OVER.   Peace, Patch;[12]
'Tis more than wonder! an astonishment
That does possess me wholly!

    LOV.   Noble lady,
This is a favour, to prevent[13] my visit,
The service of my life can never equal.

    L. ALL. My lord, I laid wait for you, and much hop'd
You would have made my poor house your first inn:
And therefore doubting that you might forget me,
Or too long dwell here, having such ample cause,
In this unequall'd beauty, for your stay,
And fearing to trust any but myself
With the relation of my service to you,
I borrow'd so much from my long restraint
And took the air in person to invite you.

    LOV. Your bounties are so great, they rob me, madam,
Of words to give you thanks.

    L. ALL.   Good Sir Giles Overreach. *Salutes him.*

---

         [12] Fool.   [13] Anticipate.

—How dost thou, Marrall? Lik'd you my meat so ill,
You'll dine no more with me?

GREEDY.   I will, when you please,
And it like[14] your ladyship.

L. ALL.   When you please, Master Greedy;
If meat can do it, you shall be satisfied.
And now, my lord, pray take into your knowledge
This gentleman; howe'er his outside's coarse. .

Presents WELLBORN.

His inward linings are as fine and fair
As any man's; wonder not I speak at large:
And howsoe'er his humour carries him
To be thus accoutred, or what taint soever,
For his wild life, hath stuck upon his fame,
He may, ere long, with boldness, rank himself
With some that have contemn'd him. Sir Giles Over-
     reach,
If I am welcome, bid him so.

OVER.   My nephew!
He has been too long a stranger. Faith you have,
Pray let it be mended.

LOVELL *confers aside with* WELLBORN.

MAR.   Why, sir, what do you mean?
This is "rogue Wellborn, monster, prodigy,
That should hang or drown himself;" no man of worship,
Much less your nephew.

OVER.   Well, sirrah, we shall reckon
For this hereafter.

MAR.   I'll not lose my jeer,
Though I be beaten dead for't.

WELL.   Let my silence plead
In my excuse, my lord, till better leisure
Offer itself to hear a full relation
Of my poor fortunes.

LOV.   I would hear, and help 'em.

OVER. Your dinner waits you.

LOV.   Pray you lead, we follow.

L. ALL. Nay, you are my guest; come, dear Master Well-
     born.   *Exeunt all but* GREEDY.

[14] If it please.

GREEDY. "Dear Master Wellborn!" so she said: Heaven!
    Heaven!
If my belly would give me leave, I could ruminate
All day on this: I have granted twenty warrants
To have him committed, from all prisons in the shire,
To Nottingham gaol; and now, "Dear Master Wellborn!"
And, "My good nephew!"—but I play the fool
To stand here prating, and forget my dinner.

Re-enter MARRALL

Are they set, Marrall?
    MAR.   Long since; pray you a word, sir.
    GREEDY. No wording now.
    MAR.   In troth, I must. My master,
Knowing you are his good friend, makes bold with you,
And does entreat you, more guests being come in
Than he expected, especially his nephew,
The table being full too, you would excuse him,
And sup with him on the cold meat.
    GREEDY.   How! no dinner,
After all my care?
    MAR.   'Tis but a penance for
A meal; besides, you broke your fast.
    GREEDY.   That was
But a bit to stay my stomach. A man in commission
Give place to a tatterdemalion!
    MAR.   No bug[15] words, sir;
Should his worship hear you——
    GREEDY.   Lose my dumpling too,
And butter'd toasts, and woodcocks!
    MAR.   Come, have patience
If you will dispense a little with your worship,
And sit with the waiting women, you'll have dumpling,
Woodcock, and butter'd toasts too.
    GREEDY.   This revives me:
I will gorge there sufficiently.
    MAR.   This is the way, sir. *Exeunt.*

[15] Terrifying.

SCENE III[1]

[Enter] OVERREACH, *as from dinner*

OVER. She's caught! O women!—she neglects my lord,
And all her compliments appli'd to Wellborn!
The garments of her widowhood laid by,
She now appears as glorious as the spring,
Her eyes fix'd on him, in the wine she drinks,
He being her pledge, she sends him burning kisses,
And sits on thorns, till she be private with him.
She leaves my meat to feed upon his looks,
And if in our discourse he be but nam'd,
From her a deep sigh follows. And why grieve I
At this? It makes for me; if she prove his,
All that is hers is mine, as I will work him.

Enter MARRALL

MAR. Sir, the whole board is troubled at your rising.
OVER. No matter, I'll excuse it. Prithee, Marrall,
Watch an occasion to invite my nephew
To speak with me in private.
MAR.   Who! "The rogue
The lady scorned to look on"?
OVER.   You are a wag.

Enter LADY ALLWORTH *and* WELLBORN

MAR. See, sir, she's come, and cannot be without him.
L. ALL. With your favour, sir, after a plenteous dinner,
I shall make bold to walk a turn or two,
In your rare garden.
OVER.   There's an arbour too,
If your ladyship please to use it.
L. ALL.   Come, Master Wellborn.
            Exeunt LADY ALLWORTH *and* WELLBORN
OVER. Grosser and grosser! Now I believe the poet
Feign'd not, but was historical, when he wrote
Pasiphaë was enamour'd of a bull:
This lady's lust's more monstrous.—My good lord,

Another room in Overreach's house.

Enter Lord Lovell, Margaret, *and the rest*

Excuse my manners.

Lov.   There needs none, Sir Giles,
I may ere long say father, when it pleases
My dearest mistress to give warrant to it.

Over. She shall seal to it, my lord, and make me happy.

Re-enter Wellborn *and* Lady Allworth

Marg. My lady is return'd.

L. All.   Provide my coach,
I'll instantly away. My thanks, Sir Giles,
For my entertainment.

Over.   'Tis your nobleness
To think it such.

L. All.   I must do you a further wrong
In taking away your honourable guest.

Lov. I wait on you, madam; farewell, good Sir Giles.

L. All. Good Mistress Margaret! Nay, come, Master
          Wellborn,
I must not leave you behind; in sooth, I must not.

Over. Rob me not, madam, of all joys at once;
Let my nephew stay behind. He shall have my coach,
And, after some small conference between us,
Soon overtake your ladyship.

L. All.   Stay not long, sir.

Lov. This parting kiss: [*Kisses* Margaret] you shall every
          day hear from me,
By my faithful page.

All.   'Tis a service I am proud of.
          Exeunt Lord Lovell, Lady Allworth, Allworth,
              and Marrall.

Over. Daughter, to your chamber.—   *Exit* Margaret
                            —You may wonder, nephew
After so long an enmity between us,
I should desire your friendship.

Well.   So I do, sir;
'Tis strange to me.

Over.   But I'll make it no wonder;

And what is more, unfold my nature to you.
We worldly men, when we see friends and kinsmen
Past hopes sunk in their fortunes, lend no hand
To lift 'em up, but rather set our feet
Upon their heads, to press 'em to the bottom;
As, I must yield,[2] with you I practis'd it:
But, now I see you in a way to rise,
I can and will assist you. This rich lady
(And I am glad of 't) is enamour'd of you;
'Tis too apparent, nephew.

WELL.   No such thing:
Compassion rather, sir.

OVER.   Well, in a word,
Because your stay is short, I'll have you seen
No more in this base shape; nor shall she say
She married you like a beggar, or in debt.

WELL. (*Aside.*) He'll run into the noose, and save my
    labour.

OVER. You have a trunk of rich clothes, not far hence,
In pawn; I will redeem 'em; and that no clamour
May taint your credit for your petty debts,
You shall have a thousand pounds to cut 'em off,
And go a free man to the wealthy lady.

WELL. This done, sir, out of love, and no ends else——

OVER. As it is, nephew.

WELL.   Binds me still your servant.

OVER. No compliments, you are staid for. Ere you have
    supp'd
You shall hear from me. My coach, knaves, for my nephew.
To-morrow I will visit you.

WELL.   Here's an uncle
In a man's extremes! How much they do belie you,
That say you are hard-hearted!

OVER.   My deeds, nephew,
Shall speak my love; what men report I weigh not. *Exeunt.*

² Admit.

ACT IV

Scene I[1]

[Enter Lord] Lovell *and* Allworth

Lov. 'Tis well; give me my cloak; I now discharge you
From further service. Mind your own affairs;
I hope they will prove successful.

All.   What is blest
With your good wish, my lord, cannot but prosper.
Let aftertimes report, and to your honour,
How much I stand engag'd, for I want language
To speak my debt; yet if a tear or two
Of joy, for your much goodness, can supply
My tongue's defects, I could——

Lov.   Nay, do not melt:
This ceremonial thanks to me's superfluous.

Over. (*within.*) Is my lord stirring?

Lov. 'Tis he! oh, here's your letter. Let him in.

Enter Overreach, Greedy, *and* Marrall

Over. A good day to my lord!

Lov.   You are an early riser,
Sir Giles.

Over. And reason, to attend your lordship.

Lov. And you, too, Master Greedy, up so soon!

Greedy. In troth, my lord, after the sun is up,
I cannot sleep, for I have a foolish stomach
That croaks for breakfast. With your lordship's favour,
I have a serious question to demand
Of my worthy friend Sir Giles.

Lov.   Pray you use your pleasure.

Greedy. How far, Sir Giles, and pray you answer me
Upon your credit, hold you it to be
From your manor-house, to this of my Lady's Allworth's?

Over. Why, some four mile.

Greedy.   How! four mile, good Sir Giles——
Upon your reputation, think better;

        [1] A room in Lady Allworth's house.

For if you do abate but one half-quarter
Of five, you do yourself the greatest wrong
That can be in the world; for four miles riding
Could not have rais'd so huge an appetite
As I feel gnawing on me.

MAR.　　　　　　　Whether you ride,
Or go afoot, you are that way still provided,
An it please your worship.

OVER.　　　　　　　How now, sirrah? Prating
Before my lord! No difference! Go to my nephew,
See all his debts discharg'd, and help his worship
To fit on his rich suit.

MAR.　　　[*Aside.*] I may fit you too.
Toss'd like a dog still!　　　　　　　　　*Exit.*

LOV.　　　　　　I have writ this morning
A few lines to my mistress, your fair daughter.

OVER. 'Twill fire her, for she's wholly yours already.—
Sweet Master Allworth, take my ring; 'twill carry you
To her presence, I dare warrant you; and there plead
For my good lord, if you shall find occasion.
That done, pray ride to Nottingham, get a licence,
Still by this token. I'll have it dispatch'd,
And suddenly, my lord, that I may say,
My honourable, nay, right honourable daughter.

GREEDY. Take my advice, young gentleman, get your break-
　　　fast;
'Tis unwholesome to ride fasting. I'll eat with you,
And eat to purpose.

OVER.　　　　Some Fury's in that gut:
Hungry again! Did you not devour, this morning,
A shield of brawn, and a barrel of Colchester oysters?

GREEDY. Why, that was, sir, only to scour my stomach,
A kind of a preparative. Come, gentleman,
I will not have you feed like the hangman of Flushing,
Alone, while I am here.

LOV.　　　　　　Haste your return.

ALL. I will not fail, my lord.

GREEDY.　　　　　　Nor I, to line
My Christmas coffer.　　　*Exeunt* GREEDY *and* ALLWORTH.

OVER.　　　　To my wish: we are private.

I come not to make offer with my daughter
A certain portion,—that were poor and trivial:
In one word, I pronounce all that is mine,
In lands or leases, ready coin or goods,
With her, my lord, comes to you; nor shall you have
One motive to induce you to believe
I live too long, since every year I'll add
Something unto the heap, which shall be yours too.

   Lov. You are a right kind father.

   Over.   You shall have reason
To think me such. How do you like this seat?
It is well wooded, and well water'd, the acres
Fertile and rich; would it not serve for change,
To entertain your friends in a summer progress?
What thinks my noble lord?

   Lov.   'Tis a wholesome air,
And well-built pile; and she that's mistress of it,
Worthy the large revénue.

   Over.   She the mistress!
It may be so for a time: but let my lord
Say only that he likes it, and would have it,
I say, ere long 'tis his.

   Lov.   Impossible.

   Over. You do conclude too fast, not knowing me,
Nor the engines[2] that I work by. 'Tis not alone
The Lady Allworth's lands, for those once Wellborn's
(As by her dotage on him I know they will be,)
Shall soon be mine; but point out any man's
In all the shire, and say they lie convenient
And useful for your lordship, and once more
I say aloud, they are yours.

   Lov.   I dare not own
What's by unjust and cruel means extorted;
My fame and credit are more dear to me,
Than so to expose them to be censur'd by
The public voice.

   Over.   You run, my lord, no hazard.
Your reputation shall stand as fair,
In all good men's opinions, as now;

               [2] Devices.

Nor can my actions, though condemn'd for ill,
Cast any foul aspersion upon yours.
For, though I do contemn report myself
As a mere sound, I still will be so tender
Of what concerns you, in all points of honour,
That the immaculate whiteness of your fame,
Nor your unquestioned integrity,
Shall e'er be sullied with one taint or spot
That may take from your innocence and candour.[3]
All my ambition is to have my daughter
Right honourable, which my lord can make her:
And might I live to dance upon my knee
A young Lord Lovell, born by her unto you,
I write *nil ultra*[4] to my proudest hopes.
As for possessions and annual rents,
Equivalent to maintain you in the port
Your noble birth and present state requires,
I do remove that burthen from your shoulders,
And take it on mine own: for, though I ruin
The country to supply your riotous waste,
The scourge of prodigals, want, shall never find you.

    Lov. Are you not frighted with the imprecations
And curses of whole families, made wretched
By your sinister practices?

    OVER.   Yes, as rocks are,
When foamy billows split themselves against
Their flinty ribs; or as the moon is mov'd,
When wolves, with hunger pin'd, howl at her brightness.
I am of a solid temper, and, like these,
Steer on a constant course. With mine own sword,
If called into the field, I can make that right,
Which fearful enemies murmur'd at as wrong.
Now, for these other piddling complaints
Breath'd out in bitterness; as when they call me
Extortioner, tyrant, cormorant, or intruder
On my poor neighbour's right, or grand incloser
Of what was common, to my private use;
Nay, when my ears are pierc'd with widows' cries,
And undone orphans wash with tears my threshold,

          [3] Stainlessness.   [4] Nothing beyond.

I only think what 'tis to have my daughter
Right honourable; and 'tis a powerful charm
Makes me insensible of remorse, or pity,
Or the least sting of conscience.

  Lov.   I admire
The toughness of your nature.

    OVER.   'Tis for you,
My lord, and for my daughter, I am marble;
Nay more, if you will have my character
In little, I enjoy more true delight
In my arrival to my wealth these dark
And crooked ways, than you shall e'er take pleasure
In spending what my industry hath compass'd.
My haste commands me hence; in one word, therefore,
Is it a match?

    Lov.   I hope, that is past doubt now.

    OVER. Then rest secure; not the hate of all mankind here,
Nor fear of what can fall on me hereafter,
Shall make me study aught but your advancement
One story higher: an earl! if gold can do it.
Dispute not my religion, nor my faith;
Though I am borne thus headlong by my will,
You may make choice of what belief you please,
To me they are equal; so, my lord, good morrow.   *Exit.*

    Lov. He's gone—I wonder how the earth can bear
Such a portent! I, that have liv'd a soldier,
And stood the enemy's violent charge undaunted,
To hear this blasphemous beast am bath'd all over
In a cold sweat: yet, like a mountain, he
(Confirm'd in atheistical assertions)
Is no more shaken than Olympus[6] is
When angry Boreas loads his double head
With sudden drifts of snow.

    Enter LADY ALLWORTH, *Waiting Woman, and* AMBLE

    L. ALL.   Save you, my lord!
Disturb I not your privacy?

    Lov.   No, good madam;
For your own sake I am glad you came no sooner,

                    ⁸ Apparently a slip for " Parnassus."

Since this bold bad man, Sir Giles Overreach,
Made such a plain discovery of himself,
And read this morning such a devilish matins,
That I should think it a sin next to his
But to repeat it.

L. ALL.　　　　　I ne'er press'd, my lord,
On others' privacies; yet, against my will,
Walking, for health' sake, in the gallery
Adjoining to your lodgings, I was made
(So vehement and loud he was) partaker
Of his tempting offers.

Lov.　　　　　Please you to command
Your servants hence, and I shall gladly hear
Your wiser counsel.

L. ALL.　　　　'Tis, my lord, a woman's,
But true and hearty;—wait in the next room,
But be within call; yet not so near to force me
To whisper my intents.

AMB.　　　　We are taught better
By you, good madam.

W. WOM.　　　And well know our distance.

L. ALL. Do so, and talk not; 'twill become your breeding.
　　　　　　　　　　　　Exeunt AMBLE *and Woman.*

Now, my good lord; if I may use my freedom,
As to an honour'd friend——

Lov.　　　　　You lessen else
Your favour to me.

L. ALL.　　　I dare then say thus:
As you are noble (howe'er common men
Make sordid wealth the object and sole end
Of their industrious aims) 'twill not agree
With those of eminent blood, who are engag'd
More to prefer[6] their honours than to increase
The state left to them by their ancestors,
To study large additions to their fortunes,
And quite neglect their births:—though I must grant,
Riches, well got, to be a useful servant,
But a bad master.

Lov.　　　　Madam, 'tis confessed;

* Promote.

But what infer you from it?

L. ALL.   This, my lord;
That as all wrongs, though thrust into one scale,
Slide of themselves off when right fills the other
And cannot bide the trial; so all wealth,
I mean if ill-acquir'd, cemented to honour
By virtuous ways achiev'd, and bravely purchas'd,
Is but as rubbish pour'd into a river,
(Howe'er intended to make good the bank,)
Rendering the water, that was pure before,
Polluted and unwholesome. I allow
The heir of Sir Giles Overreach, Margaret,
A maid well qualified and the richest match
Our north part can make boast of; yet she cannot,
With all that she brings with her, fill their mouths,
That never will forget who was her father;
Or that my husband Allworth's lands, and Wellborn's,
(How wrung from both needs now no repetition,)
Were real motives that more work'd your lordship
To join your families, than her form and virtues:
You may conceive the rest.

Lov.   I do, sweet madam,
And long since have consider'd it. I know,
The sum of all that makes a just man happy
Consists in the well choosing of his wife:
And there, well to discharge it, does require
Equality of years, of birth, of fortune;
For beauty being poor, and not cried up
By birth or wealth, can truly mix with neither.
And wealth, where there such difference in years,
And fair descent, must make the yoke uneasy:—
But I come nearer.

L. ALL.   Pray you do, my lord.

Lov. Were Overreach's states thrice centupl'd, his
     daughter
Millions of degrees much fairer than she is,
Howe'er I might urge precedents to excuse me,
I would not so adulterate my blood
By marrying Margaret, and so leave my issue
Made up of several pieces, one part scarlet,

And the other London blue. In my own tomb
I will inter my name first.

    L. ALL.   (*Aside.*) I am glad to hear this.——
Why then, my lord, pretend your marriage to her?
Dissimulation but ties false knots
On that straight line by which you, hitherto,
Have measur'd all your actions.

    Lov.   I make answer,
And aptly, with a question. Wherefore have you,
That, since your husband's death, have liv'd a strict
And chaste nun's life, on the sudden given yourself
To visits and entertainments? Think you, madam,
'Tis not grown public conference?[7] Or the favours
Which you too prodigally have thrown on Wellborn
Being too reserv'd before, incur not censure?

    L. ALL. I am innocent here; and, on my life, I swear
My ends are good.

    Lov.   On my soul, so are mine
To Margaret; but leave both to the event:
And since this friendly privacy does serve
But as an offer'd means unto ourselves,
To search each other farther, you having shewn
Your care of me, I my respect to you,
Deny me not, but still in chaste words, madam,
An afternoon's discourse.

    L. ALL.   So I shall hear you. [*Exeunt.*]

SCENE II[1]

[*Enter*] TAPWELL *and* FROTH

    TAP. Undone, undone! this was your counsel, Froth.

    FROTH. Mine! I defy thee. Did not Master Marrall
(He has marr'd all, I am sure) strictly command us,
On pain of Sir Giles Overreach' displeasure,
To turn the gentleman out of doors?

    TAP.   'Tis true;
But now he's his uncle's darling, and has got

----

       [7] Gossip.
       [1] Before Tapwell's house.

Master Justice Greedy, since he fill'd his belly,
At his commandment, to do anything.
Woe, woe to us!

    FROTH.   He may prove merciful.

    TAP. Troth, we do not deserve it at his hands.
Though he knew all the passages of our house,
As the receiving of stolen goods, and bawdry,
When he was rogue Wellborn no man would believe him,
And then his information could not hurt us;
But now he is right worshipful again,
Who dares but doubt his testimony? Methinks,
I see thee, Froth, already in a cart,
For a close² bawd, thine eyes ev'n pelted out
With dirt and rotten eggs; and my hand hissing,
If I scape the halter, with the letter R³
Printed upon it.

    FROTH.   Would that were the worst!
That were but nine days wonder: as for credit,
We have none to lose, but we shall lose the money
He owes us, and his custom; there's the hell on't.

    TAP. He has summon'd all his creditors by the drum,
And they swarm about him like so many soldiers
On the pay day: and has found out such A NEW WAY
TO PAY HIS OLD DEBTS, as 'tis very likely
He shall be chronicled for it!

    FROTH.   He deserves it
More than ten pageants. But are you sure his worship
Comes this way, to my lady's?

                 A cry within: Brave master Wellborn!

    TAP.   Yes:—I hear him.

    FROTH. Be ready with your petition, and present it
To his good grace.

Enter WELLBORN *in a rich habit,* [*followed by* MARRALL,]
    GREEDY, ORDER, FURNACE, *and Creditors;* TAPWELL
    kneeling, delivers his bill of debt

    WELL.   How's this! petition'd to?⁴——
But note what miracles the payment of

---

        ² Secret.   ³ For " Rogue."   ⁴ Q. *too.*

A little trash, and a rich suit of clothes,
Can work upon these rascals! I shall be,
I think, Prince Wellborn.

  MAR.   When your worship's married,
You may be—I know what I hope to see you.

  WELL. Then look thou for advancement.

  MAR.   To be known
Your worship's bailiff, is the mark I shoot at.

  WELL. And thou shalt hit it.

  MAR.   Pray you, sir, despatch
These needy followers, and for my admittance,[5]
Provided you'll defend me from Sir Giles,
Whose service I am weary of, I'll say something
You shall give thanks for.

  WELL.   Fear me not, Sir Giles.

  GREEDY. Who, Tapwell? I remember thy wife brought
   me
Last new-year's tide, a couple of fat turkeys.

  TAP. And shall do every Christmas, let your worship
But stand my friend now.

  GREEDY.   How! with Master Wellborn?
I can do anything with him on such terms.—
See you this honest couple; they are good souls
As ever drew out faucet; have they not
A pair of honest faces?

  WELL.   I o'erheard you,
And the bribe he promis'd. You are cozen'd in them;
For, of all the scum that grew rich by my riots,
This, for a most unthankful knave, and this,
For a base bawd and whore, have worst deserv'd me,
And therefore speak not for 'em. By your place
You are rather to do me justice. Lend me your ear:
—Forget his turkeys, and call in his license,
And, at the next fair, I'll give you a yoke of oxen
Worth all his poultry.

  GREEDY.   I am chang'd on the sudden
In my opinion! Come near; nearer, rascal.
And, now I view him better, did you e'er see
One look so like an archknave? His very countenance,

      [5] Appointment.

Should an understanding judge but look upon him,
Would hang him, though he were innocent.

TAP. FROTH. Worshipful sir.

GREEDY. No, though the great Turk came, instead of
turkeys,
To beg my favour, I am inexorable.
Thou hast an ill name: besides thy musty ale,
That hath destroy'd many of the king's liege people,
Thou never hadst in thy house, to stay men's stomachs,
A piece of Suffolk cheese or gammon of bacon,
Or any esculent, as the learned call it,
For their emolument, but sheer drink only.
For which gross fault I here do damn thy license,
Forbidding thee ever to tap or draw;
For, instantly, I will, in mine own person,
Command the constable to pull down thy sign,
And do it before I eat.

FROTH. No mercy?

GREEDY. Vanish!
If I shew any, may my promis'd oxen gore me!

TAP. Unthankful knaves are ever so rewarded.

Exeunt GREEDY, TAPWELL, *and* FROTH.

WELL. Speak; what are you?

1ST CRED. A decay'd vintner, sir,
That might have thriv'd, but that your worship broke me
With trusting you with muscadine[6] and eggs,
And five pound suppers, with your after drinkings,
When you lodg'd upon the Bankside.

WELL. I remember.

1ST CRED. I have not been hasty, nor e'er laid to arrest
you;
And therefore, sir——

WELL. Thou art an honest fellow,
I'll set thee up again; see his bill paid.—
What are you?

2ND CRED. A tailor once, but now mere botcher.[7]
I gave you credit for a suit of clothes,
Which was all my stock, but you failing in payment,
I was remov'd from the shopboard, and confin'd

[6] Wine from muscadel grapes. [7] Repairer.

Under a stall.

WELL.   See him paid;—and botch no more.

2ND CRED. I ask no interest, sir.

WELL.   Such tailors need not;
If their bills are paid in one and twenty year,
They are seldom losers.—O, I know thy face,

            [*To* 3RD CREDITOR.]

Thou wert my surgeon. You must tell no tales;
Those days are done. I will pay you in private.

ORD. A royal gentleman!

FURN.   Royal as an emperor!
He'll prove a brave master; my good lady knew
To choose a man.

WELL.   See all men else discharg'd;
And since old debts are clear'd by a new way,
A little bounty will not misbecome me;
There's something, honest cook, for thy good breakfasts;
And this, for your respect: [*To* ORDER] take't, 'tis good gold,
And I able to spare it.

ORD.   You are too munificent.

FURN. He was ever so.

WELL.   Pray you, on before.

3RD CRED.   Heaven bless you!

MAR. At four o'clock; the rest know where to meet me.

            Exeunt ORDER, FURNACE, *and Creditors.*

WELL. Now, Master Marrall, what's the weighty secret
You promis'd to impart?

MAR.   Sir, time nor place
Allow me to relate each circumstance,
This only, in a word: I know Sir Giles
Will come upon you for security
For his thousand pounds, which you must not consent to.
As he grows in heat, as I am sure he will,
Be you but rough, and say he's in your debt
Ten times the sum, upon sale of your land;
I had a hand in't (I speak it to my shame)
When you were defeated* of it.

WELL.   That's forgiven.

MAR. I shall deserve't. Then urge him to produce

            * Robbed.

The deed in which you pass'd it over to him,
Which I know he'll have about him, to deliver
To the Lord Lovell, with many other writings,
And present monies; I'll instruct you further,
As I wait on your worship. If I play not my prize
To your full content, and your uncle's much vexation,
Hang up Jack Marrall.
    WELL.   I rely upon thee.   *Exeunt.*

SCENE III[1]

Enter ALLWORTH *and* MARGARET

    ALL. Whether to yield the first praise to my lord's
Unequall'd temperance or your constant sweetness
That I yet live, my weak hands fasten'd on
Hope's anchor, spite of all storms of despair,
I yet rest doubtful.
    MARG.   Give it to Lord Lovell;
For what in him was bounty, in me's duty.
I make but payment of a debt to which
My vows, in that high office regist'red,
Are faithful witnesses.
    ALL.   'Tis true, my dearest:
Yet, when I call to mind how many fair ones
Make wilful shipwrack of their faiths, and oaths
To God and man, to fill the arms of greatness,
And you rise up [no][2] less than a glorious star,
To the amazement of the world,—hold out
Against the stern authority of a father,
And spurn at honour, when it comes to court you;
I am so tender of your good, that faintly,
With your wrong, I can wish myself that right
You yet are pleas'd to do me.
    MARG.   Yet, and ever.
To me what's title, when content is wanting?
Or wealth, rak'd up together with much care,
And to be kept with more, when the heart pines
In being dispossess'd of what it longs for

---

[1] A room in Overreach's house.   [2] Inserted by Dodsley.

Beyond the Indian mines? or the smooth brow
Of a pleas'd sire, that slaves me to his will,
And, so his ravenous humour may be feasted
By my obedience, and he see me great,
Leaves to my soul nor faculties nor power
To make her own election?

 ALL.   But the dangers
That follow the repulse——

 MARG.   To me they are nothing;
Let Allworth love, I cannot be unhappy.
Suppose the worst, that, in his rage, he kill me,
A tear or two, by you dropt on my hearse
In sorrow for my fate, will call back life
So far as but to say, that I die yours;
I then shall rest in peace: or should he prove
So cruel, as one death would not suffice
His thirst of vengeance, but with ling'ring torments
In mind and body I must waste to air,
In poverty join'd with banishment; so you share
In my afflictions, which I dare not wish you,
So high I prize you, I could undergo 'em
With such a patience as should look down
With scorn on his worst malice.

 ALL.   Heaven avert
Such trials of your true affection to me!
Nor will it unto you, that are all mercy,
Shew so much rigour: but since we must run
Such desperate hazards, let us do our best
To steer between them.

 MARG.   Your lord's ours, and sure;
And, though but a young actor, second me
In doing to the life what he has plotted,

        Enter OVERREACH [*behind.*]

The end may yet prove happy. Now, my Allworth—
            [*Seeing her father.*]

 ALL. To your letter, and put on a seeming anger.
 MARG. I'll pay my lord all debts due to his title;
And when with terms, not taking from his honour,

He does solicit me, I shall gladly hear him.
But in this peremptory, nay, commanding way,
To appoint a meeting, and, without my knowledge,
A priest to tie the knot can ne'er be undone
Till death unloose it, is a confidence
In his lordship will deceive him.

  ALL.   I hope better,
Good lady.

  MARG. Hope, sir, what you please: for me
I must take a safe and secure course; I have
A father, and without his full consent,
Though all lords of the land kneel'd for my favour,
I can grant nothing.

  OVER.   I like this obedience: [*Comes forward.*]
But whatsoe'er my lord writes, must and shall be
Accepted and embrac'd. Sweet Master Allworth,
You shew yourself a true and faithful servant
To your good lord; he has a jewel of you.
How! frowning, Meg? Are these looks to receive
A messenger from my lord? What's this? Give me it.

  MARG. A piece of arrogant paper, like th' inscriptions.

  OVER. (*Reads.*) "Fair mistress, from your servant learn
    all joys
That we can hope for, if deferr'd, prove toys;[3]
Therefore this instant, and in private, meet
A husband, that will gladly at your feet
Lay down his honours, tend'ring them to you
With all content, the church being paid her due."
—Is this the arrogant piece of paper? Fool!
Will you still be one? In the name of madness what
Could his good honour write more to content you?
Is there aught else to be wish'd, after these two,
That are already offer'd; marriage first,
And lawful pleasure after: what would you more?

  MARG. Why, sir, I would be married like your daughter;
Not hurried away i' th' night I know not whither,
Without all ceremony; no friends invited
To honour the solemnity.

  ALL.   An't please your honour,

      [3] Trifles.

For so before to-morrow I must style you,
My lord desires this privacy, in respect
His honourable kinsmen are afar off,
And his desires to have it done brook not
So long delay as to expect[4] their coming;
And yet he stands resolv'd, with all due pomp,
As running at the ring, plays, masques, and tilting,
To have his marriage at court celebrated,
When he has brought your honour up to London.

   OVER. He tells you true; 'tis the fashion, on my knowl-
      edge:
Yet the good lord, to please your peevishness,
Must put it off, forsooth! and lose a night,
In which perhaps he might get two boys on thee.
Tempt me no further, if you do, this goad
                        [*Points to his sword.*]
Shall prick you to him.
   MARG.   I could be contented,
Were you but by, to do a father's part,
And give me in the church.
   OVER.   So my lord have you,
What do I care who gives you? Since my lord
Does purpose to be private, I'll not cross him.
I know not, Master Allworth, how my lord
May be provided, and therefore there's a purse
Of gold, 'twill serve this night's expense; to-morrow
I'll furnish him with any sums. In the mean time,
Use my ring to my chaplain; he is benefic'd
At my manor of Gotham, and call'd Parson Willdo:
'Tis no matter for a licence, I'll bear him out in't.

   MARG. With your favour, sir, what warrant is your ring?
He may suppose I got that twenty ways,
Without your knowledge; and then to be refus'd
Were such a stain upon me!—If you pleas'd, sir,
Your presence would do better.
   OVER.   Still perverse!
I say again, I will not cross my lord;
Yet I'll prevent[5] you too.—Paper and ink, there!
   ALL. I can furnish you.

               [4] Wait for.   [5] Anticipate your objections.

Over.   I thank you, I can write then.
                                        Writes on his book.

All. You may, if you please, put out the name of my lord,
In respect he comes disguis'd, and only write,
" Marry her to this gentleman."

Over.   Well advis'd.
'Tis done; away;—(Margaret *kneels.*)   My blessing, girl?
          Thou hast it.
Nay, no reply, be gone.—Good Master Allworth,
This shall be the best night's work you ever made.

All. I hope so, sir.   *Exeunt* Allworth *and* Margaret.

Over. Farewell!—Now all's cocksure:
Methinks I hear already knights and ladies
Say, Sir Giles Overreach, how is it with
Your honourable daughter? Has her honour
Slept well to-night? or, will her honour please
To accept this monkey, dog, or paraquit,[6]
(This is state in ladies), or my eldest son
To be her page, and wait upon her trencher?
My ends, my ends are compass'd—then for Wellborn
And the lands; were he once married to the widow——
I have him here—I can scarce contain myself,
I am so full of joy, nay, joy all over.   *Exit.*

ACT V

Scene I[1]

[*Enter* Lord] Lovell, Lady Allworth, *and* Amble

L. All. By this you know how strong the motives were
That did, my lord, induce me to dispense
A little, with my gravity, to advance,
In personating some few favours to him,
The plots and projects of the down-trod Wellborn.
Nor shall I e'er repent, although I suffer
In some few men's opinions for't, the action;
For he that ventur'd all for my dear husband

---

[6] Parrot.
[1] A room in Lady Allworth's house.

Might justly claim an obligation from me
To pay him such a courtesy; which had I
Coyly or over-curiously[2] denied,
It might have argu'd me of little love
To the deceased.

  Lov.   What you intended, madam,
For the poor gentleman hath found good success;
For, as I understand, his debts are paid,
And he once more furnish'd for fair employment:
But all the arts that I have us'd to raise
The fortunes of your joy and mine, young Allworth,
Stand yet in supposition, though I hope well;
For the young lovers are in wit more pregnant
Than their years can promise; and for their desires,
On my knowledge, they are equal.

  L. All.   As my wishes
Are with yours, my lord; yet give me leave to fear
The building, though well grounded: to deceive
Sir Giles, that's both a lion and a fox
In his proceedings, were a work beyond
The strongest undertakers; not the trial
Of two weak innocents.

  Lov.   Despair not, madam:
Hard things are compass'd oft by easy means;
And judgment, being a gift deriv'd from Heaven,
Though sometimes lodg'd i' the hearts of worldly men,
That ne'er consider from whom they receive it,
Forsakes such as abuse the giver of it.
Which is the reason that the politic
And cunning statesman, that believes he fathoms
The counsels of all kingdoms on the earth,
Is by simplicity oft over-reach'd.

  L. All. May he be so! Yet, in his name to express it,
Is a good omen.

  Lov.   May it to myself
Prove so, good lady, in my suit to you!
What think you of the motion?

  L. All.   Troth, my lord,
My own unworthiness may answer for me;

       [2] Fastidiously.

For had you, when that I was in my prime,
My virgin flower uncropp'd, presented me
With this great favour; looking on my lowness
Not in a glass of self-love, but of truth,
I could not but have thought it as a blessing
Far, far beyond my merit.

Lov.   You are too modest,
And undervalue that which is above
My title, or whatever I call mine.
I grant, were I a Spaniard, to marry
A widow might disparage me; but being
A true-born Englishman, I cannot find
How it can taint my honour: nay, what's more,
That which you think a blemish is to me
The fairest lustre. You already, madam,
Have given sure proofs how dearly you can cherish
A husband that deserves you; which confirms me,
That, if I am not wanting in my care
To do you service, you'll be still the same
That you were to your Allworth: in a word,
Our years, our states, our births are not unequal,
You being descended nobly, and alli'd so;
If then you may be won to make me happy,
But join your lips to mine, and that shall be
A solemn contract.

L. All.   I were blind to my own good,
Should I refuse it; [*Kisses him*] yet, my lord, receive me
As such a one, the study of whose whole life
Shall know no other object but to please you.

Lov. If I return not, with all tenderness,
Equal respect to you, may I die wretched!

L. All. There needs no protestation, my lord,
To her that cannot doubt.—

              Enter Wellborn, [*handsomely apparelled*]
                          You are welcome, sir.
Now you look like yourself.

Well.   And will continue
Such in my free acknowledgment, that I am

Your creature, madam, and will never hold
My life mine own, when you please to command it.

Lov. It is a thankfulness that well becomes you.
You could not make choice of a better shape
To dress your mind in.

L. ALL.   For me, I am happy
That my endeavours prosper'd. Saw you of late
Sir Giles, your uncle?

WELL.   I heard of him, madam,
By his minister, Marrall; he's grown into strange passions
About his daughter. This last night he look'd for
Your lordship at his house, but missing you,
And she not yet appearing, his wise head
Is much perplex'd and troubl'd.

Lov.   It may be,
Sweetheart, my project took.

L. ALL.   I strongly hope.

OVER. [within.] Ha! find her, booby, thou huge lump of
     nothing,
I'll bore thine eyes out else.

WELL.   May it please your lordship,
For some ends of mine own, but to withdraw
A little out of sight, though not of hearing,
You may, perhaps, have sport.

Lov.   You shall direct me. *Steps aside.*

Enter OVERREACH, *with distracted looks, driving in*
     MARRALL *before him,* [*with a box*]*

OVER. I shall *sol fa* you, rogue!

MAR.   Sir, for what cause
Do you use me thus?

OVER.   Cause, slave! Why, I am angry,
And thou a subject only fit for beating,
And so to cool my choler. Look to the writing;
Let but the seal be broke upon the box
That hast slept in my cabinet these three years,
I'll rack thy soul for't.

MAR.   (*Aside.*) I may yet cry quittance,
Though now I suffer, and dare not resist.

* In Q. after "took," above.

OVER. Lady, by your leave, did you see my daughter lady?
And the lord her husband? Are they in your house?
If they are, discover, that I may bid 'em joy;
And, as an entrance to her place of honour,
See your ladyship be on her left hand, and make courtsies
When she nods on you; which you must receive
As a special favour.

L. ALL.   When I know, Sir Giles,
Her state requires such ceremony, I shall pay it;
But in the meantime, as I am myself,
I give you to understand, I neither know
Nor care where her honour is.

OVER.   When you once see her
Supported, and led by the lord her husband,
You'll be taught better.——Nephew.

WELL.   Sir.

OVER.   No more?

WELL. 'Tis all I owe you.

OVER.   Have your redeem'd rags
Made you thus insolent?

WELL.   (*in scorn*) Insolent to you!
Why, what are you, sir, unless in your years,
At the best, more than myself?

OVER.   [*Aside.*] His fortune swells him:
'Tis rank[4] he's married.

L. ALL.   This is excellent!

OVER. Sir, in calm language, though I seldom use it,
I am familiar with the cause that makes you
Bear up thus bravely; there's a certain buzz
Of a stol'n marriage, do you hear? of a stol'n marriage,
In which, 'tis said, there's somebody hath been cozen'd;
I name no parties.

WELL.   Well, sir, and what follows?

OVER. Marry, this; since you are peremptory. Remember,
Upon mere hope of your great match, I lent you
A thousand pounds: put me in good security,
And suddenly, by mortgage or by statute,
Of some of your new possessions, or I'll have you
Dragg'd in your lavender robes[5] to the gaol. You know me,

---

[4] Obvious.   [5] Clothes in pawn were said to be " laid up in lavender."

And therefore do not trifle.

WELL.   Can you be
So cruel to your nephew, now he's in
The way to rise? Was this the courtesy
You did me "in pure love, and no ends else?"

OVER. End me no ends! Engage the whole estate
And force your spouse to sign it, you shall have
Three or four thousand more, to roar and swagger
And revel in bawdy taverns.

WELL.   And beg after;
Mean you not so?

OVER.   My thoughts are mine, and free.
Shall I have security?

WELL.   No, indeed you shall not,
Nor bond, nor bill, nor bare acknowledgment;
Your great looks fright not me.

OVER.   But my deeds shall.
Outbrav'd!   *Both draw.*

L. ALL.   Help, murder! murder!

Enter Servants

WELL.   Let him come on,
With all his wrongs and injuries about him,
Arm'd with his cut-throat practices to guard him;
The right that I bring with me will defend me,
And punish his extortion.

OVER.   That I had thee
But single in the field!

L. ALL.   You may; but make not
My house your quarrelling scene.

OVER.   Were't in a church,
By Heaven and Hell, I'll do't!

MAR.   Now put him to
The shewing of the deed.   [*Aside to* WELLBORN.]

WELL.   This rage is vain, sir;
For fighting, fear not, you shall have your hands full,
Upon the least incitement; and whereas
You charge me with a debt of a thousand pounds,
If there be law, (howe'er you have no conscience,)
Either restore my land, or I'll recover

A debt, that's truly due to me from you,
In value ten times more than what you challenge.

OVER. I in thy debt! O impudence! did I not purchase
The land left by thy father, that rich land,
That had continued in Wellborn's name
Twenty descents; which, like a riotous fool,
Thou didst make sale of it? Is not here inclos'd
The deed that dost confirm it mine?

MAR.   Now, now!

WELL. I do acknowledge none; I ne'er pass'd over
Any such land. I grant, for a year or two
You had it in trust; which if you do discharge,
Surrend'ring the possession, you shall ease
Yourself and me of chargeable suits in law,
Which, if you prove not honest, as I doubt it,
Must of necessity follow.

L. ALL.   In my judgment,
He does advise you well.

OVER.   Good! good! Conspire
With your new husband, lady; second him
In his dishonest practices; but when
This manor is extended[6] to my use,
You'll speak in an humbler key, and sue for favour.

L. ALL. Never: do not hope it.

WELL.   Let despair first seize me.

OVER. Yet, to shut up thy mouth, and make thee give
Thyself the lie, the loud lie, I draw out
The precious evidence; if thou canst forswear
Thy hand and seal, and make a forfeit of
          Opens the box, [and displays the bond.]
Thy ears to the pillory, see! here's that will make
My interest clear—ha!

L. ALL.   A fair skin of parchment.

WELL. Indented, I confess, and labels too;
But neither wax nor words. How! thunderstruck?
Not a syllable to insult with? My wise uncle,
Is this your precious evidence? Is this that makes
Your interest clear?

OVER.   I am o'erwhelm'd with wonder!

          [6] Seized.

What prodigy is this? What subtle devil
Hath raz'd out the inscription, the wax
Turned into dust? The rest of my deeds whole
As when they were deliver'd, and this only
Made nothing! Do you deal with witches, rascal?
There is a statute[7] for you, which will bring
Your neck in an hempen circle; yes, there is;
And now 'tis better thought for, cheater, know
This juggling shall not save you.

    WELL.   To save thee,
Would beggar the stock of mercy.

    OVER.   Marrall!

    MAR.   Sir.

    OVER. (*flattering him*) Though the witnesses are dead,
        your testimony
Help with an oath or two: and for thy master,
Thy liberal master, my good honest servant,
I know thou wilt swear anything, to dash
The cunning sleight: besides, I know thou art
A public notary, and such stand in law
For a dozen witnesses: the deed being drawn too
By thee, my careful Marrall, and delivered
When thou were't present, will make good my title.
Wilt thou not swear this?

    MAR.   I! No, I assure you:
I have a conscience not sear'd up like yours;
I know no deeds.

    OVER.   Wilt thou betray me?

    MAR.   Keep him
From using of his hands, I'll use my tongue,
To his no little torment.

    OVER.   Mine own varlet
Rebel against me!

    MAR.   Yes, and uncase[8] you too.
" The idiot, the patch, the slave, the booby,
The property fit only to be beaten
For your morning exercise," your " football," or
" The unprofitable lump of flesh," your " drudge,"
Can now anatomise you, and lay open

       [7] The law against witchcraft.   [8] Flay.

All your black plots, and level with the earth
Your hill of pride, and, with these gabions[9] guarded
Unload my great artillery, and shake,
Nay pulverize, the walls you think defend you.
    L. ALL. How he foams at the mouth with rage!
    WELL.   To him again.
    OVER. O that I had thee in my gripe, I would tear thee
Joint after joint!
    MAR.   I know you are a tearer,
But I'll have first your fangs par'd off, and then
Come nearer to you; when I have discover'd,[10]
And made it good before the judge, what ways
And devilish practices you us'd to cozen
With an army of whole families, who yet live,
And but enrolled for soldiers, were able
To take in[11] Dunkirk.
    WELL.   All will come out.
    L. ALL.   The better.
    OVER. But that I will live, rogue, to torture thee,
And make thee wish, and kneel in vain, to die,
These swords that keep thee from me should fix here,
Although they made my body but one wound,
But I would reach thee.
    Lov.   (*Aside.*) Heaven's hand is in this;
One bandog[12] worry the other!
    OVER.   I play the fool,
And make my anger but ridiculous:
There will be a time and place, there will be, cowards,
When you shall feel what I dare do.
    WELL.   I think so:
You dare do any ill, yet want true valour
To be honest, and repent.
    OVER.   They are words I know not,
Nor e'er will learn. Patience, the beggar's virtue,

Enter GREEDY *and* PARSON WILLDO

Shall find no harbour here:—after these storms
At length a calm appears. Welcome, most welcome!

---

  [9] Wicker baskets filled with earth used to protect soldiers when digging trenches.   [10] Revealed.   [11] Capture.   [12] Fierce watchdog.

There's comfort in thy looks. Is the deed done?
Is my daughter married? Say but so, my chaplain,
And I am tame.
    WILLDO.   Married! Yes, I assure you.
    OVER. Then vanish all sad thoughts! There's more gold
        for thee.
My doubts and fears are in the titles drown'd
Of my honourable, my right honourable daughter.
    GREEDY. Here will[13] be feasting! At least for a month,
I am provided: empty guts, croak no more.
You shall be stuff'd like bagpipes, not with wind,
But bearing[14] dishes.
    OVER.   Instantly be here? *Whispering to* WILLDO.
To my wish! to my wish! Now you that plot against me,
And hop'd to trip my heels up, that contemn'd me,
Think on't and tremble.—(*Loud music*)—They come! I
        hear the music.
A lane there for my lord!
    WELL.   Think sudden heat
May yet be cool'd, sir.
    OVER.   Make way there for my lord!

        Enter ALLWORTH *and* MARGARET
    MARG. Sir, first your pardon, then your blessing, with
Your full allowance of the choice I have made.
As ever you could make use of your reason,   *Kneeling.*
Grow not in passion; since you may as well
Call back the day that's past, as untie the knot
Which is too strongly fasten'd: not to dwell
Too long on words, this is my husband.
    OVER.   How!
    ALL. So I assure you; all the rites of marriage,
With every circumstance, are past. Alas! sir,
Although I am no lord, but a lord's page,
Your daughter and my lov'd wife mourns not for it;
And, for right honourable son-in-law, you may say,
Your dutiful daughter.
    OVER.   Devil! are they married?

        [13] Q. *will I.*   [14] Solid.

WILLDO. Do a father's part, and say, Heaven give 'em joy!

OVER. Confusion and ruin! Speak, and speak quickly,
Or thou art dead.

WILLDO.   They are married.

OVER.   Thou hadst better
Have made a contract with the king of fiends,
Than these:—my brain turns!

WILLDO.   Why this rage to me?
Is not this your letter, sir, and these the words?
"Marry her to this gentleman."

OVER.   It cannot—
Nor will I e'er believe it, 'sdeath! I will not;
That I, that in all passages I touch'd
At worldly profit have not left a print
Where I have trod for the most curious search
To trace my footsteps, should be gull'd by children,
Baffl'd and fool'd, and all my hopes and labours
Defeated and made void.

WELL.   As it appears,
You are so, my grave uncle.

OVER.   Village nurses
Revenge their wrongs with curses; I'll not waste
A syllable, but thus I take the life
Which, wretched, I gave to thee.

Offers to kill MARGARET.

Lov. [*coming forward.*] Hold, for your own sake!
Though charity to your daughter hath quite left you,
Will you do an act, though in your hopes lost here,
Can leave no hope for peace or rest hereafter?
Consider; at the best you are but a man,
And cannot so create your aims, but that
They may be cross'd.

OVER.   Lord! thus I spit at thee,
And at thy counsel; and again desire thee,
And as thou art a soldier, if thy valour
Dares shew itself where multitude and example
Lead not the way, let's quit the house, and change
Six words in private.

Lov.   I am ready.

L. ALL.   Stay, sir,

Contest with one distracted!

WELL.　　　　　　　　　You'll grow like him,
Should you answer his vain challenge.

OVER.　　　　　　　　　　Are you pale?
Borrow his help, though Hercules call it odds,
I'll stand against both as I am, hemm'd in thus.
Since, like a Libyan lion in the toil,
My fury cannot reach the coward hunters,
And only spends itself, I'll quit the place.
Alone I can do nothing; but I have servants
And friends to second me; and if I make not
This house a heap of ashes (by my wrongs,
What I have spoke I will make good!) or leave
One throat uncut,—if it be possible,
Hell, add to my afflictions!　　　　　　　　　*Exit.*

MAR.　　　　　　　　　Is't not brave sport?

GREEDY. Brave sport! I am sure it has ta'en away my
　　　　stomach;
I do not like the sauce.

ALL.　　　　　　　Nay, weep not, dearest,
Though it express your pity; what's decreed
Above, we cannot alter.

L. ALL.　　　　　　　His threats move me
No scruple, madam.

MAR.　　　　　　　Was it not a rare trick,
An it please your worship, to make the deed nothing?
I can do twenty neater, if you please
To purchase and grow rich; for I will be
Such a solicitor and steward for you,
As never worshipful had.

WELL.　　　　　　　I do believe thee;
But first discover the quaint[15] means you us'd
To raze out the conveyance?

MAR.　　　　　　　They are mysteries
Not to be spoke in public: certain minerals
Incorporated in the ink and wax—
Besides, he gave me nothing, but still fed me
With hopes and blows; but that was the inducement
To this conundrum. If it please your worship

[15] Crafty.

To call to memory, this mad beast once caus'd me
To urge you or to drown or hang yourself;
I'll do the like to him, if you command me.

    WELL. You are a rascal! He that dares be false
To a master, though unjust, will ne'er be true
To any other. Look not for reward
Or favour from me; I will shun thy sight
As I would do a basilisk's. Thank my pity,
If thou keep thy ears; howe'er, I will take order
Your practice shall be silenc'd.

    GREEDY.   I'll commit him,
If you'll have me, sir.

    WELL.   That were to little purpose;
His conscience be his prison. Not a word,
But instantly be gone.

    ORD.   Take this kick with you.

    AMB. And this.

    FURN.   If that I had my cleaver here,
I would divide your knave's head.

    MAR.   This is the haven
False servants still arrive at   *Exit.*

Re-enter OVERREACH

    L. ALL.   Come again!

    LOV. Fear not, I am your guard.

    WELL.   His looks are ghastly.

    WILLDO. Some little time I have spent, under your favours,
In physical studies, and if my judgment err not,
He's mad beyond recovery: but observe him,
And look to yourselves.

    OVER.   Why, is not the whole world
Include in yourself? To what use then
Are friends and servants? Say there were a squadron
Of pikes, lin'd through with shot, when I am mounted
Upon my injuries, shall I fear to charge them?
No: I'll through the battalia, and, that routed,
                 Flourishing his sword sheathed.[26]
I'll fall to execution.—Ha! I am feeble:

[26] Q. *unsheathed.*

Some undone widow sits upon mine arm,
And takes away the use of't; and my sword,
Glu'd to my scabbard with wrong'd orphans' tears,
Will not be drawn. Ha! what are these? Sure, hangmen,
That come to bind my hands, and then to drag me
Before the judgment-seat: now they are new shapes,
And do appear like Furies, with steel whips
To scourge my ulcerous soul. Shall I then fall
Ingloriously, and yield? No; spite of Fate,
I will be forc'd to hell like to myself.
Though you were legions of accursed spirits,
Thus would I fly among you.

    [*Rushes forward and flings himself on the ground.*]

  WELL.   There's no help;
Disarm him first, then bind him.

  GREEDY.   Take a *mittimus,*[17]
And carry him to Bedlam.

  LOV.   How he foams!

  WELL. And bites the earth!

  WILLDO.   Carry him to some dark room,
There try what art can do for his recovery.

  MARG. O my dear father!   *They force* OVERREACH *off.*

  ALL.   You must be patient, mistress.

  LOV. Here is a precedent to teach wicked men,
That when they leave religion, and turn atheists,
Their own abilities leave them. Pray you take comfort,
I will endeavour you shall be his guardians
In his distractions: and for your land, Master Wellborn,
Be it good or ill in law, I'll be an umpire
Between you, and this, th' undoubted heir
Of Sir Giles Overreach. For me, here's the anchor
That I must fix on.

  ALL.   What you shall determine,
My lord, I will allow of.

  WELL.   'Tis the language
That I speak too; but there is something else
Beside the repossession of my land,
And payment of my debts, that I must practise.
I had a reputation, but 'twas lost

        [17] A writ of committal.

In my loose course; and until I redeem it
Some noble way, I am but half made up.
It is a time of action; if your lordship
Will please to confer a company upon me
In your command, I doubt not in my service
To my king and country but I shall do something
That may make me right again.
    Lov.   Your suit is granted,
And you lov'd for the motion.
    WELL. [*coming forward.*] Nothing wants then
But your allowance—

THE EPILOGUE

But your allowance, and in that our all
Is comprehended; it being known, nor we,
Nor he that wrote the comedy, can be free,
Without your manumission; which if you
Grant willingly, as a fair favour due
To the poet's and our labours, (as you may,
For we despair not, gentlemen, of the play,)
We jointly shall profess your grace hath might
To teach us action, and him how to write.   [*Exeunt.*]

FINIS

THE PUBLISHERS OF THE HAR-
VARD CLASSICS · DR. ELIOT'S
FIVE-FOOT SHELF OF BOOKS · ARE
PLEASED TO ANNOUNCE THE
PUBLICATION OF

THE JUNIOR CLASSICS
A LIBRARY FOR BOYS AND GIRLS

"The Junior Classics constitute a set
of books whose contents will delight
children and at the same time
satisfy the legitimate ethical require-
ments of those who have the children's
best interests at heart."

CHARLES W. ELIOT

THE COLLIER PRESS · NEW YORK
P · F · COLLIER & SON